THE POLITICS OF EUROPEAN TREATY REFORM

THE 1996 INTERGOVERNMENTAL CONFERENCE AND BEYOND

EDITED BY

GEOFFREY EDWARDS AND ALFRED PIJPERS

PINTER

LONDON AND WASHINGTON

PINTER
A Cassell imprint
Wellington House, 125 Strand, London WC2R 0BB, England
PO Box 605, Herndon, VA 20172, USA

First published 1997
© Geoffrey Edwards, Alfred Pijpers and the contributors 1997

British Library Cataloguing in Publication Data
A catalogue record for this book is available from the British Library.

ISBN 1 85567 358 4 (Hardback)
      1 85567 359 2 (Paperback)

Library of Congress Cataloging-in-Publication Data
The Politics of European Treaty Reform / edited by Geoffrey Edwards and Alfred Pijpers
      p. cm.
   Papers presented at the Intergovernmental Conference held in Turin in March 1996.
   Includes bibliographical references and index.
   ISBN 1-85567-358-4 (hardcover). — ISBN 1-85567-359-2 (pbk.)
   1. European Union — Congresses. 2. European federation — Congresses. I. Edwards,
   Geoffrey. II. Pijpers, Alfred.
JN30.A14 1997   96-49889
341.242'2—DC21   CIP

Typeset by Patrick Armstrong, Book Production Services
Printed and bound in Great Britain by Biddles Ltd, Guildford and King's Lynn

CONTENTS

LIST OF CONTRIBUTORS

IAIN BEGG   Professor of International Economics, The Business School, South Bank University, London.

PIET DANKERT   Member of the European Parliament.

DESMOND DINAN   Associate Professor of History and Director of the Center of European Integration Studies, George Mason University, Arlington Va., USA.

GEOFFREY EDWARDS   Jean Monnet Director of European Studies, Centre of International Studies, University of Cambridge, Fellow of Pembroke College, Cambridge.

STEPHEN GEORGE   Jean Monnet Professor of Politics, Department of Politics, Sheffield University.

NIGEL GRIMWADE   Principal Lecturer and Head of Economics, South Bank University, London.

PETER VAN HAM   Professor, College of Strategic Studies and Defense Economics, George C. Marshall European Center for Security Studies, Garmisch-Partenkichen.

BRIGID LAFFAN   Jean Monnet Professor of European Integration, University College, Dublin.

FINN LAURSEN   Professor of International Relations and Director of the Thorkil Kristensen Institute, South Jutland University Centre, Esbjerg.

SONIA MAZEY   Lecturer in Social and Political Sciences, University of Cambridge and Fellow of Churchill College, Cambridge.

JORG MONAR   Jean Monnet Professor of Politics, Centre of European Politics and Institutions, University of Leicester.

NICOLAJ PETERSEN   Professor of International Relations, Aarhus University.

ALFRED PIJPERS   Senior Lecturer in International Relations, Europa Institute, University of Amsterdam and the Department of Political Science, University of Leiden.

JEREMY RICHARDSON   Professor of European Public Policy, University of Essex and editor, *Journal of European Public Policy.*

JONATHAN STORY   Professor of International Political Economy, INSEAD, Fontainebleau.

ANDREA SZUKALA   Research Fellow, Research Institute for Political Science and European Affairs, University of Cologne.

PNAOS TSAKALOYANNIS   Professor of European Politics, University of Economics and Business, Athens.

SOPHIE VANHOONACKER   Senior Lecturer, European Institute of Public Administration, Maastricht.

JOSEPH WEILER   Manley Hudson Professor of Law and Jean Monnet chair, Co-Director, Harvard European Law Research Center, Harvard Law School, Cambridge, Mass. USA.

WOLFGANG WESSELS   Jean Monnet Professor of Politics, Research Institute for Political Science and European Affairs, University of Cologne, President of the Trans European Policy Studies Association (TEPSA).

v

ACKNOWLEDGEMENTS

The project began with a workshop in Amsterdam organized by the Europa Institute and the Institute for International Legal Research of the University of Amsterdam in December 1994. The ideas put forward by the subsequent editors of this volume were enthusiastically taken up by a number of those whose final papers appear here. We all then met again at a conference, also organized in Amsterdam, in June 1995 to which a larger number of academics, officials and politicians were invited. Among those who contributed to the discussions were: Graham Avery, Roland Bieiber, Marko Bos, Deirdre Curtin, Johan de Vree, Jan Jans, Eppo Jansen, Andreas Maurer, Les Metcalfe, Gregg Orifici, André Szász, Ranieri Tallarigo, Friedl Weiss, and Hubert Wurth.

The project would not have been possible without the support of a large number of people and organizations. Among the latter, we need to single out The Hague Office of the European Commission, The Netherlands' Bank (Amsterdam) and the Europa Instituut, University of Amsterdam, for the financial support they so generously extended. Pembroke College and the Centre of International Studies at Cambridge also provided much welcome support.

Among individuals, we should like to thank Marguerite Niekoop, Eke Boesten and Anne Doeve for their secretarial support in Amsterdam; Jane Hedley-Prole, for the translation of Dankert's chapter, Matthew Shaffer (Peterhouse College, Cambridge) for his willingness to chase references as well as his sub-editing and computer skills, and Jan Ole Kiso and Arne Niemann (both at Pembroke College) for their help, especially with the index.

LIST OF ABBREVIATIONS

BEUC	Bureau Européen des Unions de Consommateurs
BLEU	Belgo-Luxembourg Economic Union
CBI	Confederation of British Industry
CD	Common Defence
CDF	Common Defence Policy
CEECs	Central and Eastern European Countries
CFSP	Common Foreign and Security Policy
CIS	Commonwealth of Independant States
CJTFs	Combined Joint Task Forces
COREPER	Committee of Permanent Representatives
CSCM	Conference on Security and Cooperation in the Mediterranean
DM	Deutschmark
EAGF	European Agricultural Guidance and Guarantee Fund
EC	European Community
ECB	European Central Bank
ECJ	European Court of Justice
ECOFIN	Council of Economic and Finance Ministers
ECSC	European Coal and Steel Community
EEA	European Economic Area
EEB	European Environmental Bureau
EFTA	European Free Trade Association
EIB	European Investment Bank
EMU	Economic and Monetary Union
EMS	European Monetary System
EP	European Parliament
EPC	European Political Cooperation
EPU	European Political Union
ERDF	European Regional Development Fund
ERT	European Round Table
ESCB	European System of Central Banks
ESDI	European Security and Defence Identity
ESF	European Social Fund
ETUC	European Trade Union Federation
EU	European Union
EURATOM	European Atomic Energy Community
FAWEU	Forces Answerable to WEU
FCO	Foreign and Commonwealth Office
FLA	Future Large Aircraft

FOE	Friends of the Earth
G-7	Group of Seven
IEPG	Independent European Programme Group
IGC	Intergovernmental Conference
JHA	Justice and Home Affairs
MEP	Member of the European Parliament
NATO	North Atlantic Treaty Organization
NGOs	Non-governmental Organizations
NORDEK	Nordic Economic Union
OECD	Organization for Economic Cooperation and Development
OEEC	Organization for European Economic Cooperation
OSCE	Organization of Security and Cooperation in Europe
PfP	Partnership for Peace
PLF	Palestine Liberation Front
PPCG	Provisional Policy Coordinating Group
QMV	Qualified Majority Voting
SACEUR	Supreme Allied Commander Europe
SEA	Single European Act
SEM	Single European Market
TENs	trans-European networks
TEU	Treaty on European Union
UDF	Union pour la démocratie française
UNICE	Union of Industrial and Employers' Confederations of Europe
UPFM	Unified Police Force of Mostar
WEAG	Western European Armaments Group
WEU	Western European Union
WWFN	World Wide Fund for Nature
WWF	World Wildlife Fund

THE SETTING

1
THE 1996 IGC:
AN INTRODUCTION

GEOFFREY EDWARDS AND ALFRED PIJPERS

Barely had the Treaty on European Union been digested than Europe was confronted by the prospective demands of further Treaty revision resulting from the Intergovernmental Conference (IGC) that opened under the Italian presidency in March 1996. The Maastricht Treaty, though formally signed on 7 February 1992, came into force only on 1 November 1993. The intervening period almost saw the complete unravelling of the compromise reached with such difficulty at the Maastricht European Council of December 1991. Ratification procedures in Denmark and France especially – the Irish case being somewhat different – allowed those hostile to the Treaty as representing a further stage in the process of integration process full rein. But the referenda were also an opportunity seized on by those hostile to the government in power, or opposed to particular Community policies (such as the Common Agricultural Policy and its reforms). This combination of both national and European factors was sufficiently potent to bring about an initial rejection of the Treaty in the Danish referendum of June 1992 and only the slimmest of margins in favour in the French referendum of September. It took considerable ingenuity on the part of member governments and the EC institutions to agree on a formula that allowed the majority of Danes finally to agree in May 1993. Meanwhile, the British Conservative government under John Major came under ever-stronger attack from the Eurosceptics on its own parliamentary backbenches, and delayed final parliamentary ratification until July 1993. In Germany, though the Treaty and the necessary constitutional amendments were ratified by the two parliamentary chambers, constitutional challenges meant that it was not until 13 October 1993 that Germany was able to deposit the instruments of ratification in Rome.

Highlighting the difficulties experienced by only four of the then twelve member states may seem to offer an odd perspective on Maastricht. Certainly, few of the Mediterranean member states had any serious problems with ratification, nor did the Benelux countries, even if there was a degree of disappointment with the obvious compromise nature of the Treaty. And yet, the fact that disillusionment and hostility characterized so much of the debate, especially in France and Germany, is too significant to overlook. Not only have these two countries provided much of the impetus for the construction of Europe, but divisions within and between them have tended to spill over to affect the state of the Union as a whole.

The period of ratification was important therefore in that it both influenced the way in which the Treaty was implemented and provided the background to preparations for the IGC. It was not simply that implementation was delayed but that delay and division tended to reinforce a sense of caution in the protection and promotion of national interests – especially perhaps in the second and third inter-governmental 'pillars', on a Common Foreign and Security Policy (CFSP) and Cooperation in Justice and Home Affairs (JHA). Moreover, the sense of disen-chantment with, and opposition to the European venture was combined with a certain sense of malaise and unease within a number of states about the course of domestic politics and the traditions of the welfare state in Western Europe. It was this element of negative symbiosis that created a sense of alarm among some lead-ers about the continued successful development of the Union. It may, of course, be that this anxiety was, to some extent, artificial; proponents of bicycle theories are always concerned about the possibilities of slowing down and falling off. But the contrast between the economic and political gloom of the first half of the 1990s with the heady days of the late-1980s was sometimes only too clearly marked. The suggestion of a much deeper crisis or malaise within Western European societies seemed to be reflected or symbolized in the difficulties of rat-ifying Maastricht. At a minimum it seemed to point, particularly in Denmark and France, to a widening gap between government and the governed. It seemed, too, to suggest that the 'Monnet-method' of integration within Europe, characterized by the closer enmeshment of sectoral elites, seemed to have reached its limits.

Maastricht, after all, raised questions not only about deepening economic cooperation but set out a timetable for Economic and Monetary Union and a single currency. It proposed not only a common foreign and security policy but declared the eventual aim, however set around with qualifications, to be a common defence. It proposed not simply free movement of people but a common European citizenship and cooperation on justice, police and other 'internal' mat-ters. Despite all the compromises on Community supranationalism versus inter-governmental cooperation, and on opting in and opting out, merely dropping overt reference to federalism did not disguise the changed nature of the relation-ship between the member states and the Union. That change raised fundamental questions about the traditional attributes and qualities of national sovereignty, cre-ating doubts about both the democratic legitimacy of the European venture and also the continued legitimacy of the nation state itself.

This sense of uncertainty was all the more challenging in view of the efforts being made in Central and Eastern Europe to liberalize and democratize, processes undertaken clearly and determinedly with future membership of the EU as an objective. Whatever the satisfaction at the ending of the division of Europe, any triumphalism engendered by the victory of Western European polit-ical and economic values was tempered by a growing unease about the potential consequences of the full assimilation of Eastern with Western Europe. The imme-diate prospect, achieved on 1 January 1995, was of enlargement to include the EFTAn countries of Austria, Finland and Sweden – the Norwegian decision to remain outside being accepted as typically idiosyncratic – which, given their size

2

and compatibility with existing member states, appeared easily containable. The enormity of the impact on the EU of the accession of perhaps a further ten or even fifteen states was often referred to – as in the conclusions of the Corfu European Council which charged the Reflection Group to consider the agenda of the IGC in the light of further enlargement – even if most governments appeared to prefer to focus more on the principle and processes of accession rather than on its longer-term consequences.

An exception which sought to tackle the issues of legitimacy and democracy in the EU as well as the consequences of the need to enlarge eastwards was the paper drawn up by the CDU–CSU Fraktion in the *Bundestag* (September 1994). Otherwise known as the Schäuble–Lamers paper, it listed the challenges facing the Union and its member states in a particularly direct, if brief, manner. It attracted most attention perhaps for its proposals rather than its analysis, not least because it broached the subject of an inner core of a hard core of the Union, that is, an enhanced Franco-German relationship, which inevitably set off a cacophony of alarm bells. Perhaps unsurprisingly, the CDU, as the major partner in government in Germany, then backpeddled somewhat, with party leaders subsequently giving a more anodyne version of the paper. However, the analysis provided in the original paper pointed to a number of vital issues, many of them taken up in this volume of papers. It put them particularly succinctly:

- a growing differentiation of interests, fuelled by differences in the level of socio-economic development which threatens to obscure the basic commonality of interests;
- a process of profound structural economic change. With its mass unemployment, which it will be impossible to overcome in the short term, this crisis poses a threat to already overstretched social systems and social stability. The economic crisis is one aspect of the general crisis of modern society in the West;
- an increase in 'regressive nationalism' in (almost) all member countries, which is the product of deep-seated fears and anxieties caused by the internal crisis of modern society and by external threats, such as migration. Fear and anxiety tempt people to seek, if not a solution, then at least a refuge in a return to the nation-state and all things national;
- the highly debilitating effect of the enormous demands placed on national governments and parliaments by the above problems. (CDU–CSU Fraktion 1994: 2)

In addition, the paper referred to the 'over-extension' of the EU institutions, different internal and especially external priorities among the member states of the EU, as well as the question of further enlargement to include the countries of Central and Eastern Europe (the CEECs). All these factors pointed, as Schäuble and Lamers suggested, to the conclusion that 'the process of European unification has reached a critical juncture' (*ibid.*: 1).

Just how critical is inevitably a matter of political judgement but other factors might also be added to the list to reinforce the uncertainties facing governments in the late 1990s. There is, for example, the whole complex of issues raised by the process of globalization, whether of the financial system or of communications. Global financial markets and global communications networks challenge particularly directly the traditional gate-keeping role of the state. In some cases the response has been to seek to reinforce national exclusiveness at least in cultural or educational terms. In others, perhaps in part because of the difficulties of such purely national responses, the pressure has been for stronger regional solutions, however partial they might be, as for example in the efforts, sponsored especially by France for a coherent European audio-visual policy. A sense of national – or even European – identity has not, however, been enhanced by government inability to reduce unemployment, as Schäuble and Lamers suggested, or to prevent a widening gap – most marked in the UK – between rich and poor. Questions of the legitimacy and not merely the effectiveness of European political systems have also been reinforced by the seemingly continuous rise in so many member states of corruption, scandal and questionable political decision-taking.

It is against these background factors that the IGC opened in Turin in March 1996. In an important sense, the Conference reflects the ability of member governments to meet a particularly profound set of issues that affect each of them within the framework of the Union, including legitimacy, democratic accountability, and efficiency and effectiveness. That expectations of the Conference were continuously dampened down by governments, not least in the final report of the Reflection Group in December 1995 (Reflection Group 1995), reinforces perhaps the critical nature of the problems. At least one lesson of the Maastricht ratification process seems to have been absorbed, that of the importance of providing at least some information for an ongoing debate on the future of the EU. The IGC thereby provides a useful lens through which to view the EU and its member states as they approach the millennium.

This is particularly the case, despite the lack of consensus in the Reflection Group on radical reform, since virtually no subject was really excluded from the IGC's agenda. The Conference was, of course, the first to be mandated by treaty rather than as a response of governments to various internal and external pressures. Article N of the Maastricht Treaty called for a further conference in 1996 'to examine those provisions of this Treaty for which revision is provided', provisions which included those dealing with defence and other aspects of the CFSP, the continuation of the pillar structure, the scope of the co-decision procedure, the hierarchy of Community legislative acts and the possibility of specific clauses in the fields of civil protection, energy and tourism (Federal Trust 1995). Various Councils and European Councils then added to the list. Foreign Ministers, for example, decided in Ioannina in March 1994, to review member states' weighting in the Council arrangements for qualified majority voting (QMV). The Corfu European Council in June 1994, again under the Greek Presidency, created the Reflection Group for a more detailed preparation for treaty revision. The Group, consisting of representatives of the fifteen member states, together with a member of the Commission (Marcelino Oreja) and two members of the European Parliament (Elmar Brok and Elizabeth Guigou, representing the two largest party groupings in the EP), began work under the Spanish Presidency (the chairman being Carlos Westendorp) with a symbolic meeting in Messina in June 1995. It presented its report to the European Council in Madrid in December. The Council clarified the IGC's mandate, placing particular emphasis on the four core objectives of the Reflection Group: bringing the EU closer to its citizens; improving its operational efficiency; equipping it for external action; and deepening cooperation on JHA (Council 1995). But it also opened the Conference up further by agreeing that the IGC: 'will in general, have to examine the improvements which will have to be made to the Treaties to bring the Union into line with today's realities and tomorrow's requirements' (ibid.). If the 1996 IGC follows the precedent of others then member states will raise new items throughout the Conference up to the very last negotiating sessions.

Meanwhile, the European institutions duly contributed their opinions to the Reflection Group on the operation of the Treaty on European Union (TEU) and any revisions that might be required or desirable (see, for example, the Commission's Report published in May 1995 and widely distributed within the EU).[1] A wide variety of government agencies, advisory bodies, political parties, think-tanks and others also proffered their advice. The opportunities for public debate have therefore been considerable – even if media headlines and Council meetings have tended to be overtaken by crises or near crises, whether relating to 'mad cow disease' and the British non-cooperation policy of the summer of 1996, or the complexities of moving towards Economic and Monetary Union (EMU). Nonetheless, the business of treaty reform has, most certainly during the 1990s, become a primary feature in contemporary European politics.

A BACKGROUND TO TREATY REFORM

From the Treaty of Rome to the Single European Act

Treaty reform has not always been such a feature. In the 1960s and 1970s, the treaty revisions under Article 236 of the Treaty of Rome (which preceded Article N of the TEU) were usually highly restricted, limited to, for example, the Convention relating to Netherlands Antilles (1962) or the Treaty amending certain provisions of the Protocol on the Statute of the European Investment Bank (1975). There were, of course, some revisions with wider implications, such as the Merger Treaty of 1965, and the Budget Treaty of 1970. But in each case, the 'conference of representatives of the Governments of the Member States' (not yet dubbed 'IGC') that was convened met only briefly. The conference on the Merger Treaty, for instance, lasted only a few hours (on 8 April 1965) since the actual negotiations had already been completed in the Council of Ministers.

Any less circumscribed use of Article 236 was regarded as either undesirable or as unnecessary. Certainly the strongest pressure for reform came from France in the early 1960s, but largely in a direction unwelcome to the other five member states. Otherwise the great bulk of the Treaties of Rome had still to be imple-

5

mented and reform was therefore unnecessary.

During the 1970s, institutional reform that required treaty revision was blocked both by the preoccupation of most of the member states with the twin issues of inflation and stagnation and by continuing problems associated with enlargement, not least Britain's budgetary problem. The Tindeman's Report on European Union of 1975 (*EC Bulletin* 1976) merely gathered dust on the shelf. What reform there was tended to be *ad hoc* and piecemeal, using Article 235, for example, for some issues (such as the environment), or moving outside the Community framework completely as in European Political Cooperation (established in 1970) or the institutionalization of summits in the form of European Councils (from 1974). The Three Wise Men's Report (1979) reflected this political evolution by focusing – as required by the European Council – on greater institutional efficiency rather than raising the issue of constitutional reform (Edwards 1996).

However, what had therefore been a circumscribed use of Article 236 changed during the 1980s, when a string of internal and external pressures on the Community and its member states led to calls for much broader reform. The Genscher-Colombo initiative of 1981 (Bonvicini 1987) and the initiatives of the so-called Crocodile Group led by Altiero Spinelli in the European Parliament (Schmuck 1987) paved the way. Even if the former led only to a 'Solemn Declaration on European Union' in 1983 and the latter to what was forced to remain merely a Draft Treaty on European Union, the issue of treaty revision reached the political agenda. When in Fontainebleau in June 1984, a solution was found to Britain's budgetary problem, the way was open. The Council established what some hoped would be a second Spaak Committee that would echo the achievements of its predecessor in leading to the establishment of the EEC. The Dooge Committee as a whole may not have aspired to such heights but despite the reservations or footnotes entered by, for example, the British, Danes and Greeks, the report set out a clear possible agenda of reform. When taken together with Delors' dynamism as President of the Commission, the Cockfield White Paper on the completion of the internal market, a proposal strongly supported by – if not led by – European business circles and others (Green Cowles 1995), the necessary incentives for constitutional change seemed to be in place – even if it took some clever manoeuvring by the Italian Presidency at the Milan Council to overcome the British predilection for 'gentlemens' agreements' rather than treaty revision and continued opposition from the Danes and Greeks (Thatcher 1993: 548–51).

At the heart of the negotiations was a consensus on the need to establish a genuine single European market (SEM) – even if some of the less developed member states demanded a financial quid pro quo. There were of course divisions between 'maximalists' and 'minimalists' in what steps to pursue beyond and 'flanking' the key agreement on the SEM in areas such as research and development and the environment. In December 1985 agreement was reached not only on the date for the completion of the SEM (31 December 1992), but also on the means of achieving the deadline, the extension of QMV to most single market questions.

European Political Cooperation was also codified but outside the framework of the EC as such. The resulting Single European Act (SEA), sporting two of the three Maastricht pillars, was signed in February 1986. After delay caused by the issue of ratification in Ireland, the SEA entered into force on 1 July 1987.

The road to Maastricht

While the driving force that led to the establishment of the Dooge Committee and the SEA was predominantly economic, the pressures leading to the two Maastricht IGCs and the TEU were very largely of a political–security nature, despite the central part played by monetary issues. Two inter-related sets of factors, roughly divided between internal and external, are distinguishable. The internal factors are those which pressed for the completion of the 1992 programme and the development of its logical monetary (and social) follow-up. The path had already been laid down in the Delors Report of 1989 and by the European Council meetings of that year in Madrid and Strasbourg, where it was agreed in principle to convene an IGC on EMU under Article 236.

This set of internal considerations became heavily influenced by an external set symbolized by the fall of the Berlin Wall in November 1989. The collapse of the Soviet Empire (and ultimately of the Soviet Union itself) and the reunification of Germany influenced the drive for treaty revision in three ways. First, it accelerated the process of monetary integration because it reinforced French concerns about the potential dominance of Germany unless the Deutschmark (DM) was submitted to a single European currency authority. Second, it led to a rethinking of the institutional structures, since Germany was intent on strengthening the institutions, especially the European Parliament, in return for giving up the DM. Third, concern over the real and potential instability in Central and Eastern Europe raised awareness of the need for closer security cooperation among EC member states.

At the same time, the completion of the internal market, together with the moves made by some member states within the Schengen agreements to move more quickly on the issue of free movement of people, contributed to a consensus that more consistent and coherent cooperation was needed on questions relating to migration, immigration, international crime and so on. The time therefore appeared ripe for a further serious overhaul of the EC treaties. In June 1990, in Dublin, the European Council decided to convene two IGCs, on Economic and Monetary Union, and on Political Union. Both were opened at the European Council meeting in Rome in December 1990.

The two IGCs began work in January 1991 under the Luxembourg Presidency, and were conducted on separate tracks. The IGC on EMU was led by Finance Ministers, assisted by their central bankers, while the IGC on Political Union was coordinated by Foreign Ministers, occasionally assisted by representatives from other departments such as justice or home affairs. Their fate was different: the negotiators in the IGC on EMU could build on the highly professional preparations made by the Delors Committee, with the result that the negotiations went relatively smoothly and outlines of the EMU provisions were ready well before the Maastricht European Council of December 1991.

The IGC on Political Union had little but the mandate of the Rome European Council on which to build. Largely, perhaps, as a result, the negotiations were marked by controversy, particularly on security issues and institutional reform (Laursen and Vanhoonacker 1992). The Dutch Presidency's proposal to bring about a more unified structure rather than the separate pillars of the Luxembourg draft caused a mini-crisis in September (Black Monday, 30 September) and delayed agreement. Agreement at the European Council meeting in Maastricht in December was made possible only after some extremely hard bargaining on opting in and opting out, with the final treaty being signed in February 1992.

Reform and treaty revision had thus transformed the brief intergovernmental conferences of the 1960s and 1970s into major political events. Given the ever-widening range of EC competences and the growing number of member states involved, as well as the range of national and transnational interests engaged, such a widening of the agenda and its impact was perhaps inevitable. While clearly inter-state negotiations, the IGCs bore little relationship to classical diplomatic conferences reviewing international treaties. Treaty revision is perhaps better looked at as a constitutional process – with an integral role being played by the representatives of the people, both at national and European level.

Moreover, it is a process that has become increasingly time consuming. Each reform cycle has five main elements: consultations leading to the decision by the European Council to begin the process; the preparatory work with committees, advisory papers, bilateral, multilateral consultations, etc. leading to the decision of the Council to convene an IGC; the negotiation and bargaining process that leads to the formulation of new texts and the signing of the new treaty; the ratification process that finally leads to the treaty's entry into force; and finally the implementation phase. Taken together, a revision cycle spans some three or four years even before one considers full implementation. If one takes the decision by the European Council at Fontainebleau in 1984 to establish the Dooge Committee as the start of the cycle for the SEA, then the member states will have spent the larger part of the final decades of the twentieth century on treaty reform. IGCs have developed into almost semi-permanent conferences of the member states; in a sense there is a fourth circuit of decision-making within the EU, alongside the three recognized pillars.

THE FUNCTIONS OF THE IGC

IGCs have thus acquired a significance beyond simply treaty reform. Perhaps four different, if overlapping, functions can be discerned.

1. Deepening

The central purpose of treaty reform is to strengthen the EU both in internal and external policy areas. 'Deepening' has become a key concept – sometimes being used as a synonym for integration itself. It remains, though, somewhat ambiguous. On the one hand, it refers to the improvement of the institutional structures of the Union, whether in terms of closer integration for integration's sake or, to echo the 1995 Madrid European Council, improving the EU's operational efficiency, by means, for example, of the extension of QMV, greater transparency, subsidiarity, etc. On the other hand, it also refers to the widening of European concerns, whether in the sense of new Community policies or, again to follow the Madrid Council, through equipping the Union for external action and deepening cooperation on JHA. IGCs have tended to combine all these elements, though the IGC that led to the SEA was perhaps more preoccupied with the first type of deepening through the extension of QMV, the introduction of the cooperation procedure, etc. The significance of Maastricht lay more in extending the range of EU concerns, with EMU, defence and JHA, though it also added co-decision, citizenship, etc.

Given the growing Euroscepticism that has characterized the post Maastricht period, it is worth recalling that the core provisions of both the SEA and the TEU have functioned reasonably well. There may still be obstacles to the completely free movement of all factors of production within the SEM, but the achievement of so much of the 1992 programme was a considerable one. Planning for EMU remains very much on schedule, despite critics and doom-merchants. Where the treaties have not worked so well, there has been perhaps a natural tendency to blame the treaty text – it was after all the result of difficult compromises – for what have been political failures. The provisions of the TEU on foreign policy and security were in some respects, though not all, fairly ambitious. Events, not least those in the former Yugoslavia, certainly tested them severely. Member governments, though, have not always been willing, for reasons not always particularly relevant to the issue at hand, to meet the collective challenge. Yet clearly, overall the IGCs have played a critically important role in the development of the EU.

Certainly the prospect of such development has been taken seriously by countries outside the EC/EU, including the USA and Japan. Moreover, despite the limitations of Maastricht and the growth of Euroscepticism within a number of member countries, the queue for membership has lengthened; the Union, whether as a market, a political system seeking to uphold democratic norms and values, or a putative defence system, remains an important magnet. To the extent that the 1996 IGC takes the implications of further enlargement seriously, it could play a vital role in bringing about the smooth assimilation of Western and Eastern Europe.

2. Adaptation

A second function of IGCs has been to review those treaty provisions which, in the light of new circumstances (or of newly defined interests) have become obsolete, or which are felt to be inadequate to meet the objectives of the Union. Enlargement, geopolitical transformations, new world trade and investment patterns, economic and environmental crises, technological revolutions and so on, may all lead to a collective desire to adapt existing institutions, procedures and policies, or to create new ones.

The preparations for Maastricht served such a function. They became an essential part of the complex re-ordering of relations accompanying German unification and change in (and eventual dissolution of) the Soviet Union. Without the prospect that the DM would become subsumed within a single European currency, German unification might have been less acceptable and the French government might have delayed the whole process – even if it could not ultimately block it. But delay could have had serious consequences for the stability of the EC and Europe at large. Moscow, for example, might well have been tempted to stick to its demands or increase them. The prospect of EMU played its part therefore in the smooth transition to German unity.

Moreover, even if there was a sense of 'Maastricht fatigue', some member governments were quick to begin to identify the gaps, ambiguities and limitations in the TEU, even if initially without too much public discussion – during 1993–94 there were perhaps too many other preoccupations such as national elections in Germany, European elections, the debacle over the appointment of a new President of the Commission, and the enlargement negotiations with the EFTAns. With the Essen European Council in 1994 attention became more focused on the future of the Central and Eastern European countries, which, as suggested above, makes several of the issues ducked in Maastricht even more acute. There are, in other words, issues such as security, democracy and legitimacy, and employment – raised by several member states – as well as enlargement which are likely to lead some governments to continue to put forward more maximalist positions, even if, perhaps, in different contexts from that of the EU as we presently know it.

3. The accommodation of national interests

Closely related to the adaptation function is the opportunity IGCs provide member governments to redefine their positions *vis-à-vis* each other and *vis-à-vis* the Community institutions in the light of new circumstances. We have already referred to the interaction of France and Germany on the issue of EMU and stronger European institutions and it is dealt with further in Chapter 5. Some of the alliances and coalitions created during an IGC might be tactical – as in the Anglo-Italian case on security and defence during the 1991 IGC – but others represent a longer-term identity of interests as in the case of the Benelux (although as Chapter 7 points out, the degree of unity among the Benelux can be exaggerated).

The 1996 IGC offers a particularly important opportunity for this national accommodation function because of the demands that will inevitably be placed on existing institutional structures and procedures by enlargement to twenty, twenty-five or even thirty states. Change of such magnitude will, sooner or later, though the forces of inertia and delay remain significant, push member states to review their position in the EU. Several of the larger member states have already demanded a readjustment of weighting in voting in the Council, as the British did with the EFTAn enlargement. The Ioannina compromise of March 1994 was in part based on agreement to review the situation of weighted voting at the IGC so that votes are more in harmony with population figures.

Moreover, enlargement also reactivates the possibilities of differentiated forms of integration, with endless opportunities for national manoeuvring in almost every policy area, including some within the first pillar. But the second pillar especially opens up a rich menu for choice given the variables of membership of NATO, WEU and the EU. There are already significant forms of different speeds of integration and even variable geometry, which were emphasized in the Maastricht Treaty and its protocols. These are likely to become more refined and extended, if only because not all member states will be in a position – or may be unwilling – to participate in EMU. And if, as the CDU–CSU paper suggests, there needs to be a hard core – and even an inner core – to maintain the momentum of integration, it raises even the question of the unanimity requirement for future treaty revision. All these issues are now regarded as legitimate items for debate – in marked contrast to the Community orthodoxy that characterized the 1960s and 1970s.

There is also a domestic dimension to the accommodation function since IGCs allow new administrations to feed their priorities into the EU framework. Changes in government, whether in membership of the ruling coalition or when parties come to power after long periods in opposition, can have important consequences for integration policies. IGCs both require and provide the opportunity for incoming governments to formulate a coherent and more comprehensive policy.

4. Socialization

The successive stages of the reform cycle have had a socializing effect on member states. This at least has been clear at élite levels, within governments, among officials, central bankers, local and regional governments and, as Mazey and Richardson suggest in Chapter 12, among non-governmental organizations and interest groups. That is not to say that familiarity with EU negotiations necessarily induces support; Szukala and Wessels, for example, in Chapter 5, discuss the significance of the fact that the cleavages caused by Maastricht among the élite in France have persisted for much longer than might have been anticipated. Given the duration of the reform cycle and the multitude of meetings at various levels, the opportunities for debate, if not endless, are considerable. A significant factor here, however, is the varying extent to which such opportunities have actually been seized by national parliaments, parties, the media, etc. There was an element, not confined to the UK or Denmark but particularly apparent in those countries, of suspiciousness during the Maastricht debate that too little serious debate had taken place on the SEA, or rather that the full significance of the Act had not been explained. That suspiciousness influenced the Maastricht debate among the wider public, reinforced perhaps by the fact that the debate at the

11

national level took place largely after the treaty had been signed. Importantly, the debates held at the European level, particularly, of course, in the European Parliament before and during the negotiations, did not make any great impact on the national debates. Nearly all the member governments have been very much more assiduous in preparing their publics for the 1996 IGC, even though, once again, any consistency has been subject to the vagaries of more immediate crises such as mad cow disease.

There is, however, little certainty that the provision of more information on European reform is enough to overcome the gap discernably in several member states between government and the governed to which the different pace and levels of socialization may have significantly contributed. The socialization impact has, after all to be seen against the problems referred to in the CDU–CSU paper (1994) relating to structural economic change, large-scale unemployment, the threat to overstretched social systems, the increase in 'regressive nationalism' and the 'debilitating' effects of resultant demands on national institutions. Such is the fundamental nature of these challenges that it is not wholly surprising that member governments are led towards different conclusions; they too often exacerbate national differences rather than emphasize commonalities.

Risks

There are therefore risks attached to the otherwise positive role of IGCs. Politicization is not always an easily controllable process. Treaty reform, to follow Moravcsik (1991), is inevitably the result of inter-state bargaining in which governments aggregate domestic demands and determine national preferences and the resultant package deal. But as the Maastricht ratification process revealed, the final package may not be wholly welcome to electorates. It could be argued, that adverse feelings and opposition are part of any developed political system, and the rise of public concern over the course of integration might be taken more as a sign of a maturing European political system than simply as an indicator of protest. That, of course, makes some fairly sweeping assumptions about the integration process. But it may also be the case that the discrepancy between the large parliamentary majorities in favour of the TEU and the negative feelings among the broader public are more a reflection of the shortcomings in the legitimacy of the political class in general. Whichever it may be, negotiating European treaty revision has become a far more complex undertaking. Balancing domestic interests and the European interest is often a delicate task; weak governments are particularly prone to emphasize the former and particular domestic sectoral interests. The semi-permanent nature of reform cycles provides a highly inter-governmental forum which offers governments even greater leeway to emphasize national approaches.

The deadlines set for the completion of IGCs – as for other decisions within the EC/EU – however self-imposed and flexible they may turn out to be (even if the clock has to be stopped) may also lead to the insertion of awkward compromises into the text. Their codification may then frustrate decision-making thereafter.

Moreover, IGCs may well be used to introduce mere cosmetic changes to paper over conflicts or disguise lack of progress. Endless negotiations over minimal institutional change, for example, may provide a welcome escape for governments unable to face real political dilemmas. They may not, on the other hand, contribute to efficiency or effectiveness in the longer term, or provide any useful rallying point among European publics.

THE ORGANIZATION OF THE BOOK

The main purpose of this collection of studies is relatively straightforward: to investigate some of the essential political, economic and legal issues at stake for the EU as it faces the millennium. Its organizing concept is the 1996 IGC, its setting, the actors involved and its agenda. But the aim has been to look beyond the formal aspects of the Conference to examine the agenda of the EU itself – in a sense those issues that should or could have been on the IGC's agenda even if they do not actually appear on it. The IGC, in other words, is the peg on which we have hung ideas about the development and evolution of the Union. That is not to deny the importance of the IGC itself – we have pointed above to the valuable functions IGCs have come to acquire. Despite its lack-lustre start, the 1996 IGC may yet provide one of the milestones along the road of half a century of integration in Europe. Few, after all, in 1986-87 conceived of the SEA as a particularly radical step. But the primary aim has been to set the IGC in a longer-term perspective of European integration.

The book has three major parts: the chapters by Story, Begg and Grimwade, and Laursen are designed to provide the setting for the IGC, to analyse the broad political and economic context of the Conference and in Laursen, to examine the lessons of Maastricht. The second part, Chapters 5 to 12, discusses the actors involved in the debate. For practical and other reasons, we did not plan a country-by-country survey for each of the present fifteen member states. Instead we have sought to cluster member states, using patterns of possible common interests as the main criterion, and, at the same time, taking care that key national actors (i.e. the larger member states) should receive adequate attention. In view of its somewhat isolated position, the UK rather demanded separate treatment while, because of their critical role in the whole integration process, the Franco-German tandem seemed more appropriate. It also seemed appropriate given their role in EU decision-making to devote three chapters to non-state players, the European Commission, the European Parliament and organized interest groups. The last part, chapters 13 to 16, cover the agenda, both of the IGC and, more generally, of the EU and its member states.

NOTE

1. The Reports of the Council, Parliament, and Court of Justice were all published though not so widely disseminated as that of the Commision. The references are: the Council's decision is reported in Europe report, Document no. 2032, 12 April 1995; European Parliament, Committee on Institutional Affairs, report on the functioning of the Treaty on European Union with a view to the 1996 Intergovernmental Conference – implementation and development of the Union Doc. A4-0102/95/, 12 May 1995; proceedings of the Court of Justice and Court of First Instance, no. 15, 1995; European Commission (1995) report on the Operation of the Treaty on the European Union SEC (95) final, Brussels, 10 May.

REFERENCES AND BIBLIOGRAPHY

Bonvicini, Gianni (1987) 'The Genscher–Colombo Plan and the "Solemn Declaration on European Union" (1981–83)', in Pryce, R. (ed.) *The Dynamics of European Integration*. London, Croom Helm; pp.174–87.
CDU–CSU Fraktion des Deutschen Bundestages (1994) *Ueberlegungen zur europaeischen Politik*. Bonn, September.
EC Bulletin (1976) 'Tindeman's Report on European Union', 1/76.
Edwards, Geoffrey (1996) 'National sovereignty versus integration: the Council of Ministers', in Richardson, J. (ed.) *European Union: Power and Policy-Making*. London, Routledge.
Federal Trust (1995) *State of the Union*. London, Federal Trust.
Green Cowles, Maria (1995) 'Setting the agenda for a new Europe: the ERT and EC in 1992', *Journal of Common Market Studies*, vol. 33, no. 4 (December), pp.501–26.
Laursen, Finn and Vanhoonacker, Sophie (eds) (1992) *The Intergovernmental Conference on Political Union*. Dordrecht, Nijhoff.
Moravcsik, Andrew (1991) 'Negotiating the Single European Act', in Hoffman, Stanley and Keohane, Robert (eds), *The New European Community*. Boulder, Colorado, Westview.
Reflection Group (24 August 1995), progress report on the 1996 Intergovernmental Conference.
Schmuck, Otto (1987) 'The European Parliament's draft treaty establishing the European Union', in Pryce, R. (ed.) *The Dynamics of European Integration*. London, Croom Helm, pp.188-216.
Thatcher, Margaret (1993) *The Downing Street Years*. London, HarperCollins.

2
THE IDEA OF THE CORE:
THE DIALECTICS OF HISTORY AND SPACE

JONATHAN STORY

The creation of the empire of a united Germany showed a new Europe. The keen word of an English diplomatist expressed what was dawning in men's minds as a new misgiving. 'Europe', he said, 'has lost a mistress and got a master' (Morley 1905: 991). But I do not know, [asked Henry Kissinger] how the President will keep Germany from dominating the Europe he has just described. "Par la guerre", he [de Gaulle], said simply' (Kissinger 1979: 110).

The great transformation in European and world affairs in the years 1989–92 marked a shift in the dynamics of European integration from one dialectics to a new and untried dialectics. The old dialectics were those of the Cold War, with the familiar and multiple interactions between the two Germanies, the two Europes, the two alliances and the two great powers. Despite the central part played by nuclear weapons in the drama, the unravelling of the status quo consolidated sometime in the mid-1950s occurred at a leisurely pace, enabling Western European peoples and states to build up their own peculiar society. But its dynamics was played out on a world scale at four levels of the global structure, the states, society and economy, whereby the creation of a competitive global market under leadership of the USA as Europe's prime power accelerated the transformation of societies and states to undermine the communist party states. The two Europes lay at the heart of the process so that the fall of the Berlin Wall in November 1989 detonated around the world, bringing the countries of Central and South-eastern Europe, plus successor states of the Soviet Union, as well as its Third World clients, and China and India into a world market where the name of the game is getting access to hard currency markets and the best technology on offer.

With the events of 1989–92, the familiar dialectics between East and West, the two Germanies and the two Europes gave way to a new dialectic prompted by the disappearance of the old structure and its substitution for an indefinite process of open-ended transition to a new world structure whose outlines are visible, but by definition hypothetical. China, India, Russia and Europe are all candidates for world status, but each must struggle with their specific inertias, leaving only the USA as a world power, with Japan as a wealthy second (Kissinger 1994: 17–28). Germany's economy, temporarily the world's third largest, is one half the size of Japan's. Yet its unification precipitated the triple moves to integration in Western Europe, self-determination in Germany and transition out of the party states. The military threat faded, to be replaced by a process of simultaneous disintegration of the party states, their import of Western ways and an accelerated integration of the world economy. This was accompanied by a precipitate expansion of Europe's peripheries to the traditional frontier regions which separate Christian Europe from Islam, and western Christianity from eastern Christianity. Familiar landmarks of the 1945–89 period vanished. Western European leaders improvised as best they could, and sought to reassure themselves and their publics that they were neither prepared to return Europe to its pre-1945 pasts, nor that the European peoples should be dismayed at venturing into an uncharted future.

Their initial reaction was one of preservation. Only through cooperation could the system of interdependence built up since the 1940s be secured. The novelty lay in the substitution of the structure of bipolarity for the much looser configuration in Europe of a core and a periphery. The fear was that the forces of disintegration and fragmentation at work in the Balkans, Central Europe or the former Soviet Union would work inwards towards core Europe, while the expansion of core Europe would so accentuate its diversity as to loosen the bonds that had been painfully sewn together in the previous decades.[1] There was also a confused sense that the collapse of the Soviet Union, with its dogma of having taken leave of history, would unleash an orgy of figurative fishing exhibitions in Europe's collective pasts, and especially in Germany where the definition of nationality remained untaintedly that of the Nationality Act of 1914. The Act defined German nationality by the law of blood, in contrast to a law of citizenship predicated, if not always practised on universal principles. Consolidation of the core therefore required agreement on its geographic limits, on its ideals, on its institutions and on its political and economic relations with the rest of the world. Yet any attempt to define it confronted the realities of differing political imaginations among Europe's leaders and peoples as to who belonged in which core, and what the criteria for membership or exclusion should be. Defining what Europe's future should be inevitably precipitated preemptive efforts to enter it now.

The speed and scope of these changes in European and world affairs introduced a vital complicating factor to the multiple dimensions of geography, ideals, institutions and markets inherent to any political arrangement defining core from periphery. The states, and the EU, face – as Pierre Hassner (1992) has written – the double dilemma of identity, 'the temporal dimension of continuity and change, and the spatial dimension of closure and overture.' The general crisis of collective identities, Hassner went on, derives from the non-coincidence of their two dimensions of optimal size and the sense of belonging over time. As Burke wrote at the opening of a previous revolutionary period in Europe, a sense of belonging ought not to be considered as nothing better than 'a partnership agreement in a trade of pepper and coffee, calico or tobacco.' It is a partnership 'not only between those who are living, but between those who are living, those who are dead and those who are yet to be born' (Burke 1995). Partnership is as much a matter of the substance of memory as a set of expectations. In Hassner's words, the states are not generally aware that the two dimensions of scope and time do not coincide for politics, currency, defence or culture. When they do, their citizens or governments tend to become nostalgic for a lost or threatened unity. The Union then may become a scapegoat, or seek to redeem itself by trying to reproduce a mythical unity as a club of states in the realms of defence or money and economy at the level of a continent.

Any discussion of the idea of the core or periphery in the Europe of the 1990s therefore requires first a sketch of some of the major inheritances which Europe was bequeathed from the period of the Cold War. Those inheritances are juxtaposed to other strata of memory, in a Europe after the Cold War that is heir also to a pre-1945 world, and that is haunted by fears or admonitions of a return under modern conditions to that past. Yet the end of the Cold War fundamentally altered Europe's acquired position in the world economy, along with its dynamics and the world markets' varied and changing expectations about how it would evolve. The EU was conceived as a club of states and peoples, distinguishable from the rest of the world in territory, law or policy procedures. It was also part only of a world market and of a world polity.

FIVE INHERITANCES FROM 1945-89

There were at least five major inheritances for Europe left over from the collapse of the system prior to 1989–92. The first was the continuing interaction between extra- and intra-European developments. The old world structure had been established through a prolonged process, starting in 1943 and the shift in the fortunes of war against Germany, Japan and Italy, and consolidated in its main features around 1955. Its content was informed by the US policy of containment, predicated on recognition by Washington of the impossibility of prolonging the wartime alliance on the grounds of incompatible views of political community. There were two variants to the policy of containment (Gaddis 1982). One stressed US support for European, and then Japanese economic revival. The other proposed political and military preparedness to restrict any geographical or ideological extension of Soviet influence. These two variants bound Asian into European affairs through the two major wars in Korea and in Vietnam, and by the rift which opened up between the Soviet Union and the party state in China. The Soviet Union proved responsive to Brandt's *Ostpolitik*, enabling it to embark on its own policy of containment of China in Asia. Twenty years of *Ostpolitik*, intended to ease the way to German 'unity in free self-determination', were punctuated by clashes between the powers in Asia. This particular chain was broken in October 1989, when Gorbachev refused to crush the demonstrators in Berlin, as Beijing had done to the students in Tienanmen Square in June; but it was replaced by global market interdependence as European businesses or governments responded to the prospective rapid emergence of China as a great power, and to the continued transformation of Pacific Asia.

The second major inheritance from the old order was rooted in the Western European deviation over 40 years from the three components to the policy mix which informed the Marshall Plan's design for Europe's reconstruction (Nau

1990). There were three key components: governments were to pursue discretionary, but conservative counter-cyclical fiscal and monetary policies; national factor markets in labour capital and products were to be made as efficient as possible; moves were to be made to freer trade and currency convertibility. Western Europe moved to currency convertibility in 1958, and accelerated the dismantling of barriers to trade and capital movements. But in the mid-1960s, cautious fiscal and monetary policies were slowly abandoned in favour of more ambitious plans to stimulate growth. Budgets slipped into permanent deficit, as expenditures grew from about 25 per cent to 50 per cent GDP by the early 1990s. European states furthermore responded to growing competition on product markets by elaborating mutually competitive national industrial policies, while legislation was introduced to facilitate cross-shareholding between national corporations. High rates of employment shifted the balance of power in labour markets away from management towards trade unions. Governments conceded a host of benefits for people in work, providing disincentives for employers to hire. By the early 1990s, Western European wage costs numbered among the highest in the world, while unemployment rose unremittingly.

The third inheritance from the policies of free trade and currency convertibility was the huge growth in world and European trade. The larger Western European countries' trade rose from 10 to about 33 per cent of GDP, with 70 per cent or more of trade going to clients within the region. The smaller European countries traded up to two-thirds of their economies, with an even higher proportion devoted to intra-regional trade. By the early 1990s, Western Europe was the world's largest market, accounting for about 28 per cent of the market economies' combined income, and a key source of hard currency for exporters from the former Soviet bloc, the southern and eastern Mediterranean, and Africa. It accounted for about one-third of exports from the Gulf oil states, and one-fifth of exports from North America, Latin America and Asia. Western Europe at the same time had become one of the world's agricultural superpowers, along with the USA, dumping its subsidized surpluses on world farm markets, and contributing to the lowering of world farm product prices. Meanwhile, trade imbalances grew within the industrialized countries of the northern hemisphere. Trade frictions multiplied between Japan and the USA, as Japanese savings and investment rates remained consistently high, while US consumption rates rose and savings rates fell. Within Europe, the Federal Republic ran consistent trade surpluses. World and intra-European negotiations to dismantle non-tariff barriers and reduce agricultural subsidies were launched in 1986 with a view to spiking mercantilist guns across the developed world.

The fourth inheritance was the existence by the 1990s of a world market. As Secretary of State Marshall had stated in June 1947, the idea of US aid in support of a cooperative regional effort to achieve a rapid reconstruction in Europe was 'the revival of a working economy in the world so as to permit the emergence of political and social conditions in which free institutions can exist'. In 1961, the Organization for European Economic Cooperation (OEEC), which had been the result, was expanded to include the US, Canada, Australia and New Zealand, followed by Japan and Spain and became the Organization for Economic Cooperation and Development (OECD), tokening the dual trend of Western economies to promote national economic growth simultaneously with global market integration. Growth in Europe and the rest of the world was fostered on a tide of low priced oil, denominated in dollars and flowing from the Gulf states. The shift of the world onto a dollar standard was accelerated by the US move to external deficit, followed by the continuous run of federal government deficits from the mid-1960s on. Dollar hegemony was consecrated by the oil price rises of 1970–74, and by the related decisions by President Nixon to end the dollar's convertibility into gold and to end restrictions on foreign loans by US banks. Over the subsequent twenty years, London became the hub of the world's money markets, whose turnover in the early 1990s exceeded commodity trade by a factor of 100 to 1. By the early 1990s, private world financial markets were judge and jury of the world economy.

The fifth inheritance from the old order was the flowering of a specifically European society of states (Bull 1980), characterized by a sharing of common interests and values, and by a density of complex political and market interdependences marking it off from the rest of the world. Its shared common values are those of constitutional government, open markets and human rights and duties. This society developed slowly within the confines of the western alliance, based on the Washington Treaty of 1949 and its NATO appendage. Its evolution was accompanied by a contradictory reconciliation between France and the Federal Republic, exemplified in the Franco-German Treaty of 1963. Reconciliation entailed French priority in relations with Germany, but Germany maintained priority in relations to the USA and in pursuit of state unity. The institutional fabric which wove the Atlantic into the continental dimension of Western Europe betrayed the complex layers of partial accords between Europe's sovereign states, tying them through accumulative treaties to each other and to the rest of the world. The Council of Europe, with its European Convention of Human Rights as a pendant to the UN Convention, was in 1990 the sole inclusive Western European organization. The European Community went through successive enlargements from the six core founders of 1957, to the twelve who negotiated the Maastricht Treaty in the course of 1991. The maturing of the European society of states had come in the years 1974–77, with the creation of the European Council, the signing of the Helsinki Final Act among 35 states in a geographic zone stretching from Vancouver to Vladivostock, and the institutionalization of the seven-power annual summits, with their contributions from the ancillary organizations of the United Nations. The Council helped to incorporate the heads of state and government into the EC's business, with the Commission as the other head of a bicephalous pair.

MEMORIES AND GLIMPSES OF POSSIBLE FUTURES

To these five inheritances from the past was added the precipitate move to a prevalence of flux over structure (Calvocoressi 1990). The structure of bipolarity in pre-1989 Europe had replaced the old European balance of power, with its distinction between the great powers and the rest, engaged in a permanent ballet of alignments and disalignments. The permanent alliances of the Cold War confirmed stability, but at the expense of equity. Statecraft operated within predictable bounds. With the end of the Cold War, political imagination was called upon to chart ways of reconciling the multiple dimensions of the new Europe. But where were the sources on which a post-1989 political imagination could draw? Historical references were charged with Europe's divisions, as much as with its unity; the evocation of recent or distant pasts served as blueprints or warnings about possible futures. Yet in the final phases of the Cold War, visions of a Europe multiplied, in which suggestions to overcome present divisions were advanced either through commemoration of a common culture or religion, or through the resurgence of distinct state traditions. Chancellor Schmidt at the SPD conference in 1979 had referred to the unity of medieval European culture as embracing 'not only Rome and Byzantium, but also Oxford, Prague and the Sorbonne, Cluny and Zagorsk, Bergen and Novgorod' (*Financial Times* 12 December 1979), a statement echoed by Gorbachev's rendering of a humanist 'common European home' or of Pope John Paul's vision, enunciated at Santiago de Compostella, of Europe's wounds healed by a return of its peoples to the roots of their Christian civilization. As Germany's unity moved closer, references to Europe's more recent histories became louder, with Prime Minister Thatcher's Bruges speech in autumn 1988 on Great Britain's long adherence to the preservation of Europe's liberties or President Mitterrand's statement in spring 1989 that his prime purpose was to 'guard (France's) status' as a great power in a changing world. Chancellor Kohl warned against the resurgence of 'nationalism', and in particular of a return to the balance of power. Germany's future, he repeatedly stated, lay in a sharing of sovereignty under the mantle of supranational institutions, coupled with 'the definitive rejection of the 19th century order in Europe, which proved incapable of ensuring durable stability' (*Financial Times* 29 October 1990).

A further ingredient of Europe's new situation was the transformation of the world's and Europe's military system, as the Cold War came to an end and the Warsaw Pact crumbled. At the London summit of the NATO powers in July 1990, the western allies celebrated the success of their strategy – laid down in the early years of the alliance and recorded in the Basic Treaty of 1955, whereby the Western allies committed themselves to both the security of the West and the unity of Germany. With the disappearance of the common enemy, though, Europe's security problem became analogous to that confronted by the League of Nations in the inter-war years: what mandate for which purpose to be executed and decided by whom and in which institutions were the peace-keepers or peace-makers to punish an errant state, if error there was? Security for Europe was no longer to be defined in terms of containing an external enemy by military means and its local allies by political or economic inducements; it was to be achieved within a Europe, defined in the CFE Treaty of November 1990 as covering the central area of NATO and the former Warsaw Pact, but, in effect, ranging over the balance of forces in a wider Atlantic and continental context. Within this core area, a key concern for Germany as a non-nuclear state was international agreement to prevent the proliferation of nuclear weapons, while, at the same time, in the Balkans or the Caucasus demands for self-determination deteriorated into war.

On a global scale, Western Europe's acquired position as the core of the world market was fundamentally altered by the fall of the Berlin Wall. Its reverberations around the world accelerated the pace at which four-fifths of humanity with per capita incomes one-sixtieth of those of developed countries were incorporated into the global market. The collapse of the party states under Soviet control, the path of accelerated growth taken by the Chinese communists and the loss of India's soft currency markets precipitated upwards of about 3 billion people onto a world labour market. Their entry marked a challenge to the privileges accumulated by the rich countries of the northern hemisphere within the confines of the Cold War's political markets under US protection, and announced the end to the apartheid that had come to segregate one rich fifth of humanity from the rest of the world's population. The EU accounts for about 6 per cent of the world's population, 28 per cent of the world product, nearly 40 per cent of trans-oceanic trade, does over 70 per cent of its trade on a regional basis, is the principal source and target of foreign direct investment in the world, and trades twice as much with developing countries as with the US or Japan. Yet Europe's high relative wages, the rapid shrinkage in its skill and education advantages and the fluidity of capital goods point to a hyper-competitive world market. Given continued growth rates, China's economy, it could be calculated, would equalize that of the USA by the end of the 1990s; sometime between 2010 and 2020, with a per capita income only one-sixth of a present Swiss, China's economy could exceed Europe's by a factor of three. On that count, post-Cold War Europe's focus on its internal unification was deeply flawed, and revealed a parochial failure to learn from the tidal wave of change running through the vast area of Pacific Asia (Mahbubani 1995). The next century would see Europe reduced to an inconsequential periphery in a world centred on the Pacific and Indian Oceans.

By contrast, many of the arguments advanced by the élites who negotiated the Single European Act (SEA), launching the internal market, and the Maastricht Treaty, which finally entered into force in November 1993, incorporated Europe's altered position in a changing world as a central feature of their appeal. Consolidating a large internal market within the territory of the Union was conceived as a pre-requisite for the Commission and the member states together to strengthen their negotiating position on trade with the USA and Japan. The strategy soon confronted two countervailing forces: the anticipation of a large internal market contributed to accelerate inward and outward investment by corporations – an area where the Commission's powers were practically non-existent; as soon as the European publics became aware in the course of 1988 that their particular habits could be challenged by the creation of the single market, they mobilized to protect themselves or to project their special interests into EC legislation. Opening up the markets within Europe kindled parochial concerns and ran parallel to the globalization of corporate strategies. The growing din of nationalist voices thus preceded the fall of the Wall: legislation on the internal market threatened national standards or traditions; member states and their corporations protected their discretionary powers with regard to investment decisions (Bourke 1995).

Differences between member states over the organization of markets translated into disputes over the purposes of the EU's market strategy, with non-member states and their corporations serving as foils in older European feuds. For Prime Minister Thatcher, the EC's internal market was one means to spike the mercantilist guns of Germany's domestic corporate-government arrangements, adding: 'no one is entitled to have a balance of payments surplus entrenched in the way in which they [the Federal Republic and Japan] run both their economy and also their society' (*Financial Times* 23 November 1987). In Germany, a more open market for corporate assets brought the prospect and practice of foreign ownership. 'If today you restrict or forbid stakeholding for German banks,' echoed Walter Seipp of the Commerz Bank, 'then you have Jimmy Goldsmith ...[to] demonstrate to you how to buy, sell and strip industrial stakes in a market economy on the American model' (Deutschen Bundestages May 1990: 130–31).

The SEA was the last time that European integration could be presented to national European publics as a series of measures designed to improve the functioning of the European economy. Since the rejection of the European Defence Community by the French National Assembly in 1954, the protagonists of European union had sought to skirt the hard core of European patriotisms by adopting utilitarian language. Benefits of economic integration were weighed and measured against the costs, as exemplified in Mr Cecchini's contribution (Cecchini 1988). If the internal market programme was implemented, the author enthused, then 'even granting a fairly broad margin of error, the micro-economic and macro-economic estimates converge on medium-term gains of around 4%–7% of EC gross domestic product' (ibid.: 103). Yet the paradox of the EC's official style was that, though couched in terms of what Keynes labelled 'one of those pretty, polite techniques which tries to deal with the present by abstracting from the fact that we know very little about the future', it was inhabited less overtly by Keynes' 'vague panic fears and equally vague and unreasoned hopes ... (that) lie but a little way below the surface' (Keynes 1937). The internal market, Jacques Delors frequently argued, was a mobilizing device, to achieve a wider political agenda for the EC. Yet the conflation of rationality and passion in Delors' style invited passionate responses. 'The Germans are growing increasingly irritated' wrote the Handelsblatt's international business correspondent, 'at what they see as France's "grand strategy" to extract Versailles-style reparations for German unity' (*Wall Street Journal* 2 June 1992).

Indeed, the internal market programme was one of a number of visions waved before the German public in the dying days of the Cold War. Another was a MittelEuropa, cosily patterned on a Swiss neutrality, with the German Michel figuratively clad in *Zipfelmütze*, naive and innocent of the calculations of this world. Another vision was 'common home', rapturously endorsed by the German public in summer 1989 at the time of Gorbachev's visit to Bonn. Meanwhile President Bush in May 1989 had offered 'partnership in leadership' to Germany, in an Atlantic alliance whose membership would extend, as Secretary of State Baker indicated, to the Pacific Ocean. What was the average German to make of all this wooing? Both Mitterrand and Delors answered in October 1989 by proposing a more rapid move to European integration. But trust between Bonn and its Western European partners was broken in November, when Kohl – suspecting that his neighbours were less than enthusiastic about the prospect of German unity – announced his own Ten Point programme for a slow and controlled passage to confederation with the GDR. There followed three months, when the reflexes of old Europe returned with a vengeance: the French President flirted with a reverse alliance with Russia; Kohl failed to allay Polish suspicions that the Oder-Neisse line was permanent; and Britain saw Germany as Europe's hegemonic power. In April 1990, the passage was passed, as Mitterrand and Kohl 'relaunched' the process of intergovernmental conferences, culminating in the Maastricht Treaty.

The ensuing debate could no longer conceal the many national agendas and visions covered during the years of the Cold War by the handy veil of the external threat and of utilitarian jargon. Yet Jean Monnet's method, which had served well enough in the past, was applied one more time. Maastricht was a pure product of European diplomatic traditions and of neo-functionalist methods. One policy area after another was spun into a seamless web, recorded in a Treaty 72 pages in length, and equal in complexity to the many other European settlements down the centuries. Yet there was no readily available European culture on which the élites who negotiated the Treaty could draw. National cultures commemorated Europe's divisions. Regional cultures were awakened to their own claims for self-determination. One historical layer below the nations and regions were the religious wars and settlements of the sixteenth and seventeenth centuries, and behind them the memory of a Catholic Europe under Pope and Emperor. Within each layer, the golden ages of some jockeyed against the nightmares of their neighbours. Fleeting moments of European unity around Rome or Charlemagne remained too far in the past; recent episodes of unity under Napoleon or Hitler were all too present in popular memories. The builders of the new Europe thus faced a double paradox: they had to build on the European society created after 1945, but the world prior to 1989 had gone for ever; 'Europe' had to be created on the basis of a memoryless project for a future beyond the Cold War.

WHICH CORES AND WHOSE PERIPHERIES?

There had been moments in the old Europe of 1945–89 when ideas seemed to challenge structures. Recalling the years immediately after the Second World War, and while the conditions and terms of the provisional European settlement were still fluid, Secretary of State Dean Acheson could record the creation of the Atlantic alliance with the words of Alphonso X the Learned, that 'had I been present at the creation I would have given some useful hints for the better ordering of the universe'. Another such period was in the early years of the Fifth Republic, when de Gaulle preempted his nightmare of an *Algérie Française* leading to a Colombey-les-deux-Mosquées, and united the prayers at Reims of 'the first among Frenchmen and the first among Germans', so that 'the works of friendship forever replace the misfortunes of war' (de Gaulle 1970: 191). A further period of change, when Cold War structures seemed to shake was in the early 1970s, as Chancellor Brandt negotiated the treaties with the GDR, Poland and the Soviet Union. His strategy to widen the area of freedom through subversive cooperation with the party states was expressed in the 'letter on German unity': 'to work toward a state of peace in Europe in which the German people regains its unity in free self-determination' (Garton Ash 1993: 71). The last period of movement encompassed the years of Delors' presidency of the Commission, where he described his vision using the words of Geoffrey Howe: 'the sovereign nations of the European Community, sharing their sovereignty freely, are building for themselves a key role in the power politics of the coming century' (Delors 1992: 326).

Each one of these visions of Europe holds its own core, and its different peripheries. All were born prior to the great transformation of 1989–92. There is the Europe of Charlemagne represented in the Franco-German relationship; the wider Europe of which Brandt and Schmidt dreamt, and which, in effect, displaces Europe's geographic centre to Berlin; there is the Western alliance with its American core and its German ally in Europe; and there is Delors' hope for a quasi-federal Europe exemplified in aspects of the SEA, and preserved in the Maastricht Treaty – most evidently in the promises of further revisions at the 1996 Intergovernmental Conference. Each contains its own stresses and strains which is introduced to or which inhabits its core, and most importantly, which is introduced into relations between France and Germany.

1. Franco-German Europe

A Carolingian Europe, formed around an inner core of France, Germany and the Benelux countries, has been a constant vision and practice at the heart of Europe. In 1994 it was embodied in the Schäuble–Lamers paper presented by the German Christian Democratic Party leadership, which suggested both the reinforcement of the European Council but also a greater use of majority voting (CDU–CSU 1994). Prime Minister Balladur placed a French accent on a similar suggestion in his Europe of concentric circles, with France and Germany at the core – adding that the EU should propose a white paper on defence to define 'precisely' its security interests and how to defend them in conjunction with NATO (*Le Monde* 30 November 1994). Both of these proposals could boast a long pedigree, stretching back to the Schuman plan of 1950 to subordinate coal, iron and steel industries to a common supranational authority. The idea was immediately welcomed by Chancellor Adenauer as it satisfied German aspirations for equality of treatment, promised an end to allied controls over production, opened a path to reconciliation with France, and was a step in the direction of binding the young Federal Republic into the Atlantic alliance. The two proposals for a hard core, or a Europe of concentric circles could also hark back to the 1963 Franco-German Treaty, with its emphasis on inter-governmental relations.

De Gaulle outlined his view of Franco–German relations in his regular conversations to Alain Peyrefitte. There were four guiding ideas, de Gaulle declared, to form a Europe that was not integrated or supranational. The first was that the 'hard core' (cited in Peyrefitte 1994: 62) states of Western Europe (who had signed the Rome Treaty) had to move so close in policy as to offset the attraction on the others of the two 'mastodants' of the Soviet Union and of the USA. Eventually, Portugal and Spain could join; Britain, when it had shed the Commonwealth and loosened its ties to the USA; Scandinavia, and then Poland and the other satellites once the iron curtain had lifted. The second guiding idea which would determine whether Europe would or would not take shape was whether or not Germany and France could be reconciled. This had perhaps been achieved at the level of élites; but it had not been done in depth: 'There will be no European construction if the accord between the two peoples is not the keystone'. The third idea is that each people is different from any other and that they were not only 'incomparable, unalterable' but that: 'They must stay as they are, as their history and culture have formed them, with their memories, their beliefs, their legends, their faith, their determination to build their own future'. The fourth idea is that Europe will only take shape when the peoples 'dans leurs profoundeurs' decide to adhere to the project. It would not be enough, de Gaulle considered, for the parliamentarians to decide: 'popular referenda are needed, preferably on the same day in all those states involved'.

What has become of this vision? The Franco-German engine has consistently proven to be the centrepiece of European construction (see also Szukala and Wessels in this volume). All of the major initiatives from the Coal and Steel Community, through to the Rome and Euratom Treaties, the Franco-German Treaty of 1963 and its revival in 1974 – under Chancellor Schmidt and President Giscard d'Estaing – have been based on Franco-German initiatives. They in turn formed the indispensable pre-requisite for all institutional initiatives, such as the development of the European Council or the trend to institutionalize majority voting as the way to overcome resistance among recalcitrant member states. French and German accord was indispensable to the setting up of the common external tariff, the CAP, the series of enlargements, direct elections to the European parliament, the launch of the EMS, the internal market and to monetary union. France and Germany furthermore account for 50 per cent of the EU's GNP and about 40 per cent of its population. They separately control the region's key currency and one of the considerable nuclear forces in Europe. Germany is Europe's prime industrial exporter and France is the number two world farm produce exporter. On a more negative note, when the two fall out, as occurred after Adenauer's retirement, or in Mitterrand's first year, little could be achieved.

Furthermore, the major effects of the lifting of the Iron Curtain and the Soviet Union's collapse, as far as French geopolitical calculations are concerned, is that Germany has no equivalent power to its east. It is easily the largest of the

European states in all relevant measures, whether population, industrial output, trade surplus, hardness of currency or numbers of orchestras. German unity has been seen in Paris as a threat to France's status as a great power, and this has been interpreted in contradictory statements by President Mitterrand about the centrality of Franco-German friendship to Europe's future, while in 1994 not inviting Chancellor Kohl to celebrate France's liberation 50 years earlier by the Anglo-American armies. Both Schmidt and Kohl had been prepared to provide the financial substance to oil the works of European construction, and leave the style of Euro-policies to the French President. As Germany moves slowly to define its own external policies in a post-Cold War world, one expectation in Paris is for German Chancellors to appropriate more of the style for their own domestic benefit to clarify the message about the principle sources of Euro-largesse.

Nor are public opinions in both countries reconciled in depth to each other. During the French referendum campaign in September 1992 on the Maastricht Treaty, both supporters and opponents of the Treaty reinforced German scepticism about the relationship with France. Those campaigning for a 'yes' vote urged their compatriots to support the Treaty on the grounds that this was France's last chance to corral Germany within a European framework. If France was to say 'no', Germany would go its own way, and dominate the continent. The DM would be emperor and king, and France would have no say in shaping either interest or exchange rate policy. It would simply have to accept whatever decision was made in Berlin or in Frankfurt. Better to co-determine policy with Germany within the EU, than to be one among many of German considerations in external policy. The opponents argued that rejection was the only way for France to escape being suffocated by united Germany's embrace.

On the German side, public opinion was awakened by the *Bild Zeitung* in December 1991 that Kohl had made an 'irrevocable' commitment to hand over the DM for a potage of ecu. The ensuing eruption of national resentment prompted Kohl to up the stakes by insisting on a more assertive German foreign policy. Bonn hurried to 'recognize' Slovenia and Croatia, ignoring the arguments of its allies that this spelt claims and counter-claims by competing ethnic and religious groups over Bosnia. Both Genscher and Kinkel, his successor at the Foreign Ministry, argued that Germany had acquired self-determination, and should not deny that right to others who claimed it, in effect laying out a stake for Germany as the champion of national self-determination. The claim was rapidly augmented by another commitment by Kohl to make Frankfurt visibly into Germany's *Finanzplatz* by making it the centre for the European Central Bank (ECB). London's counter-claim foundered when the *Bundesbank* in August 1992 clearly indicated its preference for the pound sterling's devaluation, and then meted out the same treatment to the franc in August 1993 – though the latter only after some costly support. Kohl was rewarded in October 1993, when the member states voted 11 to 1 in favour of Frankfurt as the capital for the ECB.

More seriously still, Kohl pledged in the Maastricht negotiations that the DM would only be handed over if the powers of the European Parliament would be augmented. French politicians suspect Germany of seeking to expand

Parliament's powers because both the German Christian Democrats and Social Democrats – the latter now joined by a large body of Labour MEPs – form the hard core of the Parliament's main parties, whereas the French MEPs are dispersed across the hemi-cycle. In a different vein, the German Constitutional Court's opinion on the Maastricht Treaty links future surrenders of sovereign powers to the filling of the EU's 'democratic deficit'. Further institutional progress is not going to be automatic, unless the EU's development is compatible with the principles laid down in the Basic Law. The election of a Gaullist President, with a massive majority in the National Assembly, reduces still more the probability of significant increases in the Parliament's powers. No progress on powers to the European Parliament jeopardizes the French project to end the *Bundesbank's* primacy by creating an ECB.

Finally, Kohl linked the DM's fate to further progress made in elaborating a common foreign and security policy. Optimally for Germany, all decisions regarding foreign and security policy would have to be adopted by majority voting. But at the heart of French foreign policy stands France's view of its standing as a great power, with its permanent seat on the Security Council, its *mission universelle* as the country of the Rights of Man, and its nuclear weapons. Germany has renounced ambition as a great power in the traditional sense, but seeks a permanent seat on the Security Council, and equates its eventual role there with implementing the UN Charter. Above all, Germany voluntarily renounced nuclear weapons by signing the Non-Proliferation Treaty in 1968, and lobbied heavily for its extension in 1995. Yet nuclear weapons are at the heart of French military strategy. The ultimate exchange rate in the negotiations over monetary union is thus the price of surrendering the DM for joint planning of the nuclear *force de frappe*. Joint planning means an end to French discretion in the deployment of nuclear weapons in support of a policy of deterrence from a threat which cannot readily be identified. As the French Ambassador to Australia answered in response to questioning as to the identity of a threat to France that justified the renewal of nuclear testing in Mururoa, in the South Pacific: 'Certainly, the fact that we wanted to exclude for good the possibility of any further conflict between France and Germany was at the root of our European policy' (*Financial Times* 4 September 1995).

In effect, what France asked in the Maastricht Treaty was for Germany to hand over the DM, while France retained its nuclear deterrence. French European diplomacy does therefore not accept German equality. The implication is that Germany retains a number of options: it may seek economic hegemony by retaining the DM; it may seek equality by inducing France to abandon its nuclear weapons; it may acquire a nuclear force of its own, or cling to the US as nuclear protector; or it may accept inequality, and abandon the DM while leaving France its *force de frappe*. The latter option is not so much a Carolingian as a Napoleonic Europe.

2. A wider Europe

As soon as it became evident that the people of Eastern Germany were voting on their feet for unification, Kohl made clear his view of the need to widen the EU beyond its western core. The EU had successfully appropriated the name of 'Europe', despite the fact that membership had never been inclusive of all states in the Western sphere of influence. In the dying days of the Cold War, the EU won a prolonged battle with the moribund party states to negotiate with each on a bilateral basis. Decompression in Central–Eastern Europe in 1989 set the scene for the round table meetings between opposition groups and party states, leading to the dismantlement of the regimes. After 40 years under dictatorship, the countries of Central and Eastern Europe (the CEECs) could now 'join Europe' – a shorthand for the combined process of political transition, economic restructuring and marketization, and entry to the various institutions which represented Western society. NATO extended its reach eastwards with the creation in November 1991 of the North Atlantic Cooperation Council, incorporating a gathering number of participant members; the Council of Europe opened its doors to new applicants. By October 1991, the President of the Commission, Jacques Delors, was calling on member states to prepare for a European Community numbering 24 to 30 over the coming decade.

The end of the Cold War transformed the relations of the neutral states to the EC and to NATO. Sweden had maintained its inherited form of neutrality through the world wars, as had Switzerland. Finland, as a belligerent against the Soviet Union in the Second World War, had reached its own *modus vivendi* with the Soviet Union in 1948. Austria declared its own neutrality following the withdrawal of Soviet troops from Vienna in 1955. All neutral states had sought to play a part in the prolonged negotiations between East and West, as their contribution to creating European stability under the conditions of the Cold War. The transformation of Europe's security in 1989–90, and the ensuing collapse of the Soviet Union, prompted them to reformulate their neutralities, and to participate in the EU's discussions on the 'political aspects of security'. By contrast to the public opinions of Central–Eastern Europe, their public opinions were not eager to join NATO. But their publics shared the same anxieties that an extension of NATO membership to embrace all of Europe, including perhaps the Baltic states, would have been interpreted as an aggressive act by Russia.

From Bonn's perspective, there was no alternative to embracing the CEECs within Western society. Bonn's position from the outset was that it was vital in order to fill the void left by the collapse of the Warsaw Pact and the Comecon, and to help mitigate the interstate or state–society conflicts in the region. The alternative was to build up autonomous institutions, such as attempted at Visegrad between the governments of Poland, Hungary and Czechoslovakia (as it then was). But there was little reason to consider that these weaker institutions would have been better capable of confronting the multiple agenda of transition in these countries, nor that bilateral channels between its member states and the EC/EU or NATO would not have prevailed. But the main consideration for extending the reach of Western institutions was political. The countries of Central–Eastern Europe, and in particular Poland, had been excluded from joining in the Marshall Plan, and in the OEEC, on Stalin's orders. Their peoples' aspirations for national independence had been contained by the use of Soviet force, and – in the twenty-year period of détente from 1970–89 – with the support of Western loans and of Western governments, more concerned to maintain European stability than to back local dissenters against the regimes. Western European society had first and foremost a moral obligation to welcome the 'other Europe' into it's midst.

Paris proved more reserved in extending the membership of Western institutions, on the broad grounds that the EU in particular already faced enough challenges of its own, without being burdened by the additional difficulties of enlargement and of transition. Enlargement of the EU, first through the economic area agreements and then through the accession of Austria, Finland and Sweden in January 1995, increases the EU's geographic scope, political diversity, economic divergence and institutional imbalances between small states and large states, which was symbolized by the difficulties in reaching agreement on majority voting. Widening to the CEECs creates a similar set of problems, that may be laid out in matrix form: on one plane may be placed the complex of interstate relations, including the matter of membership of the varied fora in Western society; the restructuring of the state following the collapse of the party states; and the social implications of the transition. On the other plane may be listed the rapid extension of market relations and institutions; the process of political transition out of party dictatorships; and the redefinition of external policies of the states. A third dimension of time may be added, split between one section of the line referring to layers of historical memory, and the other projecting through transition timetables into the future.

Without encompassing all the elements of this matrix, a number of dilemmas may be isolated to illustrate the impact on the discussion of cores. In the longer run, the dream is of the whole of Europe, united in diversity, free of wars and prosperous and open to multiple channels of exchange with the rest of the world. In this vision, the wider Europe becomes its own core to the rest of the world. The path there, however, entails the risk of considerable strain, and even dissolution, of the hard core of relations between France and Germany, through the extension of its scope and the concomitant import of the problems of 'the other Europe' into its midst. The attempt to consolidate a 'core EU', or a 'hard core of the core' may have served prior to 1989–92 as a means to prod the inner-peripheries of the British Isles, Spain or Greece into more cooperative attitudes with regard to agendas set in Brussels, Paris or Bonn. But after the demise of the party-states, attempts to consolidate a core Western Europe threatened to perpetuate if not the exclusion of 100 million Eastern Europeans from the mainstream of Western society, at least the continuation of their subordinate status.

There were at least two dimensions to this double fear by Easterners of exclusion or subordination, and by Westerners of dilution of Western institutions. One related to trade. Quite simply, the structure of Western European markets had been laid in the early years of the Cold War when traditional suppliers from Central or South-eastern markets were excluded on account of Europe's division. Any perpetuation of the division to protect significant lobbies within the EU risked prompting the revival of an authoritarian periphery; the political awakening of sullen rural populations (nearly 40 per cent of Poland's employed labour force), or the promotion of an Eastern diplomacy of resentment at the self-centredness of EU policy. Nonetheless, while Eastern European states have diverted trade abruptly to Western hard currency markets, protectionist groups ensconced in the entrails of the EU have provided incentives for the CEECs to move rapidly into higher valued added activities by attracting in foreign direct investment for re-export into Western European markets. One paradox of Western European conservatism towards Eastern European competitors is therefore to maximize their competitive advantage in low wages, high skill potential and as hosts for capital-intensive Western companies.

The other dimension related to the post-Cold War complexities of ensuring security throughout Europe. The demands of the Baltic states, Poland, Hungary, the Czech lands, Slovakia, or Slovenia was for as close an incorporation in or association with Western institutions as possible. This entailed the construction of constitutional and democratic institutions, reform of the armed forces alongside profound changes in economic structures, and settlement of frontier disputes and the status of minorities through negotiation rather than by force. Croatian and Serbian practices of ethnic cleansing and the revision of frontiers by force left them no alternative to seeking patrons on a bilateral basis. Croatia turned to Germany for sympathy and support, and Serbia looked to Russia. An aggravation of the conflict in the northern Balkans thus risked bringing Russia and Germany into indirect conflict through clients whose actions they did not control. As Germany set prior store to supporting President Yeltsin, not least with a view to promoting the dismantlement of nuclear plant or weapons across the length and breadth of the former Soviet Union, the Balkans were relegated to subordinate status in the hierarchy of German–Russian relations. Similarly, the Partnerships for Peace programmes, extended by NATO to the CEECs in the course of 1994, sought to defuse fears in Moscow about the extension of the Western alliance's frontiers to Russia. But they failed to win acclaim among the former member states of the Warsaw Pact, worried at the potential for militarism in a disturbed Russia, and they reinforced sentiments in the USA about presumed Western European pusillanimity.

Widening the EU on the evident grounds that 'Europe is much more than the economic Community', as Kohl stated, was not readily compatible with the other dimension of his strategy whereby 'our common aim must be to build up the EC as the kernel of a future European peace order' (Le Monde 19 January 1990). A wider Europe would require a further call on German taxpayers' contributions to facilitate the necessary side-payments in enlargement negotiations, and to transfer resources to prospective and poorer members. But German resources were absorbed in the reconstruction of Eastern Germany. That meant that the EU had to call on extra resources from The Netherlands, France or Sweden. In view of national opinions' reluctance to become net contributors to the EU budget, a wider Europe with larger transfers was likely to create less public support among net donor states. On the other hand, were Germany to resume trade surpluses, the DM's role would be confirmed as a key currency and the calls on German financial resources would resume. There were two competing sources of demand: one was from the Southern European countries, championed by France, and concerned to augment the flow of resources to themselves and to the Maghreb. The other sources of demand came from the 'other Europe', and looked to Germany as their champion. A wider Europe therefore introduced a further point of discord between France and Germany, as the core countries of the 'hard core'.

3. A Europe of states

Over the twenty years of German détente policy, France edged away from being the champion of state sovereignty and national independence towards an acceptance of a pooled exercise of sovereignty within the institutions of the EU. German diplomacy took the same direction but with a view to moving also to state unity and national self-determination. The achievement of state unity marked the re-emergence of a Europe of great powers, but one where Germany outweighed all other Western powers in terms of demography, of agricultural potential and industrial and financial prowess. The DM was the continent's key currency. Germany was the prime provider of aid and investment to the former party states, and the main target for their post-communist trade. The end of the Cold War spelt the winding down of the allied military presence to one-third of the *Bundeswehr's* manpower, and the withdrawal of Russian troops from German territory in 1994. The prospect beckoned of a Mitteleuropa, hinging on Austro-German cooperation in Central and South-eastern Europe. A Western-anchored Europe would be centred on Paris, while a wider Europe could be centred eventually on Berlin. Germany championed the EU's rapid enlargement, while nothing within the Union could be agreed on without Germany's consent. 'In these circumstances', former Prime Minister Thatcher concluded, 'the Community augments Germany's power rather than constraining it' (*The Times* 18 May 1992).

Such a Europe of the states, whose major power is Germany, perpetuates the USA as Germany's prime ally, partner and competitor. German–American relations have been at the centre of European affairs since the Second World War. The Federal Republic, as a net importer of security within NATO, consistently gave priority to relations with the USA over French aspirations to create a 'European' Europe. The *Bundesbank* emerged as the Federal Reserve's main counterpart in international financial relations. The Bank held dollars in reserves, but remained opposed to buying up the currencies of its European partners. As the Ecu was composed of a basket of European currencies, the same ban applied to its full development as European reserve currency. Germany's special financial relationship with the USA thus stood as a metaphor for its special relation with the USA on defence (Emminger 1986; Strange 1976; Calleo 1982): Germany's security was ensured by alliance with the USA, while the DM–dollar relationship was a function of domestic policy in Germany and the USA, and of the value of the dollar as the world's key currency. It formed the central relationship on which all other European currencies came to depend.

The centrality of Germany's relationship with the USA was reconfirmed in the crucial years of 1989–91 when German unity was negotiated between Bonn and Washington with Moscow, while keeping the Poles, Italians, French and British at arms length. The end of the Cold War opened the prospect for Germany of a European peace system, hinging on a continued USA presence and a network of institutions, including the EU. This implied keeping defence policy within the domain of the sovereign states, and therefore NATO. This was quite compatible with the German government's readiness to link, and eventually merge, the *Bundeswehr* in multilateral or bilateral divisions or corps under NATO command. But one inference was whether Germany's financial relationship with the USA would continue as a metaphor for its relationship on defence. Abandoning the DM to create a core currency for Europe raised both the delicate matter of the terms of the deal struck with France, and the relegation of the inner peripheries of the EU in the Mediterranean member states or in Britain to an outer periphery. The further inference was that the USA's world role after the Cold War, and its centrality in any future foreign policy for Germany, set undefined limits around Bonn's readiness to base security on prior alliance with Paris. For Britain, the advantage of such an arrangement was to remain an offshore financial centre, and a junior partner to the central German–American relationship.

The heart of the matter is that the USA is united Germany's prime ally in the maintenance of the new European balance. Successive US administrations have played a central role in restructuring NATO and have earmarked national forces for inclusion in multinational corps. The USA has insisted on retaining the post of SACEUR, despite a reduction of US forces in the European theatre to about 100,000. The USA has been an indispensable partner in managing the partial extension of NATO into the territories of the former Warsaw Pact, and has been an active supporter of Western, particularly German efforts to limit the damage to world stability resulting from a proliferation of nuclear know-how flowing from the collapse of the Soviet Union. Both Washington and Bonn have supported Yeltsin's Presidency on that account. A US presence in European security arrangements reassures smaller states against domination by one, or a combination of European powers. It shields France and Britain from a loss of status, and augments for them the significance of retaining their permanent seats in the Security Council. It reassures Russia, and receives the support of the CEECs, and Norway and Turkey, all of whom share common concerns about the turbulence around them. It binds the USA and Canada, at lesser cost into a European security structure. If Germany for the first time in its history is a satisfied power, that is the achievement of the Atlantic alliance, and in particular of America's commitment to European security.

The foundation of the argument for a Europe constructed on existing states, most eloquently presented by de Gaulle in the 1960s and also argued by Thatcher in her Bruges speech of 1988, is that they are the products of a long and complex European history. They are also varied in their forms as republics, or monarchies. Some few are nation-states, such as France, Denmark, Portugal or Ireland. Britain, Belgium, Spain or Switzerland are multi-national states. Their histories ring with their own myths, symbols and celebrations. These particularities are expressed in distinct political imaginations about the role of authority, the use or non-use of force, or the exemptions from laws of general applicability to be granted to this or that section of the population. Their parliaments and executives are constituted in subtly different ways. Their 'comparative advantages' have been created over the centuries by policies as much as by endowments. Germany's apprenticeship system was introduced to Germany in the course of the *Kulturkampf*, while the educational reforms of the Third Republic established an educational monopoly by the state, which excluded or marginalized the development of a parallel system in France. These differences worked through the culture of companies to affect the core of legitimacy and of career development in German or French corporations (Maurice *et al.* 1982). In short, their different histories have entered into the inner marrows of the states, which alone have the authority to speak on behalf of their peoples. Governance of Europe could only be by the states and for the states.

Yet a Europe of the states after the Cold War is replete with paradoxes, some overt and imminent, and others implicit and still buried beneath the layers of Europe's many complexities. How they are likely to work themselves out, either through reconciliation or through contradiction, lies more in the realm of conjecture than of analysis. We shall identify some of them rather than work through their multiple ramifications, if only for reasons of space.

One overt and imminent paradox relates to Germany's continued reliance on the US as a prime partner. The incompatibilities between Germany's reliance on the USA as a major security partner, and the relations between the dollar and DM, are continuing to widen. A US presence in European security arrangements rests in the last resort on the mood in the US Congress and in US public opinion. While opinion polls in the USA suggest continued backing for NATO, NATO stands low on the list of US domestic priorities. These continue to be focused on the problems of a multi-racial society, crime, the inner cities or on competition from the countries of Asia–Pacific. Indeed, the central dollar–DM rate is conditioned by the cloud of public debt overhanging the global financial markets, and by the continued propensity of the US to run trade deficits with the exporters of Asia–Pacific. Intra-European exchange rates remain a function of German and US domestic political and economic priorities. In the period of détente, the German economy's formula to absorb the revaluation of the DM was to ensure that national pay bargaining yielded wage rises below the increases in productivity. As a result, German labour costs are among the highest in the world. Yet the German economy since 1993, with full government support, has moved to a strategy of cost-cutting, and return to export surplus. As, and if, the DM moves up again in the late 1990s against the dollar, German business people may be expected to accelerate foreign direct investment or to become ardent supporters of monetary union in order to end the nightmare of an ever rising DM.

A Europe of the states also places economic and psychological strains on Germany, allowing Germany's national ambitions to linger in the ambiguities of a post-Cold War European security structure. State unity meant freer hands for

Germany. Bonn cited constitutional constraints on the deployment of troops out-of-NATO-area to avoid military participation in the Gulf War of August-February 1990–91. Then, Germany – with Austria – emerged as the champion of independence for Slovenia and Croatia. The Maastricht Treaty's German opponents vented their resentments at France's 'grand strategy to extract Versailles-style reparations for German unity'. France was accused, not incorrectly, of wanting to act as gravedigger for the DM; but France was also accused by the international correspondent of the *Handelsblatt* of entertaining a Napoleonic design for a Europe to be run by the 'élites of the *grandes écoles*' (*Wall Street Journal* 2 June 1992). These accusations fell on fertile ground, in a public opinion hostile to abandoning the DM, or to having its regulations tampered with by the internal market process. A more assertive Germany in Europe's counsels was the consequence.

Yet were Germany to consolidate a national position as the largest state in Europe, and explicitly assume the laurels of leadership, all praise and supplications would be directed to its representatives. No significant dispute in Europe could be settled without its say. German governments could choose to disguise the location of negotiations in the pluralistic bargaining process of Brussels, but that would not alter the reality in such a Europe that the final accord would require Germany's seal of approval. Such prominence in an interdependent Europe of states points Germany in two different directions. One is that the process of European integration promotes ambitions in sections of German opinion or of interests alienated by the thrust of EU policy, and resistant to Kohl's policy of conceding sovereign powers once they have been finally restored. Such a strand of opinion and interests may proclaim innocent intent, much as Genscher's German Michel did in the years culminating in German state unity. But a united Germany protesting innocent intent is no adequate policy for Europe's leading power. *De facto*, German unity challenges French status; united Germany cannot escape contending with the complexities of European political and economic interdependence. Another direction for German policy is therefore to consider Europe in the first instance, and Germany in the second. Any German assertion of national independence runs up against its restricted resources to meet the competing demands of a fragmented Europe. In the last resort, the reason why Germany, having acquired sovereignty, is ready to share it is that the scale of the new Europe by far exceeds its capabilities. Germany is dwarfed by the scale of Europe's intricacies and cannot hope to master them alone. Nor may Germany's domestic intricacies be overridden for the sake of 'Europe'.

One of these intricacies is that a Europe of the states widens the gap between larger and smaller states and their responsibilities. The larger states have regularly sought to create a presidium of powers, starting with de Gaulle's proposal for a world council including the USA, France and Great Britain, through the various Fouchet plans, the Franco–German Treaty, and the Group of Seven (G7). Just as regularly, the smaller states, championed within the EU by The Netherlands, have promoted majority voting and democratization through direct elections to the Parliament in order to equalize their own influence over policy, and stymie any effective return to a Europe of the powers. But with the EU's fourth enlargement to fifteen member states, the traditional arguments about democratization of the EU as a method by the smaller to tie down the larger have been turned on their head. The larger states, including an allegedly anti-federalist British government, have pointed out that the four largest states account for 80 per cent of the enlarged EU population. Under the existing voting system, the eleven smaller or medium-size states may theoretically outvote the larger states, representing the EU's majority. If the smaller states are to stick to a Dutch position on a weighted majority voting in Council, they are in effect championing a maximization of small state influence in EU counsels. If, on the other hand, the larger states champion the criteria of population size, they are taking a mighty step towards the still distant prospect of considering the European electorate as final arbiter (see also Laffan in this volume).

The apparent meeting point between these two positions of small and large states is an EU characterized by majority voting in the Council, where the smaller states in effect have considerable capacities to constrain the large; and by a further extension in the powers of Parliament. Yet decisions in Council tend by custom to consensus or to agreements to disagree, while any prospect of a European electorate as final arbiter remains in the distance. Meanwhile, the political geography of Europe is shaped by the distribution of powers and resources among the states, engaging in their permanent ballets of alignment and disalignments. Such a Europe is a Europe of states whose future peace and prosperity depends on preserving and consolidating the values of Europe's society, one of whose pillars is the states themselves and the other of whose pillars is the continued and perhaps extended presence of a reluctant USA as Europe's major power.

4. Delors' Maastricht Europe

It may be objected that Delors had little to do with the Maastricht Treaty's ultimate form, as it escaped the control of the Commission almost as soon as the negotiations began on the context of the Delors Report on monetary union in late 1989. The Treaty thus contrasted with the SEA, the heart of which was delineated in the Commission White Book, presented to the European Council in June 1985. The Commission won ownership of the internal market programme (Cockfield 1994), but lost ownership of the discussions on monetary union and on the common foreign and security policy (Ross 1995). Delors seized opportunities to tie liberalization of capital movements and the internal market legislation to the implicit commitments by the member states in the SEA to move towards monetary union. Without Delors' ardent advocacy, the intergovernmental conferences may not have been held. But because the stakes were so high, and touched at the very heart of the member states' sovereignties and ambitions, the Commission was sidelined. It was not that Britain warped the Treaty's content in the direction of a Europe of the states, so much as the Treaty was the best that the member states could negotiate under the circumstances. Delors helped set the stage for the negotiations; there could be no surprise that the major protagonists – the member states – then proceeded to write the script.

Delors' ideal was to reconcile the historical diversities of the peoples and nations of Europe with the economic and geopolitical necessities to form a European federation (Delors 1992). But, as Delors regularly recalled, the European construction had to be created and be driven by the states, with the support of an active Commission and Court. There were many novelties which distinguished Europe's relaunch in the years 1984–92 from that of 1972, when the Paris summit of October sketched a European Union by 1980, complete with its own social fund, social action programme, an industry and technology policy, a common trade position, and a commitment to full monetary and economic union. This was later elaborated with a statement on a foreign policy 'identity'. But crucial details on the balance between intergovernmentalism and EC practice remained vague, and within two years all the major leaders were either dead or out of office. By contrast, the path to Maastricht was taken by a group of travellers of unprecedented political longevity in high office. Many of the details on the balance between integovernmentalism and EC practice had been resolved in the intervening years. The broad vision of 1972 was there to serve as a blueprint. In the changed context of world affairs, the Treaty in effect envisaged the EU as the inner core of a wider Europe, and as one of two pillars in the Atlantic alliance.

The Treaty fell far short of federalist wishes, as indicated by the battle in late 1991 as to whether it should be unified under one Union roof, or support the roof on three pillars. Its eventual complexity, though, was the best that the states could manage under the conditions. Each injected their own preferences into the negotiations, and haggled over details. Whether the ultimate result was seen as laden with federal intent, or as perpetuating a Europe of the states in an open-ended process, the concessions made by all parties to the Treaty meant that none was satisfied with the result and all could claim a partial victory while arguing the need to make partial sacrifices. As the concessions had to be balanced by future rewards, and the partial victories opened a prospect of further benefits, none had the incentive to drop out and all had an incentive to stay in 'at the heart of Europe'. The Treaty also underwrote a multi-speed, variable geometry Europe of concentric circles and special relations. It left the inner core of states, led by France and Germany, to set the agenda for the union's future developments in any of the three pillars. *De facto*, the Treaty barely impaired the member states powers to act alone. If progress towards union was the goal, the Treaty left open the way for an inner core of members to make the first move, and provide an incentive to the laggards to join sooner or later. The Treaty thus incorporated Europe's diversity into its complex procedures, but provided a timetable for commitments and further amendments.

The heart of the Treaty was the member states' 'irreversible' commitment to achieve monetary union by 1997–99. The gap between signing the Treaty and making the leap was necessary for Germany to digest the costs of unification; for implementation of the internal market and its accompanying legislation; or for the member states to address the budgetary imbalances or labour market rigidities that had been built up since the 1960s. The technical arguments in favour of monetary union included the reduction in transaction costs involved in a multi-currency and highly interdependent trading area. Equally important was the promise that a single currency held a prospect of much greater transparency to customers of pricing differentials across the EU. A single currency would cement the internal market, as producers in member states whose governments were profligate would not be able to seize market shares through competitive devaluations from producers in countries whose governments pursued more virtuous policies. The major arguments in favour of monetary union on its own terms, though, were political: it would be a European System of Central Banks, not the *Bundesbank*, which in the future would set monetary policy for the Union. Other member states would gain by participating in monetary decisions. Germany would gain, because the Bank's mandate was a duplicate of its own and because it would not be making policies for others on a national mandate alone.

Maastricht's final content prompted those member states pushing for a more federalist content to prepare for the next leap towards fuller Union in 1996. There were two demands in particular: the one for an increase in the European Parliament's powers was designed to counter the accusation that the EU process centralizes legislation in the EU executive, and deprives the member states' parliaments of their legislative and other powers. The Parliament would share legislative powers with Council, where, optimally, all domains of policy would be brought under majority voting. The boundaries between the core functions of EU activity and that of the state or regions would be drawn around the principle of subsidiarity. This sharing by the states of their powers in the EU and the shifting of their functions to the regions would be underwritten by the creation of what became the Committee of the Regions, which would be expected to develop regional loyalties within the member states, and open channels for local authorities to by-pass national governments through the creation of Union-wide alliances. The other demand was to strengthen the common foreign and security policy, in conjunction with NATO and the US. A European Union had 'to speak with one voice'. Eventually in a federal Europe, all politics would become domestic, by abolishing diplomacy between the member states, the traditional and characteristic feature of European affairs. The Union, not the member states, would be the central protagonist of global politics.

One source of the Treaty's ambiguities was its incorporation of both temporal – the inherited layers of historical memory and present expectations of differing futures – and spatial dimensions – the attempt to build a territorial club in a world market and polity – of the new dialectics in European and world affairs. On the temporal dimension, the various policy areas already within the EU's competences, or moving into them, were not compatible with the mental maps of public opinions. The oldest area of common policy was in the trade arena, and the traditional differences between France's concept of its agricultural identity, and its cultural mission, came into conflict with those of other member states in the concluding months of the Uruguay Round negotiations. Chancellor Kohl figuratively bent over backwards in his eventually successful effort to meet the demands of German industrial exporters for a completion of the Round, and those of the French government to unhitch itself from the hook on which it had suspended itself by drawing on the well-worn imagery and language of 'les Anglo-Saxons' wedded to 'le grand large' and to 'free trade'. Even more significantly, the opponents in Germany of Maastricht had no trouble in mobilizing old images of France, seeking to impose Versailles-type reparations on Germany, whereby Germany would surrender the DM as the symbol of its post-war success in return for its unity. Other membranes of convention, to use William Pfaff's phrase (1989: 212), were touched in Britain, where the Tory Party was rent into near internal civil war over whether Maastricht represented a step to an expansion of British influence and values, or to the surrender of British liberties.

Furthermore, the tensions within Maastricht as consolidating a Europe of the states or as moving to a federation were mitigated in part by the promise of future amendments. The intergovernmental conference of 1996 was seen as necessarily linking concessions by the French or the British to the Germans on increasing the powers of the European Parliament, and on strengthening the common foreign and security policy. The implicit bargain is that, if satisfaction could be given the German delegation, then the monetary aspects of the Treaty might be implemented forthwith. But this is a bargain struck in inter-state negotiations. Another bargain has yet to be struck between political leaders and their domestic electorates. In Germany, the bargain's terms would have to be in response to the question: what is the German public's price for handing over the DM? Were German public opinion to become exigent, as there is every reason for it to be, then France's strategy to bind Germany into a EU, as sketched at Maastricht, would entail paying an ever higher price. In exchange for the DM, nothing short of a federal Europe would be acceptable. The future ECB had to be located in Frankfurt or Bonn. The ECB's money market operations would be decentralized, and not located primarily in London. All central banks would have to be independent. Member states would have to meet the Treaty criteria for convergence. The question of nuclear weapons, their proliferation and their control, could no longer be avoided.

There was another incompatibility between intra-state negotiations and implicit bargains in the Union, and US–German relations and public opinion in the USA. France's bid to Europeanize the *Bundesbank* pointed by the end of the decade to a European currency rivalling the dollar. Such a move would pull the centre of world finances to Europe, allow the EU to pay for oil imports in Ecu or Euros, manage a major reserve currency, and provide the EU with an integrated capital market capable of funding major Europe-wide projects or to help in the development of its surrounding peripheries to east and south. Such a Union would be the US's prime creditor, involving it in probably arduous negotiations for the restructuring of the debt of its former protector. Given the volatility of US public opinion, and the current views in the US that Europe's democrats and Europe's wealth are indebted to the generosity of the US this century, the present anticipation of future potential difficulties in German–US relations counsels the German government to pursue a very special relationship with Washington. This is only reinforced by the US role for the foreseeable future as Europe's major power. The point of reconciliation with French preferences for a 'European

Europe' is to imbue it with an Atlantic dimension. But that Atlantic dimension could entail a price to be paid to the US in financial negotiations, while the enthusiasm of any French government for an Atlantic Europe may be said to rise in proportion to the prospect of the US withdrawing. As French diplomacy in the past decade indicated repeatedly, France's nightmare is to be left alone in a face-to-face with Germany.

The spatial dimensions of post-Cold War dialectics are no more readily compatible with Maastricht's ambiguities. Each state continues to be the focus of its own network of regional and global relations. Germany not only has its own very special relationship with the USA, but like other major European states, engages in its own aggressive trade and business diplomacy outside the boundaries of the EU. Chancellor Kohl in his visit to China in November 1993 clinched a contract to build the Canton metro, from which the French had been excluded on account of their arms sales to Taiwan, and then proceeded to accept the Chinese offer to take over the French consulate there, which the French had had to vacate a year earlier. Similarly, President Mitterrand rushed to South Africa after the ANC's electoral victory in April 1994 in order to be the first to congratulate President Mandela and in the hope of snatching defence contracts from British suppliers. Prime Minister Major was not far behind. A different example of the same phenomenon was when British fishermen flew the Canadian flag during the fisheries dispute of early 1995 between Spain and Canada over Newfoundland fisheries. Spain's official arguments that the UK should respect the principle of supporting member states against outsiders represented a legalistic argument in the face of powerful sentiments of 'kith and kin'.

Global or regional developments therefore operate more as stimulants to differentiate one state from another, than they provide opportunities to 'speak with one voice'. A prime concern in Germany is to stabilize the countries of Central and South-eastern Europe, whereas France, Italy and Spain are increasingly preoccupied by the demographic imbalances in the Maghreb. The prospects of growing markets in China and the Pacific beckon European businesses, but present a long-term competitive challenge on labour costs and skills to European workforces. Hoover may have closed their factory in Bordeaux in order to open in Glasgow, but a more significant item was SKF's decision in 1994 to place its most advanced factory for the manufacture of ball-bearings in Malaysia, rather than in Western Europe. Conversely, the rise of the yen and the incentive for Japanese corporations to invest outside their home market provides multiple benefits for the UK, as a low wage economy well-equipped with golf courses, but the inward investment to the UK is seen by the French or Italian automobile producers as a threat to their position on European markets. Similarly, a fall in the dollar generally interprets into a rise of the DM, providing a price advantage for non-German exporters into German markets. Rises in world oil prices have and will continue to exert a differentiating impact on European national markets, as in the past.

The seamless web which binds European states together, and into the world system of states, implies that its core members will have to expand their numbers into the periphery in order to retain the consensus on which they function by choice and by method. There are few effective coercive instruments in the hands of the Union, not least because the states both legislate and execute. There is an imminent rather than an actual division of powers in the political system of the EU. All states retain a *de facto* veto if their vital interests are at stake. They may resist a consensus for a while, but each state has its own bundle of interests represented so that any set of linkages may be bound into negotiations at any time. The EU is thus a permanent process, whose dynamics derive from the relations among the states and of their external attachments. These ensure a graduated overture to all other European countries, and to all other existing European institutions. It is thus not just that the prospect is of a dilution of the European core into a widening periphery, but also of an ambitious Union which absorbs as many tasks as possible from other international institutions. Just as the dilutant to the core may only weaken when a consensus is reached on what the cultural boundaries of 'Europe' are, so the explosive in the Union is its ambitions to absorb tasks distributed around other institutions in the old world of pre-1989. The danger to the Union is that all disputes from across the whole of Europe and all member states are internalized within its processes.

Were the core ever to gel into a real Union, it would inevitably have to acquire all the symbols of authority and power, such would be the internalization of conflicts within a European polity with an ill-defined political culture, composed of multiple layers of historical memory. The rift developing among those favouring a more federal content in the EU, is between those who find allies among proponents of states' rights, and those who seek to drive ambitiously forward and outwards to absorb member states and other institutional functions. Before it would be ever likely to gel, though, the EU would have to overcome the hard core of resistance it has bumped into in the course of the period 1985–92. This was well expressed by former Commission President Delors in his announcement in December 1994 that he would not run for the French presidency. After ten years of militancy in the Commission's highest post, he stated that his reason for not running was that there would not be enough support for his ideas in France.

THE DANGER OF THE FUTURE

The danger facing Europe is not the emergence of a dominant Germany, but of a new and wider and deeper Europe. This is not the wider and deeper Europe, initially discussed at The Hague summit of 1969, and at numerous successive occasions. The wider and deeper Europe of yore involved a parallel effort to use the opportunities afforded by a widening of EU membership to deepen the scope and reach of commonly elaborated policies. The novelty is that the widening of Europe in the 1990s has its boundaries merge into the rest of the world; the deepening of Europe through the development of common policies involves a voyage into Europe's many historical layers which lie one on top of another in the manner of an onion. The top layer is the layer of the states, formed at varying times over the past millennia, with a tendency inherited from the pre-1945 period to a competition between the states through the play of shifting alliances, as well as the distinct but changing structures and purposes of the states. From post-1945 Europe is inherited the complex political and market interdependencies within Eastern Europe, with multiple strands and ties into the rest of the world, and the society established in Western Europe on the basis of institutions and values, and now extended at least in principle to the rest of Europe. The end of the Cold War has prompted a struggle between the two, one pulling backwards to the re-nationalization of policies and public opinions, and beyond that to Europe's multiple historical layers and memories, and the other calling for patience and perseverance in establishing a grand compromise for the whole of Europe in a new world for which there is no historical precedent.

The paradox of Maastricht was to have been designed in the spirit of a grand compromise, open to further elaboration, but to have been inspired by the renewed competition between states, and to have promoted a trend to a re-nationalization of policies and public opinions. Its implementation, however partial, rests on the drive and support of the member states, anchored in their own historical identities, with their particular external attachments and domestic alignments and interests to consider. Its ambitions are a token of the Union's weight in a global economy which perforates its frontiers and ignores its territorial limits. As there is no final agreement about its destination, the Union must meanwhile deal with the extension of Europe's periphery eastwards and the lengthening list of candidates who wish to join. That extension shifts the balance of Europe towards its geographic centre in Germany, away from the EC's own inner periphery of Britain and Ireland or Southern Europe. It places a great burden on Germany, economically and psychologically, and may be expected to drive up Germany's price for cooperation. It not only challenges, but fosters national identities. It proclaims an ultimate objective of a Europe beyond the powers, but it was written because of the collapse of the 1945–89 inter-regnum and the re-mergence of a Europe differentiated between greater and smaller powers.

The Maastricht Treaty envisaged the European Community as the core around which a wider, open Europe would be organized. But the fragmentation from the peripheries of Europe was quite capable of entering the core, destroying the achievements of the past four decades. Europe's society of states had flowered within the confines of the Atlantic alliance. Its rationale of containment disappeared with the Soviet Union. The novelty for Europe thus lay in the opening of a parenthesis in European history, where the continent would be in transition from a containment which had provided it with a degree of unity in opposition to a common enemy, to an as yet undefined polity capable of containing its historic diversity. Europe, in short, is in transition from one containment to another. It triumphed in the first; it has just embarked on the second. Maastricht I of 1992 was the first step: Maastricht II of 1996–97 will be the second step. Further 'Maastrichts' would be required thereafter.

There can be little doubt that the real Europe of historical layers, of culturally disputed geographic boundaries and of local diversity in a world market and a world polity has entered on revolutionary times, and is tearing at the fragile edifice of institutional Europe. The real Europe is once again pregnant with conflicts. A positivist belief that politics and institutions still have purchase on European affairs would urge that Europe's many latent conflicts may be promoted and contained by the only institutional fabric of which the real Europe permits: beyond blueprints into a Europe of the Atlantic alliance, and within that of an EU of concentric circles, inner groups, many speeds and multiple geometry – the only Europe of which Burke may ever have approved. A more negative belief in the purchase of politics over events in the world market and polity as it is developing may suggest, though, that the EU of concentric circles, inner groups and many speeds is merely an older and differentiated Europe in new guise. Accepting that Europe would be yielding the ideal to the diktat of events. Rather than becoming trapped in such dichotomies, it may be worth returning to the simplicity and wisdom of the founding fathers of Europe's longest peace: the preservation of the peace and the reconciliation of the peoples must remain at the very forefront of political action and imagination.

NOTE

1. For an analysis of the problem of diversity in managing the European Community in the mid-1980s, see Helen Wallace and Adam Ridley (1985) *Europe: the Challenge of Diversity.* London, Routledge and Kegan Paul.

REFERENCES AND BIBLIOGRAPHY

Bourke, Thomas (1995) *EC–Japan relations 1985–93: the impact of foreign direct investment on regional political integration.* Doctoral thesis. Florence, European University Institute.

Bull, Hedley (1980) *The Anarchical Society: A Study of Order in World Politics.* London, Macmillan.

Calleo, David P. (1982) *The Imperious Economy.* Cambridge, MA, Harvard University Press.

Calvocoressi, Peter (1990) 'World Power, 1920–1990', *International Affairs*, vol. 66, no. 4 (October 1990), pp. 663–74.

Cecchini, Paolo (1988) *The European Challenge 1992.* Aldershot, Wildwood Park.

CDU–CSU Fraktion des Deutschen Bundestages (1994) *Ueberlegungen zur europäischen Politik.* Bonn, September.

Cockfield, Lord (1994) *The European Union: Creating the Single Market.* London, John Wiley.

Delors, Jacques (1992) 'Réconcilier l'idéal et la nécessité', Devant le Collège de l'Europe à Bruges, le 17 Octobre 1989, in Delors, Jacques *Le Nouveau Concert Européen.* Paris, Odile Jacob.

Deutschen Bundestages (1990) Offentliche Anhörung. Protokoll No. 74 (May 1990), pp.130–31.

Emminger, Otmar (1986) *D-Mark, Dollar, Währungskrisen.* Stuttgart, Deutsche Verlags-Anstalt.

Gaddis, John L. (1982) *Strategies of Containment: A Critical Appraisal of Post-War American National Security Policy.* New York, Oxford University Press.

Garton Ash, Timothy (1993) *In Europe's Name: Germany and the Divided Continent.* London, Jonathan Cape.

de Gaulle, Charles (1970) *Mémoires d'Espoir: Le Renouveau, 1958–1962*. Paris, Plon.

Hassner, Pierre (1992) 'Construction européenne et mutations à l'est', in Lenoble, Jacques and Dewandre, Nicole (eds) *L'Europe aus oir du siècle*. Paris, Editions Esprit.

Keynes, J.M. (1937) 'The general theory of employment', *Quarterly Journal of Economics* (February 1937), pp. 209–23.

Kissinger, Henry (1994) 'The new world order', in *Diplomacy*. New York, Simon and Schuster, pp.17–28.

Kissinger, Henry (1979) *White House Years*. Boston, Little Brown.

Mahbubani, Kishore (1995) 'The Pacific impulse', *Survival*, vol. 37, no. 1 (spring 1995), pp.105–20.

Morley, J. (1905) *The Life of William Ewart Gladstone, vol. 1*. London, Macmillan.

Maurice, M., Sellier, F., and Silvestre, J-J. (1982) *Politique d'éducation et organisation industrielle en France et en Allemagne*. Paris, Presses Universitaires Francaises.

Nau, Henry (1990) *The Myth of America's Decline: Leading the World Economy into the 1990s*. New York, Oxford University Press.

Pfaff, William (1989) *Le Réveil du Viex Monde: Vers un Nouvel Ordre International*. Paris, Calmann-Lévy.

Peyrefitte, Alain (1994) *C'était de Gaulle*. Paris, Fayard.

Ross, George (1995) *Jacques Delors and European Integration*. Cambridge, Polity Press.

Strange, Susan (1976) *International Monetary Relations, Vol. 2 of International Economic Relations in the Western World, 1959-1971*. Oxford, Oxford University Press.

Wallace, Helen and Ridley, Adam (1985) *Europe: The Challenge of Diversity*. London, Routledge and Kegan Paul.

3
ECONOMIC AND BUDGETARY CHALLENGES

IAIN BEGG AND NIGEL GRIMWADE

INTRODUCTION

As the single market is consolidated and the EU moves towards economic and monetary union, a re-allocation of responsibility between tiers of government for different elements of economic policy will take place. This will occur partly because of formal agreements to shift the locus of power, but will also reflect new circumstances induced by economic integration. For some fields of policy, the Treaty provides clear guidelines for the division of responsibilities. Monetary policy, for example, will move 'up' to the European tier, while fiscal policy will remain with member states. Yet is not obvious that this division will make it easy to conduct a coherent macroeconomic policy either in individual member states or in the EU as a whole. In other policy areas, there is little guidance either from the Treaty or from the way in which policy has developed.

The uncertainty surrounding the future assignment of policy is most pronounced in areas in which the EU tier has had little to offer in the past (for example, industrial policy) or in which integration itself has created new demands on policy that are not easily dealt with under the existing policy framework. In particular, there is a lack of consensus on the degree to which the EU tier of governance should become involved in policies to redistribute between social groups or to ensure that 'losers' from the integration process are not excessively penalized.

This chapter highlights some of the areas in which there are either difficulties and inconsistencies in the way in which responsibility for important areas of economic policy is assigned, or a need for new thinking about how policy responsibility should evolve as the Union becomes closer. Both sets of issues raise awkward problems, not least because of the need, first, to reconcile demands for subsidiarity with equity and efficiency in policy delivery, and second, to fit in with existing and planned institutional structures of the EU. There are also awkward budgetary questions to confront. The Community budget at present is small (1.2 per cent of GDP) and largely earmarked for specific spending programmes, especially agricultural subsidies. This is due to increase to 1.27 per cent by 1999 under the Financial Perspective agreed at the 1992 Edinburgh Council, which sets the expenditure framework for the seven-year period from 1993–99. Notwithstanding the 'Euro-sceptic' view that the Community's budget is already overblown, the question remains of whether an altogether different approach to EU public finance is now needed.

Many of the questions raised here are unlikely to be resolved at the 1996 Intergovernmental Conference (IGC). Budgetary questions, for instance, are likely to come to the fore only when negotiations start for the renewal in 1999 of the EU's Financial Perspective. Our contention, however, is that these are matters that cannot and are unlikely to be ignored in the meantime, but will have to be settled one way or another, with the implication that they will remain firmly on the agenda. By the same token, the eventual choices will provide a clear signal about the future character of the EU. Those member states whose governments want, essentially, to limit the EU to being a single market will strongly resist any moves to reassign further economic policy powers; but if economic and monetary union is to be complemented by moves towards political union, as Germany appears to want, the case for a substantial reassignment of economic powers to the supranational (federal?) level will become compelling.

THE POWERS OF THE EU

Although the EU is a closer form of union than other free-trade areas, the supranational tier of government stops well short of the powers vested in federal governments in countries such as the US or Germany for economic policy. Some of the main areas where the EU tier of government takes the lead in economic policy are:

- international trade negotiations; the EU negotiated as a bloc in the GATT Uruguay Round completed in 1994;
- setting of rules affecting business; European directives now underpin the regulatory framework facing business in several areas, including competition policy and various aspects of labour relations;
- mergers and acquisitions involving large companies;
- funding of an increasing number of technology and research programmes;
- more notoriously, the common agricultural policy and the common fisheries policy.

In some other areas, policy developed or funded by the EU level complements national policies. These include:

- macroeconomic policy, in which the European Commission and the Councils of Ministers make some effort at coordination. The balance here will change markedly if monetary union proceeds;
- regional policy, through the 'Structural Funds' – the European Regional Development Fund (ERDF) and the European Social Fund (ESF). There are also smaller funds aimed at change in agriculture and fisheries and at boosting the economic performance of the least well-off member states;
- transport and communications, especially with the initiative to develop trans-

European networks (TENS);
- overseas development aid;
- training schemes;
- elements of consumer protection;
- environmental and energy policies.

Most other policy areas are, and are likely to remain, under the control of member states, including welfare policies and tax policy (the exception being the few small taxes directly hypothecated to the EU as 'own resources'). The question is whether this configuration of policy assignment is appropriate for the EU. The next section of the chapter appraises the arguments for and against a reassignment of powers over economic policy to the European tier of government.

THE ARGUMENTS FOR A 'EUROPEANIZATION' OF KEY ECONOMIC POLICIES

Although economic or political theory can give some guidance on how policy responsibilities in the EU should be assigned, more pragmatic considerations are all-important and it is a safe bet that political horse-trading will inevitably settle the matter. Nevertheless, it is useful to start by reviewing the conceptual case for and against shifting more policy-making to the EU level. A variety of considerations inform the selection of the appropriate tier. As Olson (1986) has observed, the starting point for any analysis is market failures. Such failures may not be a sufficient justification for government, but to the extent that government intervention enables a better outcome, the next question is where jurisdictional boundaries should be drawn. Olson argued forcefully that government boundaries should match the geographical area in which a policy takes effect.

The political conditions clearly do not exist for a further substantial transfer of power from member states to the European level, but this does not exclude the possibility that an economic case exists for some change. One area which warrants scrutiny is macroeconomic policy where the Maastricht agreement means that the two main instruments – fiscal and monetary policy – will be largely set by different levels of government. Apart from macroeconomic policy, at least some responsibility for other broad areas of policy could also be shifted to the EU level. For example, in the provision of social welfare policies, it is customary in federal systems for the higher tier of government both to set broad parameters for the administration of welfare systems and to provide or organize a significant proportion of the funding for such policies. There are also persuasive arguments for the higher tier to be involved in regional or structural policies.

An obvious immediate difficulty is that there is little room for manoeuvre in the Financial Perspective. This provides for an increase in commitment appropriations of nearly 22 per cent over the seven years. However, because the CAP will, by 1999, still absorb 46 per cent of funds (compared with 51 per cent in 1993) and much of the rest of the budget is already hypothecated, there is little room left for developing other common policies. Some improved scope for redistribution from richer to poorer member states is possible because of an increase in the scope of structural operations (up 41 per cent compared with 1993 and taking 36 per cent of the budget in 1999 compared with 31 per cent in 1993) and increased reliance on the GNP-based 'fourth resource'. The problem is compounded by the fact that Germany – traditionally the major net contributor – now has major commitments in its new *Länder*. This means that it will be virtually impossible to consider action that makes calls on the EU budget, so that in the short term, any initiatives at the European level will have to be administrative actions rather than expenditure. This need not preclude substantial shifts in policy assignment, nor does it rule out the use of funding mechanisms outside the budget.

Reasons for supranational involvement in policy

Conceptually, a number of arguments can be adduced to support a reassignment to the supranational level. A first issue is the degree to which the impact of a policy falls within national boundaries. In many policy fields, it is becoming increasingly apparent as the EU economy becomes more integrated that, to use Olson's term, the 'domain' of policy is wider than national boundaries (Olson 1986). In addition to macroeconomic management or social welfare, this would point to the European level as the appropriate one for a number of other policy areas such as consumer protection or regulation, where national boundaries have become less meaningful.

The progressive integration of European financial markets, for example, has undermined the ability of individual member states to conduct monetary policy, because decisions on interest rates have to take into account the influence of cross-border financial flows. The EMS crises in 1992 and 1993 highlighted the problems that can arise in this context in reconciling differing monetary objectives. Indeed, avoidance of the monetary turmoil that arises from the conjunction of integrated capital markets and separate monetary policies is one of the more persuasive justifications for monetary union. However, much the same reasoning can be applied to justify a 'Europeanization' of prudential controls aimed at ensuring the solvency and stability of the banking system.

A second class of reasons for policy integration is that policy choices in one jurisdiction may have a significant effect in another. Such spillover effects give rise to concerns that the national policy-maker will be able to impose costs elsewhere while securing benefits for the home nation. The phrase 'exporting unemployment' – perhaps by a snap devaluation – exemplifies this. Spillover effects of this sort arise in numerous other fields including controls aimed at safeguarding the environment, regulation of major industries and the administration of social protection systems.

The issue is not just that spillovers distort the pattern of costs and benefits. A related cause for concern is that, collectively, the policy decisions of the member states could become sub-optimal and inefficient. French antagonism to Britain's devaluations over the last five years, and to the British opt-out from the single currency, though largely self-interested, has at least partly been prompted by the fear that a wave of competitive devaluations would be damaging overall to the EU.

A number of reasons can be identified for a decline in the ability of member states to internalize the costs and benefits of policy actions, many of which flow from the process of economic integration in Europe. These can be split into three broad groups: industrial integration; policy efficiency; and mediation among national interests.

To take industrial integration first: as cross-border activities and alliances grow in importance, the impact of any individual national policy regime on the corporate sector is bound to diminish. Yet, in the absence of supranational policies, it is the collective effect of member state policies that will impinge on economic actors. This can take differing forms. In some spheres of policy, such as macroeconomic management, it will be the average of the member state policies that matters. Where there are competing regulators, by contrast, it may be the lightest or least effective regulation that emerges: one interpretation of the BCCI débâcle is that the bank was able to exploit the option of being formally based in Luxembourg to undermine what might have been more intensive scrutiny in other member states.

The second class of reasons involves the pursuit of policy efficiency. A compelling reason for the single market programme was to eliminate duplication in areas such as certification or controls on movements. Such duplication is wasteful from all sides and plainly to be deplored. The Schengen agreement, notwithstanding French ambivalence, is one example of a solution involving inter-governmental cooperation, and a variety of other ways to avoid duplication can be envisaged. Thus, rather than full harmonization of, for instance, technical standards, a less rigid 'approximation' may suffice. Indeed, even when an EU directive is the basis for policy, member states continue to implement these rules. As Daintith (1995) shows, this 'indirect rule' can often lead to substantial differences in implementation, giving rise to costs in enforcement where discretion is contested. This raises the question of whether the sheer complexity of coordination and cooperation between member states should be abandoned in favour of conferring additional competences on the supranational tier in the interests of reducing the cost of administration. No doubt, it will not only be Euro-sceptics who question the ability of 'Brussels' to achieve this efficiently.

The third set of reasons revolve around mediation among national interests. Just as a national government has to balance the claims of local and regional authorities in its country, the supranational tier is the appropriate level to hold the ring between member states. A good illustration is EU competition policy, reinforced by many of the measures in the single market programme. The use of state aids such as subsidies favours some companies, and such distortions will not only tilt the 'playing field' away from level, but may also undermine allocative efficiency. It can be argued that if the supranational tier assumes the role of honest broker, these distortions will be lessened, although the risks of 'regulatory capture' – that is producer interests holding sway over the way a policy operates – are far from negligible (Woolcock 1995). Similarly, a higher tier of government is better placed to judge the net winners and losers from any policy change and thus to justify any off-setting response. An illustration of this is using the Structural Funds to promote cohesion, where the reasoning is that economic integration damages the competitive position of some regions. Inevitably, the member states which stand to benefit most from such transfers are most inclined to support their existence, while those that are net contributors to the EU budget are dubious that the Structural Funds actually do much to promote economic adjustment. It is worth noting that the setting up of the Cohesion Fund became the price that the Southern member states, led by Spain, demanded for agreeing to the Financial Perspective at the 1992 Edinburgh European Council.

Reasons for preferring the member state or lower tiers

The case for a decentralization of policy decision-making is partly political in that issues of accountability and legitimacy are bound to feature in any debate on shifts in economic powers. The widespread presumption is that if power is exercised by too remote a level of government, it will be less subject to democratic checks. Appeals to preserve national sovereignty are, however, apt to be used as a blunt instrument for resisting change, irrespective of the merits of the case. Application of the principle of subsidiarity also sets limits on possible reassignments of economic policy, but this principle has, arguably, been incorrectly invoked on occasion by some member states to oppose 'Europeanization'. After all, subsidiarity is about locating policy responsibility at the lowest tier consistent with effective policy, and this may mean the European tier. Good reasons can nevertheless be put forward for leaving responsibility for various domains of economic policy with member states or, indeed, lower tiers of government.

First, a policy-maker close to indigenous markets will often have superior knowledge of the economic actors. This allows more appropriate policy choices to be made and prevents actions that are either ineffective or might lead to unfortunate side-effects. Equally, economic actors learn how to interpret policy signals. In so far as financial markets and the corporate sector become accustomed to interpreting hints from national monetary authorities, part of the case against monetary union turns on such arguments. It also has to be recognized that national policy-makers can be poorly attuned to regional or local circumstances that might be better served by decentralization to sub-national levels. Recent thinking on economic development, for instance, emphasizes the benefits of such an approach (see OECD 1993; Begg *et al.* 1995).

Second, competence and experience often go together with proximity to economic actors. If a policy authority has not been through a learning process, good policy will be more difficult to develop. This will be compounded where there is a tangible risk that the supranational policy-maker, for political reasons, succumbs to the temptation to go for a consensus policy that is the lowest common denominator, rather than the 'correct' option. National policy-makers are far from immune to such temptations, but the resulting damage may be lesser, at least for the EU in aggregate.

Third, in an economic area as large as the EU there is inevitably diversity in institutions which makes the design and implementation of common policies either impractical or potentially damaging. Policies ultimately have to operate through existing channels, so that they must be adapted to the limitations of institutions. The complexities and, indeed, the various political accommodations that have gone into the design of social protection systems, for example, help to explain why harmonization in this area is so problematic.

Liberal opponents of centralization such as Vaubel (1995) see other virtues in decentralization. In particular, it permits better satisfaction of individual preferences and, through competition between governments, protects individual freedom. Strong local and regional preferences exist in the provision of public goods and services within Europe due to differences in income levels, geographical conditions and social traditions. These preferences can be better satisfied if decisions about how much provision should be made for public goods and services are made at the most decentralized level. Again, this could warrant an increased role for sub-national policy-makers. Competition between governments protects the freedom of the individual because it allows individuals to express their views by leaving the country or withdrawing their money and capital, the so-called 'power of exit'. 'Classic liberals' – as these proponents of the free-market tend to be called – see in these arguments a case for preferring market (or negative) integration to political (or positive) integration.

KEY POLICY AREAS

The present array of policies assigned to the EU level is partly the result of historical accident and would struggle to survive a dispassionate 're-engineering' exercise. It is easy to defend common external trade policies, while the desire to assure the transparency of the single market justifies harmonization of the regulatory framework. Agricultural subsidies, by contrast are more problematic. Indeed, on objective criteria, the case for a European policy in the agricultural sector is probably weaker than that for a common industrial policy. That the CAP survives, and continues to absorb the lion's share of the EU budget, illustrates the balancing of political interests that shape economic policy assignment.

Political considerations will, similarly, affect any prospective policy reassignment, but economic imperatives must also be expected to exert an influence. This section looks at how the inter-play between economic and political factors can be expected to affect the development of policy in two key areas: macroeconomic management and social protection. Possible changes in both policy areas would have implications for the size of the EU budget and for the procedures by which it is set and administered. This, in turn, raises difficult questions of accountability and legitimacy, which have to be reconciled with a search for economic efficiency. How these matters are eventually resolved in the EU will, consequently, provide pointers to the nature of the Union that will emerge from the IGC and the implementation of the TEU. Indeed, it can be argued that choices made in

50

these key economic policy areas will play a large part in determining whether the EU moves beyond intergovernmentalism (as Germany appears to want), or calls a halt now to the integration process (thereby accepting the UK line).

Macroeconomic policy

Assuming monetary union proceeds as set out in the Treaty, responsibility for monetary policy will be transferred from member states to the European Central Bank (ECB) acting together with national central banks in the European System of Central Banks (ESCB). Yet although there is a clear remit to pursue price stability, what this will mean in practice has not been specified. No government will openly admit to being 'soft' on inflation, but experience suggests that many member states – notably in the south of the EU – have found it expedient to allow moderate inflation as a means of facilitating structural change. If the ESCB were to set the target to be very low inflation (as has happened consistently in Germany), this would imply what many would consider to be an excessively tight monetary policy, that would make life difficult for a number of member states. In this regard, it is important to note that enthusiasm for price stability also varies between interest groups within a member state.

More disconcerting is the absence of agreed mechanisms for the setting of fiscal policy. With each member state free (within the prescribed deficit limits) to set its fiscal stance, two categories of problems could conceivably arise. First, it may prove difficult to ensure that *aggregate* fiscal policy is compatible with monetary policy. That this can create difficulties in a national context was illustrated in the early 1990s in Germany when fiscal and monetary policy appeared to be at odds.

Second, a problem could arise in ensuring that the overall policy stance is the one best suited to the prevailing macroeconomic conditions. For example, if the EU economy should suffer from inadequate growth and rising unemployment due to lack of demand, a need would arise to ensure that macroeconomic policy is adjusted accordingly. This could be better achieved if fiscal policy were set at a EU-wide level. This would presume a larger budget and could necessitate the power for the EU to run a budget deficit and thus to borrow within prescribed limits. This may, at the present time, be seen by member states as bestowing an excessive and undesirable degree of power on the EU. It could also conflict with the deeply-cherished autonomy of national administrations in imposing taxes (although a given fiscal target can be achieved by widely different combinations of taxes and public expenditure). Nevertheless, the issue may have to be faced in the future if macroeconomic policy formulation and execution is to be conducted efficiently. Additional reservations will be expressed about the ability of macroeconomic policy to influence the level of output or employment in the long run. However, even if a minimalist view of macroeconomics is accepted unconditionally, it can be argued that an incoherent policy would also undermine supply-side reform.

Some scope for influencing the fiscal stance of individual member states after monetary unification does exist within the Treaty. Thus, it contains measures for dealing with a member state which runs an excessive budgetary deficit. The latter is defined as a ratio of planned or actual government deficit to GDP exceeding 3 per cent and/or a ratio of government debt to GDP exceeding 60 per cent. A phrase allows for account to be taken of whether or not the ratios are tending to decline 'substantially and continuously' towards the required level and whether or not any excess is 'only exceptional and temporary' (Article 104c). Where a member state is failing to fulfil these requirements, it may be reported by the Commission to the Council and the Council, acting by a qualified majority vote, may require the member state to bring the situation to an end within an agreed period of time. Failure to comply may result in sanctions against the member state. These could take the form of a requirement that the member state publish additional information specified by the Council before issuing bonds and securities, an invitation to the European Investment Bank (EIB) to reconsider its lending policy towards the member state concerned, a requirement that the member state make a non-interest-bearing deposit of an appropriate size with the Community until the deficit has been corrected and/or the imposition of a fine.

However, it remains questionable how effective these provisions will prove to be in practice. In particular, it is difficult to see how a recalcitrant member state could be forced to abide by any sanctions imposed. Reliance will necessarily be placed on the unwillingness of member states to be ostracized. A state may prefer to correct a fiscal deficit rather than risk being identified by its peers as being 'fiscally unsound'. Even then, the provisions are limited to situations where member states are pursuing over-expansionary fiscal policies. A genuine EU-wide fiscal policy must also include scope for making fiscal policy slightly more expansionary if and when EU-wide aggregate demand is considered to be inadequate and/or incompatible with the monetary stance of the ECB.

There are also aspects of EU macroeconomic policy that have to be addressed during the remainder of the second stage of the transition to EMU (for an overview, see Amato *et al.* 1994). EU macroeconomic growth since the middle of the 1970s has been lacklustre, and is one of the main explanations for the high and persistent unemployment that has characterized the EU in recent years. Although it is accepted that growth alone cannot provide a complete solution to high unemployment (see the discussion in Drèze and Malinvaud 1994), there are fears that an over-zealous application of the nominal convergence criteria for monetary union could compromise attempts to relaunch the EU economy.

This is further complicated by the potential for conflict between the aims of nominal convergence (that is in inflation rates and public finances) and real convergence (meaning relativities in the standard of living). Attempts to bear down too heavily on the economies of inflation-prone member states in order to be eligible for stage three of EMU could, perversely, make them relatively worse off (Crockett 1994). EU policy-makers will, consequently, have to tread a careful line on fiscal and monetary rectitude. The imperative of cohesion reinforces this, but also raises the question of complementary policies. A fund to assist member states with 'temporary' macroeconomic problems brought about by an economic shock might, for instance, be envisaged. In principle, this could be accomplished with relatively modest interventions (European Commission 1993).

Social protection and cohesion

Redistribution has long been accepted as one of the functions of government, and it is generally the case that the highest tier of government plays a prominent part in achieving it. Within a member state, redistribution takes place principally through the tax and public expenditure systems, and these 'solidarity' mechanisms are legitimized by a national consensus worked out, in some cases, over several generations. No such consensus exists between member states in the EU, with the result that cross-border solidarity is lacking. Although payments from the Structural Funds do involve fiscal flows which favour some member states at the expense of others, their intention (though possibly not their true incidence) is meant to be to achieve structural objectives, not to redistribute.

The issue to be confronted is whether the elevation of 'cohesion' to one of the fundamental principles the EU seeks to respect (in Article 2 of the Treaty) requires integration of policy on redistribution. With social protection budgets averaging 25 per cent of GDP in the EU, this is bound to be a contentious issue, if only because of the scale of funding. In addition, as Quintin (1992) notes, such proposals have consistently been rejected and were again ruled out in the Treaty. This can be explained, in part, by worries about the budgetary implications, but also because most member states continue to regard social protection as a domestic policy concern. Yet as Sanchez (the Spanish contributor to a study by Jacquemin and Wright 1993, on the challenges facing the EU) warns, there may be serious dangers in an 'economic Europe going faster than social Europe. If this relative gap widens, the Community project may not be viable'.

In considering the merits of greater involvement by the EU in social protection, it has to be recognized that there is no necessary link between economic union and social union. An economic space can, in principle, function without any provision for social integration. The difficulty in the EU, however, is that social protection policies are well-entrenched in what is sometimes referred to as the European social model. Although the implications of social security charges for competitiveness are increasingly under scrutiny (see the OECD 1994), the broad structure of European social protection continues to be supported by the 'social partners'. Yet if national systems remain separate, there may be incentives for member states to dismember them to achieve short-term competitive gains, but ultimately with damaging consequences. There are parallels, in this respect, with competitive devaluations. As Berghman (1991) observes, 'in most federal states, the core social protection schemes are organized on a federal level in order to prevent social competition amongst states and in order to guarantee solidarity and equity of distribution'. The question, therefore, is whether the 'rules' currently in place and consolidated in the 1992 Council Recommendation go far enough. This Recommendation set out targets for the harmonization of the objectives of social protection, but left member states free to use their own systems.

Economic justifications for a social dimension to the integration process can be grouped into three, the most straightforward of which is the mobility of workers between member states, one of the 'four freedoms' sought from the single market programme. Very simply, if the costs and benefits of social protection are too disparate, the result will be to distort labour markets. *Ceteris paribus* employers may prefer to recruit in areas where social charges are low, whereas employees will want to be assured of high levels of social protection. In practice, this neat dichotomy is very difficult to demonstrate. Indeed, the relationships between social charges, social protection and competitive advantage tend to elicit an excess of ill-informed debate.

A second set of reasons for an EU involvement stems from the uneven effects of economic integration on different social groups and regions. Again, the case can be simply put: if disparities are a direct consequence of the single market or EMU, it can be argued that the beneficiaries should be expected to compensate the losers, failing which there is little incentive for the latter to proceed. This philosophy already underpins the Structural Funds.

A third argument is that the long-term coherence and cohesion of Union depends on there being common responsibilities for welfare in different segments of the Union. In both respects, it is only at the highest level of government that there is likely to be a political process capable of mediating demands. This goes to the heart of the debate about what the EU aspires to be.

Various possible developments have been envisaged to encourage convergence in social provision in what has been an extensive debate (see for example: Room 1991; Pieters and Vansteenkiste 1993). Perhaps the best developed is the 'social snake' scheme (Dispersyn *et al.* 1992) under which agreed minimum standards would be gradually raised towards those prevailing in the member states with the best developed systems of social protection. The essence of this proposal is to limit the difference between the most extensive social provision and the least by ensuring that if some member states increase their provision, efforts would be made to obtain improvements in other member states. Another proposal is 'The Thirteenth State' (Pieters and Vansteenkiste 1993), a scheme to create a system of social insurance operated at the supranational level, and aimed primarily at migrant workers. This is advocated as an alternative to the complexities of regulations which govern the entitlements of those who move between national jurisdictions, and would involve the establishment of a system administered at the supranational level which would operate alongside existing national ones. It would, therefore, be an evolution directly inspired by the philosophy of free movement in the single market programme.

Proposals have been made also for the EU to offer complementary social protection in regions or to social groups most affected by short-term economic crisis, as advocated in the MacDougall report (1977) and by Begg and Mayes (1991). Such schemes, which could take the form of supplementary unemployment benefits, would provide a further layer of social protection, and, at the same time, help to reduce socio-economic differences between EU regions, hence contributing to cohesion. A study of such a scheme in France (Melitz 1993) suggested that it would find it difficult to avoid two problems. First, if the benefits are to be financially relevant for significantly reducing differentials between regions, they would become a permanent transfer from rich to poor countries, likely to be politically and socially rejected by richer regions. If, on the contrary, the transfer payments are kept low, and are organized such that they can only be of short duration, then they would have little impact in the recipient areas.

Budgetary constraints have also inhibited serious consideration of such proposals since they would imply at least a doubling of the European budget to have a meaningful impact. Moreover, even relatively unambitious schemes would require that the member states concede a critical point, namely that cross-border transfers for income support rather than structural purposes are justifiable. Many of the richer member states, especially those with right of centre governments, are strongly opposed to concessions on this principle. Transfers do, however, tend to attract support from the socialist group in the European Parliament and recent indications suggest that the Swedish government might support some initiative along these lines. The strength of feeling from the four least-favoured member states in the negotiations on the establishment of the Cohesion Fund suggests that they, too, would be receptive. These political dividing lines coincide, to some degree, with those on the debate on real and nominal convergence. EMU could, as a technical proposition, function provided that the nominal convergence criteria set out in the Treaty are respected. But if adherence to the nominal convergence criteria aggravates disparities in real convergence – real incomes per head – the result could be to undermine support for European integration. There are echoes of this in the policy debate in France since the election of President Chirac.

CONCLUSIONS

'Classical liberal' arguments concerned with diversity of preference and policy competition as a means of protecting individual freedom will always be used to oppose centralization of policy-making at the EU level. In addition, at the political level, the desire to retain power and to keep control of economic instruments is certain to act as a powerful force opposing any shift of responsibilities to EU institutions. Considerations of economic efficiency, however, may demand that these matters are rationally examined in a different light. The deepening process of economic and monetary integration within Europe must be expected to create pressures for some shift in policy-making to the European centre. As a result, member states will need to reach new accommodations on a much wider range of policy areas than hitherto. In that case, it is highly desirable that some of the ground is prepared now.

One issue clearly concerns the size of the EU budget. There needs to be some recognition of the necessity for a budget which commands a greater share of Union GDP than is envisaged in the current expenditure plans of the Union. However, much can still be achieved without the necessity for a substantial increase in the budget, a change likely to be politically difficult to bring about as the Edinburgh Summit demonstrated. By devising new forms of cooperation or coordination, or, perhaps, by setting up new intergovernmental organizations to deal with specific policy areas, much change can be brought about. Some form of pooled social security or unemployment fund, for example, could be constructed in this way without control being vested in the European Commission. Similarly, many of the regulatory challenges of integration can be met with little more than a slightly higher administrative budget. Majone (1993), for example, in an appraisal of European social policy, concluded that 'a European welfare state seems politically unfeasible and, at the present level of political development of Community institutions, perhaps even undesirable'. He argued that the thrust of EU policy should be on social regulation: consumer protection; health and safety; and environmental protection – that is, factors affecting the quality of life – rather than direct income support.

Nevertheless, as the EU becomes more closely integrated, the limits of cooperation and coordination are likely to be tested. National systems which are too disparate may undermine the underlying principles of the single market. Similarly, even if common policies are adopted, but implemented indirectly via national legal and institutional systems, anomalies in interpretation and enforcement can arise. More pointedly, if the EU is serious about cohesion, it is difficult to escape the conclusion that mechanisms to secure cross-border transfers will be required. Whether this need be on the scale suggested by the MacDougall report is open to question. Equally, it will not be feasible within the present EU budget. More effective demand management at a European-wide level may also imply an increased budget and, perhaps, provisions for the financing of demand-stimulating deficits, implying borrowing powers.

The latter would be highly contentious and is unlikely to gain easy acceptance from even a small number of member states. There may, however, be scope for revising the fiscal provisions already contained in the Treaty which are currently limited to measures for curtailing an excessive fiscal deficit in an individual member state. Such measures are justified because they curb the spillover effects on other member states of any one member state over-borrowing. However, there may also need to be provisions for dealing with the equally damaging situation where one or more of the larger member states is pursuing a fiscal policy which is unduly deflationary when viewed from an EU point of view. This suggests that, at the very least, much stronger procedures for coordinating member states' fiscal policies are required.

Given that there is no compelling reason to expect the European tier to be any more efficient in the delivery of social protection, the case for EU involvement hinges largely on the acceptability of cross-border transfers. However, it can also be justified as a response to common problems. Thus, recent trends suggest that the role of social protection will have to be widened to incorporate action to promote employment and address exclusion. In other words, the boundary between social protection policy and labour market policies is becoming increasingly blurred as social protection aims to do more than provide replacement income. The establishment of an agency for social protection at the EU level could, consequently, provide a valuable complement to the activities of the Social Fund in these domains.

These considerations lead to the conclusion that the present allocation of policy responsibilities may well become increasingly untenable as the single market becomes ever closer integrated. Notwithstanding the attachment of many member states to the principle of subsidiarity, this is bound to be a matter for intense debate at the IGC and beyond.

REFERENCES AND BIBLIOGRAPHY

Amato, G. et al. (1994) 'Is European Monetary Union Dead?' Discussion Paper No. 3, *The Philip Morris Institute for Public Policy Research*.

Begg, I.G. and Mayes, D.G, with Shipman, A. and Levitt, M. (1991) *A New Strategy for Social and Economic Cohesion after 1992*. Luxembourg, Office for Official Publications of the European Community.

Begg, I.G., Lansbury, M. and Mayes, D.G., (1995) 'Decentralised industrial policies', in Cheshire, P. and Gordon, I. (eds) *Territorial Competition in an Integrating Europe*. Aldershot, Avebury.

Berghman, J. (1991) '1992 and social security', in Room G. (ed.) *Towards a European Welfare State*. Bristol, SAUS Publications.

Crockett, A. (1994) 'The role of convergence in the process of EMU', in Steinherr, A. (ed.) *30 years of European Monetary Integration from the Werner Plan to EMU*. London, Longman.

Daintith, T. (ed..) (1995) *Implementing EC Law in the United Kingdom: Structures for Indirect Rule*, Chichester, Wiley.

Dispersyn, M. *et al.* (1992) 'La construction d'un serpent social européen', *Revue Belge de Sécurité Sociale*, vol. 36, pp. 315–656.

Drèze, J.H. and Malinvaud, E. (1994) 'Growth and employment: the scope for a European growth initiative', *European Economy Reports and Studies*, vol. 1, pp. 77–106.

European Commission (1993) 'Stable money – sound finances', *European Economy*, no. 53.

Jacquemin, A. and Wright, D. (1993) *The European Challenges Post-1992: Shaping Factors, Shaping Actors*. Aldershot, Elgar.

MacDougall, D. (1977) *Report of the study group on the role of public finance in European integration*. Brussels, Commission of the European Communities.

Majone, G. (1993) 'The European Community between social policy and social regulation', *Journal of Common Market Studies*, vol. 31, pp. 153–70.

Melitz (1993) 'Faut-il une assurance commune centre des différences de conjonture?', *Economie et Statistique* No. 262263, pp. 101–7

OECD (1993) *Territorial Development and Structural Change: A New Perspective on Adjustment and Reform*. Paris, OECD.

OECD (1994) *The Jobs Study*. Paris, OECD.

Olson, M. (1986) 'Towards a more general theory of governmental structure', *American Economic Review*, vol. 76, Papers and Proceedings, pp. 120–25.

Pieters, D. and Vansteenkiste, S. (1993) *The thirteenth state: towards a European Community social insurance scheme for intra-community migrants*. Leuven.

Quintin, O. (1992) 'The convergence of social protection objectives and policies: a contribution to solidarity in Europe', *Social Europe*, supplement 5/92, pp. 9–12.

Room, G. (ed.) (1991) *Towards a European Welfare State*. Bristol, SAUS Publications.

Vaubel, R. (1995) *The Centralisation of Western Europe: The Common Market, Political Integration and Democracy*. London, Institute of Economic Affairs.

Woolcock, S. (1995) 'Regulatory competition in the European Community', paper presented to the ECSA Biennial conference, Charleston, South Carolina (mimeo).

4

THE LESSONS OF MAASTRICHT

FINN LAURSEN

INTRODUCTION

We are all supposed to learn from history. The 'lessons' of the past are used in the present and thus contribute to determining the future. The historian, Ernest R. May wrote a book relating such 'lessons' to American foreign policy. The three theses are: framers of foreign policy are often influenced by beliefs about what history teaches or portends; policy-makers ordinarily use history badly; policy-makers can, if they will, use history more discriminatingly (May 1973: ix–xii). The last thesis is comforting for any historian. It gives some utility to his *metier*.

In this chapter we discuss the 'lessons' from the negotiation and ratification of the Maastricht Treaty as well as its operation. It is an interesting research project to investigate to what extent the difficulties of getting the Treaty ratified affected the 'cognitive maps' of European political leaders. Although such a task goes beyond what is possible in only one chapter, the reports from the Commission, the European Parliament and the so-called Reflection Group, established to prepare the 1996 Intergovernmental Conference (IGC) provide some possible answers. But we need to go beyond the question of what policy-makers have learned to touch on the question of what we think they should have learned. The basis on which such prescription rests is a belief in the need to upgrade the institutional capacity of the European Union (EU) before further enlargements take place. This requires leadership, a topic not dealt with in the reports analysed.

A reminder

In their approach to the IGC, a number of member states were only too acutely aware of the serious problems encountered in ratifying the Treaty. First, the Danes voted 'no' to the Treaty in June 1992 and accepted it only when it was combined with the special Edinburgh arrangements in a second referendum in May 1993. The British finally ratified the Treaty in the summer of 1993. The French government gained only a *petit oui* in its referendum in September 1992. It was a referendum which was not formally necessary, but which was called by President Mitterrand after the 'no' vote in the first Danish referendum in June 1992. Finally, in Germany, the government had to wait for a judgement by the Constitutional Court before it could complete the ratification process. The judgement linked further integration with the democratic nature of the EU. The Treaty thus turned out to be controversial not only in two of the countries that joined the

European integration process in the first enlargement of the European Communities (EC) in 1973, namely the UK and Denmark, but also in two of the founder countries, France and Germany, usually considered to be the motors behind European integration.

At the same time, however, it should not be forgotten that the ratification process went smoothly in a majority of the member states. Member governments received consent to ratify the Treaty by large parliamentary majorities in all the southern member states, Greece, Italy, Spain and Portugal as well as in the three Benelux countries, Belgium, the Netherlands and Luxembourg. And the Irish public accepted the Treaty by a rather substantial majority in their referendum in June 1992 (Laursen and Vanhoonacker 1994).

LEARNING LESSONS

Caution, pragmatism and simplicity

Judging from the reports from the European Parliament, the Commission and the Reflection Group, it seems that our policy-makers have concluded that the difficulties of the Maastricht Treaty should lead to caution and pragmatism. 'The main issue during the conference will not be an increase in the Union's powers,' said the Commission Report on the operation of the Maastricht Treaty (European Commission 1995: 6). The new President of the Commission, Jacques Santer, talked about doing less, but doing it better (see Chapter 10). Along similar lines it was stated in the report from the Reflection Group: 'The general feeling within the Group is that the Community should try not to do more but better' (Reflection Group 1995: 40). In a Parliament report, David Martin said proposals should be 'practical as well as desirable'.

This does not mean that Parliament should be cautious in all fields and in a number of questions it will have to put forward bold solutions. However, it should seek to work to the maximum extent on the basis of what exists. In many areas it might be more attractive and indeed coherent to start again from scratch, but this is not a realistic option. The 1996 Conference will be difficult enough as it is without adding to the difficulties (European Parliament 1995: 5).

A difficult conference was therefore regarded as unavoidable. As Dinan and Dankert point out (Chapters 10 and 11), the two main Community actors, the Commission and the European Parliament, seemed to approach the IGC with much more caution than the 1991 Conference. That government representatives in the Reflection Group also seemed rather cautious should probably surprise us less.

Another conclusion that was widespread was that the IGC needed to be discussed more openly this time. A revised treaty should not come as a surprise; it should be simpler, more easy to understand and, as David Martin suggested in his report, it should be 'more inspiring' (European Parliament 1995: 6). To make it simpler, Martin proposed a restatement of the basic principles, including a new

Article B. The existing treaties should be consolidated in 'a single clear and concise document' (ibid.). This, however, should also lead to the abolition of the 'pillars'. There should be judicial review by the European Court of Justice (ECJ) in all areas, and the Union should have legal status. However, some of the features of the separate pillars could be kept, at least for transitional periods. But special procedures should be kept to a minimum.

The members of the Reflection Group also called for simplification. For instance, a majority of the members favoured reducing legislative procedures to three: consultation, co-decision and assent (Reflection Group 1995: 9). Although they favoured improvements in the two intergovernmental pillars, a majority did not favour abolition of the pillar structure. But some members felt that the third pillar, Cooperation in Justice and Home Affairs (JHA), should 'at least partially' be brought into the Community sphere (ibid.). A majority did see structural problems in the second pillar, Common Foreign and Security Policy (CFSP), but disagreed on what to do about it.

Efficiency, openness and democracy

Another principle suggested by David Martin was 'more efficient, open and accountable institutions and decision-making mechanisms' (European Parliament 1995: 6). In a similar vein the Commission suggested that 'the Union must act democratically, transparently and in a way people can understand'. The second principle put forward by the Commission was that 'the Union must act effectively, consistently and in solidarity' (European Commission 1995: 4). The Reflection Group said 'Ways must be found of increasing citizens' confidence in the European institutions.' Institutional reform, therefore, had to 'be subjected to the test of more democracy, more efficiency, more solidarity and more transparency' (Reflection Group 1995: 7).

These principles take us into the hard core of the 1996 IGC: institutional changes. Such changes are called for partly because parts of the Maastricht Treaty, especially the second and third pillars, have not worked very well, and partly because of future enlargements with Cyprus, Malta and Central and Eastern European countries (CEECs). With membership now being offered, with conditions, to 12 states we may be moving towards an EU of 27 members. It is widely recognized that such enlargement will require institutional changes to avoid a serious weakening of the institutional capacity of the EU, although some may have a hidden agenda to achieve that. Thus a dilemma has emerged: how can one make existing institutions both more democratic and more efficient? Are we moving towards a wider, but weaker Union?

David Martin wanted the role and independence of the Commission to be reasserted. The Council and the European Parliament should be 'established as equals in all fields of EU legislative and budgetary competence' (European Parliament 1995: 11). The question was raised whether it was necessary to have unanimity for the appointment of the President of the Commission. Or, would it not be better to have the Parliament elect the president? This would also make the elections to the European Parliament more interesting. Concerning the role of national parliaments, he had this to say: 'a pragmatic improvement of current networks for cooperation and of exchanging information between the European Parliament and national parliaments should be encouraged' (ibid.: 16).

The Reflection Group was not very specific about the Commission. The Group was inclined to maintain the Commission's monopoly of legislative initiative in Community matters. In respect to comitology, the Group was in favour of simplifying procedures (Reflection Group 1995: 14–15; for a discussion of existing procedures, see Docksey and Williams 1994).

On Council voting, David Martin was in favour of some adjustment of the weighting of votes, but only a slight adjustment, for example, a scale from two to fifteen instead of two to ten under existing provisions. He was against 'double majorities' since that would make the system more complicated (European Parliament 1995: 18). In the Reflection Group, some members took the position that 'the system should be corrected so that greater account is taken of population by means of new weightings for votes'. Other members, however, disagreed. They pointed out that 'there is no systematic pattern of small-population countries forming coalitions against the large-population countries'. (Reflection Group 1995: 12). However, a majority of the members of the Group maintained 'that the enlarged Union would appear to require the extension or even the generalization of the qualified majority, for reasons of efficiency' (ibid.: 11).

The Commission Report dealt with some of these issues in part one on 'Democracy and transparency in the Union'. It also dealt with European citizenship, outlining what was already in the Maastricht Treaty, concluding with the assessment that 'the citizen enjoys only fragmented, incomplete rights which are themselves subject to restrictive conditions. In that sense, the concept of citizenship is not yet put into practice in a way that lives up to the individual's expectations.' (European Commission 1995: 10).

David Martin had called for 'a European union which is as close as possible to its citizens' (European Parliament 1995: 6). In this connection he suggested greater substance for the concept of Union citizenship, more open decision-making, and improved implementation of subsidiarity.

One may wonder whether such suggestions would make it easier to sell a revised treaty to the electorates in the member states. If we compare them with the Edinburgh arrangements that eventually helped to sell the Maastricht Treaty to Danish voters, it probably would not help to give the concept of EU citizenship more substance. Some Danes feared that they were losing their national citizenship. Indeed, as the members of the Reflection Group put it, in some countries:

there was a failure to put across the idea that citizenship of the Union is not intended to replace national citizenship but actually to complement it. In some cases the perception has been precisely the opposite, and in societies where this occurs there is undoubtedly a need to make a special effort to explain the facts. (Reflection Group 1995: 17)

We can guess that they were thinking of Denmark in particular. Danish – and other – politicians need to explain things better the next time.

On legitimacy, the Commission argued that the greater legislative role of the European Parliament and its increased role in appointing the Commission had increased legitimacy. But it concluded: 'there has also to be a reservation concerning the weakness, not to say the absence, of democratic control at Union level in the fields of activity where the intergovernmental process still holds sway,' i.e., in the fields of the CFSP and JHA (European Commission 1995: 18).

In the section on decision-making, the Commission found three major weaknesses: the continuing divergence between legislative procedures and the budget procedure; the complexity of the decision-making system; and the lack of logic in the choice of the various procedures and the different fields of activity where they apply (ibid.: 23).

Indeed, as the Commission went on to point out, the Union had more than twenty different decision-making procedures. The number and the complexity of some of these 'renders the Union's *modus operandi* extremely obscure' (ibid.). Simplification in the area of procedures was therefore considered necessary.

As for the role of the European Court of Justice (ECJ), the Commission saw a weakness in the Court's non-involvement in the two intergovernmental pillars, 'where vital personal rights and freedoms can be affected' (ibid.: 28).

On the question of transparency, the Commission looked at subsidiarity, access to information and clarity of legislation. It was admitted that subsidiarity needed further development and that 'the public's expectations are far from satisfied' in respect to openness and transparency. The latter was particularly wanting in JHA (ibid.: 35). For its part, the Reflection Group, *inter alia*, recommended 'allowing individuals more information and greater access to documents and improving the quality of legislative texts' (Reflection Group 1995: 20).

Various proposals to improve the institutions and enhance the legitimacy of the EU were therefore put forward. How they were meant to inter-relate was left unclear. Indeed, none of the reports prepared for the IGC had any explicit theory or conceptual framework linking the different proposals together into a simple vision of a wider and stronger Union which might help the citizens understand the rationale of the whole endeavour.

Effectiveness and consistency of policies

The three reports also dealt with policies. David Martin suggested the following policy goals. As a minimum, the European Union must:

- tackle unemployment more effectively;
- ensure that its industries and services remain internationally competitive;
- ensure that there is a true internal market without barriers for people as well as goods and services;
- reduce the existing discrepancies between its richer and poorer countries and regions;
- ensure high environmental and consumer protection standards;
- maintain its cultural identity and diversity;

- tackle fraud and waste more effectively;
- ensure that it has firm but fair controls at its external borders;
- develop an effective framework for foreign policy;
- develop a stronger security and defence policy dimension. (European Parliament 1995: 19).

The Reflection Group stressed 'the urgent need to meet the challenge of job creation, in response to pressing demand from Europe's citizens'. Most members also wanted to strengthen the social content of the treaty, and the Group concluded that 'priority should be given to taking account of environmental aspects of Community policies' (Reflection Group 1995: 40–41). There was little doubt in anyone's mind, perhaps, that the EU would have a better press and more support if it could create more jobs. But, unemployment and the reduction of discrepancies between richer and poorer regions requires an increased Community budget, a doubtful outcome of the IGC, even if more fiscal federalism might return to the agenda in the move towards EMU.

The last four points in David Martin's list, from fraud to defence, more or less fall under the intergovernmental pillars of the TEU. The likelihood of any fundamental change in the pillar structure was dashed early by the opposition of 'some member states' to ending the pillar structure in the Reflection Group. For its part, the Commission reported mainly on the differences between supranational integration in the first pillar and intergovernmental cooperation in the second and third pillars and the problem of consistency between them. The Maastricht Treaty produced progress in the first pillar with plans for, strengthened policies in some areas (e.g. environment) and by introducing some new policy chapters. Adding cooperation in JHA was also regarded as a 'major innovation' (European Commission 1995: 47). However, the results were seen as meagre with the Council unable to adopt a single common position, and able to agree only on two joint actions and one Convention within the third pillar. The legal instruments of the JHA pillar were ineffective, partly because of disagreement over their nature. Decision-making by unanimity was, the Commission believed 'a major source of paralysis, either preventing any action or decision at all or reducing the decision taken to the lowest common denominator' (ibid.: 52).

On the interface between the first and third pillars, the Commission pointed to the fact that the free movement of persons fell under both pillars. Visa policy was offered as an example of the complications:

> The list of non-member countries whose nationals require a visa is laid down in a Community regulation, while the conditions for the issue of visas are to be decided through intergovernmental cooperation (ibid.: 52).

Questions of consistency also exist in external policy, where commercial policy (Articles 110–116), development cooperation (Articles 130u to 139y) and sanctions against non-member countries (Article 228a) fall within the first pillar. The scope of Article 113, limited by the ECJ to trade only in goods, has been regarded, especially by the Commission, as a growing problem. International commercial policy has developed hugely to include new areas, such as trade in services, foreign direct investments, protection of intellectual property rights, etc., as was very clearly revealed in the GATT Uruguay Round. According to the Commission, therefore, shared powers in, say, the services sector (some 25 per cent of total world trade and growing), which involve lengthy processes of national ratification of agreements, reduce effectiveness in negotiation, add to the complexity of decision-making and risk the benefits negotiated within the World Trade Organization go well beyond the remit of Article 113: 'the structure of Community law has manifestly been overtaken by commercial reality' (ibid.: 58).

In the case of the creation of an integrated system for the control of exports of dual-use goods, i.e., goods that can be used for both civilian and military purposes, the Commission has been critical of the duplication of decision-making involved. Under the TEU, it is necessary to adopt both a Community regulation and a CFSP common position (ibid.: 60). Looking at the second pillar as such the Commission welcomed the novelties: its own right of initiative, the possibility of joint actions and the inclusion of defence policy. By the time the IGC opened in Turin some 23 common positions and 24 joint actions had been adopted (the majority of the latter in connection with the former Yugoslavia). It was not too impressive a record, for which the Commission provided one answer:

> Unanimous voting, even where the Treaty allows qualified-majority voting, is one of the problems of foreign and security policy and one of the reasons why it is so ineffective. (ibid.: 67)

Moreover, the lack of clarity over CFSP expenditures, which might be charged either to the EC budget or to member states, also created problems: 'the hybrid structure of the Treaty, with decisions under one pillar requiring funding under another, has introduced an additional source of conflict (ibid.: 68).

Another inter-institutional aspect which had not worked well was that between the EU and the Western European Union (WEU). The WEU had been 'used rarely and with limited success' (ibid.: 69). Indeed, in practical terms, the use of WEU in joint actions under the CFSP was limited to the provision of a policing contingent for the administration of Mostar.

Other problems in the second pillar included those created by rotating presidencies, inadequate analytical capacity, and the ill-adaptation of the troika to representing the Union externally. Again, as the Commission put it:

> Better common background analysis, better decision-making and clearer representation of the Union will all contribute to giving substance to the common foreign and security policy. They will have to become practical realities if the policy is to make real progress. (ibid.: 67)

In its final conclusion the Commission expressed two concerns that very well summarize its argument:

- first, the less-than-convincing experience with intergovernmental cooperation under the second and third pillars suggests that there can be no question of trying to accommodate further enlargements with the present arrangements for their operation;
- second, it is not certain that the Treaty has actually brought the Union closer to the general public: the subsidiarity principle has in some instances been used for other than its intended purpose, and there is still a shortage of openness in the fields of justice and home affairs. (ibid.: 70)

The issue of institutional capacity, especially of CFSP and JHA, has thus been clearly presented as an important point on the agenda of the IGC. The Commission put forward a realistic analysis of the shortcomings of the intergovernmental pillars. While they were raised in the deliberations of the Reflection Group, the lack of unanimity found in its report creates severe doubts that all member states are willing to tackle the issues with any great seriousness. But even if governments were prepared to make the necessary progress at the IGC, itself, they are likely to be only too aware of the possibly problematic issue of ratification.

If not all the member states are able to agree on reform or ratify the results of the IGC, will we get more multi-speed integration or even variable geometry? The question raises some decisive issues for the future of European integration, which have either not been dealt with at all in existing reports or memoranda or have been done so only marginally. Indeed, a worrying part of past reports has been the discrepancy between the problems analysed and the remedies suggested. One can only wonder sometimes whether policy-makers are aware of past efforts at reform and are using or abusing history for their own purposes.

THE ISSUE OF DIFFERENTIATION

There are already elements of differentiation, i.e. multi-speed integration or variable geometry in the Maastricht Treaty and there will probably be more of it in the future. The UK and Denmark obtained opt-out (or rather opt-in) clauses in respect to the third phase of EMU, and certain convergence criteria have to be fulfilled by the countries which will take part in that phase. At best it will probably be a core group of countries that will start the European Central Bank (ECB) and the single currency in 1999 (or later).

The UK also negotiated a clear opt-out on social policy, which takes us from multi-speed integration to variable geometry or à la carte integration. As long as there is agreement on the goal, we can have multi-speed integration. If there is disagreement on the goal we get variable geometry or à la carte integration, which is widely seen as more dangerous than multi-speed integration. With multi-speed integration the idea is that slower members will catch up.

Within the Maastricht Treaty's second pillar on the CFSP, five of the fifteen – Denmark, Ireland and the three newcomers, Austria, Finland and Sweden – are not members of the WEU. Ireland has stayed out because of its special version of neutrality policy. To persuade the Danish people to accept the Maastricht Treaty in the second referendum in May 1993 it was decided, *inter alia*, to announce that Denmark did not intend to join the WEU. This was despite the fact that some political circles in Denmark, especially the Liberal Party, realized that Europe's defence-related problems would increasingly be discussed in that forum. The three newcomers have maintained a policy of military neutrality (or non-align-ment) that at least for the moment seems to rule out NATO and WEU member-ship because of the collective defence commitments of these organizations (Keatinge 1995). As the Reflection Group Report put it:

> A number of members, chiefly representing countries which are not members of the WEU, do not think a merger [of the EU and WEU] feasible, at any rate not in the fore-seeable future. The reason for this is that their countries' special position does not allow them to take on all of the obligations under the Brussels Treaty, in particular the auto-matic territorial guarantee in Article V. (Reflection Group 1995: 31).

For the moment Austria, Sweden and Finland have joined Ireland and Denmark as observers in the WEU. They have also joined NATO's Partnership for Peace (PfP) Programme, in which Ireland, however, does not yet take part. A learning process may well have been started that will take the 'neutrals' in the direction of a possible future EU defence policy, but it is certainly moving very slowly.

If some core members of the European Union decide to press ahead with developing the European defence identity much further, it may, and probably will, leave some members on the side-lines, i.e., lead to more differentiation. However, the merger of the WEU with the EU is not very likely. With NATO playing a larger role in Bosnia, the 'lesson' may also be that it is not really necessary, at the moment at least. However, some kind of 'progressive integration', as the Reflection Group called it (1995: 31) may have started.

In respect to JHA cooperation, there is also the possibility of more multi-speed integration or variable geometry. Some members, including Ireland, the UK and Denmark have not joined the Schengen agreement, for instance. Some countries are more eager to move some of the policy areas under the third pillar to the first pillar than others. Some are more eager to introduce aspects of Community law in the third pillar than others.

If we look towards the future with more countries joining the EU, we have to expect more multi-speed integration within the EU and possibly also more vari-able geometry. The role of the EFTAn newcomers has already created some uncertainty. In the future, will the poorer CEECs be ready to join EMU? When can they meet EU environmental standards? Will an Eastern European enlarge-ment require the Union to drop the established doctrine that newcomers must accept the *acquis communautaire*? Can the Common Agricultural Policy (CAP) and regional policies be reformed to allow for integration of the CEECs? (Baldwin 1994) The difficulties of CAP reform in connection with the Uruguay Round do not suggest any great optimism (Nedergaard 1995).

In his report to the European Parliament, David Martin suggested that multi-speed integration might be accepted on certain conditions: a single institutional framework, the *acquis communautaire* and the maintenance of the concept of EU-wide solidarity (European Parliament 1995). Certain core areas of EU action should be defined for which opt-outs should be avoided:

> The European Union should continue to set the same objectives for all its Member States to the maximum possible extent, with flexibility being permitted when individual Member States have genuine difficulty in meeting certain commonly agreed objectives or decisions.

He added: 'any proposals which would lead to a "Europe à la carte", and which could undermine the European Union's internal market and solidarity and its external identity, should be resisted' (ibid.: 20).

If the EP can envisage multi-speed integration, but rejects variable geometry, so, too, can the Commission. Indeed, the Commission is 'utterly opposed' to *à la carte* integration (European Commission 1995: 6). The Reflection Group suggested similar considerations, but was clearly not unanimous about it (Reflection Group 1995: 6).

Multi-speed integration is probably becoming the only way to proceed among a much bigger group of countries. One can hope that there will continue to be a core group of countries which will keep pressing on. The 'laggards' can then 'graduate' and join the inner circle later.

THE RATIFICATION PROBLEM

According to Patrick Keatinge: 'Ultimately, selling the outcome of the IGC to their publics is the critical consideration (Keatinge 1995: 33). He added that none of the three new states that confirmed their membership with referenda would require a mandatory referendum to endorse ratification. However, both Denmark and Ireland would require a referendum to become members of the WEU, and in the Danish case other changes in the Edinburgh arrangements would require a referendum. Earlier in their report, Keatinge *et al.* (in this instance, Gunilla Herolf assisted by Rutger Lindahl) wrote of Sweden:

> Given the narrow margin of success in Sweden's accession referendum (52.3% in favour), it might be difficult for political leaders to ignore demands that if other states require popular approval the same procedure should be followed in Sweden. A referendum in Denmark might well provoke such a situation. (Keatinge 1995: 26)

Even if a Danish referendum was not necessarily followed by others, governments are still caught in a two-level game – to follow Putnam (1988) – where much depends on national situations and capacities. If national governments are unable to win change at the EU level that meets domestic demands, it may be impossible to achieve the required consensus or majority at the European level.

Governments will only accept what they think will be accepted domestically. Some governments have clearly been concerned about what their electorates can accept at home, especially, perhaps Denmark and Sweden (see Chapter 9). It was also clear in the run-up to the IGC that some governments were worried about John Major's United Kingdom. Indeed, it looked as if the Conservative government would be able to accept very little of what other member states considered essential. Given the need for a general election in the UK in the first half of 1997, few governments appeared to be in favour of a rushed Conference, in the hope that a new Labour government in the UK would be able to accept more.

Should Denmark and Ireland need a referendum to ratify a revised treaty, with other member states following, then the unpredictability of referenda becomes a major issue. Yet most pre-IGC reports largely ignored the issue. It was not even mentioned in the report by the Danish Foreign Ministry published in June 1995 (Udenrigsministeriet 1995).

The ratification of the Maastricht Treaty took four referenda, including two in Denmark. The 'no' vote in the first Danish referendum led to more discussion of the Maastricht Treaty, not only in Denmark, but also in many other member states. Such discussion should, of course, be welcomed in democratic societies. But it should not be forgotten that the Danish 'no' contributed to create a situation of great uncertainty, including costly speculation on the currency markets. And to get the Maastricht Treaty ratified in Denmark the special Edinburgh arrangements were necessary. Denmark's decisions not to join the WEU or take part in the third phase of EMU points in the direction of more differentiation in the integration process.

In his report to the European Parliament, David Martin had this to say about referenda:

> It has also been suggested that any referendum to ratify treaty revisions should be Union-wide on the grounds that a collective decision affecting the whole of Europe is at stake, and that such a referendum would minimize the domestic considerations which frequently play a major role in national referendums on Europe. (European Parliament 1995: 22)

However, more realistically he added: 'although this idea merits further reflection, your rapporteur is of the view that it is unlikely to prove acceptable at this stage'. The question of referenda therefore remains an open one.

Whether the use of referenda is a good or bad thing is, of course, a political question. One can see such use as a way to further participatory democracy, and one can argue that the process of European integration involves important steps, especially the transfer of national powers to supranational institutions, that should be authorized by the people. Surely, popular acceptance of integration steps adds to the legitimacy of the process. However, the counter question is whether the issues involved are sometimes too complex for the average voter? Don't we have parliaments to make that kind of decision for us?

Summarizing a discussion of direct democracy, a great student of constitutional democracy, Carl Friedrich, concluded: 'direct popular action in its several forms can serve to strengthen the democratic element. But if the dose is too strong, it will seriously strain the system' (Friedrich 1968: 556).

If we do move towards increased use of referenda it becomes imperative for governments to explain the issues fully to their electorates. Such a move will also demand considerable leadership on the part of pro-integration political leaders, who will need to communicate the rationale of integration a good deal better than in the past.

The question of leadership

History teaches us that it is not easy to reach joint decisions among a group of sovereign nation-states, and there are theories that suggest that the difficulties are correlated to the size of the group (Olson 1965). A larger European Union therefore is more likely to have 'collective action' problems than a Union with a small number of members. If enlargement does not go hand-in-hand with measures to increase decision-making capacity we must expect to see more 'collective action' problems in the future in Europe. A wide but weak Union will 'underproduce' public goods such as peace, security and welfare. One device to try to overcome 'collective action' problems is obviously the building of institutions and regimes (Stein 1983). Political entrepreneurs or leaders can also help solve collective action problems (Taylor 1987: 24–7).

The EC founding fathers invented the 'Community method' to try to 'upgrade the common interest' among the original six member countries (Haas 1961). This included an important role of initiative and leadership for the Commission and some decisions by qualified majority voting in the Council. The Luxembourg Compromise in 1966 weakened the method for about two decades. The SEA constituted a 'return' to the Community method and extended it somewhat in connection with the internal market programme. The Maastricht Treaty also extends the use of this method to the new policy areas, but, despite talking about a single institutional framework, does not extend the method to CFSP and JHA (Laursen 1992). Thus we have some of the problems of the second and third pillars singled out not only by the Commission and the European Parliament but also by the Reflection Group and some national reports – as in the case of the Dutch, for example (Netherlands Foreign Ministry 1995). But, even if that would be the logical thing to do, accepting the Community method for CFSP and JHA seems impossible for many of the member states.

It is doubtful whether the political leadership exists to overcome the shortcomings of intergovernmentalism. The Commission can play the role of supranational leader, especially within the first pillar. Member governments, especially the country holding the presidency, can play a role that subsumes simply national leadership. Historically the leadership roles of France and Germany have been of fundamental importance. But treaty revision requires leadership on the part of all member states in order to sell the outcome during the ratification process.

Leadership is especially needed in the countries where the publics are sceptical, including the UK, Denmark and Sweden. At present at least, such leadership does not appear to exist.

To take this discussion further, some distinctions can help. Oran Young (1991) has argued that there are three kinds of leadership. Structural leadership relies on 'devising effective ways to bring [a] party's structural power (that is, power based on the possession of material resources) to bear in the form of bargaining leverage over the issues at stake in specific interactions'. The role played by the USA in establishing the international monetary system at Bretton Woods is a good example of such structural leadership. Entrepreneurial leadership, on the other hand, is based on the 'use of negotiating skill to influence the manner in which issues are presented ... and to fashion mutually acceptable deals'. Finally, there is intellectual leadership which 'relies on the power of ideas to shape the way in which participants ... understand the issues at stake and to orient their thinking about options available to come to terms with these issues' (Young 1991: 288).

Applied to the process of European integration it is easy to find examples of at least entrepreneurial and intellectual leadership. Jean Monnet combined the two, as did Jacques Delors. Jacques Santer, on becoming Commission President, had not the same reputation as Delors and has perhaps suffered in comparison – not assisted by the fact that he was member governments second choice after the British had vetoed the Franco-German proposal of Jean-Luc Dehaene, the Belgian Prime Minister (for a discussion of the possible role of the Commission see Chapter 10).

The question whether structural leadership has played a role is a little more difficult. The EC has not had a dominant power – or hegemony – playing a role comparable to the role played by the USA in the early post-Second World War period, although the Franco-German alliance has played a vital role (at least so far). As the two most powerful states in the EC one may see Franco–German leadership as a kind of shared structural leadership.

The notion of collective action problems in international relations is often associated with the Prisoners' Dilemma (Hardin 1982). This is a situation which in a one-shot experiment will normally lead to suboptimal outcomes. Leadership can help overcome the problem. But with many actors more than one leader may be needed. Thomas C Schelling developed the notion of the 'k-group', the minimum coalition that it would require in a given situation to overcome the dominant strategies that lead to suboptimal outcomes (1978: 218). The Franco-German alliance can be seen as such a k-group in European integration. Much in the future will depend on its continued existence. Chancellor Kohl survived the parliamentary elections in Germany in the autumn of 1994. In May 1995 France elected a new president who is a Gaullist. Inevitably these factors have had an impact on the Franco-German relationship and its leadership. Initially, the new French leadership appeared somewhat ambivalent towards the German wish to deepen integration and the British wish to loosen it. France may have moved closer to Britain on defence policy, but still needs Germany for EMU. And Germany may require more political union to move ahead with EMU (see also

Chapter 5). There is perhaps a serious question about the availability of leadership during the 1996 IGC and beyond which may be a decisive factor for the future of European integration.

CONCLUSIONS

Europe since Maastricht is very much a new Europe. The Cold War is over. Central and Eastern European countries are striving to modernize economically and politically. The EU is assisting through association agreements, partnership and cooperation agreements as well as the PHARE and TACIS programmes (Laursen 1993). The EU may have had serious internal problems in the aftermath of Maastricht, and it is still fighting to come to grips with a severe unemployment problem. Seen from outside, however, the Union does not look all that bad. More countries want to join. Politically it is not possible for the Union to keep disappointing them. It must upgrade its capacity to respond favourably to the other countries in Europe.

The Union must therefore find adequate institutions to respond to the challenge. Such institutions must be democratic and transparent as well as efficient. The low turnout at the elections for the European Parliament in June 1994 was disappointing because it suggests the continued problem of legitimacy of the whole integration project (*Economist* 18 June 1994). The issues are on the IGC's agenda; the Reflection Group went at least some way in preparing the discussion unlike the last IGC. But there has also been a lack of vision and an unwillingness to lead. The question remains therefore as to whether lessons have been learned from Maastricht about meeting the challenges of the future.

NOTE

1. This and the following sections rely heavily on the concluding part of the author's 'The not-so-permissive consensus: thoughts on the Maastricht Treaty and the future of European integration', in Laursen and Vanhoonacker (eds), op. cit., pp. 295–317.

REFERENCES AND BIBLIOGRAPHY

Baldwin, Richard E. (1994) *Towards an Integrated Europe*. London, Centre for Economic Policy Research.
Docksey, Christopher and Williams, Karen (1994) 'The Commission and the execution of Community policy', in Edwards, Geoffrey and Spence, David *The European Commission*. London, Cartermill.
European Commission (1995) *Report on the Operation of the Treaty on European Union*, SEC(95) final, Brussels, 10 May.
European Parliament (1995) Committee on Institutional Affairs, *Report on the functioning of the Treaty on European Union with a view to the 1996 Intergovernmental Conference – implementa-*

tion and development of the Union Doc. A4-0102/95/Part I.B, 12 May.

Friedrich, Carl J. (1968) *Constitutional Government and Democracy: Theory and Practice in Europe and America.* Fourth edition. Wantham, MA, Blaisdell Publishing Company.

Haas, B. (1961) 'International integration: the European and the universal process', *International Organization*, vol. 15, no. 4, pp. 366–92.

Hardin, Russell (1982) *Collective Action.* Baltimore, The Johns Hopkins University Press.

Keatinge, Patrick (1995) *The Security Doctrine of the New States, Denmark and Ireland*, report for DG 1A, the European Commission, May.

Laursen, Finn (1992) 'The Maastricht Treaty: a critical evaluation', in Laursen, Finn and Vanhoonacker, Sophie (eds) *The Intergovernmental Conference on Political Union.* Dordrecht, Nijhoff, pp. 249–65.

— (1993) 'The EC in Europe's future economic and political architecture', in Andersen, Svein S. and Eliassen, Kjell A. (eds) *Making Policy in Europe: The Europeification of National Policy-making.* London, Sage Publications, pp. 215–36.

Laursen, Finn and Vanhoonacker, Sophie (eds) (1994) *The Ratification of the Maastricht Treaty.* Dordrecht, Martinus Nijhoff and Maastricht, EIPA.

May, Ernest R. (1973) *'Lessons' of the Past: The Use and Misuse of History in American Foreign Policy.* London, Oxford University Press.

Nedergaard, Peter (1995) 'The political economy of CAP reform', in Laursen, Finn (ed.) *The Political Economy of European Integration.* The Hague, Kluwer.

Netherlands Foreign Ministry (1995) *The Netherlands and Europe: The Intergovernmental Conference 1996.* The Hague, Foreign Ministry.

Olson, Mancur (1965) *The Logic of Collective Action.* Cambridge, MA, Harvard University Press.

Putnam, Robert D. (1988) 'Diplomacy and domestic politics: the logic of two-level games', *International Organization*, vol. 42, no. 3 (summer), pp. 427–60.

Reflection Group (1995) *Progress Report from the Chairman of the Reflection Group on the 1996 Intergovernmental Conference* Doc. SN 509/95 (Reflex 10), Madrid, 24 August.

Schelling, Thomas C. (1978) *Micromotives and Macrobehavior.* New York, W. W. Norton & Company.

Stein, Arthur A. (1983) 'Coordination and collaboration: regimes in an anarchic world', in Krasner, Stephen D. (ed.) *International Regimes.* Ithaca, Cornell University Press, pp.115–40.

Taylor, Michael (1987) *The Possibility of Cooperation.* Cambridge, Cambridge University Press.

Udenrigsministeriet (1995) *Dagsorden for Europe: Regeringskonference 1996.* Copenhagen, Schultz.

Young, Oran R. (1991) 'Political leadership and regime formation: on the development of institutions in international society', *International Organization*, vol. 45, no. 3 (summer), pp. 281–308.

THE ACTORS

5

THE FRANCO-GERMAN TANDEM

ANDREA SZUKALA AND WOLFGANG WESSELS

INTRODUCTION: '1989' AND THE DECLINE OF BILATERALISM?

The real challenge of '1996' cannot be understood without looking at '1989'. Franco-German relations had become almost the natural object of any consideration about what revolutionary change in the international and European system meant for the process of integration. But, by the mid-1990s, the steadfastness of the Franco-German tandem was being questioned as was its indispensability for the integration. Indeed, in some quarters, the very enterprise of a European Union seemed to be considered anachronistic.

One school of thought has argued that since 1989 Europe has been thrown back into history and that the end of the post-war period has led to a renaissance of the polycentric European state system (Schwarz 1995: 15–33). The Franco-German partners have now come to recognize that integration had only been forced on them by superpower bipolarity. With 'history taken out of the refrigerator', a return of nation-state thinking is to be expected with a traditional balance of power logic as its inevitable consequence (Mearsheimer 1990). According to this perspective, the EC and the EU have lost their major *raison d'être*. Maastricht was out of touch with the new reality even at its signature; it was a desperate attempt to continue certain habits and long-term objectives even though the basic constellation of forces had already changed fundamentally. Franco-German friendship was therefore no longer vital. Their cooperation and resolution had clearly been determined by a very specific political context. The 1996 IGC could only be a final farewell to a period that is now a part of history. Franco-German bilateralism, as a strategy to stimulate the dynamics of integration, is out of date if one recognizes that the 'New Europe' will be a 'Grand Europe', driven by heterogeneous forces – and perhaps even by a 'great power' Germany (Waltz 1993: 77). Moreover, the new realities render common Franco-German long-term initiatives, if not impossible, at least improbable.

The opposing view claims that even if '1989' changed many basic factors, these have not acted against European integration and Franco-German cooperation but, rather, have given them fresh impetus. Now that both partners have finally become 'adults', their friendship can achieve maturity as well. The changing realities have not eroded but reinforced the needs and potential benefits of common policy-making. According to this perspective, post-Maastricht 'blues' are nothing but one of the well-known cyclical down-swings that can be reversed by a new Franco-German initiative. '1996' can open the door to a new qualitative step forward within the EU or – if necessary – within a core Europe.

Some aspects of these two extreme positions in the debate can be seen in some of the political conceptualizations of Europe's future. '1989' not only changed the political landscape, it also increased the impact of old sensibilities and perceptions, of ancient 'mental maps' of the political actors (Wallace 1990a: 7). In France, its self-perception as a legitimate Cold War leader now in decline could only be reinforced (*Herodote* 1993; Nicolas and Stark 1992; Korinmann 1995). In the context of possible treaty reforms and eastern enlargement, this discourse, which had calmed down after the achievement of German unification and the troubles over the ratification of Maastricht, has regained importance once again. The underlying question – even if raised explicitly only by the 'geopoliticians' and some right- and left-wing nationalists – is still one of how to deal with the fear of becoming Germany's 'junior partner' in a new Europe whose geographic centre had shifted only too clearly eastwards (Korinmann in *Le Monde* 3 February 1995; Chévènement in *Le Monde* 12 October 1994).

The German debate has as yet been less fundamentalist. There has been no drastic upheaval of general orientations on European politics, although with the prospect of eastern enlargement, political leaders have attempted to develop a new European vision and mission. However, it was widely recognized that Germany, having had to cope with the first years of its enormous unification programme, was politically ambivalent when confronted with the immediate prospect of the 1996 IGC, particularly in the foreign and security policy domains. The economic and social burdens of unification have weighed longer than perhaps foreseen in the minds (and purses) of the population.

This context does not seem to be particularly conducive to the establishment of a common agenda for the rest of the twentieth century. This was reinforced with the first public debates about the 1996 IGC's agenda provoked by the report of the German Christian Democrat group in the *Bundestag* (CDU–CSU 1994). This included an unforeseen reaction among French political leaders, and, indeed, in the rest of Europe. In France at the start of the consultation period, the agenda seemed to focus on basic concepts: Alain Lamassoure, France's former European Minister, for example, suggested that with the achievement of the single market and Maastricht, the policy list was more or less closed and the 'Old Europe' had now to deal with the challenge of becoming the 'New Europe' (*Le Monde* 31 May 1994). Although the dynamics of the negotiation process as well as political exigencies might open up some of the reforms envisaged early in the consultation period, the crucial point remains that of the further impact of the more fundamental issues in Franco-German cooperation. Are such issues only a rhetorical swan-song, as the first school of thought would argue, or are they preparation for a new phase of European construction? In attempting to draw some conclusions, we first need to sum up these fundamentals of the Franco-German tandem in order to isolate the factors that formerly contributed either to the dynamic development or to the slowing down of the integration process. Here the lessons of Maastricht and the shortcomings of the Treaty's implementation in the fields of economic and security policies provide some indication of the practical problems for future cooperation.

THE FUNDAMENTALS: MYTHS AND REALITIES OF THE FRANCO-GERMAN TANDEM

The Franco-German relationship has been the crucial element determining war and peace during the nineteenth century. The ways in which both countries perceived and treated each other was of vital national consequence. The experience of two world wars brought home to them that friendly relations were key to the peaceful development of both countries and, indeed, of Europe. This can be seen, for example, in the declarations by the resistance movement as well as the Zurich speech of Churchill calling for a Franco-German alliance (*Centre d'action pour la fédération européenne* 1945; Churchill 1948). The breakthrough came with the Monnet–Schuman declaration of 9 May 1950 in which the key terms were: '*Le rassemblement européen exige que l'opposition séculaire de la France et de l'Allemagne soir éleminée*'.

The French position, while in part the product of considerable external pressure from the USA, was full of constructive ambiguities which set the tone of its relationship with Germany up to now. The Schuman declaration can be seen either as an essential element of France's European conviction, in the interests of a new European, federal construction, or as part of a French strategy motivated by a determination to dominate Germany, even if through the use of different, supranational methods because the use of military means (as in the aftermath of the First World War) were no longer acceptable. In fact a pro-European strategy could serve as the vehicle for the exercise of friendly control of Germany (Ziebura 1970). On the German side, the national interest most clearly discerned was the process of emancipating the country from occupation and dependence to *de facto* equality. It was a strategy of rehabilitation that perforce had to rely on the agreement of the former enemy.

Beyond the calculation of national interests and pro-European commitments and ideas, the self-perception of both countries was – and remains – based on particular attitudes. The notion of *Schicksalgemeinschaft* (community of destiny) may have become something of a cliché but it has made sense to the generation that lived through the Second World War (including Kohl and Mitterrand). It has served as a kind of symbolic political programme with, sometimes puzzling, long-term effects. Terms like 'special partnership', the 'tandem' etc. have sought to catch something of this spirit, which is difficult to grasp and explain. In view of the deeply-rooted divergencies in national approaches on so many important policy issues – whether economic, foreign and defence, and even on integration policy itself – such statements may appear simply as rhetoric. Indeed, the Franco-German policies that have emerged since the conclusion of the Elysée Treaty of 1963 may well point more to a pragmatic mistrust than to a belief in the myth of 'arch-friendship' (Schwarz 1992). But on an axis where the rhetoric of the Franco-German 'motor' of European integration is at one pole and the divergent interest hypothesis is at the other, 'reality' perhaps lies somewhere in the middle. The myth of the Franco-German tandem has had utility insofar as it has supported an obligation to achieve consensus and to adopt common positions 'as far as possible' – to use the language of the Elysée Treaty (Picht *et al.* 1990: 25). The ratification struggles that followed the signing of the Treaty in 1962 provided only the first indication that the adoption of common positions could not be taken for granted.

However, since the period 1962–68, there has been a harmony of interests that has often constituted a major precondition for the deepening of the European framework. Bilateral disagreements were handled in a different way: alternative options could only be mobilized to a limited extent (as in the Genscher–Colombo Initiative of 1981–83) and were for the most part of only limited success. The special status of the relationship was never seriously called into question; its durability has been fostered through intensive institution-building and relatively steady patterns of cooperation among key actors. From the Schuman declaration which was immediately accepted by Adenauer, via the EEC treaty, the Brandt–Pompidou and Giscard–Schmidt tandem, up to the Kohl–Mitterrand partnership, major initiatives were prepared by France and Germany and, in some ways, were even expected by their European partners. The tandem served almost as a laboratory for testing potential European cooperation – one example being perhaps the Franco-German Brigade.

But not all bilateral initiatives have been successful. Changing European coalitions and new strategies of issue-management have been significant factors that have impeded the exercise of any systematic Franco-German leadership. As Helen Wallace has put it: 'congruent Franco-German positions, however necessary, were never a sufficient condition of wider Community agreement' (Wallace 1989: 146). The opportunities to reach agreement on policy positions within the framework of multilateral bargaining and package deals increased with the widening of the Community's competences, the number of negotiators and the policy-mix itself (Wessels 1994a: 502). Similarly, over time, the rhetoric became as routinized as the summits, personal meetings, and the extensive range of interactions at ministerial and administrative levels. And yet, the steady enlargement of the system of Franco-German councils and the scope of their activities, the range of instruments used, and the general quality of bilateral cooperation have been such to make it difficult to conceive of what further value might be added with another Franco-German treaty (Balladur in *Le Monde* 30 November 1994).

From the beginning, the dynamics of the bilateral relationship were conditional on a certain fundamental division of labour. De Gaulle's assumption, taken up by later presidents, was that France would look for a partnership with Germany that gave a strong common leadership in Europe without diminishing France's status as the pre-eminent political power in Europe (Kolboom 1991: 144). The inherent logic of the Cold War European bargain for France was based on the simple premise: French political leadership (symbolized *inter alia*, by the possession of nuclear weapons) on the one hand, against German economic power and political stability, on the other. Germany, for its part, needed a greater political 'voice'.

Both sides, however, always showed a certain degree of mistrust: the French felt the economic competitiveness of Germany to be a constant challenge; Germany sometimes resented the implied bar to a more independent political status. The problems and failures in the division of labour derived very largely from mutual misperceptions about the other's intentions and scope for action. This applied particularly in the field of defence, whether suspiciousness about de Gaulle's dreams of the European 'third way', or disconcertedness over Chirac's sudden change in French defence policy in 1995.

Shortcomings in the management of the relationship were also clearly revealed in the rapid process towards German reunification. Although Kohl's lack of consultation over his Ten Point Plan or Mitterrand's attempt to resurrect a Franco-Russian axis could – with a degree of generosity – be characterized as 'policy overload' in a unique historical situation (Attali 1995), the fundamentals of the relationship have had to be reassessed. From 1989 on – even with the common interests shown in Maastricht – the old Franco-German 'corridor of power' has been slowly changing (Cole 1993). Again, perceptions of the new distribution of power are telling: the French have believed their position and status to have been devalued while those of Germany have been enhanced. The lack of alternatives for France has seemed stark for neither a Mediterranean group with Spain and Italy (see Chapter 8) nor an Anglo-French marriage have seemed at all promising. The latter might offer a certain identity of interests in seeking to maintain great power status (in the UN Security Council, or through nuclear weapons) but it lacks a European dimension (see Chapter 6). For the Germans, the concept of *Mitteleuropa* is linked to the trauma of being isolated. Neither the USA nor Russia could seriously act as a substitute for France in terms of 'partners in leadership'. Nor are other groupings such as a 'northern group' of Austria, The Netherlands and the countries of Scandinavia any more promising.

If the lowest common denominator is a shared lack of alternatives, France and Germany are now hard-pressed to revive their strategic interest in mutual cooperation. At the level of policy preferences, new patterns of pragmatic cooperation and coalition-building may emerge, though the reconciliation of fundamentally different approaches to integration that have often been hidden behind the demands of day-to-day negotiation in Brussels may well require considerable effort. But, neither partner can act alone and the new relationship has obviously to be based on the recognition of this, whatever the divergencies on particular issues.

PROSPERITY AND SECURITY AFTER MAASTRICHT: PACKAGE DEALS WITHOUT VISION?

A major characteristic of past Franco-German practices was what might be described as 'a package deal with vision', that is, a future-oriented project that neatly synthesized the divergent demands of both countries. The achievement of the Single European Act (SEA) and the Maastricht Treaty are forceful illustrations of this practice. Combinations of French and German interests served the basic purpose and, at the same time, served the integration of Europe inasmuch as it provided a setting broad enough to encompass the specific interests of all the member states in the common framework. But the problems over the ratification of Maastricht preoccupied national politicians and bilateral coordination tended to take second place. Certainly efforts at political entrepreneurship through a coordinated exercise for the 1994–95 Council Presidencies came to little, and not only because of the demands made on both governments by national elections. The two very low profile Presidencies generated neither new concepts nor any substantive policy innovation. Instead they gave the impression that there had been little political coordination at all. And, even if one should not jump to the conclusion that the lack of concerted action since Maastricht indicates a lack of commitment to any new package deal, with or without vision, post-Cold War realities seem to reveal some crucial changes of attitude. The 1996 IGC will have been shaped by these inherited problems, many of which Maastricht failed to deliver, not least in the terms of the economy and of security.

Economic and monetary interdependence

The economic and monetary interdependence of France and Germany is undisputed. Clearly, however, divergences remain. Many of the German economic élite still view French economic policy as inherently protectionist, interventionist and deficit-prone – in spite of all the French government's efforts and its success in achieving a lower inflation rate than Germany and despite the acceptance of many German demands including the independence of the Bank of France. Germans remain suspicious that they are somehow being lured into a supranational structure which will allow the French to continue their traditional economic policies by different means – to the detriment of German interests and the economic principles that have lain behind them. Behind the German approach has been a general wish to establish a kind of *Ordnungspolitik* at the European level; monetary sacrifices in favour of nebulous ideas about European unification are unacceptable. It has been a view widely shared among politicians, whether Adenauer, Schmidt or Kohl, who emphasizes the instrumental character of economic integration for positive political purposes.

The French position has had three dimensions. First, the supranational solution has been regarded as the means of escape from the asymmetrical relationship with the dominant economy, and especially from the monetary hegemon in Europe, the German *Bundesbank*. It is a position that makes even considerable transfers of sovereignty acceptable in the French national interest, and has been a factor in all phases of European integration since the European Coal and Steel Community (ECSC). A second dimension has been the need to make the French economy more competitive, a kind of 'cold shower' strategy that demands the modernization of industry and society and which will prevent France from falling behind other economies. Finally, the third factor making for French support for economic integration has been the potential international influence to be gained through the reinforcement of Europe's weight in the world's monetary markets.

During the bargaining leading to the Maastricht Treaty, these French positions became clear. They agreed without any particular fuss on the issues such as the convergence criteria and the European Central Bank (ECB) which followed the German model. At the national level, too, the French accepted the need to grant independence to the French Central Bank. Even if Bérégovoy continued to insist on the necessity of European economic government (*Les Notes Bleues de Bercy* 24 March 1991), France's negotiators ultimately accepted the fact that they could not achieve more than a partial control over monetary policy through EMU and counter the structural power of the German Central Bank in the EMS (de Larosiére 1993: 59). But the independence of the *Banque de France* did at least reinforce the credibility of France's policy of *rigeur*, under which France has achieved an average current account surplus of some 2 per cent (OECD 1994). And, at the same time, the liberal deregulatory thrust of the single market programme should be complemented by a social dimension for which the French socialist government had pressed. Since then, French parties have somewhat quietly changed their positions: the Union pour la démocratie française (UDF), for example, in its 1994 European elections programme demanded a lengthening of the second stage with no reference to the ECB at all; the opposition socialists, for their part, talked increasingly of the need to weaken the convergency criteria (Balleix 1994: 42).

Clearly German unification had a profound impact on Europe's economy as well as on its politics. The immediate costs of Germany's monetary union were inflation, high interest rates and, for the first time, a budgetary deficit, but these had the effect of slowing down recessionary pressures in the rest of Europe. However, thereafter Germany's economic growth slipped from 4.5 per cent to 2.2 per cent in 1994. Financial transfers in Germany from West to East reached DM180 billion in 1993, some 5 per cent of West Germany's GDP. Germany became a huge net capital importer. Fearing hyperinflation, the *Bundesbank* continued its hardline interest rate policy, which led to a fall in growth, investments and tax revenues in Germany, and had adverse repercussions on all the economies of the member states. The first speculative attacks against the franc were during the uncertainties of the 1992 Maastricht referendum but calmness had been restored in March 1993 with the election of a conservative government determined on the continuation of monetary austerity and the implementation of legislation making for the independence of the French Central Bank. However, the new government's insistence on maintaining pre-unification parities within the EMS – a dramatic error in the eyes of many French economists (Fitoussi 1995;

Saint-Etienne 1995) – led to a second speculative wave and the crisis in the EMS of August–September 1993. As a result, and despite the announcement of a five-year austerity programme, France's public deficit increased from 3.8 per cent of GDP in 1992 to 6 per cent in 1994, double, that is, the figure set down in the convergence criteria of Maastricht (Article 104.2).

The general consensus was that the French, in return for limited concessions on political union, had gained rather more then Germany from EMU (see Chapter 2). There was, indeed, a growing belief that the 'win-set' (to follow Putnam 1988) in economic and monetary policies had become increasingly limited once the debate over the DM had begun and after the judgement of the *Bundesverfassungsgericht* (Federal Constitutional Court) on the Maastricht Treaty (Pierre Lellouche in *Le Monde* 23 November 1994). On this basis the German position *vis-a-vis* its European partners might well have hardened during 1995. The 'stability pact' proposal was designed to exercise additional pressure on member states to reign in budgetary expenditures (with deficits not normally to be more than 1 per cent of GDP, the establishment of a 'Stability Council' and so on). The German position also owes something to the swing in opinion in Germany from a loss of confidence in the EMU provisions of Maastricht to a belief, after the breakdown of the EMS, that they provided *the* major disciplinary instrument for strengthening European monetary cohesion. The battle over the implementation of EMU has therefore become highly politicized and this inevitably influenced the position of both countries towards the IGC.

There are three central aspects to the Franco-German debate about EMU: the procedures for its implementation, and the issues of the convergence criteria and economic policy cohesion.

AGENDA AND PROCEDURE

Despite President Chirac's call for a referendum to decide on the final step to a single currency in 1995, there has been little question in France of the irreversibility of the movement towards EMU. The majority of French economic and political leaders – with perhaps the exception of M Balladur during the 1995 presidential campaign – have expected the third stage to begin in 1999, the 1997 option having been described by Chirac as 'not only unrealistic but dangerous' (Chirac 1995: 23). In Germany, on the other hand, there has been a big public debate over the move to the third stage, and indeed, on the Commission's competence in evaluating the criteria and interpreting their fulfilment. Not only was there concern over the shortcomings in the Treaty's provisions, there are now also doubts about Germany's own ability to meet the criteria. The majority view in public and in parliament is that if there is conflict between meeting the criteria and the timetable, Germany should call for a delay in the latter rather than dilute the criteria. Given the divisiveness of the issues in France, public and parliamentary pressures are increasingly likely to weigh with the government despite its eagerness to move rapidly to the third stage.

THE CRITERIA

The fear among some economic leaders in Germany has been that despite the urgency of some treaty reforms, the IGC would be misused to reopen the debate over the strictness with which the convergence criteria should be applied (see the *Frankfurter Allgemeine Zeitung* (FAZ) 11 July 1995 for the views of the President of the German Chambers of Commerce, Hans-Peter Stihl). Some of the discussions in the Reflexions Group on treaty reforms seemed to confirm such concern (ibid. 6 September 1995). The idea of a new criterion relating to employment, which emerged in March 1995 – raised by, for example, the President of the French National Assembly, Philippe Séguin – threatened further cleavages, with a German government unable to compromise over the strict maintenance of a European *Stabilitatspolitik* with, above all, a rigorous enforcement of the budgetary discipline and price stability criteria. Warnings about France's shortcomings in terms of budgetary discipline and distributive policies came *inter alia*, from Hans Tietmeyer, president of the *Bundesbank* in February 1995 (*Le Monde* 12 February 1995). Significantly, while pressing for the strict maintenance of the criteria at the European level, the German government is also using the need for rigour for domestic reasons, to counter wage increases – or so many in France suspect.

During the first six months of the Chirac–Juppé government, economic policy guidelines remained uncertain. Despite measures aimed at consolidating the budget, such as increasing VAT from 18.6 to 20.6 per cent in 1995, the planned budgetary deficit was still set to rise to about 5.3 per cent of GDP. This was largely because of the end of privatization and the fall in corporation tax receipts. The Juppé government's attempt to reform the French social security system and the resulting 'hot' autumn and winter of 1995 was seeming proof of the efforts France is willing to undertake to meet the threat of being marginalized in terms of failing the convergence criteria.

ECONOMIC POLICY COHESION

After 1993, all member governments had to accept that convergence could not be decreed but had to be the result of substantive and not merely institutional efforts to change economic policy as a whole. Even if, after unification, the traditional divergence over the nature of the market economy between French economic voluntarism and German *Ordnungspolitik* continued to narrow (Uterwedde 1995: 207), political priorities in the fields of employment, industrial and trade policies remain distinctive. Indeed, the political impact of the debate on employment in France is matched in Germany by that on industrial location (*Standort*). In June 1995, a statement from the French government revealed that the two most crucial issues for France at the European level were the future of agriculture (especially, even if implicitly, in view of the potential consequences of an Eastern enlargement) and the future of the French civil service (*Le Figaro* 1 June 1995). The German coalition's priorities, on the other hand, related to the problem of production costs – on average some 12 per cent higher than in other Western industrialized states (Uterwedde 1995: 200).

France has had to deal with an unemployment rate (12.5 per cent in 1994
has reached almost the levels in Eastern Germany. Its structural character (s
28 per cent youth unemployment) has made it a particularly heavy burden on ᵤₑ
cohesion and stability of French society (Franzmayer 1995: 252). As a result
labour market deregulation (for example, *contrat initiative emploi*) is far easier to
implement in France than in Germany – even if the latter has begun to suffer
markedly from this competition between the two partners. In this context,
Germany is far from being the model example as far as market liberalization is
concerned. The government's obvious tendency to regulative protectionism and
Community subventions – sometimes even bigger than those of France – point to
only a slow and unobtrusive change in old behaviourial patterns.

Trade policy remains one of the most sensitive issues between France and
Germany, not only for structural reasons (such as France's greater dependence on
intra-European trade and the greater price sensitivity of French exports), but also
for deep-rooted national attitudes towards trade and each other's position in the
global economy. The GATT Uruguay Round was a difficult, costly and perhaps
crucial test for Franco-German solidarity. After all, as in the case of industrial
policy, the differences were rather in terms of a 'south-west' grouping more
inclined to protectionism and the 'north-east' grouping more in favour of free
world trade, as the CDU–CSU paper of 1994 put it (CDU–CSU 1994). An
Anglo-German agenda on trade policy would be more likely to show a greater
convergence than a Franco-German one.

Finally, the general asymmetry of the Franco-German economic relationship
underwent a silent change after Maastricht. France remains the *demandeur* in monetary matters. But, although still relatively steadfast in opposition to changing the
rules to expedite EMU, Germany itself has been suffering from recession and
unemployment far longer and far more severely than had been foreseen. Societal
and structural problems, including winning support for the policies necessary to
bring about the modernization of the country's industry, as well as the need to
face the adverse impact on its exports of an overvalued currency have progressively weakened old positions. A convergence of policies to respond to global competition is still lacking as is a greater meeting of minds on employment policies.
The EMU framework may be decisive in bringing about changes in political attitudes, not least during debates on institutional flexibility and 'core' options in the
IGC. A scenario of France and Germany fixing exchange rates when neither
meet the convergence criteria is inconceivable.

Changing foreign policy interests and the new agenda

Since the Four-Power system has disappeared, France has suffered from the loss
of that psycho-political element that provided compensation for the economic
superiority of Germany. It has also had to recognize that, in the age of regional
and local conflicts, nuclear power contributes less to the maintenance of military
power than it did in a bipolar world (Grosser 1993: 18). However, at Maastricht
the concept of a new security order and its institutionalization at the level of the

EU was far from clearly perceived or realized – hence the importance of the CFSP as a central issue on the 1996 agenda. But, the extent to which the changing European security landscape and the experiences of implementing the CFSP could clarify the position is limited (see also Chapter 15). Unknown variables, including future Russian foreign policy as well as relations with the USA have combined with those continued differences in perception that have been historically determined. France and Germany, in other words, still do not always have converging expectations of either Europe or its foreign policy.

Although the establishment of the Franco-German Brigade in 1987 and the Defence and Security Council in 1988 showed a clear willingness on the part of both governments to cooperate on 'difficult' issue areas (Manfrass-Sirjacques 1993), the changes since 1989 have thrown up fundamental challenges. French nuclear policy was not called into question during the 1980s, even if a 'two-key system' was discussed. In the 1990s, French proposals have included both a change in nuclear policy, addressed to Germany for a system of 'concerted dissuasion', and steps towards France's reintegration into NATO's integrated military structure. These suggest a fairly radical adaptation to the changing security constellation in Europe, perhaps brought about, above all, because it has become increasingly clear that the EU lacks any capacity to provide stability in Eastern Europe. In the longer run, therefore, the considerable distances between the two countries on transatlantic relations may well decrease.

Public opinion in Germany has not been enthusiastic about changing the country's foreign policy towards a more traditional 'power politics' approach. The experience of not having military sovereignty yet achieving an economic strength that brought considerable prestige to the Federal Republic has created among many a self-perception of Germany as a Swiss-like 'civilian power' (Maull 1992). On the other hand, political leaders have become more and more aware of growing international expectations – even if at first they sought to assuage them by shifting responsibilities for any inaction or change onto the Constitutional Court (*Neue Juristische Wochenschrift* 1994). There remains a significant consensus that Germany could not and should not undertake foreign and defence policy initiatives either on its own or bilaterally with France (*FAZ* 11 September 1995). German abstinence from such policies may have contributed to a certain, but possibly deliberate, intellectual vagueness when interests and instruments of foreign policy have to be defined; a 'moral pathos' at critical moments. Moreover, Franco-German defence cooperation has always entailed an economic dimension, especially at moments of real or potential crisis that coincide with periods of restricted defence budgets and economic recession. But there is still little consensus on basic questions such as the future structure and primary mission of both countries' armies and their cooperation within the Eurocorps or whether they should be concentrating on flexible intervention forces or armed forces directed towards territorial and alliance defence. For Germany, bilateralism within the common frameworks of the UN and the Organization for Security and Cooperation in Europe (OSCE), and multinational operations within NATO and WEU, constitute the primary approach in foreign policy-making, with France as a major partner, of course, but alongside the USA.

One substantial obstacle for France remains the interface between defence and the economy so that the competences in the Community and the second pillar-frameworks of the EU are of particular significance. Questions of market access continue to influence Franco-American relations even if the old clash of doctrines in security policy has slowly begun to disappear as old Gaullist ideas have less and less influence on French foreign policy (Schrader 1993). The proposed 'Atlantic Pact' in the spring of 1995 and the later rapprochement with NATO's integrated military structure indicate the move towards 'normalization' and French 're-association' with the Alliance. Now to ignore the pre-eminent role of NATO within the future European security order would impede any confirmation of the WEU as the EU's vehicle for establishing a European Security and Defence Identity (ESDI). It seems to have gained general acceptance in France that a European defence policy is now inconceivable outside the NATO framework. The crucial question is how to integrate the existing structures of the Eurocorps and WEU into that common framework. The Chirac–Juppé government seems to have shifted its institutional priorities since the decision of the NATO Summit in Brussels in January 1994. The emphasis has been less on WEU and more on a (reformed) Atlantic Alliance that would provide cooperation in resources and command structures in Combined Joint Task Forces (CJTFs) (*Le Figaro* 20 December 1995).

Within the EU, the structure and effectiveness of the second Pillar has been seriously criticised. The shortcomings of the CFSP in the conflict in the former Yugoslavia provoked reservations, above all perhaps from the French. The Europeans were obliged to accept that without American participation there was little chance of any peace-making or enforcement. On the other hand, there have been bilateral initiatives in the second pillar that suggest that a 'European' approach has gradually taken root. Complementary action and a sense of joint responsibility seem to have characterized the first 'joint action' – the European Stability Pact – and again when Germany strongly supported the Barcelona Conference on the Mediterranean. Differences in perception of 'interests' do seem to have diminished – even in the Serbian–Croatian war, France and Germany were far from being on opposite sides.

The prospect of the IGC focused attention further. The joint proposal of a senior permanent representative for CFSP (a 'Monsieur PESC' – *Le Monde* 22 September 1995) underlined a willingness to make political leadership more visible and seems to have been widely accepted in the Reflections Group Report. There have, though, been problems about quite how to integrate such an individual into the EU structure. The French rapprochement with NATO can also been seen as part of the strategy to operationalize the WEU, though it has been agreed by both France and Germany that the WEU must remain subordinate to the EU – and closely linked to NATO.

All in all, the traditional cleavages between the two countries continue to exist. While the German approach has tended to favour getting rid of the pillar structure and the extension of majority voting (*FAZ* 1 September 1995), the French have insisted on the maintenance of a genuinely intergovernmental CFSP and a 'positive abstention' approach in decision-making (*Le Figaro* 20 February 1996). Similarly on the question of the financing of the CFSP, France has been reluctant to envisage Community-financing, which would open the door to a significant role for the Commission and the EP. Nevertheless, according to Deubner, at the practical level both have been increasingly prepared to minimize their differences (Deubner 1995). France's approach of 'reinforced cooperation' in defence policy within the WEU and the proposal that Eurocorps' participation could be decided on 'objective criteria' suggests a necessary acceptance of 'variable geometry' solutions in CFSP that is common to both countries. The definition of common interests in CFSP and the role of the EU as a global player, demand efforts to share approaches and burdens even if basic preference structures in defence policy continue to differ, while in the field of foreign policy positions seem to have converged more than might have been expected in the early 1990s.

CONVERGENT AND DIVERGENT CONCEPTS ON THE POLITICAL AND INSTITUTIONAL FUTURE OF THE EU

The debate on the nature of the future Europe which, in the aftermath of Maastricht, was characterized by a turning away from Europe, has become focused on concepts such as legitimacy and sovereignty (see Chapter 13). Several factors contributed to this development: in a small number of member states, including France, the Maastricht discussion was the occasion for the first serious politicization of Europe as an issue. The potential impact on national institutions that have been at the core of what has symbolized national sovereignty was a vital factor in creating this 'spill-back', that is, a public focus on questions of identity, social cohesion and democracy (Wessels 1994b: 446). Whatever the political bargaining and its outcome, there remains a central political preoccupation about the nature of the new European order and the distribution of power and influence within it.

The concept of legitimacy: public opinion as a new factor in European affairs?

Whatever doubts academics may have had about the impact of popular consent on the substantive development of integration (Moravcsik 1993), political actors are constrained by electoral pay-offs. In France, as in Germany, there was a consensus in the run up to the 1996 IGC that it would be a disaster if the reasons why further steps in the construction of Europe were not made comprehensible and credible to their populations. Since Maastricht (and the period of economic recession) public approval of European integration has progressively decreased, according to Eurobarometer polls; from 61 per cent in Germany in 1990 to 43 per cent in 1994, and from 57 per cent to 39 per cent over the same period in France (*Eurobarometer* July 1994). Inevitably the circumstances in which the IGC's outcome would need to be ratified were unpredictable, but member governments were generally very much more aware of the need to foster legitimacy for the political system of the EU than they were before Maastricht.

However, the context of the IGC has been markedly different. As the 1994 European elections showed, European issues were very largely irrelevant in European as well as national elections (Hrbeck 1994: 158). This was not quite the case, though, in France for the analysis of electoral behaviour showed that 'Maastricht' cleavages persisted into the elections. The problem of the 'de-legitimization' of Europe and its politics seems to have endured and to have split the French political élite for much longer than had been anticipated. Much of this has been attributed to Mitterrand's strategy of importing and implementing social and economic modernization through European policies – an attribution made particularly by those who lost from the process (Duhamel and Grunberg 1993). Since the politicization of the European issue in the referendum (ibid.), the French party system has shown the greatest variety of anti-European groupings than anywhere else in the Union. In view of the anti-European vote of some 39 per cent at the 1994 elections (compared to 48.95 per cent in the referendum), it is possible to discern the establishment of a relatively stable anti-European force. About 71 per cent of French voters maintained their 1992 positions on Maastricht in the equivalent party lists in 1994. Nonetheless, as Grunberg shows, the social cleavages that shaped the referendum's electorate has lost its impact. The perception of the role of the state, especially in the economy, was the more decisive factor in the 1994 elections. The lesson from this politicization of Europe is that the public debate about France's future in the Union does not necessarily reflect the extent of social and economic Europeanization.

Since Maastricht, Europe has become a 'dangerous issue' – but not only in France (Moreau Defarges 1995: 345), for, to a different degree, a similar trend can be seen in Germany. In the latter, the winners and losers of the process of modernization tend to hold the opposite views to those in France. The economic actors who are 'modernizers', especially globally, tend to see the EU as an inward-looking bureaucratic monolith that inhibits rather than fosters market liberalization and the adaptation of European economies to global competition. The average German citizen, on the other hand, despite the heightened profile of EMU on the political agenda, has shown a surprising lack of interest in such European issues, in that only 24 per cent of the population consider that monetary union will have a major impact on their personal situation (*FAZ* 16 December 1995).

Ultimately, efforts to stimulate debate among the public rather than simply the institutions may have some odd consequences. Among these may be the transference of at least elements of the crisis of social identity and modernization to the European level. Public envy of richer member states and the costs of burden-sharing – not uniquely but especially in financial terms – may well become a major future problem. The French example in the autumn and winter of 1995 suggests that there is an institutional tendency among national politicians to favour national solutions while shifting the blame for any threat to collective welfare onto the EU. Some of the statements made by minister-presidents of the German

Länder on Germany's contribution to the EU's budget seem to confirm the tendency (*FAZ* 12 December 1995). The Reflection Group emphasized the need for 'legitimacy in the eyes of citizens' but even if there was a greater willingness of governments to encourage the domestic debate on Europe, there has been little or no evidence that they have done so on core issues such as the single market or EMU, on which public opinion might be mobilized (Wessels 1996).

A new discourse on states, nations and identity

In his analysis on the geopolitical debate during the Maastricht ratification process in France, Sur departed from the thesis that '*dans les rélations bilatérales comme dans la construction européenne, les intérêts des états comptent plus que jamais, car leur politique extérieure et de défense doit beaucoup moins se définir de manière négative par réaction à un danger établi*' (Sur 1993: 128). But do we need to deal with a 'return of the state' in European politics as French electoral behaviour also suggests? What impact has the fundamentally different approaches in France and Germany towards the state, nation and sovereignty had on the debates on the IGC?

The most animated reactions to the CDU–CSU paper of September 1994 were over the hypothesis that the sovereignty of the nation-state today is nothing more than an 'empty cover'. The French debate rapidly focused on the questions about the nature of national identity and popular sovereignty in a federal Europe. Dominque Boquet, Secretary General of the European Movement, for example declared: '*mais la France tient une certaine idée d'elle même: une nation porteuse de valeurs et de visions, et donc légitime dans l'influence*' (Boquet 1995). From the Jacobin Left, the message is much the same, for as Jean-Pierre Chévènement put it:

> *Mais la France ne'est pas un peuple (Volk), c'est une nation éminemment politique. C'est une commu-nauté de citoyens, ou ce n'est rien. Qu'est-ce qu'un Français? C'est un citoyen français ... L'idée d'une féderation ne menace en aucune manière l'identité culturelle de la nation allemande. Par contre elle agi-rait comme un puissant dissolvant de l'identité politique de la nation française. (Le Monde* 12 October 1994)

Others have been more restrained: the UDF Deputy, Dominique Baudis, for example, spoke of a French '*réalité nationale*' (*Le Monde* 10 November 1994); while the former Minister for European Affairs, Alain Lamoussure, sought to explain France's particular character in terms of:

> *Le jugement exprimé par M. Lamers selon lequel la souveraineté de l'Etat-nation ne constitue plus depuis longtemps qu'une enveloppe vide heurte profondément en France ... c'est pourquoi lorsqu'on évoque un transfert de souveraineté, au tréfonds de la conscience collective française s'éveille la crainte de voir perdre un droit fondamental acquis par la Révolution ... chez beaucoup de Français, l'Europe fédérale' evoque un ensemble politique où l'identité nationale ne pèserait pas plus que celle du Massachusetts ou de la Louisiane auz Etats-Unis.* (Lamassoure 1994: 55)

In the first report of the National Assembly on the issue of the IGC, the rapporteurs declared that:

En France, au Royaume-Uni et au Danmark notamment, l'identité nationale
ressentie... Aussi, l'Europe est-elle perçue par eux dans un perspective d'un équ
commun volantaire de certaines compétences et la preservation de l'identité
Assembly 1995: 49)

Finally, Jacques Delors demanded that: *'nous avons à montrer au*
pleinement français ... et puisqu'on parle beaucoup en France ... de cohésion so ..., soyons nets,
seule la nation peut aider à maintenir ou à reconstituer le lien social' (Delors 1995: 17). He
went on to attempt to reconcile French and German positions by pointing out
that: *'La structure fédérale et celle qui permet le mieux de conforter la nation'* (ibid. 18).

The Franco-German debate on the state, the nation and identity is not at all
new – as Kolboom showed when writing about the deep misunderstanding
between the two countries on such issues (1991). Friction was evident, for example, in 1962 when de Gaulle in one of his press conferences made clear his conception of Europe as a *'Europe des Etats'* and not a *'Europe des Patries'* (de Gaulle
1970: 406). Whereas in France, nation-building was accomplished through the
formation of a secular state symbolized by the attachment to such republican
institutions as the *'Service publique'*, and the *'Ecole Laique'*, Germany's historical
experience fostered a tendency which allowed for the delegation or 'pooling' of
state sovereignty – such sovereignty either not having been fully acquired for some
time or else it had been discredited. The ethnocentric definition of German
nationality had largely determined the country's self-perception as apolitical and
pointed to an important difference from the French notion of citizenship and
nationality (Brubaker 1992). Since it begins therefore from a very different
premise, German public interest does not hold the sovereignty of the state as its
central concern.

The assumptions behind the German debate have remained fairly stable. The
federal system has made its citizens familiar with the exercise of multiple loyalties
which fits the pattern of European policy-making, and, indeed, is seen by many
as providing a model for Europe (Wallace 1990b: 17). At the same time, the concept of constitutional democracy has been fundamental – though the Karlsruhe
Constitutional Court decision implied difficulties when applied to Europe. By
defining the EU as a *'Staatenverbund'* (a union of states), the Court denied any legitimacy to the EU itself and upheld the classical definition of the nineteenth-century nation-state, i.e., one defined in terms of territory, people and a common
language. The state thereby remained the only political body within which legitimate governance could be provided (Everling 1994; and see also Chapter 13).

Despite the different roots of French and German conceptions of the state,
nation and identity, they have not prevented some convergence of attitudes
towards the EU. The ruling of the Constitutional Court and subsequent com-
mentaries by constitutional lawyers (Kirchhof 1992) and political scientists
(Kielmannsegg 1996) have stressed the point that the EU offers no constitutional
guarantee of genuine democracy and lacks the qualities of common learning and
solidarity necessary for a real political community. Moreover, although they may
not be predominant in élite opinion, there is a convergence of views on nature of

...he Union, the Constitutional Court insisting that the member states should remain 'masters of the treaty', which tallies closely with the French approach of intergovernmentalism. So, neither in France nor in Germany can support for concepts such as state fusion or shared sovereignty and interdependence be taken for granted. Maastricht led to a common resurgence of thinking about the state and the nation rather than reflection on the nature of a common European citizenship.

In such a context the very different approach that suggests that the European political system shows some of the characteristics of statehood has become more and more divisive. What Safran calls the French 'paradox' distinguishes the new post-reunification setting:

> France's influence in Europe has been in a process to be eclipsed by that of a reunited Germany, so that ... a safeguarding of France's relative political power might be achieved only with still more European integration, namely a further reduction of France's sovereignty. (Safran 1991: 225)

Since Maastricht, especially, France has been painfully seeking to bring about further integration yet preserve its identity. It is not without importance that the constitutional reform that led to the ratification of the Treaty also introduced a new Article 2, which stated that '*la langue de la République est le français*'. The symbolism of the cultural and language policies of the French government under Chirac's presidency is likely to acquire even greater political impact (Bastien 1992).

It could be argued that the Franco-German debate over nuclear tests in 1995 follows a similar pattern. After Chirac's first irrevocable gesture in exercising France's sovereign power – which also, of course, re-emphasized its nuclear status – the debate became more one on misconceptions of the function of the modern stateq. Subsequently, the French also sought – even more unrealistically – to safeguard the continuity of the *force de frappe* by suggesting its integration into a Franco-German framework. Perhaps, therefore, the debate is less about the 'return of the state' in its geopolitical sense, but the re-emergence of the symbolism of the state. But, nevertheless, in practical terms these symbolic politics strengthen the demands for the Europeanization of opportunities to formulate political objectives at the national level.

The political debate on reform

Since the beginning of the debate over reform, differences emerged between France and Germany. The issue of 'political power' still dominates the French discourse, much more so than in Germany. The French remain more explicitly concerned with the systematic exercise of *political* leadership in Europe, while in Germany there remains, especially at the top, a 'European conviction'. In terms of the 1996 IGC agenda, it was generally accepted even in France that the Conference had to deal with two main issues at the same time: the achievement of a more efficient and democratic Europe; and preparations for enlargement eastwards. Early ideas about new fundamental contracts (Lamassoure, *Le Monde*, 31 May 1994) that ignored the challenge of enlargement were rapidly discarded, although for most French participants in the debate, agreement to enlargement was regarded largely a function of relations with Germany.

Two basic cleavages have dominated the Franco-German debate on enlargement: the correlation between deepening and widening and Communitization and intergovernmentalism; and the rationalization of the existing order with some sort of attention being paid to the relationship between big and small member states. Agreement has emerged that enlargement is inevitable. The shape of the future Union has been clearly identified, with membership achieved by the six CEECs, Malta and Cyprus, plus the Baltic states and the states of the former Yugoslavia led by Slovenia (Balladur in *Le Monde* 30 November 1994; Juppé in *Le Monde* 18 November 1994). But there remain differences as to the nature of the future Europe, and rival conceptions of a 'big' and 'little' Europe.

In Germany the 'old' approach, of widening and deepening at the same time has remained the basic assumption but with a somewhat different agenda associated with a smaller 'core' Europe as the fall-back position if enlargement should prove possible only with the strengthening of intergovernmentalism and the dilution of the Union. The EFTAn enlargement clearly showed the difficulties of institutional 'deepening' before widening. With Germany's domestic judicial and parliamentary constraints provoked by the Maastricht ratification process, a two speed approach has appeared increasingly inevitable (Deubner 1995). French reactions have been divided. The most substantive answer to the CDU–CSU 'hard core' approach came from former President Giscard d'Estaing who saw the need for a fundamental change in the basic Community bargain. He differentiated between a European 'space', a 'community of nations' within a free trade zone, and a Europe of 'power', a political Europe with a federal vocation. He underlined the point that it would be inappropriate to mix these two competing projects because the more traditional French (as well as German) approach of widening and deepening would be mutually destructive. On the contrary, he believed that France should avoid pressing for any further steps towards political integration in order to concentrate its efforts on achieving EMU. In his view, monetary integration offers the most significant opportunity for the realization of political union.

The sharpness of the Giscardian 'either/or' approach was in marked contrast to that of President Chirac and Prime Minister Juppé. They have spoken about a common '*socle*' or pillar for economic policy, political cooperation and common borders, and *solidarités renforcées* in other areas of cooperation (Chirac 1995: 28). Such an approach has characterized the Gaullist position. The first Balladur proposals in response to the CDU–CSU paper, of concentric circles, derived from the same basis. The biggest circle would be the circle of common law, the single market, its common policies and foreign and security policies, a wider circle of those waiting for membership or linked by agreements through the Stability Pacts and Partnership for Peace and a third, tighter, more limited circle covering EMU and defence (*Le Monde* 30 November 1994). In a similar way, the two conservative rapporteurs of the National Assembly's *Delegation pour l'Union Européene* proposed a 'big Europe' with a common market, and two further levels of *solidarités renforcées* in the economic and monetary and defence sectors (National Assembly 1995).

In effect, therefore, the two governments seem to converge on questions of flexibility and differentiation, with both favouring a strong Union. If consolidation and further deepening within the EU is not possible because other member states are unwilling or unable to accept it, further steps would be considered, either within or without the Union framework. The major prerequisite, however, would be that the Franco-German tandem remained intact; no core Europe would be conceivable without it.

Before the IGC, few in French government circles had been particularly interested in abolishing the pillar structure that was still considered to be the real French contribution to Maastricht. Important new European policy initiatives were not expected; the focus was on institutional consolidation and preservation, including, with the prospect of further enlargement, the re-establishment of the balance between the big and small member states and the rationalization of the existing political order in the Union. Otherwise France was not interested in major changes in the institutional equilibrium – even if Germany had long been an advocate of greater influence for the EP and the German position even envisaged the participation of EP rapporteurs in the IGC. Nor were the French enthusiastic about the participation of regional actors (to meet German fears over ratification) or the communitization of the CFSP or the JHA pillars of Maastricht.

The focus for both countries was the Council, still the heart of the system. The guidelines laid down by the Chirac/Juppé government were fairly opaque in terms of the institutional structures of the circles, though there was extensive agreement on the more effective functioning of the Council and the European Council. The rotating Presidency in an enlarged Union was considered likely to be inefficient and favoured the smaller member states who might prove inadequate to meet the task. The concepts of 'team presidencies', gathering several small member states together with one larger one – eventually perhaps on a regional base (Senat 1995) – and of a presidency–vice presidency system (Chirac 1995) emerged. Several French proposals also suggested the replacement of the Committee of Permanent Representatives (COREPER) with a Brussels-based minister from each member state (Senat 1995: 17; Bourlanges 1995: 239). There was also an idea of prolonging each presidency. Chirac (1995: 30) suggested the election of a 'president' by the European Council for a set term of office, as did Elizabeth Guigou (one of the two representatives of the EP on the Reflections Group), although she wished to preserve the rotating Presidency for the Council (Guigou 1995: 39). The CDU–CSU group in the *Bundestag* held not dissimilar views with their suggestion of an elected presidency serving for one year with the office rotating among groups of small states together with larger ones (CDU–CSU 1993).

There seems, too, to have been something of a convergence of views on voting in the Council. Even if there has been little enthusiasm in France for extending the system of Qualified Majority Voting (QMV), there has been a growing acceptance of the idea of a 'double majority', i.e. decisions taken on the basis of a majority of member states and a majority of their populations (*Le texte confidentiel* in *Le Figaro* 20 February 1996). Other differentiated procedures have also been suggested, Bourlanges, for example, proposed a triple system, with an additional reinforced majority (a 'quasi-consensus') together with an 'optional initiative right', similar to the German idea of 'positive abstention'. Others, including the Prime Minister and the President were concerned both with the dangers of immobilism in decision-making and the continued existence, albeit latent, of the Luxembourg Compromise where vital national interests were involved, a point noted in the French Government's discussion paper of November 1995 (Chirac 1995: 29; *Le Figaro* 20 February 1996). That raised the crucial question of whether the Gaullists were willing to tolerate any majoritarian rule, there being a clear preference for votes in such fields as the budget, structural funds, fiscal and financial harmonization and association treaties to be on the basis of consensus, and foreign policy etc. on 'super-qualified majority votes' (National Assembly 1995: 82).

Given such views, it is not perhaps surprising that there was extensive agreement among French leaders that the Commission should be more responsible to the Council. In the *Texte Confidentiel*, the Government's attitude to the Commission was that its main function was the application of Council decisions, and that it should be bound more strictly to the mandate set out by the Council (*Le Figaro* 20 February 1996). The National Assembly rapporteurs went further to demand the abolition of the Commission's right of initiative and calling in effect for the negation of any political role for it.

One of the major differences between the two governments has been, however, in their attitudes towards the EP. While the *Texte Confidentiel* favoured greater efficiency in the legislative process, based on a hierarchy of norms, this was not to be achieved by modifying Parliament's relationship with the Council. For France the emphasis lay not on the greater democratic legitimacy of the EP but in the role of national parliaments. For Germany there was a much greater preoccupation with the EP's role and particularly in the use of majority voting in the Council and the co-decision procedure and in new rights in relation to the second and third pillars. For the rapporteurs of both the French Senate and National Assembly, there was considerable suspicion of the EP's efforts to have a greater role in the second and third pillars and to become more involved through the co-decision procedures (National Assembly 1995: 141). The *Bundestag*, on the other hand, put the emphasis squarely on the linkage between treaty modifications and greater democratizsation.

French proposals for the greater representation of national parliaments at the European level appeared to have widespread parliamentary support, and especially among the Gaullists (ibid.) *Le Figaro* 7 December 1994; de la Malène in *Agence Europe* 30 December 1994). Most seemed to suggest a new second chamber, a European senate, that *'pouvait être opportunément compensé par la suppression du Comité des Regions'* (National Assembly 1995: 141). The notion that the principle of subsidiarity needs to be applied to allow for the systematic involvement of the national parliament is an interpretation that contrasts markedly with that of Germany where subsidiarity is conceived on regional lines (*Bundesrat* 1995). The Senate and the Assembly put forward two proposals, the Senate suggesting a European Senate responsible for exercising parliamentary control over the second and third pillars and with a general responsibility for the application of the principle of subsidiarity (Senat 1995: 14), while the National Assembly built more on existing structures. The latter's position was similar, indeed, to that of the Government as expressed in the *Texte Confidentiel* that, based on COSAC (the biannual meetings of the Conference of European Affairs Committees), national parliaments would cooperate on exercising supervision over the third pillar as well as subsidiarity questions.

In neither the German nor the French case were revolutionary changes envisaged as far as the institutions were concerned. Both actors follow the same line, as long as neither sees 'relative gains' such as, for example, Germany in respect of the Council's voting system. In the eyes of both governments there was much greater emphasis on institutional consolidation and prservation rather than change. The perspectives were still those of the 'old Europe'; the challenge of enlargement has not been taken into account.

CONCLUSIONS: FRANCE AND GERMANY IN THE FUTURE EUROPEAN CONTEXT – MORE THAN A CORE?

Certainly before the IGC opened, debates among the general public and political and economic élites of both countries suggested that there was little clarity and considerable muddle. Much of the debate concerned what was left of the Maastricht Treaty still to implement rather than new initiatives. This created additional difficulties for both governments and widened still further the scope for conflict and cooperation.

The common challenge for both France and Germany has been to adapt their economic and social systems both to Maastricht and the circumstances of the 1990s. This painful process of modernization has had to be realized not only in a European but also a wider, global context. In that sense, 'Maastricht' is only a metaphor for 'globalization' or 'de-nationalization'. So far, it remains unclear whether in either country, the legitimacy of the European project will suffer as a consequence; shifts of hitherto national responsibilities to the European level open up the possibility of the EU becoming a political scapegoat, thereby weakening it seriously.

There is, according to this perspective, a new dynamic to the symbolic dimension of the state. For some political actors, what is being created is a new opportunity for addressing the loss in social coherence within Western societies since the end of the Cold War. In both France and Germany there are those who see bilateral and European cooperation as the only way out of the dilemma facing the state over the provision of prosperity and stability. The framework for finding a common approach is shaped by such a convergence of ideas – even if some basic cleavages, as over economic policy, may still persist. But in both countries there is opposition to such ideas; 'Maastricht' remains a potent symbol in the political discourse. In such circumstances it is difficult to see any great eagerness to consider any widening beyond the 'old' Europe.

The Reflection Group report in December 1995 demonstrated the dilemma – that is, the failure to achieve a post-Maastricht Political Union for the fifteen, and at the same time, the failure to confront an enlargement that might make them all losers. There is little sense of a willingness to share burdens despite the uncertainties of the outcome of the crisis affecting Western European welfare states (Wessels 1996: 22). The implicit repercussions of that dilemma for the debate on EU reform have, though, begun to emerge: neither the discourse on legitimacy nor the debate on the Maastricht 'order' suggest any major changes are to be expected.

A new pragmatism is gaining ground in Franco-German relations. This is largely because both recognize that they remain extremely interdependent and without alternatives to closer cooperation and integration. The post-Maastricht debate did not suggest – in spite of some temptations on the French side – that the Franco-German political partnership had run its course. Given all the dangers that derived from their relative size and geo-economic position in the global system, they remain geared to cooperation and solidarity; the 'swan-song' thesis has not yet won the day in public debates. At the same time, however, there is an impression that, with the conclusion of the TEU, the integration process as a whole has reached such a level that additional progress will be more and more difficult to achieve (Sauder 1995). Very few 'easy' policy areas are left at the disposal of political actors to be used for the drive towards further integration. There are, indeed, other areas, especially those relating to the completion of EMU, that are still full of pitfalls for both France and Germany. The Maastricht 'acquis' has not yet been fully implemented.

At the same time, new and different problems are emerging on the European agenda for the last years of the century that may further a new type of initiative within the framework of a 'smaller' Europe. Both the move to the third stage of EMU and the prospect of enlargement to include another twelve states has led to a reassessment of the validity of the EU as the major framework for common policy-making. The risk that countries 'unwilling or unable' to tackle vital issues jointly could hinder the pursuit of shared interests in areas of major importance will constantly lend itself to Franco-German consideration of complementary and/or alternative options. Whether these options – as constituting the only way to overcome blockage in an inefficient and ineffective enlarged EU – will be used depends to a large degree on the partners who are reluctant to continue and extend common policy-making. A 'smaller' Europe may not be the optimal strategy but may come to be regarded as the only option in the last resort that will enable the EU to tackle future issues.

However, in spite of convergence of ideas on major areas in the IGC negotiations, it remains uncertain if there is a shared conviction that deepening and widening at the same time would inevitably lead to a successful 'core'. So far at least, both member states have preferred to work within the framework developed over the last few decades. It is impossible to predict if and when they might decide, simultaneously and together, that a point of no return had been reached. The 1996 IGC may only perhaps have prepared the ground for debating unorthodox ideas and concepts; certainly the history of Franco-German bilateral relations has shown that 'smaller' solutions are not necessarily easier.

REFERENCES AND BIBLIOGRAPHY

Attali, Jaques (1995) *Verbatim III*. Paris, Fayard.

Balladur, Edouard (1994) 'Pour un nouveau traité de l'Elysée', *Le Monde*, 30 November.

Balleix, Corinne (1994) 'La Banque Centrale Européenne dans le discours politique français', *RPP*, vol. 96, no. 974, pp. 38–45.

Bastien, Francois (1992) 'Maastricht, la constitution et la politique. Breves considérations sur la dimension symbolique des révisions constitutionelles', *RFDC*, vol. 11, pp. 469–78.

Boquet, Dominique (1995) 'Paris, Bonn, Delors: L'Europe en quête de centre', *Le Débat*, no. 83, pp. 4–41.

Bourlanges, Jean-Loius (1995) 'L'Europe à trente: un objet virtuel', *Commentaire*, no. 78, pp. 229–42.

Brubaker, Roger (1992) *Citizenship and Nationhood in France and Germany*. Cambridge, MA, Harvard University Press.

Bundesrat (1995) 'Entschliesseung des Bundesrats zur Vorbereitung der Regierungskonferenz 1996', Drs. 169/95.

CDU–CSU Fraktion des Deutschen Bundestages (1993) 'Frieden und Wohlstand – fuer ein handlungsfaehiges und einiges Europa', *Positionspapier zur Europaeischen Union*. Bonn, 26 October.

— (1994) *Ueberlegungen zur europaeischen Politik*. Bonn, September.

Centre d'action pour la fédération européenne (ed.) (1995) *L'Europe de demain*. Neuchatel.

Chévènement, J.P. (1994) 'A l'Allemagne, parlons franc', *Le Monde* 12 October.

Chirac, Jaques (1995) 'Pour le contrat initiative-emploi, pour la monnaie unique en 1999 et un élargissement du référendum', *RPP*, vol. 97, no. 976.

Churchill, R.S. (ed.) (1948) *The Sinews of Peace; post-war speeches*. London.

Cole, Alistair (1993) 'Looking on: France and the New Germany', *German Politics*, vol. 2, no. 3, pp. 358–76.

De Gaulle, Charles (1970) *Discourse et message, vol. 3 (1958-1962)*. Paris, Seuil.

Delors, Jaques (1995) 'Le moment et la méthode', *Le Débat*, no. 83, pp. 4–23.

Deubner, Christian (1995) *Deutsche Europapolitik: Von Maastricht nach Kerneuropa?*. Baden-Baden: Nomuos Verlag.

Duhamel, Oliver and Grunberg, Gerard (1993) 'Référendum: les dix France', in Duhamel, Oliver and Jaffré, Jérôme (eds) *L'état de l'opinion 1993*. Paris: Seuil, pp. 12–28.

Everling, Ulrich (1994) 'Das Maastricht-Urteil des Bundesverfassungsgerichts und seine Bedeutung fuer die Entwicklung der Europaeischen Union', *Integration*, vol. 17, no. 3, pp. 165–75.

Fitoussi, Jaques (1995) *Le Débat interdit. Monnaie, Europe, Pauvreté*. Paris, Arléa.

Franzmeyer, Fritz (1995) 'Was braechte eine deutsch-franzoesische Beschaefti-gungsinitiative? – Zur Rezeption des EU-Weissbuchs in Deutschland und Frankreich', *CIRAC/DFI/DGAP/IFRA*, op.cit., 242–63.

Guigou, Elisabeth (1995) 'Les Enjeux de la Conférence de 1996, *Revue des Affaires Européennes*, vol. 1, pp. 35–40.

Grosser, Alfred (1993) 'Petit bilan des relation franco-allemandes dans le contexte de l'integration europeennne,' in Beutler, Bernhard (ed.) *Reflexions sur l'Europe*. Bruxelles, Editions Complexes, pp. 15–22.

Grunberg, Gérard (1995) 'Les élections européennes en France', in Duhamel, Oliver and Jaffré, Jérôme (eds) *L'état de l'opinion 1993*. Paris, Seuil, pp. 12–28.

Guerin-Sendelbach, Valery (1993) 'Ein Tandem fuer Europa? Die deutsch-franzoesische Zusammenarbeit der achtziger Jahre', *Arbeitspapiere zur Internationalen Politik*, no. 77, Bonn: Europa Union Verlag.

Héredote no. 68 (1993) 'La question allemagne', Paris, La Decouverte.

Hrbek, Rudolf (1994) 'Das neue Europaeische Parlament: mehr Vielfalt – weniger Handlungsfaehigkeit?', *Integration*, vol. 17, no. 4, pp. 157–64.

Kielmannsegg, Graf Peter (1996) 'Integration und Demokratie', in Jachtenfuchs, Markus and Kohler-Koch, Beate (eds) *Europaeische Integration*. Opladen, Leske und Buderich, pp. 47–71.

Kirchhof, Paul (1992) 'Der deutsche Staat im Prozess der europaeischen Integration', in Isensee, Josef and Kirchhof, Paul (eds) *Handbuch des Staatsrechts der Bundesrepublik Deutschland*. Heidelberg, pp. 855–78.

Kolboom, Ingo (1991) 'Charles de Gaulle und ein deutsch-franzoesisches Missverstaendnis ueber Nation und Europa', in Loth, Wilfried and Picht, Robert (eds) *De Gaulle, Deutschland und Europa*. Opladen, Leske und Buderich, pp. 135–50.

Korinmann, M. 'Pour l'Union franco-allemande, tout de suite', *Le Monde*, 3 February 1995.

Lallement, Henri (1995) 'Handelspolitik – Ein Zankapfel zwischen Deutschland und Frankreich?' *CIRAC/DFI/DGAP/IFRI*, op. cit., 225–41.

Lamassoure, Alain (1994) 'Pour un nouveau contrat fondateur', *Le Monde*, 31 May 1994.

—— (1995) 'La question de confiance portera sur la politique étrangère et de défense', *RAE*, no. 1, pp. 51–5.

Larosiére, Jacques (1993) 'L'Union Economique et Monétaire et le traité de Maastricht', in Lloyd, Alexis and Winckler, Antoine (eds) *Europe en chantier*. Paris, Hachette, pp. 57–1.

Les Notes Bleus de Bercy. No 532, 24 March 1991.

Manfrass-Sirjacques, Françoise (1993) 'La coopération militaire franco-allemande depuis 1963', in Ménudier Henri (ed.) *Le couple franco-allemand en Europe*. Publications de l'Institut d'Allemand d'Asnières, no. 17: Asnières, pp. 99–111.

Maull, Hans W. (1992) 'Zivilmacht Bundesrepublik Deutschland. Vierzehn Thesen fuer eine neue deutsche Aussenpolitik', *Europa-Archiv*, vol. 47, no. 10, pp. 269–78.

Mearsheimer, John J. (1990) 'Back to the future: instability in Europe after the Cold War', *International Security*, vol. 15, pp. 5–56.

Moravcsik, Andrew (1993) 'Interests and ideals in the European community: the french referendum', *French Politics and Society*, vol. 11, pp. 45–56.

Moreau Defarges, Philippe (1995) 'Frankreich und die Europaeische Union: Vom Maastrichter Vertrag zur Regierungskonferenz 1996', *CIRAC/DFI/DGAP/IFRI*, op. cit., pp. 338–51.

National Assembly (1995) 'Rapport d'information sur les réformes institutionelles de l'Union européenne', *Rapport d'informations no. 1939*.

Neue Juristische Wochengschrift (1994) *Constitutional Council decisions* (12 July), pp. 2207—19.

Nicolas, F. and Stark, H. (eds) (1992) *L'Allemagne. Une novelle hégémonie?* Paris, Dunod.

OECD (1994) *OECD Economic Surveys, 1993*. Paris.

Picht, Robert, Wessels, Wolfgang and Uterwedde, Henrik (1990) 'Deutsch-franzoesischer Bilateralismus als Motor der europaeischen Integration: Mythos oder Realitaeten?', in Picht, Robert and Wessels, Wolfgang (eds) *Motor fuer Europa? Deutsch-franzoesischer Bilateralismus und europaeische Integration*. Bonn, Europa Union Verlag, pp. 15–31.

Putnam, Robert D. (1988) 'Diplomacy and domestic politics, the logic of two-level games', *International Organization*, vol. 42, pp. 427–60.

Safran, Wiliam (1991) 'State, nation, national identity, and citizenship: France as a test case', *IPSR*, vol. 12, pp. 219–38.

Saint-Etienne, Christian (1995) 'Fur eine deutsch-französische Währungsunion', in *CIRAC/DFI/DGAP/IFRI*, pp. 213–24.

Sauder, Axel (1995) 'Realismus statt Vision. Bonn und Paris bleiben aufeinander angewiesen', *Internationale Politik*, vol. 50, no. 9, 31–6.

Schrader, Lutz (1993) 'Mitterrands Europapolitik oder der lange Abschied vom Gaullismus', *Aus Politik und Zeitgeschichte*, B 32/93.

Schwarz, Hans-Peter (1992) *Erbfreundschaft: Adenauer und Frankreich*. Bonn,

— (1995) 'Die neue Weltpolitik am Ende des 20. Jahrhunderts – Rueckkehr zu den Anfaengen vor 1914?', in Kaiser, Karl and Schwarz, Hans-Peter (eds) *Die neue Weltpolitik*. Bonn, pp. 15–33.

Senat (1992) *Rapport d'information sur l'application du principe de subsidiarité*, no. 45, session 1992–93.

— (1995) *Rapport d'information no 224 sur la réforme des insitutions de l'Union européenne*, 15 February.

Sur, Etienne (1993) 'Maastricht, la France et l'Allemagne', *Héredote* no. 68, pp. 125–37.

Uterwedde, Henrik (1995) 'Wettbewerbsfaehigkeit und Industriepolitik: Deutschland und franzoesische Strategien', *CIRAC/DFI/DGAP/IFRI*, op. cit., 192–212.

Wallace, Helen (1989) 'Institutionalized bilateralism and multilateral relations: axis, motor or detonator?', in Picht, Robert and Wessels, Wolfgang (eds) *Motor fuer Europa? Deutsch-franzoesischer Bilateralismus und europaeische Integration*. Bonn, Europa Union Verlag, pp. 145–57.

Wallace, William (1990a) *The Transformation of Western Europe*. London, Pinter.

— (1990b) 'Introduction: The Dynamics of European Integration', in Wallace, William (ed.) *The Dynamics of European Integration*. London, Pinter, pp. 1–24.

Waltz, Kenneth (1993) 'The emerging structure of international politics', *International Security*, vol. 18, no. 2, pp. 44–79.

Wessels, Wolfgang (1994a) 'Integrationspolitische Konzepte im Realitaetstest', *Wirtschaftsdienst*, vol. 10, pp. 499–503.

— (1994b) 'Rationalizing Maastricht: the search for an optimal strategy of the new Europe', *International Affaires*, vol. 70, pp. 445–57.

— (1996) 'Weder Vision noch Verhandlungspaket – Der Bericht der Reflexionsgruppe im integrationspolitischen Trend', *Integration*, vol. 19, no. 1.

Ziebura, Gilbert (1970) *Die deutsch-franzoesische Beziehungen seit 1945. Mythen und Realitaeten*. Pfullingen Neuke.

6
BRITAIN AND THE IGC

STEPHEN GEORGE

Britain has acquired a reputation for being an awkward partner in the European Union (EU), for not being fully committed to the project of European integration, for remaining semi-detached from the organization and its goals. There is plenty of historical evidence to support such a view: the initial refusal to join the European Community (EC); the acrimonious renegotiation of the terms of entry under the Wilson Government in 1974–75; the even more acrimonious dispute over British budgetary contributions during the first five years of Margaret Thatcher's premiership; the refusal of the same Prime Minister to accept that the 1992 single market programme should be extended to be given a social dimension, or to embrace monetary union (for further detail see George 1994).

Margaret Thatcher was replaced as Prime Minister shortly before the opening of the 1991 IGCs. Her successor, John Major, said that he wanted to put Britain 'at the centre of the debate' on the future of the EC, as 'an enthusiastic participant' (HMSO 1991). However, he still refused to accept a social chapter in the Treaty on European Union (TEU), agreeing only to the other member states going ahead without Britain under a Protocol to the Treaty; and he negotiated an opt-out for Britain on monetary union.

Subsequently, in the latter half of 1992, Britain held the Presidency of the EC. Although there are different interpretations of the conduct of the Presidency (Ludlow 1993; Garel-Jones 1993) it is difficult to argue that it did anything to enhance Britain's pro-EC credentials, particularly because during the Presidency the pound was forced out of the exchange rate mechanism of the EMS, amidst recriminations against Germany for the alleged failure of the *Bundesbank* to support the efforts of the Bank of England to relieve speculative pressure on sterling.

To understand the record of successive British governments in the EC, it is necessary to look at the domestic political constraints that they face. This analysis will also allow an understanding of the position that the Government was preparing for the 1996 IGC. First, however, it is important to understand exactly what the bases of British policy in the EC have been.

THE BRITISH POSITION ON EUROPEAN INTEGRATION

Despite frequent presentations in the media of the British position on Europe as being simply negative, it is not difficult to construct a picture of the underlying principles of the policies of successive governments. These have applied to both Labour and Conservative governments in the past, as can be seen from the quotations compiled by Martin Holmes (1991). The continuity of the policies of the last two Conservative Prime Ministers can be seen very clearly if Margaret Thatcher's Bruges speech of September 1988 (Thatcher 1988) is compared with an article by John Major that appeared in *The Economist* five years later, in September 1993 (Major 1993). (A close textual comparison of the two pieces, highlighting their similarities, can be found in George 1995.)

The principles that emerge from comparing these various statements are as follows:

1. A BELIEF IN A EUROPE OF NATION STATES
British policy has never subscribed to the idea that nationalism is a spent force, and that nation states should be superseded by a federal Europe. Because the language associated with this federalist ideal had become the dominant form of discourse about the EC by the time Britain became a member, British interventions in the debate sounded negative even when they were intended to be positive contributions to building a sustainable EC.

2. PRAGMATISM
Because British governments never subscribed to the teleological idea of European integration as a process designed to lead to a federal Europe, they always demanded positive and practical reasons for adopting common policies or for changing decision-making procedures. For the British, Europe is a 'journey to an unknown destination' (Shonfield 1973), and the only justification for taking a further step on that journey is that there are present problems which can best be solved by joint action.

3. RELEVANCE
Closely related to the pragmatism of the British approach is an impatience with what from a British perspective are irrelevant 'doctrinal' debates. Long before the rest of the EU decided it was a priority, the British government was insisting that action to tackle unemployment was more urgent than endless discussion about how far the powers of the European Parliament ought to be extended, or whether citizens of one member state ought to be allowed to vote in European elections in another member state. As John Major put it, 'unless the Community is seen to be tackling the problems which affect [the electorates of Europe] now, rather than arguing over abstract concepts, it will lose its credibility' (Major 1993: 23).

4. ECONOMIC COMPETITIVENESS
Conservative governments always put a strong emphasis on the need for policies

to encourage enterprise. Many of the restrictive practices that persisted throughout the EU were swept away in Britain by the Thatcher governments. The single market programme was seen as an opportunity to extend the competitive environment to the rest of the EC, which would be beneficial to the EC as a whole because it would make it more competitive in global terms with the USA and Japan.

5. A Europe open to the world

Linked to this commitment to a competitive Europe, but of even older vintage, because it was also a theme of the Labour governments of Wilson and Callaghan, is the idea that the EC should not become a fortress, but should be open to the world. In particular, both Labour and Conservative politicians repeatedly stressed during the period of the Cold War that the EC was not the whole of Europe, and that the states of Eastern Europe should not be forgotten.

6. A commitment to NATO

All British governments stressed the importance of the Atlantic Alliance, and resisted any suggestion that the EC should somehow emerge as a 'third force' in world affairs, distancing itself from the USA.

7. Financial probity

Finally, a point not mentioned explicitly by either Thatcher or Major, but one that underpinned many interventions by British governments in EC debates, is a consistent demand that EC expenditure be justified in detail, and be accounted for in detail.

THE DOMESTIC DETERMINANTS OF THE BRITISH POSITION

The consistency of British positions on Europe reflect underlying political realities, the values of the civil service, and a cultural pragmatism that pervades the thinking of the political and administrative élites.

Because Britain was undefeated in the Second World War, and did not experience occupation, nationalism was not discredited as it was in parts of continental Europe. The British public remained responsive to nationalist appeals, and political parties never adopted the rhetoric of European integration as part of their political discourse. When Britain applied to join the EC, the reasons given to the British people were pragmatic rather than idealistic; but the fact that membership was not achieved until after the end of the long post-war period of economic growth meant that the EC did not become associated with increasing prosperity in the minds of the British people as it had in the minds of the populations of the original six member states.

As well as reflecting the nationalism of the electorate in their statements about the EC, politicians actually reinforced it. The confrontational attitude to the EC that was first adopted by Wilson in the renegotiation of the terms of British entry, was developed much further by Thatcher. Faced with the need drastically to restructure the British economy, her governments followed policies that precipitated record bankruptcies and high unemployment. In response to the social unrest that this provoked, Thatcher liked to pose as a national leader taking on a common external enemy. One such enemy was the Soviet Union, the 'evil empire'. Eventually another presented itself when Argentina invaded the Falkland Islands, allowing Thatcher to become briefly a real war leader. In between, the EC served as a substitute. In fighting the battle over budgetary contributions, Thatcher was able to call on historically deep-seated British prejudices against the French, and more recent ones against the Germans (Currid 1995). Her campaign on the issue reinforced the prejudices that she played upon, although it did not prevent British public opinion as a whole becoming steadily more favourable towards membership of the EC (Nugent 1992).

The association of Thatcher with this nationalistic line towards the EC had different effects in different groups of the population as a whole. It probably helped the Labour Party to evolve in a more pro-EC direction (Seyd and Whiteley 1992: 47–8); but it left her Conservative successor facing a party membership which was divided on the issue, with a majority strongly negative about further European integration, but with a significant pro-European sentiment persisting among about one-third of the membership, making party management extremely difficult (Seyd et al.1994: 57–8).

There are other bases, though, for the consistency of British attitudes. There is also within the British establishment a belief in the importance of avoiding a narrow regionalism in the EU, which dates back to the period of British global hegemony in the late nineteenth and early twentieth centuries. To argue this point fully would require a separate chapter, but it has been developed at length elsewhere (George 1989). The institutional source of continuity on this issue lies within Whitehall, and perhaps particularly in the Foreign Office, rather than in the arena of party politics, just as the consistent demand for parsimony in public expenditure can be seen as a value of the Treasury. However, it is important not to overlook the importance of such ideas in their own right in conditioning the outlook of British politicians, irrespective of any pressure that they may get from civil servants.

The other important political actors who have not yet been considered are interest groups, and particularly the big economic interests represented by large manufacturing concerns and by the financial institutions of the City of London. Although not always pushing government in the same direction, there has been an adjustment by British economic interests to the reality of membership of the EC-EU, and this has tended to put them on the side of the more pro-European elements in the national debate (Butt Philip 1992). For example, British industrialists were an important pressure group in favour of the single market programme, and their pressure may have been significant in getting Mrs Thatcher to swallow her principles on majority voting when signing the Single European Act (SEA).

On some issues that separated the British government from the governments of other member states, the economic interest groups were on the British side. Indeed, it was not only British industry that was opposed to some of the plans for social legislation drawn up by the European Commission: the Union of European Employers' Confederations (UNICE) was opposed to many items in the 'social charter'. However, it is difficult to argue that business pressure was the real reason for Britain's opposition to the social dimension, as the British government had other, more party political reasons for its opposition.

On the other important issue that followed in the train of the single market programme, monetary union, a gap did emerge between the policy of the Thatcher government and the interests of British economic actors. The government as a whole tried to find a way through the pragmatic doubts of the Treasury about the viability of monetary union and the concerns of industrial and financial interest groups that if there were to be a monetary union, it would be damaging to their business to be left outside of it. John Major, first as Chief Secretary to the Treasury and later as Chancellor of the Exchequer, worked with officials to devise the scheme for the 'hard Ecu' as an evolutionary route to monetary union. Unfortunately, the then Prime Minister undermined the credibility of her own Government's alternative to the Delors plan by stating in the House of Commons that she did not believe that anyone would use the envisaged parallel European currency (*Hansard* 30 October 1990: col. 878). What was intended to be a genuine and serious contribution to the debate was made to look like a British wrecking tactic.

The gap that had opened up between the Prime Minister and the rest of her government can ultimately only be explained in terms of ideals. Margaret Thatcher was often described as a 'conviction politician', and one of her convictions was that to surrender monetary sovereignty to the EC would be wrong. As a result she was not prepared to go along with the pragmatic line that the government as a whole was prepared to support. It was against this background that Sir Geoffrey Howe made his famous resignation speech in the Commons in which he expressed the dismay of many supporters of the Conservative Party from business and financial circles about the direction in which Thatcher was leading the party (*Hansard* 13 November 1990: cols. 461–5). This was the blow from which Thatcher never recovered. However, her successor was faced with a party that still generally backed the Thatcher line on Europe, and so he had to move cautiously in the negotiation of the TEU.

NEGOTIATING MAASTRICHT: BRITAIN AT THE HEART OF EUROPE

In understanding British diplomacy in the approach to Maastricht, it should first be noted that the British view of the nature of the EC was never as eccentric as the media presented it. There was always an undertow of hypocrisy about the *communautaire* statements of politicians from other member states. All states in the EC pursued their national interests, and all were capable of being awkward partners when those national interests were threatened (Buller 1995: 36). However, because European integration was generally considered a good thing in most other states, it was difficult for Ministers from those states to oppose even proposals which they knew were damaging to their interests in the forthright way that British Ministers could. Indeed, British Ministers using the veto in the Council of Ministers were often aware of a widespread sigh of relief around the table before their colleagues went outside to condemn British intransigence to the awaiting press.

In other respects, Britain had been in the process of becoming a more normal member of the EC for some years prior to Maastricht. When it first joined, there were certain structural problems that made it difficult for Britain to fit into the EC, but these gradually receded in importance. The most important issue was Britain's budgetary contributions, which bedevilled relations during the first five years of Margaret Thatcher's premiership. Whatever may be thought of the then Prime Minister's approach to the problem, there was certainly a genuine problem; Britain's partners admitted as much. The problem was solved in one sense by the deal struck at the Fontainebleau meeting of the European Council in June 1984. But in another sense the problem began to solve itself because of changes in Britain's pattern of trade, and changes in the structure of the budget.

Enlargement of the EC brought in three poorer states (Greece, Spain, and Portugal), and led directly to the expansion of the structural funds, which, taken together with some reining-in of expenditure on agricultural support, produced a clearer division between contributing and receiving member states. Britain remained a net contributor to the budget, but was on the same side of the debate as other contributory states, including both the states that were often seen as the dominant actors in the EC, Germany and France.

During the latter years of Margaret Thatcher's premiership relations with both these countries cooled, especially with Germany. It was certainly no coincidence that John Major's first speech abroad as Prime Minister was made in Bonn. The Franco-German axis was always central to the unity of the EC, and in order to have any influence on the direction in which the Community would go in the future it was clearly necessary for Britain to be involved in dialogue with both these states. That is not to say, though, that the aim of British diplomacy under the Major Government was to break apart the close links between France and Germany. British policy had never involved trying to force France and Germany apart, and officials even saw the special relationship as beneficial. There were issues where Britain was closer to one of the partners, and where it would have been counter-productive for the British to try to persuade the other to modify its policies. On such issues it was sensible for the British to agree a line with the partner to whom they were the closer, and then leave it to them to persuade the other.

Although the Franco-German partnership will always remain important to developments in European integration, it is a mistake to see that relationship as the sole driving force of the EU. This mistake is made not only by the media. In academic writing on the EC, the realist position insisted that the future direction of the EC could be discerned if the balance of power between the big three states was correctly analysed (for example, Moravcsik 1991). This position misunderstands the complex nature of the EC diplomatic game. It was probably never an accurate picture, but successive enlargements made it less accurate, as did the introduction of qualified majority voting (QMV) in the Council of Ministers in the SEA.

QMV changed the nature of the diplomatic game. Once a state did not have a veto, it had constantly to be thinking in terms of constructing coalitions with other states, not only to achieve majorities on issues that it favoured, but also to construct blocking minorities on issues that it did not want to see agreed. Such alliances were extremely fluid, changing from issue to issue; and the habit of coalition-building spread even into those areas that were not formally subject to QMV.

In this fluid diplomatic game it became increasingly difficult for the Franco-German axis to give a lead to the EC. Indeed, many of the other states resented the closeness of the links between France and Germany, and the way in which there was a joint Franco-German position paper presented to every European Council. This made it easier for Britain to enlist other states in support of British positions ahead of Maastricht.

Italian leaders, for example, thought of themselves as representing a big country, and reacted strongly to any slight on Italy's competence, as the British Government discovered to its cost in October 1990 when jibes about the competency of the Italian Presidency provoked the Italian Prime Minister to call a vote at the Rome European Council on setting a target date for movement to stage 2 of the Delors plan for monetary union. Despite this incident, Italy was only too happy to join Britain in presenting a joint paper on Common Foreign and Security Policy (CFSP) to the IGC on political union as a counter to the Franco-German paper. Italy was traditionally more Atlanticist than France, but also resented being left out. Admittedly this was the only example of Anglo-Italian collaboration in the Maastricht negotiations, but it was an important intervention in the debate, and showed the potential for alliances in the future.

Another potentially formidable ally for Britain was Spain. There was a considerable degree of respect for the professionalism and pragmatism of the Spanish administration among their British counterparts. If Spain and Britain could form an alliance, it would carry a great deal of weight. Unfortunately there were not many issues on which the Spanish Socialist government and the British Conservative Government did see eye-to-eye. A change of government in either country might have produced interesting results. Nevertheless, there was some cooperation behind the scenes during the negotiation of the TEU, no doubt assisted by the fact that the chief British negotiator was Tristan Garel-Jones, a well-known hispanophile.

So far as the smaller member states were concerned, there was a fund of goodwill among several of them towards the British government. One reason for this was the reaction in the past of the Foreign and Commonwealth Office (FCO) to requests for assistance. When small states held the presidency, they sometimes found it difficult to prepare briefing papers on all the issues that came onto the agenda. If a request for information did come through on the Coreu telex link, the FCO always responded promptly with a full briefing paper. This was done without condescension and without publicity.

So even before Maastricht the British were not without potential allies. These were not permanent alliances, but permanent alliances are the exception, not the rule in the EU. The Franco-German relationship, the Benelux relationship, and the close Benelux link with Germany are the exceptions. Otherwise the coalitions shift on different issues. During the 1991 IGCs, Britain was as centrally involved in the game of building coalitions on specific issues as any of the other member states. The success of this strategy can be seen in the terms of the TEU.

Although represented by Conservative Euro-sceptics as a great defeat for the British view of Europe, it is difficult to see the political union provisions of the TEU, the subject of review in the 1996 IGC, as anything other than a consider-able triumph for British diplomacy, and an indication that the British view was not as eccentric as the media wished to present it.

There were two elements of the TEU with which the British government was particularly pleased: the three-pillar structure of the EU which embodied inter-governmentalism in the areas of Common Foreign and Security Policy (CFSP) and Justice and Home Affairs (JHA); and the writing of subsidiarity into the Treaty as a justiciable concept, so new legislative proposals would have to meet the test of there being a need for action at EU-level. In addition, the extension of QMV was largely limited to areas where the government felt it was justified on subsidiarity grounds; and the increase in the powers of the EP was mostly limited to areas where the introduction of QMV indicated a weakening of the democra-tic control that could be exercised by national parliaments. (In two areas, the multi-annual R&D framework programmes and culture, unanimity was retained but the co-decision procedure still applies.)

Of course there were concessions to other viewpoints. That is the nature of diplomatic bargaining. A Committee of the Regions was created, although only as an advisory body. The role of the EP in most areas where QMV existed was strengthened beyond that agreed in the SEA. There was agreement to review the three-pillar structure in 1996. Overall, though, far from being 'a Treaty too far', as Thatcher insisted, the TEU was nearer to the retreat from federalism which Major presented it as being (*Hansard* 11 December 1991: cols. 859–62; ibid. 18 December 1991: cols. 275–86).

Given this starting point, it was understandable that in its approach to the 1996 IGC the British government intended to negotiate to preserve the TEU from amendments that would undermine its congruence with British objectives. As Douglas Hurd put it in a newspaper interview: 'We shall try to preserve the present architecture [of the EU] which actually suits us by and large.' (*Financial Times* 11–12 March 1995)

BRITISH OBJECTIVES IN THE 1996 IGC

From the outset it was clear that the 1996 agenda would largely be set by other actors. First, this was because of the position of Britain as a *status quo* state, its government being generally satisfied with the existing Treaty whatever Conservative backbenchers (and members of the House of Lords) might say about it. Second, given the delay in ratification, 1996 was seen as too early to have a review anyway, especially as three new member states had just joined in January 1995. Third, the British government felt there were more urgent issues that the EU ought to be addressing, particularly entrenching democracy in Central and Eastern Europe, and working out ways of increasing the competitiveness of the European economy. Finally, although not unimportantly, the extreme sensitivity of the EU in domestic politics, with a general election due in 1997 at the latest, made 1996 a very inconvenient time to be forced to negotiate Treaty changes.

As the EU was committed to holding an IGC, the British aim was to turn it so far as possible into a non-IGC, that is a conference that would not make far-reaching changes to the Treaties, and to use the occasion to anticipate the future shape of an EU enlarged even further to take in several states from Central and Eastern Europe.

It was not anticipated that monetary union would be discussed at the IGC, as there were no further Treaty changes that were needed: all the provisions necessary had been laid out in the TEU. The only possible changes would be to the target dates, or to the convergence criteria, but it was not the intention of the British government to raise either issue, and it did not expect others to do so.

It was also the view of the government that there would have to be discussions about reform of the budget, including the common agricultural policy and the structural funds, before enlargement negotiations could proceed. However, these were seen as matters to be discussed in parallel with the IGC, not as part of the IGC itself. They might affect the pattern of alliances around IGC issues, though, since the questions involved were of fundamental importance to both net recipient and net contributory states.

The main issues that were anticipated as forming the basis for negotiation in advance of the IGC were: the further extension of the competences of the EC; the three-pillar structure of the EU; defence cooperation; the operation and extent of QMV; and changes to the structure and powers of the central institutions.

Extension of the competences of the EC

In the view of the British government the TEU had made all the extensions to the competences of the EC that were necessary. There were three policy areas that had been considered at Maastricht for inclusion in the competences of the EC but left until the review: civil nuclear protection, energy policy, and tourism. There was certainly a case for the inclusion of energy in EC competences, and under other circumstances the British government might not have been unsympathetic; but given the extreme sensitivity of the issue of European integration in domestic politics, the Government's view was that the less change in the Treaty rules the better because the less ammunition there would be for the Euro-sceptics who wished to push for a referendum on the outcome of the IGC.

The three-pillar structure

At the pre-Maastricht IGC on political union the British government gave a high priority to heading off an attempt by the French and Germans to bring JHA and CFSP under the umbrella of the EC, and to introduce some degree of QMV in those areas. This was not too difficult, because the French government was less committed to it in practice than in rhetoric. It was Helmut Kohl who really wanted this, particularly with respect to the internal security issues that eventually formed the JHA pillar of the TEU.

The British view immediately after the signing of the TEU, with its provision for a review in 1996, was that they had five years in which to prove to the Germans that real progress could be made in these sectors on an intergovernmental basis. Because of the delay in ratification of the Treaty they only had two.

Making Maastricht work in these pillars was never going to be easy, and as the 1996 IGC approached it was clear that the Germans were dissatisfied with progress, and would be pressing for the absorption of the intergovernmental pillars into the EC pillar. The British position ahead of 1996 was that the protection of the three-pillar structure remained a fundamental objective, in line with the general British commitment to building a Europe of cooperating nation-states rather than transferring powers to a supranational super-state.

Defence cooperation

Defence remained a more difficult issue for the EU than the generality of CFSP because of the membership, after the 1995 enlargement, of four neutral states (Austria, Finland, Ireland, and Sweden). There remained also an underlying question about the role of the USA in the defence of Europe. The British view was set out in a paper presented to Foreign Ministers at a meeting in Carcassonne in March 1995. The paper opposed integrating the Western European Union (WEU) into the EU, arguing the advantages of having a forum in which the non-EU Nato members (Turkey, Iceland, and Norway) could participate as observers alongside the non-Nato members of the EU (Austria, Finland, Ireland, and Sweden). It proposed twice-yearly back-to-back summits of the EU and the WEU. The EU would be able to request action from the WEU in the areas of peace-keeping, crisis management, and assisting a regional ally against aggression (as in the Gulf). Nato would remain the vehicle for the defence of Europe itself, but the staffing of WEU would be strengthened, and in a crisis it would be able to use Nato infrastructure, such as communications systems and transport. This was consistent with the long-term British belief that Nato must form the basis for the defence of Europe.

Qualified majority voting

It is wrong to believe that the position of the British government prior to Maastricht was hostile to QMV *per se*. That may well have been Margaret Thatcher's position, but the general position was much more pragmatic. Where QMV could be seen to be needed, it should be adopted. This applied to the single market programme, where even Thatcher could see the logic, hence her signing of the SEA; but it also applied to those other areas that were brought under QMV in the TEU, such as environmental questions where the effects crossed national boundaries. However, the British government did not want to see any further extension of QMV in 1996. On the other hand, it did want to discuss whether the weighting of votes and the size of the blocking minority of votes should be changed, particularly with an eye on future enlargement.

This issue had already caused difficulties when the accession of Austria, Finland, Sweden, and (as it seemed at the time) Norway was under discussion in March 1994. Britain and Spain had argued that the size of the blocking minority that was needed to stop proposals under QMV should not be increased from the existing 23. The Commission had proposed that it be increased to 27, in proportion to the increase in the total votes post-enlargement. Britain and Spain pointed out that because votes were only very approximately proportionate to population size, this would mean that 41 per cent of the population of the EU could be outvoted on any particular issue.

The outcome in 1994 had been a compromise to lift the blocking minority (as it turned out to 26 because Norway did not agree to join) while accepting that if there were 23 votes against a measure it should be withdrawn for a period of reflection rather than pushed through. It was also agreed to consider the issue further at or before the 1996 IGC. It remained important to the British government not to allow the continued dilution of the ability of the larger member states to block legislation, and to get the issue settled before the next round of enlargement negotiations began so as to avoid being put in the position of having to threaten an enlargement that they wished to see in order to defend a principle that they did not wish to see go by default.

The European Parliament

The most ambitious of the EC institutions, the EP indicated in its own position papers for the IGC that it was looking for an extension of the Article 189b procedure, or co-decision. This legislative procedure, introduced in the TEU, gave the EP its strongest basis for forcing amendments to proposed legislation, and ultimately blocking any legislative instrument which did not take sufficient account of its views. It was, however, only one of four procedures applying to legislation, depending on the Articles of the Treaty under which it was introduced (Nugent 1994: 304–23). Ideally the EP wanted the procedure extending across the board of EC legislation. This also had the implication that QMV would be extended further, as the co-decision procedure was linked to the practice of QMV in the

Council of Ministers. Besides its opposition to the further extension of QMV, the British Government's position on this demand, ahead of the IGC, was that it was too soon to consider extension of a procedure that had not yet been adequately tested. The potential for institutional gridlock inherent in the procedure was a possible threat to the efficient working of the EC, which was a fundamental British commitment; and the whole issue of increasing the powers of the EP was likely to be highly controversial in domestic politics.

To counter the existence of a democratic deficit in EC decision-making, and in line with its stress on the importance of subsidiarity, the British alternative to increasing the legislative powers of the EP was to find ways to involve national parliaments more actively in the scrutiny of EC proposals. On the other hand, in line with the British emphasis on efficiency, the government was prepared to propose increases in the EP's role in detecting fraud against the EC budget and ensuring value for money.

It was also recognized in Whitehall that the size of the EP would have to be reconsidered, again with an eye on the situation following further enlargement. This was not a controversial issue, though; it was generally recognized in the EU that there would have to be some limit set, with seats being re-distributed when further enlargements took place, perhaps more in line with population size than previously (Cameron 1995: 6).

The Commission

Just as further enlargement would have implications for the size of the EP, it also raised questions about the size of the College of Commissioners. Already the 1995 enlargement had produced a situation where there were too many Commissioners (20) for them all to have significant portfolios. Clearly the size of the College of Commissioners could not simply be increased each time there was another member state, especially as in the British view there were unlikely to be commensurate increases in the competences of the Commission. The government had since 1986 supported the reduction in the number of Commissioners for the large states from two to one; but it also wished to explore the possibility of not every small state having a Commissioner in every Commission, and the establishment of a hierarchy of Commissioners along the lines of domestic Ministers and Junior Ministers.

The nomination of the President of the Commission had caused some discontent when the successor to Jacques Delors was being sought. Moves to involve the EP more at the nomination stage were very likely to emerge from other member states (Cameron 1995: 6). The British government, given the domestic sensitivity of the issue, could be expected to oppose such moves; however, given the British emphasis on ensuring that the populations of Europe were fully involved in developments in the EU, such opposition might put them in a difficult position.

111

The Council of Ministers

In addition to the question of QMV and the blocking minority, enlargement raised the issue of the rotating presidency of the Council. With fifteen member states it was already the case that the presidency would only be held by any one state once every seven and a half years. Further expansion would reduce the frequency further, making it more difficult to maintain continuity in policy, and meaning that by the time the presidency did come round, any lessons learned from the previous tenure would be less likely to be remembered. In response to this the British government favoured team presidencies, grouping one large and two smaller member states for a twelve-month period.

THE PROSPECTS FOR A SUCCESSFUL IGC FOR BRITAIN

It was still possible in the approach to the IGC to find media commentary which suggested that Britain's would be a lone voice arguing against a coherent block of federalists. Even the generally well-informed *Financial Times* managed to carry a piece beginning: 'The UK government now seems set on a collision course with its European partners over the future of the Union. The collision point will lie in the 1996 intergovernmental conference (IGC) that will revise the Maastricht Treaty' (Davidson 1995).

This view seriously underestimated the extent to which events in Europe had moved the debate in Britain's direction, even before Maastricht, but even more so after it.

The problems in getting the TEU ratified showed a deep disillusionment with the EC among the electorates of Europe. One hope of the British government ahead of the IGC was that nobody would want to risk another round of referendums to ratify Treaty changes, with the opportunity that would give for further expressions of discontent both with the EU and with national governments. This might lead to a conspiracy to keep changes to the absolute minimum.

Britain's own role in the ratification crisis had not helped its position with Germany. In particular, the German Chancellor did not understand why the British government withdrew the ratification bill from Parliament following the Danish referendum result that rejected the TEU. Also, the revelation that Major had only been able to obtain a majority on the vote in the Commons to re-introduce the bill by promising backbench rebels that final ratification would not take place until after the second Danish referendum, ran counter to everything that the government had been saying to its EC partners, and gave a signal of weakness (Ludlow 1993: 256).

Even more damaging to the Anglo-German relationship had been the acrimony surrounding the withdrawal of sterling from the exchange rate mechanism of the European Monetary System (EMS) in the autumn of 1992, which was accompanied by an unseemly public exchange with the *Bundesbank* over the level of support that the German monetary authorities had been prepared to give to the British currency.

However, against that Britain and Germany had been on the same side in the internal EU dispute about the GATT agreement, a prime example of Britain encouraging the working of the Franco-German special relationship to achieve its own aim of persuading France to accept the deal. Britain and Germany were also allies in pressing for enlargement to the East, and on a range of other issues. As Douglas Hurd expressed it in a speech in Berlin: 'Britain and Germany have set much of the agenda for Europe in the last decade: budgetary discipline, sub-sidiarity, deregulation, tackling fraud, promoting free trade in the GATT' (Hurd 1995: 8).

Relations with France had also developed. On defence, Britain and France had moved much closer to a common position as a result of their joint involvement in Bosnia, which had led to the setting up of a joint air command; and the studied silence of the British government amidst the outburst of international protests about French nuclear tests in the Pacific had sent a message of solidarity to President Chirac. There was no real dissent on the defence and security propos-als in the British paper presented at Carcassonne, and with the two main military powers in the EU backing the proposals it seemed unlikely that they would not be accepted at the IGC.

In terms of its relations with the smaller states, the reaction of the British gov-ernment to the Danish referendum result was deeply appreciated, and not only in Copenhagen. The small states felt that they were in danger of being relegated to a minor role in the post-Maastricht EU, and the suggestion by both the French and German governments that the Danish referendum result was unimportant because it was only little Denmark and not an important member state went down very badly. Although Britain would inevitably be in the position of sup-porting any moves at the IGC to make the balance of the institutions reflect more accurately the balance of population in the EU, it was starting from a point of goodwill on the part of the smaller states, and might therefore be in a position to play a central role in the negotiations around this sensitive issue.

Relations with Spain were not quite so good following the resignation from his ministerial post of Garel-Jones, and they had been soured by disputes over fishing. Yet there was some goodwill among Spain's political leaders as a result of John Major's handling of the issue of the structural funds at the Edinburgh European Council in December 1992. Although representing a net contributor state, Major had brokered an agreement that the Spanish government could accept as fair. Clearly Spain could not be expected to be delighted at the prospect of further enlargement reducing its own share of the structural funds, but again the British were in a good position to broker an agreement. Within the IGC itself, the agree-ment of Spain and Britain on the issue of re-calibrating votes under QMV has already been noted. Essentially Spain had proved itself to be a pragmatic actor within the EU, defending national interests which in some respects were similar to those of Britain.

Against these positive factors, the British government recognized the determi-nation of the German Chancellor to press ahead with integration in an attempt to tie down his own country. Helmut Kohl had guaranteed his place in the history books when he presided over the reunification of Germany. He did not want those books to portray him as a Frankenstein who re-created a nationalistic German monster. However, the strength of the forces favouring a centralizing view of federalism had been considerably weakened.

The collapse of the Italian Christian Democratic and Socialist Parties meant the Italian vote for closer integration was no longer guaranteed. The election of Jacques Chirac to succeed Francois Mitterrand as President of France in May 1995 replaced a convert to European integration with someone more pragmatic, and even sceptical about the process. Enlargement to bring into membership Austria, Sweden and Finland certainly did not strengthen the federalist tendencies; although these states could not be expected to see eye-to-eye with the British Conservative government on all issues, especially social policy, they were not expected to be keen to surrender more sovereignty so soon after joining.

In the Commission also there had been changes that had strengthened the British view of where the EU should be going. The shock of the unpopularity of the TEU had led national politicians to turn their fire on the Commission, whose President Jacques Delors had played a high-profile role in the run-up to the ratification debacle. Even Helmut Kohl, the most pro-federalist of the national leaders, told the press that the Commission was 'too powerful, constantly expanding, and exterminating national identities' (*Financial Times* 22 September 1992). The effect of Maastricht on the self-confidence of the Commission should not be underestimated. The new President, Jacques Santer, declared that the Commission was not seeking any further extension of its competences in the 1996 IGC, but was intent on improving the efficiency of the EU. In a speech to the Confederation of British Industry (CBI) he stressed, as he had elsewhere, the need for the Commission to do less, but to do it better, and the importance of respecting subsidiarity (Santer 1995). Santer's words could have come from the mouth of Douglas Hurd, and indeed had done on a number of occasions.

So the British government approached the 1996 IGC with a reasonable prospect of being able to pursue successfully its objectives. However, there were problems facing it because of its difficult domestic political situation. With a slender majority in the House of Commons, John Major faced a rebellion from backbench members on the precise issue of membership of the EU. The so-called Euro-sceptics were so hostile to any concessions in the negotiations that there was no chance of the government pleasing them. Indeed, even complete success in defending the TEU would not have pleased them because they had convinced themselves that the TEU itself was a dangerously federalist Treaty.

The domestic problems of the government raised the distinct possibility that the IGC might be completed by a Labour government. There was much sympathy in other European capitals for the idea that the proceedings should be dragged out beyond the British General Election, because nobody really wanted to see the election fought on a European agenda which might push the Conservatives into adopting an even more intransigent attitude. There might even have been the hope in some quarters that a Labour government would adopt a different and more *communautaire* line.

What would change under a Labour government?

Labour had certainly tried to suggest that it was more favourable to the EU than the Conservatives, but on both the broad objectives and the specifics of policy it was difficult to detect any fundamental difference. On most of the objectives out-lined earlier, there was nothing in Labour's position to suggest that they would pursue a very different path from the Conservatives.

On the broad objectives of policy, Tony Blair outlined six priorities in a speech in Bonn on 30 May 1995:

- to make the case for Europe from first principles, not taking public opinion for granted;
- to address the issue of enlargement to the East and how it is facilitated;
- to take on the agenda of reform of the EU, defending what should be defended and changing what should not;
- to make the European Union more democratic and open;
- to take steps towards building a stronger European foreign and defence policy in harmony with the Atlantic Alliance;
- to ensure that the EU remains against protectionism and opens up its markets and becomes a stronger voice for free trade in the world (Blair 1995: 3–4).

This list differs in some respects from those provided by Thatcher and Major, especially in the emphasis placed on a more democratic and open Europe. However, in other respects it is remarkably similar, especially in the stress on the need for an EU that is a force for free trade.

The similarities came out even more markedly in a speech to a conference on 'Britain and Europe 1996' in which the Shadow Foreign Secretary, Robin Cook, set out what Labour's approach to the IGC would be (Cook 1995). The basic principles were:

- that European Union must be based on a sharing of national interests and not on the surrender of national identity;
- that the CFSP should not be merged 'into the bureaucratic machinery of Brussels', but that the existing intergovernmental arrangements should be maintained;
- that greater democracy should be achieved by the EP working more closely with national parliaments, with national parliaments having more influence over the Council of Ministers and the EP having wider scrutiny over the Commission;
- that the national veto should be retained over matters of vital national interest, and for important decisions on the budget or revision of the treaties, but that it should be used sparingly;
- that the CAP should be reformed;

- that the creation of jobs should be at the top of the European agenda.

On these issues, some of which went beyond the IGC's agenda, there was no discernible difference between the Government and the Opposition. In one area, though, there was a clear difference. Labour was committed to ending the British opt-out from the Social Protocol of the TEU. This would mean that the Protocol could be restored to the body of the Treaty as a Social Chapter (which it had been in the first place).

The other difference came back to the matter of the tone in which the negotiations would be conducted. A Labour government would be able to negotiate free of the extremely unhelpful 'voices off' that bedeviled the EU diplomacy of the Major Government during 1994–95. Even if there were doubters on the Labour backbenches, they would be unlikely to cause trouble for their Prime Minister so soon after attaining office again for the first time in over sixteen years.

CONCLUSION

British policy in the EC-EU has shown a remarkable consistency in its objectives over a considerable period of time. The idea that this position is out of line with the rest of the EU is simply incorrect. Even before Maastricht, Britain was centrally involved in all the debates about the future of the EU, and had allies on particular issues. This showed in the outcome of the negotiations: the TEU was much more in line with British policy than with the federalist aspirations of Jacques Delors or Helmut Kohl.

These same consistent objectives informed the British approach to the 1996 IGC. It was an IGC that the British government believed to be unnecessary and even a distraction from the really pressing business facing the EU in 1996. However, given that there had to be an IGC, the British position was well prepared. In particular, the British paper on defence cooperation, presented to Foreign Ministers in advance even of the meetings of the preparatory group for the IGC, showed real thought about how to address the problem in a way likely to attract support from other member states, particularly from France, the other major player in this policy area.

What apparently threatened to damage British credibility in the negotiations more than any other factor were domestic political constraints. The demands of the Conservative backbench Euro-sceptics were pushing the Prime Minister into adopting an uncompromising tone that increasingly resembled that of his predecessor before the opening of the 1991 IGCs. As Lord Howe put it:

A new language of semi-detachment is being created. The world outside Britain is being recast in the hope of making political life at home easier to manage. The UK's capacity to define, articulate and pursue credible, coherent interests at the European negotiating table risks being cast away. (Howe 1995: 16)

From this point of view an objective observer might have come to the conclusion that British interests could be better served under a Labour government which would be likely to follow the same agenda, with the important exception of social policy, but which would be less constrained in pursuit of a satisfactory outcome by domestic interference with the necessary diplomacy. However, despite the consensus in the pro-European press that Britain's credibility was being undermined by the demands of domestic party management, there had to be a suspicion that it might be convenient for some other member states to pedal this line in advance of the negotiations, for the Labour Party to pedal it for domestic political reasons, and for dissident Conservative pro-Europeans to reinforce it for reasons of internal party politics. Not for the first time the press might have been rather gullible on Britain and Europe.

REFERENCES AND BIBLIOGRAPHY

Blair, T. (1995) *Britain in Europe: An Agenda for Reform*, speech by the Rt Hon Tony Blair MP, Leader of the Labour Party, to the Friedrich-Ebert Stiftung, Bonn, 30 May (press release, British Embassy, Bonn).

Buller, J. (1995) 'Britain as an awkward partner: reassessing Britain's relations with the EU,' *Politics: Surveys and Debates for Students of Politics*, vol. 15, pp. 33–42.

Butt Philip, A. (1992) 'British pressure groups and the European Community', in George (1992), op. cit., pp. 149–71.

Cameron, F. (1995) *The 1996 IGC: A Challenge for Europe*, paper presented to the Fourth Biennial Conference of the European Community Studies Association (USA) in Charleston, South Carolina, 12 May.

Cook, R. (1995) Speech to conference on 'Britain and Europe 1996' News Release, 30 January (London, Labour Party Campaigns and Communications Directorate).

Currid, N. (1995) 'Explaining "anti-EC" nationalism in Britain', paper presented to the UACES Research Conference, Birmingham, 18–19 September (available from UACES Secretariat, King's College, London, WC2R 2LS).

Davidson, I. (1995) 'Weak kind of wooing: British hopes of a special partnership with the French are doomed', *Financial Times* 18 January, p. 20.

Garel-Jones, T. (1993) 'The UK Presidency: an inside view', *Journal of Common Market Studies*, vol. 31, pp. 261–7.

George, S. (1989) 'Nationalism, liberalism and the national interest: Britain, France, and the European Community', *Strathclyde Papers on Government and Politics*. Glasgow, Department of Government, University of Strathclyde.

— (1992) *Britain and the European Community: The Politics of Semi-Detachment*. Oxford, Clarendon Press.

— (1994) *An Awkward Partner: Britain in the European Community*, 2nd edition. Oxford, Oxford University Press.

— (1995) 'Britain and the European Union after Maastricht', in Furlong, P. and Cox A. (eds) *The European Union at the Crossroads: Problems in Implementing the Single Market Project*. Boston, Lincs., Earlsgate Press.

HMSO (1991) *Developments in the European Community, July – December 1990*. (Cmnd 1457) February.

Holmes, M. (1991) 'Mrs Thatcher, Labour and the EEC', *The Bruges Group Occasional Paper 12*, London, Bruges Group.

Howe, G. (1995) 'A better European policy for Britain', *Financial Times* 30 January, p.16.

Hurd, D. (1995) *The Future in Europe*, speech to the German Society for Foreign Affairs, Berlin, 28 February. Verbatim Service VS07/95 (London, Foreign and Commonwealth Office).

Ludlow, P. (1993) 'The UK Presidency: a view from Brussels', *Journal of Common Market Studies*, vol. 31, pp. 246–60.

Major, J. (1993) 'Raise your eyes, there is a land beyond', *Economist*, 25 September, pp. 23–7.

Moravcsik, A. (1991) 'Negotiating the Single European Act: national interests and conventional statecraft in the European Community', *International Organization*, vol. 45, pp. 19–56.

Nugent, N. (1992) 'British Public Opinion and the European Community', in George (1992), op. cit., pp.172–201.

—— (1994) *The Government and Politics of the European Union*. London; Macmillan.

Santer, J. (1995) Speech to the Confederation of British Industry (untitled), 16 May, Ref. SPEECH/95/99 (Brussels, European Commission).

Seyd, P. and Whiteley, P. (1992) *Labour's Grass Roots: The Politics of Party Membership*. Oxford, Clarendon Press.

Seyd, P., Whiteley, P. and Richardson, J. (1994) *True Blues: The Politics of Conservative Party Membership*. Oxford, Clarendon Press.

Shonfield, A (1973) *Europe: Journey to an Unknown Destination*. Harmondsworth; Penguin Books.

Thatcher, M. (1988) Britain and Europe: Text of the speech delivered in Bruges by the Prime Minister on 20 September 1988, London, Conservative Political Centre.

7

THE POSITION OF THE BENELUX COUNTRIES

ALFRED PIJPERS AND SOPHIE VANHOONACKER

INTRODUCTION

Among the smaller member states, the Benelux countries have always occupied a rather privileged position in the EU. They were co-founders of the Communities, and their own integration schemes (BLEU since 1921; customs union since 1948; Benelux Economic Union since 1958) stood partly as a model for the development of the common and internal market. A Benelux Memorandum (based on the Beyen Plan) paved the way for the *rélance* of Messina (which might have been worth a pilgrimage by the Reflection Group in June 1995), and the history of European integration is littered with the reports of personalities like Spaak, Mansholt, Werner, or Tindemans.

Comparatively speaking the three countries (Belgium and Luxembourg in particular) are well represented in the EU institutions, which, with only a few exceptions, have their seat in Brussels or Luxembourg. A large number of the EU-officials have Belgian nationality. Though the Benelux countries represent only 7 per cent of the total population of the EU, they dispose of 14 per cent of the votes in the Council; 15 per cent of the Members of the Commission (now again with a Luxembourg President, rather soon after Gaston Thorn who held the office 1981–85); and they provide 10 per cent of the MEPs. Because of its prominent share in, and virtual blending with, the EU institutions, its mediating role in times of conflict, and to its limited national profile, Luxembourg appears sometimes to act almost as an EU institution in its own right.

It remains uncertain whether all three countries will be promoted to the third stage of EMU (the large national debt of Belgium in particular may be an obstacle), but it seems not unlikely that this will occur. Certainly, in the various concepts of differentiated integration which have been floated since the summer of 1994, the Benelux countries have been considered as part of the 'core group', either in the sense of the Lamers–Schäuble paper (CDU–CSU 1994), or in the looser sense of Balladur's concentric circles (*Le Monde* 30 November 1994). Belgium and the Netherlands are considerable trading nations in comparative terms, and the Benelux is, after the USA, Germany and Japan the largest trading bloc (import plus export figures combined) in the world. In itself, then, the signs bode well for a continuous comfortable position of the 'Little Three' in the heart of the

European Union.

Yet, the European revolutions of 1989–90 have not left this position unaffected. The collapse of the Soviet Union, German unification, and the enlargement of the EU have done much to divert some of the traditional foreign policy objectives of the Low Countries. Internal developments, such as the completion of the internal market, and the federalization of Belgium (and of Belgian foreign relations) have added to this pattern. The Benelux Economic Union has lost much of its economic functions since the realization of '1992' and the Treaty of Maastricht. Its pioneering role is largely over. The political weight of the three is obviously diminishing further in a Union with fifteen or twenty members (of whom many belong to the same class of smaller states). It may be true that, in the present EU, the institutional share of the Benelux is still comparatively large, but this share has steadily declined with each successive round of enlargement. In the 1960s, the combined voting weight of the three in the Council added up to about 25 per cent of the total number of votes. Today this figure has dropped to less than 14 per cent. What, then, is the position of the Low Countries in the present EU? What are their convergent or divergent interests in the 1996 process, and in which ways is the Benelux as such still figuring in the EU and its reforms?

BELGIUM AND EUROPEAN INTEGRATION

Being one of the founder members of the European Communities, Belgium's position with respect to European integration has been characterized by a high level of continuity. As a small country which is highly dependent on exports, it had everything to gain from closer political and economic cooperation with its neighbours and the establishment of a framework for closer European cooperation.

Throughout the post-war period, European integration has been the cornerstone of Belgium's foreign policy and, on several occasions, the country has been a driving force in this process (Coolsaet 1987; Dumoulin 1987; van Meerhaeghe 1992). As chairman of the expert committee in charge of drafting the Treaties of Rome, the Belgian Minister of Foreign Affairs, Paul-Henri Spaak, played an active role in the creation of the European Economic Community (EEC) and Euratom. Belgium's blueprint for integration has always been that of a federal Europe and, in the early 1960s, the government did not hesitate to support the Dutch veto against the French proposals for political union. It was argued that the intergovernmental character of the Fouchet proposals endangered the supranational character of the EC and was to the detriment of the small member states. In the 1970s, the Belgian Prime Minister, Leo Tindemans, attempted to give new impetus to the stagnant process of European integration by elaborating a report which outlined the necessary steps to be taken to establish a fully fledged EU (Tindemans 1976). Many European governments considered Tindemans' proposals to establish an Economic and Monetary Union (EMU) and to develop a common foreign and security policy far too ambitious and the report was not given any concrete follow-up.

Belgium does not want the EC to become an exclusive club but, at the same time, considers it imperative that any new accessions be counterbalanced by a deepening of European integration. By defending a maximalist approach during the Intergovernmental Conferences leading to the adoption of the Single European Act (SEA) and the Treaty on European Union (TEU), Belgium tried to realize this objective of further strengthening the European Communities.

In general, the Euro-enthusiasm of the governing élite is shared by the population. If one considers the process of national and European federalization as two complementary developments, Belgians usually have little difficulty in accepting the transfer of sovereignty to either the regional or the supranational level. However, this support is not reflected in the form of an intense popular debate. Even the ratification of the TEU, containing provisions on the creation of an EMU and the development of a Common Foreign and Security Policy (CFSP) did not elicit a major discussion (Vanhoonacker 1994). It is interesting to note that, in the debate preceding the national elections of May 1995, the issues of 'Europe' and the 1996 Intergovernmental Conference (IGC) were largely absent. The campaign was dominated by domestic problems such as unemployment and the future of the Belgian social security system (Eppink 1995). According to an opinion poll by Europinion, prior to the inaugural session of the Reflection Group in June 1995, only 16 per cent of Belgians were aware of the IGC (*De Standaard* 3–5 June 1995). The first policy note of the Belgian government on the 1996 IGC (July 1995) received hardly any attention in the press, let alone stirred Belgian public opinion (Keukeleire 1995).

A slow start to preparations

Contrary to the 1991 Intergovernmental Conference on Political Union, for whose agenda Belgium was one of the first countries to put forward concrete proposals (*Europe Documents* 29 March 1990), the debate on the 1996 IGC was slow to get under way. The political agenda of the first half of 1994 was entirely dominated by the national elections of 21 May. Given that it was far from certain whether the electorate would endorse a continuation of the coalition between the Christian Democrats and the Socialists,[1] it is understandable that the question of the 1996 IGC had to take a back seat.

In the first half of 1995, the Belgian Prime Minister, Jean-Luc Dehaene (of the Flemish Christian Democrat party), who continued to lead the government after the May elections, gave a number of speeches, in which he gave some first indications with regard to the emerging Belgian position. By the summer of 1995, the Government had further elaborated these ideas in a special IGC policy note (Belgian Government 28 July 1995), which was to be the basis for further discussion with the country's federal entities, the Regions and Communities.[2] On the basis of their comments, a new position paper was drafted which was then submitted for discussion to the national parliament.

The increased involvement of the Communities and the Regions in the definition of the Belgian position towards the 1996 IGC was the result of two parallel developments whereby the position of Belgium's federated entities has considerably been strengthened both *vis-à-vis* the national as well as the European level. Since the summer of 1993, Belgium has become a fully-fledged federal state and foreign policy, including Belgium's policy towards the EU, is no longer a purely exclusive federal competence. When today the federal government wants to conclude a treaty which also impinges upon the competencies attributed to the federated level, it has to define its position in close consultation with the Communities and the Regions. The body in charge of coordinating the positions of the different players is the Interministerial Conference on Foreign Policy. Once the treaty has been concluded, the provisions related to competencies falling under the responsibility of the Regions and Communities require ratification by their respective Councils.

At the same time, a reinforcement of the role of regional entities at the European level has also taken place. Through the adoption of non-binding opinions on draft proposals for European legislation, the newly created body of the Committee of the Regions (Article 198, TEU) can make regional and local voices heard in the European decision-making process for the first time.[3] Another important novelty introduced by Maastricht is the possibility for members of the federal entities capable of committing their national government to participate directly in EU Council meetings (Article 146, TEU). Belgium, which together with Germany had played an important role in achieving the amendment in question, decided to make use of this new possibility and, in Council meetings related to areas where the three Communities or Regions are exclusively or predominantly competent, it is a representative of a federated entity which represents Belgium, participation of the three being organized on a rotational basis (*Moniteur Belge/Belgisch Staatsblad* 17 November 1994: 28209–25).

Priorities for Belgium

In its policy note on the 1996 IGC to the parliament, the Belgian government left no doubt that the long-term objective of the European integration process should be the development of an EU on a federal basis (Belgian government 13 October 1995). The Community method whereby the European Commission has the exclusive right of initiative and the Council decides by qualified majority voting (QMV) continued to be seen as providing the best guarantee to realize this final goal. For the Belgian government, one of the major challenges of the 1996 IGC has been to prevent further enlargement towards the east and the south neither dilutes the European integration process nor reduces the EU to a mere free-trade area (Derycke 1995). Its position has been that it is only by ensuring that the next enlargement is preceded by the further internal strengthening and deepening of the EU that such scenarios can be avoided. The key, according to the Belgian Prime Minister, Jean-Luc Dehaene, to realizing this objective of deepening the Union is the further development of a Political Union, which must provide the political framework for EMU (Dehaene 21 February 1995). Although EMU might not constitute the final phase, it is seen as the element which will transform

European integration into an irreversible process.[4] The fulfilment of the convergence criteria as laid down in the TEU has been the Belgian government's foremost priority and, although the country has been undergoing some serious problems relating to the criterion of government public debt[5], it is radical in its rejection of any proposal suggesting the relaxation of these criteria.

An EU of more than twenty member states will require the substantial transformation and simplification of the decision-making process. Belgium has favoured the further extension of the use of QMV, including its use in the second and the third pillars (though the Flemish government, while supporting this position, has insisted on maintaining unanimity for decisions related to European citizenship and cultural policy). The co-decision procedure, which has led to a considerable increase in the European Parliament's (EP) role in the legislative process, should become the general rule, but should be simplified considerably (Dehaene 29 March 1995). Being a small country, Belgium has supported the case for safeguarding the European Commission's strong role (Dehaene 13 January 1995). The Commission, as a collegial and independent body designed to represent Community interests, is seen as the best guarantee against the larger member states dominating the Union.

The concept of deepening as advocated by the Belgian government implies, in the first place, the further strengthening of some Community policies. Belgium has favoured increased integration within the fields of social and environmental policy as well as within the area of taxation (Dehaene 22 March 1995). Its position has been that the continuation of incongruous regulations within these areas will lead to unfair competition and will seriously hamper the functioning of the internal market. Belgium has therefore been extremely critical of the British optout on social policy and considers that similar constructions should definitely be avoided in the future. Another example of incongruous rules leading to unfair competition within the EU is within the area of fiscal policy. As a result of the absence of a minimum Community levy on revenues from financial investments, Belgium has suffered from serious flights of capital to neighbouring countries. Even though Belgium has endorsed reinforced Community action within a certain number of areas, it has also warned against over-regulation and has encouraged the Community bodies to weigh very carefully any new initiatives which are opposed to the principle of subsidiarity.

Throughout the history of European integration, Belgium has always been a fierce advocate of increased foreign-policy integration among the EC member states. At the same time, however, it has never been satisfied with the purely intergovernmental organization of European Political Cooperation (EPC) and, together with The Netherlands, it was dismayed by the fact that the provisions on Common Foreign and Security Policy (CFSP) as agreed in Maastricht were not incorporated into the Community pillar. In their initial evaluation of the CFSP, Dehaene and the Belgian government pointed to its unsatisfactory results and have continued to plead the case for a strengthened role of the European Commission in the field of CFSP, as well as for the increased use of QMV (Belgian government 13 October 1995: 2). To reinforce the Commission's role in the

CFSP, it was suggested that it should be provided with a European analysis and evaluation capability or what Dehaene referred to as a *'centre d'impulsion'* – a suggestion that echoed the proposals of the High-level Group of Experts in their report of December 1994 (*European Security Policy Towards 2000* 1994: 8). In addition, the possibility of strengthening the role of the Presidency and the Council Secretariat, with the latter perhaps being led by a political personality, who could also possess the right of initiative, have also been considered. In order to address the problem of the democratic deficit within the field of foreign policy, the government has proposed that the EP should be consulted on important foreign policy choices and that the EP be entrusted with the annual adoption of the CFSP budget.

On the highly sensitive area of defence, Belgium has pleaded the case for continuing along the path chosen at Maastricht. While, the long-term objective is to realize a merger between the EU and the Western European Union (WEU), in the short-term both fora should intensify their cooperation. More concretely, a proposal was put forward for the CFSP unit of the Council Secretariat and the WEU Secretariat to intensify their cooperation and for the WEU Secretary-General to be provided with the opportunity to participate in CFSP discussions. The WEU should become involved in joint actions by the Union, and Community financing of WEU operations decided upon by the Fifteen should be considered (Dehaene 22 March 1995).

Ultimately, the deepening of European integration should also include the further strengthening of cooperation within the field of Justice and Home Affairs (JHA). Third pillar issues related to the free movement of persons and goods such as asylum policy, customs cooperation and fight against drugs should be transferred to the Community pillar (Belgian government 13 October 1995). As within the second pillar, the Belgian government has been in favour of going beyond intergovernmental cooperation to increase the role of the European Commission. It has been suggested that one or two Commissioners in charge of JHA should be appointed (Dehaene 22 March 1995).

One of the major repercussions of an enlarged EU will be its increasingly diverse membership. Although it has not abandoned its federalist ideals, Belgium is realistic enough to recognize the fact that it will be extremely difficult to maintain the European momentum and that there is a risk that what has been achieved to date might start to crumble. In order to cope with these challenging new realities, Belgium is ready to accept what Dehaene has referred to as 'a strategy of differentiation', allowing some member states to move towards the commonly defined goals of European integration at a slower pace (Dehaene 21 February 1995). However, the Belgian government has strongly rejected the development of a Europe à la carte, according to which each member state may choose from the menu those policy fields most suitable to its needs. Even the differentiation method or what in Euro-jargon is known as the 'multi-speed Europe' can only be a last-resort solution and is regarded as the exception rather than the rule. It has therefore been proposed that any demand for a differentiated approach be submitted to the European Commission and be decided upon by the member states by qualified majority. Nevertheless, for this model to be functional, it is absolutely necessary for a 'hard core' of countries to participate in all aspects of the European integration process. Belgium has left no doubt as to the fact that it sees itself as one of the key participants within this core (Dehaene 26 October 1994).

In general, Belgium's Communities and the Regions could have identified themselves fairly easily with the position of the federal government as presented in its policy note of July 1995.[6] With regard to three issues, however, they asked the federal government to adopt a more specific and outspoken posture. In the first place, the federated entities pleaded for the upgrading of the Committee of the Regions to the status of a fully-fledged institution and for the extension of the obligatory consultation of the Committee to areas such as the environment, country and urban planning and vocational training.[7] Furthermore, they advocated giving the Committee of the Regions the right to introduce cases before the European Court of Justice (ECJ) when, for example, there had been an infringement of the principle of subsidiarity.

Although the Communities and the Regions agree that the introduction of the principle of subsidiarity has been one of the major achievements of Maastricht, they consider that its definition as laid down in the Treaty needs some further elaboration and improvement, including a specific reference to the role of the regions. Furthermore, the Flemish Community has also pleaded for a clear delimitation of the competencies belonging to the European, the national and the regional level and for the introduction into the Treaty of a list summing up EU competencies.

A final very sensitive issue, especially for the Flemish Community, has been the question of the official languages within the EU. The government of the Flemish Community has defended the principle that every citizen should be able to address the EU institutions in his/her own language and, furthermore, that it should be possible for representatives of citizens within the EP and other bodies, such as the Economic and Social Committee and the Committee of the Regions, to speak and to work in their own language.

In conclusion, it can be said that the Belgian stance with respect to the IGC has been very much in line with the position which the country has traditionally defended *vis-à-vis* European integration. Many of the proposals put forward for the IGC, such as the extension of QMV, the application of the Community method within the field of foreign policy, a reduction in the democratic deficit by increasing the role of the EP, and the extension of the Community's social dimension, had already been put forward in the Belgian memorandum of 1990 outlining the country's position during the 1991 IGC (de Wilde d'Estmael and Franck 1993; Vanhoonacker 1992). In view of the controversy raised by Maastricht, the Belgian government realized that the time was not ripe to put forward very ambitious blueprints for European integration. It therefore adopted a pragmatic approach, consolidating what has already been achieved and gradually building on the *acquis communautaire*; as Dehaene put it: `*Sur le plan interne comme sur le plan européen, mes compatriotes sont foncièrement pragmatiques et cela nous porte à favoriser les procédures qui donnent des résultats*' (Dehaene 26 October 1994). Contrary to Messina

1955, where Belgium and its Minister for Foreign Affairs, Paul-Henri Spaak, were one of the main locomotives behind the following phase of European integration, it seems that, by Messina 1995, prudence and pragmatism had become the Belgian government's two major guiding principles.

THE NETHERLANDS

The Dutch attitude on European integration has gone through a number of significant changes over the past five years, though the basics still bear the imprint of the previous periods. As ever, priority is given to the preservation of the Community legal order, and to the further development of the internal market and of the *acquis communautaire*. Strong support for the Community method, an open window to enlargement, and a permanent watch on the manoeuvres of the larger member states, still determine much of the Dutch EU position.

Changes in the Dutch EU approach

The transformation of the European international system after the fall of the Berlin Wall, with all its profound consequences for the internal and external affairs of the EU, however, did not fail to affect Dutch integration policies. The upheaval partly reinforced some of the traditional federal elements, but it also added new features to the Dutch EU-position. These more recent developments may be summarized as follows:

1. While in the first decades of its existence the European Community was just one sector of Dutch foreign policy (though a very important one), it developed over the years to become the main framework for nearly all Dutch external relations, as well as for considerable parts of its domestic politics. The three pillars of the EU leave hardly an area of national policy untouched. Most aspects of the Dutch external relations are now to a large extent conceived and implemented through the widening EU-CFSP-prism. And, though the nature of EU policies and their degree of domestic penetration can vary considerably, the whole European complex has more or less reshaped The Netherlands from a country with active sectoral EC policies like trade or agriculture, into a part of a federalizing system.

2. Because of the steady involvement of so many departments, subnational authorities, regions, and interest groups in the European political process, Dutch views on European integration have become more heterogeneous. Other domestic voices make themselves heard in Brussels alongside traditional departments and lobbies, sometimes in open conflict with the 'federal' orthodoxy of the Foreign Ministry. The Ministry of Social Affairs, Home Affairs, or Justice, for instance, prefer intergovernmental forms of cooperation in their field, with the fall-back position of a veto, rather than using the full Community method (van Schendelen 1995: 64). The Prime Minister, as well, sees the role of intergovernmentalism in and around the European Council in a more favourable light than

does the Foreign Ministry.

3. The decline of the federal orthodoxy is partly related to the fact that, since the early 1990s, The Netherlands has turned from being a net recipient of Community funds into a net payer. From 1970 until 1991 the Dutch received on average 2 billion guilder (about 1 billion ecu) each year (apart, that is, from the overall benefits of the common market). Beginning with the implementation of the Delors I package, this has changed. Under the Delors II package and the McSharry reforms, The Hague, in 1994 and 1995, was paying a net contribution of about 4 billion guilder (2 billion ecu) annually, a sum likely to rise to 3 billion ecu in 1999. Both as a percentage of GNP, as well as in per capita terms, the Dutch now belong to the foremost net payers in the EU.

This development has caused the Ministry of Finance to complain, not only about the size of the contribution, but also about the ways in which money is spent in Brussels. An in-depth review of the cohesion policies and of the way the structural funds are operating has been called for, in terms akin to the principle of *juste retour*, which the Dutch government so fiercely rejected in the 1970s.

4. These changing attitudes have been reflected in party politics and public (or at least élite) opinion. The media coverage of internal and external EU affairs since Maastricht has been much more salient than before. By and large, the broad consensus on European integration among the foreign policy élite, and within (and between) the principal political parties, seems to have shrunk. Or rather, while the broad consensus over the *acquis communautaire* and the necessity of preserving it still exists, the more ambitious objectives as well as the implications of the EU have encountered criticism and sometimes even rejection. Frits Bolkestein, the leader of the Liberal Party, for instance, openly cast doubt on any further political aspirations beyond Maastricht, and can only reluctantly accept EMU. His views are in some respects close to those of the Euro sceptics in the British Conservative Party. Though his ideas may not be representative of the Liberal Party as a whole, the fact that the leader of a main coalition party (and with Michiel Patijn, the Liberal State Secretary for European Affairs as the Dutch representative in the IGC), openly questioned some of the federal objectives of European integration, is in itself a novel feature in the Dutch EU approach. The other major parties (Christian Democrats, Social Democrats, and Liberal Democrats) remain more within the confines of traditional pro-Europeanism. Yet, even here, dissident voices have been heard, in particular among the Social Democrats. At the same time, discussions on the 'national interest' or 'national identity' have become fashionable themes among Dutch intellectuals. Since the Danish and French referendums in the wake of the Maastricht Treaty, calls for a Dutch referendum can be heard to ratify Maastricht II.

The opinion of the wider public remains uncertain. Eurobarometer polls give a consistent pattern of pro-Europeanism among the population (with only a slightly downward tendency in recent years), but active support for the EU or its institutions has become less visible, at least as suggested in the steady decline in voter turn-out for EP elections. In 1979, the percentage of voters was 57.8 per cent, in 1984 50.6 per cent, in 1989 47.2 per cent. In 1994, the figure dropped to

35.6 per cent, the lowest of all member states. It was a remarkable record for a country which still counts as one of the champions for a stronger position of the EP. Though, as yet, no satisfactory explanation has been given for this diminishing popularity of the EU institutions, the government can no longer be as certain of automatic domestic and parliamentary support for treaty reforms as it was in the pre-Maastricht period.

Hence we meet the paradox that while the EU is becoming more federal in several respects (EMU, subsidiarity, citizenship, the idea of a common defence, or increasing administrative interdependence), Dutch perspectives, as reflected in government departments, political parties, and public opinion, are less so. Dutch 'supranationalism' in the early EC years was, essentially, confined to the Community method, and not necessarily to radical ideas of political union. It seems that the Dutch were only in favour of a 'European Union' only so long as the concept remained vague and ill-defined.

5. A fifth cluster of differences from earlier periods in Dutch integration policy relate to the metamorphosis of the East–West order and to German reunification. These processes have redirected the course of Dutch foreign policy in several respects. Dutch relations with Washington or London, for instance, are now conducted in a different way from, say, the early 1960s, when the UK still was considered as an essential link in the Atlantic security chain, and a useful counterweight to Franco-German bilateralism. Then, a close relationship with London was seen in The Hague as vital for Dutch Atlantic and European priorities. Today, a similar British contribution is less obvious, though for several reasons the UK remains an important bilateral trading and security partner for The Netherlands.

At the same time, the Franco-German relationship is being reappraised. Deals made by Paris and Bonn are still viewed with misgiving, but a leading role for the two in a European Union with fifteen and more members is acknowledged as perhaps necessary, and the Dutch are increasingly prepared to support it. A much stronger and open orientation towards Germany fits within this scheme and reflects the present continental-European priorities of the Dutch government, next to, and often above traditional overseas and Atlantic ones (Pijpers 1996).

6. Though enlargement as such has never been a controversial element in Dutch foreign policy, the forthcoming widening to include Eastern and Southern European countries has called for a new philosophy. The government has stuck to the principles set out in Copenhagen and Essen, holding the view that, in order to avoid chaos in the former orbit of the Soviet Union, 'the only possible solution is to integrate the countries of Central and Eastern Europe into western economic and political structures' (Dutch Ministry of Foreign Affairs 1994: 3). But it realizes that a number of obstacles need to be cleared before the road to membership is open: 'The institutional adjustment of the Union is not the least of these obstacles. It is therefore of great importance to find a balance between the wish, on the one hand, to bring forward the moment at which the countries of Central and Eastern Europe accede, and, on the other, attempting to ensure that the existing Union maintains its cohesion and decisiveness' (ibid.).

To find this balance the Dutch government has used a number of guidelines, which aptly summarize some Dutch core interests on the eve of the 1996 IGC: (i) achieving a stable security policy, socio-economic development, and democratic stability in Central and Eastern Europe; (ii) maintaining the active participation of Germany in the European integration process and in the joint European and Atlantic security structure; (iii) maintaining the internal market and the common legal order and thus a European Union that is capable of decisive action; (iv) achieving the aforementioned objectives at acceptable cost (ibid.: 5).

The Netherlands and the 1996 process

In order to prepare itself for the 1996 IGC, and to invoke a proper public debate on possible treaty revisions (a process omitted from preparations for the Maastricht Treaty), the Dutch government presented four discussion papers to the States-General on the eve of the IGC: on the implications of enlargement; on the CFSP; on cooperation in JHA; and one focusing on the role and composition of the institutions. From these documents the following picture emerges as to the principal preferences and viewpoints (though not final positions) of the Dutch government.

One basic feature stands out: the Dutch attitude towards further treaty reform is cautious and middle-of-the-road. The government has emphasized that the objectives of the EU do not need to be adapted or supplemented with new policy areas. Deepening is only called for in the sense of institutional improvements. Most if not all Dutch documents and advisory reports have, in a striking way, been empty of any reference to the need, or the possibility, for creating a true federal EU in the near or not so near future. The Foreign Ministry in The Hague and its advisory bodies tended to regard the IGC mainly as a means for consolidating the *acquis communautaire* and *acquis politique* in the context of broadening Union membership, with the internal market and its functionally related policy areas (including monetary unification, cooperation in the fields of justice and home affairs, the social chapter) as its most essential elements. If the IGC contributes to preserving these core elements of the EU under the trying circumstances of further enlargement, chronic instability and crises in the immediate external environment of the EU, and the impact of a globalizing economy, then it may already be considered a success.

At the 1991 IGC on Political Union, the Dutch government had still been prepared to launch outspoken federal concepts – including the ill-fated 'tree structure' presented by the Dutch Presidency in September 1991 (Wester 1992; van Hulten n. d.; Penders and Kwast 1992) – for a new Union treaty with strong support from all the large fractions in the Second Chamber, opposition parties included. By 1995, the government's proposals implicitly or explicitly acknowledged the pillar structure to be the most realistic option for the near future, though its view was also that the role of the EC institutions should be expanded, especially in the second and third pillars. Some politicians have even come to think that the pillar structure has the advantage of safeguarding the proper

129

Community domain from the problems of stagnation that have beset the CFSP or the area of police cooperation. Communautarian decision-making in the first pillar 'remains sacrosanct' in the view of the government (Dutch Ministry of Foreign Affairs 1995: 22). But the political ideal of a federal Europe has almost completely disappeared from political debate in The Netherlands.

Institutional matters

The Dutch share the general consensus that the application of a simple extrapolation model for the institutional set-up of a further enlarged Union should be rejected. It is felt that 'the accession of the EFTA countries has already stretched the extrapolation model to the limit', and that a continued application of this model 'will cause the decision-making machinery to grind to a halt' (Dutch Ministry of Foreign Affairs 1994: 19–20). The voting weight per member state, the number of Commissioners and MEPs, will have to be established in a different way than before, and so will the procedures necessary to obtain a qualified majority. This to avoid a situation in the foreseeable future where a group of small countries, representing only a minority of the population in the EU, will be able to overrule all larger member states under existing QMV procedures. The Netherlands and other smaller states encounter here the dilemma between a proper national representation in the EU institutions, and the necessity to streamline decision-making.

The overall approach of the government is to maintain the principle of disproportionality[8] (which gives the smaller countries a larger share in terms of institutional representation as compared to the larger ones), but to mitigate it. This appears in a number of suggestions made by the Dutch government on issues like decision-making in the Council, voting weights, the rotation of the Council Presidency, or the number of national representatives in Commission, EP and Court.

The government is of the opinion that all decision-making in the first pillar should, in principle, be taken on the basis of QMV, except for fiscal matters, 'own resources', and for decisions with a constitutional character such as treaty revision, enlargement, and the number of languages used in the Union (Dutch Ministry of Foreign Affairs 1994: 13). The government rejects the further application after the IGC of the Ioannina Agreement, which, though establishing the threshold for a blocking minority at 26 votes, has stipulated that if 23 to 25 votes appear to be cast against a certain measure, the Presidency should continue consultations, without taking the issue under consideration to a vote. The threshold for a blocking minority in the Council should remain at 30 per cent of the total amount of votes.

The Hague has also expressed itself in favour of introducing a double key for QMV: one reflecting the present number of votes per member state, and an additional one which stipulates that the majority should also represent at least 50 per cent of the total EU population. Such a double key formula has the advantage of maintaining the principle of disproportionality, but it makes it more acceptable to the larger states. The Netherlands, with its comparatively large population, would not itself be badly off. But the government is reluctant to mitigate the idea of disproportionality by simply giving the large members more votes. Such a move might lead to new calculations among the four big states, with the potential for friction between them.

A similar compromise formula has been conceived for a better functioning of the EU Council Presidency. In the present arrangement, adopted by the European Council in December 1993, the former alphabetical order was substituted by a rotation scheme of successive troikas, each with a large member state taking part in it. The scheme is rather flattering for The Netherlands, appointed an 'honorary' large state to take on the troika with Luxembourg and Ireland during the first half of 1997 . Yet, the government realizes that in a Union with 20 and more members (when a member state might occupy the Presidency only once each decade) other measures are called for, such as extending each presidential term to one year, splitting the tasks among 'internal' and 'external' presidencies, to opt for an elected President, or a team presidency. The Dutch government itself favours a team presidency in which the tasks are divided among the members of a troika serving a term of one year (ibid.: 15). A more sensitive point concerns the composition of the Commission. According to most analysts, a ceiling has already been reached with 20 Commissioners. A college of more members can hardly work effectively, and makes it difficult to create a relevant portfolio for each of the Commissioners. At the same time, the Dutch government is well aware of the importance of the role of the Commission in the EU. It remains of the opinion that each member state ought to be represented in the Commission, preferably with one Commissioner (ibid.: 16). At the beginning of the IGC debate, the government was still fairly flexible on the point, not being wholly opposed, for instance, to smaller states having fewer Commissioners than the larger members, on the strict condition that all members would in principle be prepared to forsake their right on a seat in the Commission. This possible concession was dropped after domestic pressure and discussions in the Benelux framework.

Common Foreign and Security Policy (CFSP)

The pragmatic approach of the Dutch government was also reflected in its proposals for the second pillar. The Hague accepted that there had been several 'significant weaknesses' in the operation of the CFSP (Dutch Ministry of Foreign Affairs 1995: 16): divisiveness over Bosnia and Rwanda; slow decision-making and insufficient joint analysis; difficulties of consistency between the first and second pillars; and lack of democratic control. It did not, however, see any need to reformulate CFSP objectives as listed in Article J.1.2. of the Treaty on European Union: 'The existing wording allows sufficient scope, and experience to date with the CFSP gives no grounds for reformulation' (ibid.: 16).

The problems with the CFSP are seen not as technical but political. Some procedures, however, could be improved. The 'capacity for analysis' or the ways policies are prepared could be strengthened, through, for instance, a better staffing of the CFSP unit, or even the creation of a new unit halfway between the Council and the Commission, and possibly headed by a 'Secretary-General of its own'. The Hague has also traditionally favoured the strong involvement of the Commission in the CFSP, which could be extended 'to include preparations for decision-making.' Similarly, Article J.3 procedure could be improved, the government agreeing with the German idea of allowing the adoption of joint actions by QMV. But a true communitarization of the CFSP was regarded as only 'an option for the longer term' (ibid.: 17,18, 20); the lessons of Black Monday have been taken well to heart.

The Dutch are aware of the necessity of further developing a common defence policy. To this end they have favoured the future integration of the WEU in the EU, not by establishing a new, fourth pillar in the EU treaty, but through the incorporation of the WEU into the second pillar. This would have the advantage of 'smoothing the transition from CFSP to common defense policy', while preserving the single institutional framework of the EU better than a separate fourth pillar (ibid.: 29). It was recognized that this had to be a gradual process which could only be completed in the long run, given the divergencies between EU, WEU and NATO membership in the wider Europe. An 'Atlantic contract' should in the meantime bridge the possible gap between NATO and EU membership (ibid.: 32, 26).

Multiple speed

The Dutch government has always tried to ban 'inner circles', 'directorates' or other informal clubs outside the regular channels for decision-making and consultation in the EU (Voorhoeve 1979: 187–8). Such tendencies are regarded as undermining the legal order of the Community and likely to lead to a hegemony of the larger states. But it has gradually occurred to the Dutch that even though the classical concept of a 'directorate' should remain taboo, certain forms of differentiated integration are unavoidable in a Union of more than fifteen members, with considerable economic and monetary divergencies, and different strategic interests. The government, though, is of the opinion that differentiated forms of integration should remain the exception, and that such forms, in whatever variant, should not detract from the single institutional framework of the EU (Dutch Ministry of Foreign Affairs 1994: 17). Each variant should also be compatible with the following criteria: (i) 'differentiated integration must be compatible with the objectives of the TEU; (ii) each member state must be free to participate if it can and wants to meet the requirements for the fast track; (iii) differentiated integration must not undermine the Community legal order or, in principle, impair the cohesion of the internal market; (iv) member states which elect to opt out must not be allowed to oppose the formation of a leading group which does meet the above-mentioned criteria' (Dutch Ministry of Foreign Affairs 1994: 23–4).

Though these criteria would seem to allow for a variety of modes of integration, it transpires that the only form the Dutch government believes meets all the criteria is multiple speed integration, whereby the policy objective is the same for all the member states, though the speed at which they are achieved may vary. Multiple speed integration is not an end in itself, but a means to an end: 'it enables a core group, or rather a leading group of member states to proceed with further cooperation and integration', or to achieve 'gradual convergence when new member states join the EU' (ibid. 22).

The government has been less enthusiastic about the concept of variable geometry, whereby not just the speed, but also the integration objectives may vary among the member states. Variable geometry should, it holds, be avoided in the Community sphere, since 'allowing our objectives to diverge will only encourage disintegration' and may easily undermine the Community legal order. For the second and third pillar, however, The Hague 'would not exclude the option of variable geometry altogether'. This is perhaps clear already from the Dutch participation in Schengen and several forms of European military cooperation.

Needless to say, the Dutch resist any form of opting-in or opting-out at will. European integration 'cannot survive a Europa à la carte' (ibid.: 23).

LUXEMBOURG

Luxembourg belongs to the group of EU member states who defend a 'maximalist' position towards European integration. Being part of a wider European framework has always been a highly attractive option for a country which, for the major part of its history, has been dominated by large powers and whose independence, gained in 1839, was threatened by its mighty neighbours on several occasions. Although the German *Zollverein* (1842), the Belgo-Luxembourg Economic Union (BLEU) (1921), and the Benelux (1944) imposed clear limitations on its sovereignty, Luxembourg realized that membership of these organizations was also the best guarantee for the country's autonomy. As Colette Flesch has argued, integration in a broader forum is, for Luxembourg, not so much a question of choice, but is in the first place a matter of survival (Flesch 1983: 154).

In view of this foreign policy tradition, it is not surprising that Luxembourg became an enthusiastic supporter of post-war attempts to integrate closely the Western European countries' coal and steel industries[9] and became one of the founding member states of the European Coal and Steel Community (ECSC) (and indeed, the seat of the ECSC's High Authority and Court of Justice). The important role attributed to the supranational body, the High Authority, created to defend the Community rather than national interests, was seen as the best safeguard against the domination of the ECSC by the large member states. After the abortive attempts to establish a European Defence Community (1952–54), Luxembourg, together with Belgium and The Netherlands, played a major role in establishing the European Economic Community (EEC) and the European Atomic Energy Committee (EURATOM) (Wurth-Rentier 1981).

Throughout the short history of European integration, Luxembourg has played an active role on the European stage. As a small country situated between

France and Germany, the two key protagonists of the EU, Luxembourg has put to good use its knowledge of both of those countries' languages and culture by functioning as a package-broker in difficult European negotiations. Through personalities such as Joseph Bech (Prime Minister and Minister of Foreign Affairs from 1926 to 1959; see Trausch 1978), Pierre Werner (Prime Minister and Minister of Foreign Affairs, chairman of the working group that drafted the *'Report on the Creation of a European Economic and Monetary Union'* in 1970; see Werner 1991) and Commission Presidents Gaston Thorn (1981–85) and Jacques Santer (1995–), Luxembourg has definitely left its mark on the European integration process. The most famous example of Luxembourg's skills as mediator is its role in the forging of the 'Luxembourg Compromise' (January 1966), which succeeded in bringing to an end several months of France's 'empty chair' policy (Jansen and De Vree 1985). Luxembourg's capacities as a compromise-builder again came to the fore during the negotiations leading to the conclusion of the SEA (De Ruyt 1987) and the TEU (Vanhoonacker 1992). On both occasions the Luxembourg Presidency proved to be extremely active in forging the divergent views of the EC member states into one single text.

Proud of its important contribution to the gradual development of 'an ever closer union among the peoples of Europe', Luxembourg is wary of the diluting effects of further enlargement on the European integration process. In its *'aide-mémoire'* on the 1996 IGC, the Luxembourg government advocated giving top priority to the further deepening of the EU (Luxembourg government, June 1995; Poos, 3 April 1995). More concretely, the paper pleaded for a further consolidation of the internal market through the establishment of EMU, for a strengthened social and environmental policy, and for the reinforcement of the Maastricht Treaty's second and the third pillars.

Conscious of the EU's poor performance in the field of foreign policy, Luxembourg put forward a number of concrete proposals intended to improve the effectiveness of the CFSP. These included a proposal to equip the Council Secretariat with a special foreign policy analysis unit, to make increased use of QMV, to associate the European Commission more effectively with CFSP joint actions and to finance all undertakings in the field of CFSP through the EU budget. As regards the development of a European security and defence identity, Luxembourg adopted a more cautious approach. It pleaded for a further strengthening of the European pillar of the North Atlantic Alliance which it views as the linchpin of European security. Although, for the time being, the WEU remains a separate organization, Luxembourg was in favour of further strengthening the WEU's relations with the EU and introducing a specific provision on the gradual integration of the WEU in the EU into the Treaty (Luxembourg government June 1995: 8–10; Poos 16 February 1995).

The Luxembourg paper adopted a critical attitude with regard to the EU's achievements in the field of JHA. Although it acknowledged that the third pillar deals with extremely sensitive matters, it considered that progress under this pillar had been too often hindered by decision-making by unanimity, by it being excluded from the jurisdiction of the European Court of Justice, and by its complicated working structures. Luxembourg proposed therefore the possibility of referring questions related to cooperation in the field of JHA to the ECJ for preliminary rulings and of allowing the Court to intervene between member states, as well as between member states and the European Commission, in disputes related to the third pillar (Luxembourg government 1995: 10-11).

By making the further deepening of the European integration process the central theme of its paper, Luxembourg defended a position characteristic of those member states that favour the development of the EU into a fully fledged Union. Clearly, not all EU member states support this approach and, as happened in Maastricht, some countries might again try to obtain authorization to opt out from certain provisions. Such an approach is strongly rejected by the Luxembourg government. Although it should be possible for some countries to receive special authorization from the Council and the European Commission to enjoy longer transitional periods to fulfil certain obligations, all new provisions introduced by the 1996 IGC should be endorsed by all member states. In other words, Luxembourg accepts the concept of a multi-speed Europe, but radically rejects that of a Europe à la carte (ibid.: 12; Poos 16 February 1995).

The Luxembourg government's *aide mémoire* on the 1996 IGC not only voiced a series of worries with regard to the future of the EU, it also reflected some concern about its own future position and role in an EU of more than twenty Member States. Discussions about reducing the number of Commissioners and the ideas being floated of several small countries sharing the Presidency have raised fears that the principle of the equality of all EU member states will come under increasing pressure. Conscious that there is a serious risk of being marginalized in the enlarged EU of the 21st century, Luxembourg has announced that it is not ready to abandon its right on a seat in the European Commission, neither does it intend to give up the rotating Presidency, the symbol which embodies the equality of all EU member states (Luxembourg government 1995: 15).

A final characteristic of the Luxembourg paper was its emphasis on the need for the closer involvement of Europe's citizens in the debate on the future of Europe. Although the Luxembourg Parliament ratified the TEU without any major problems, the government realized that there had been very little public debate on the Treaty and that European affairs increasingly risked becoming the *domaine réservé* of a small group of politicians, officials and academics that has all too often lost touch with the concerns of the wider public (Pauly 1992). To remedy this situation, the government has proposed the improvement of information channels to the citizens and equipping the EU with more transparent decision-making procedures. Furthermore, the government also proposed the closer association of the Luxembourg Parliament with the EU's decision-making process. At the government's request, the Luxembourg MEP, Charles Goerens, member of the Liberal opposition, drafted a report (1994), making concrete proposals to achieve this objective and suggesting the introduction into the Treaty of a 'charter' defining the minimal obligations of a government towards its national parliament and creating the possibility for national parliaments to lodge an appeal for annulment of a Community act with the ECJ.[10]

A NEW ROLE FOR THE BENELUX?

Though in several respects the Benelux have played a pioneering role in the field of European integration, and though it has become a household word in Europe's political vocabulary, its actual unity has always lagged behind the Benelux-image held by outside observers – a fate it perhaps shares with the EU itself, which is also often considered more of a unity by the outside world, than by the European participants themselves.

Unity has lagged, first, because ambitions for Benelux as a grouping have always been restricted. The three countries have never aspired to create a real economic and political (let alone military) union, with supranational bodies and QMV. On the contrary, they have always carefully opted for the intergovernmental model (with only a very limited competence on, mainly, trade mark law for the Benelux Court of Justice), and have tried to keep their cooperation efforts as pragmatic as possible. As a pure intergovernmental organization, the Benelux is not a suitable model of or for the EU (at least not for those who want to develop the EU in a communautarian direction). The attitudes of Belgium and The Netherlands are not very consistent on this point. While both are very much in favour of preserving the Community legal order, with all its supranational features, they opt squarely for intergovernmentalism in the Benelux context (with exactly the same arguments used by France and the UK in the EU).

Furthermore, economic union proved difficult to realize, due to different traditions in such areas as agriculture, trade policy, industrial policy. The French-speaking community has always resisted closer political union among the three, out of fear of becoming dominated by a forceful Dutch-speaking majority (Kersten and Boekestijn 1994). There have been regular political consultations among the three, with the occasional joint statements or memoranda on the eve of important meetings of the European Council on for instance, institutional matters. In EPC as well, a number of common proposals have been presented. But the three countries for many historical and cultural reasons have never shown the common will to build a real political bloc, and their initiatives have lacked, therefore, always a certain political clout.

Moreover, since the virtual completion of the internal market and the conclusion of the Maastricht Treaty, most of the original tasks of the Benelux Economic Union, in such fields as trade, the free movement of persons, economic and monetary cooperation, have become more or less obsolete, or taken over by an organization like Schengen. In a sense, the Benelux is in these areas a victim of its own success.

The federalization of Belgium has, furthermore, made coordination in the Benelux context more problematic. The responsibility for the external relations in Belgium is now shared among three regions, three communities, and the federal government, each with substantial powers to conduct foreign policy and to conclude treaties. This devolution has led, quite naturally, to new patterns of bilateral relations. Flanders, for instance, has intensified its relations with The Netherlands in order to solve longstanding common problems in the fields of environment, the

High Speed Train network, the accessibility of the river Scheldt, and culture. The Walloon Region and the French Community do their own bit *vis-à-vis* France. Benelux as such is only partly relevant to such specific bilateral issues.

A Committee of Wise Men from the three, established in 1994 to investigate the future of Benelux, has admitted these developments in so many words. In its report, it recommends a thorough reorganization of the many Benelux commissions and working groups, while the Secretariat-General should reduce its number of staff (Three Wise Men Report 1994). Benelux should mainly confine its tasks to facilitating cross-border arrangements, and to providing a common platform for political consultations, in particular concerning institutional matters, such as the 1996 IGC – a recommendation that has, in fact, been followed up through a series of summits between the three in 1995 and early 1996, and also through the adoption of the Benelux Memorandum for the IGC (March 1996). Apart from a paragraph on employment as an issue for the IGC, the Memorandum contains no viewpoints which fundamentally differ from the national positions presented above, being, essentially a catalogue of the three countries' well-known viewpoints on the importance of preserving the Community's legal order and the *acquis communautaire*.

The Committee of Wise Men admits, however, that in such instances Benelux encounters a dilemma. If it behaves too openly as one political bloc during negotiations for institutional reform, it could boomerang with the common Benelux position being translated into a single Benelux member in the Commission, or one Benelux Presidency. The Committee has acknowledged this risk, and proposed that the three should consult each other on issues of common interest, but without presenting themselves as a real political bloc; it is a dilemma akin to the squaring of the circle.

The political dimension of Benelux consultations has received an additional impetus by the emerging discussion on the role of core groups in the future EU. The Schäuble–Lamers paper is particularly relevant in this respect (CDU–CSU 1994). The central argument of this CDU–CSU document (which was in all likelihood supported by Chancellor Kohl) was to maintain in any further enlarged union one of the principal driving forces in the process of European integration: Franco-German cooperation. This might be done, in the view of Schäuble–Lamers, through the creation of a core group around the French–German axis. In such a way the capacity of the axis would be increased so as to be able to support the growing demands of integration in a much enlarged EU. In the German paper the three Benelux countries were explicitly named to become members of this core group, which should not only operate in the monetary field, but also in a more general political sense. The three will probably meet the EMU convergence criteria by the end of this century; they are longstanding NATO and WEU members, and they were among the founding fathers of the EC, with a positive integration record. Being smaller states, they are also useful, of course, in legitimizing the continuous leadership role of the two biggest West European powers (Wallace and Wallace 1995: 90).

Though the core concept as such was not on the opening agenda of the 1996

IGC, it will probably remain on the European agenda in a broader sense for quite some time to come. For the Benelux countries the concept harbours some advantages and some risks. A positive aspect is, of course, to have a seat at the first table. In a sense, the Schäuble–Lamers idea restores the position which the Benelux had in the Community of Six. But appearances may be deceptive. Firstly, the core is not an exclusive affair (there are more candidates), and the parameters for current small state influence differ considerably from those in the 1950s and 1960s. In those years, with the UK still out and Germany still rather subdued, the Benelux countries had a relatively strong position. Now the game is different. The central function of a core is not to give the Benelux countries more influence, but to better organize support for Franco-German proposals. The Benelux would probably be asked first to support certain Franco-German ideas, and then to help implement them in a wider European circle.

We may conclude, then, that the Benelux Economic Union has become obsolete in a number of respects. At the same time, however, an enlarged EU urges the three countries to consult each other on common (institutional) concerns, and the formation of a core group – formal or informal – also requires coordinated positions and policies. In a political sense the role of the Benelux, which has celebrated its 50th anniversary in 1994, is not yet over. On the contrary, their longstanding record of initiating integration projects, their deep involvement in all sectors of the EU and in related organizations such as WEU or Schengen, and their *esprit d'équipe* (created over the years through the numerous working groups and commissions in the proper Benelux framework) are all indispensable to sustain the comprehensive deepening operation needed in the future EU. In a Union encompassing Cyprus or Estonia it is essential that the European patrimony of Monnet is preserved. The Benelux countries took a disproportional large share in creating this patrimony. That contribution should be acknowledged when it comes to the further institutional build-up of the EU.

NOTES

1. It was expected that the Socialist Party, who was accused of corruption in having accepted money from the Italian helicopter firm Agusta would suffer from heavy losses. The Party, however, maintained its position.
2. Belgium has two kinds of federated entities, the Communities and the Regions, each with their own specific competencies. The three Communities are the French, the Flemish and the German-speaking Communities. The three Regions are the Walloon, the Flemish and the Brussels-Capital Regions. Each Community and Region has its own parliament or 'Council' and its own government or 'Executive'. The Communities are competent in cultural matters, education, the use of language and 'personalized matters' (health care, social and family policy). The Regions are competent in the field of environmental policy, foreign trade, energy, public works and transport, urban planning, regional aspects of credit policy, provincial and municipal institutions, scientific research and monuments and sites. See: André Alen, *Treatise on Belgian Constitutional Law*

(Deventer-Boston: Kluwer Law and Taxations Publishers, 1992).

3. Belgium has twelve representatives in the Committee of Regions, all of them representatives of the governments of the federated entities.

4. By bringing about a compromise on the location of the EMI, the Belgian Presidency, in the second half of 1993, played an important role in preparing the ground for the launching of the second stage of EMU foreseen to start in January 1994. See Christian Franck and Tanguy de Wilde d'Estmael, 'L'Union européenne et la présidence belge. Juillet-décembre 1993', *Courrier hebdomadaire (CRISP)*, nos. 1432–1433, 1994, pp. 28–30.

5. In 1994, the public debt was equivalent to 128 per cent of GDP. However, Belgium fulfils the criteria on the level of inflation and interest rates without any problem, and possesses stable exchange rates. In 1996, it will for the first time also fulfil the criterium according to which the public deficit should not amount to more than 3 per cent of GDP.

6. Only the Flemish and the French Community as well as the Brussels Region presented written versions of their respective positions *vis-à-vis* the 1996 IGC. See 'Nota aan de Vlaamse Regering. Ontwerp van Vlaams standpunt betreffende de intergouvernementele conferentie (IGC) van 1996', Brussel, n.d.; 'Note au gouvernement de la Communauté française. Conférence intergouvernementale de 1996 (CIG). Révision du Traité de l'Union', Bruxelles, le 11 septembre 1995; 'Europese Unie. Intergouvernementele Conferentie 1996. Standpunt van de Brusselse Hoofdstedelijke Regering', Brussel, n.d.

7. Currently consultation of the Committee of the Regions is obligatory for five areas of Community policy: education; culture; public health; trans-European networks; economic and social cohesion.

8. In a joint Benelux memorandum, presented to the Lisbon meeting of the European Council in June 1992, it is stated: 'the basic idea which should be endorsed is that in the Commission, the Council, and the European Parliament the larger countries will have to accept some over-representation of the smaller member states'. L.J. Bal a.o., "Institutionele hervorming van de Europese Unie", *Internationale Spectator*, vol. 48 (1994), p. 112.

9. In the 1920s, Emile Mayrisch, a Luxembourg engineer and director of the Luxembourg steel firm ARBED, launched the idea of creating an 'Entente internationale de l'acier' with the aim of reducing the mistrust between France and Germany. Created in 1926, it grouped together the steel industries of France, Belgium, Luxembourg and the Saar. With Hitler's advent to power in 1933, the committee ceased to exist. See: Henri Rieben, *Des guerres européennes à l'Union de l'Europe* (Lausanne: Fondation Jean Monnet pour l'Europe et Centre de Recherches Européennes, 1987), pp. 63–67.

10. The national parliament in question could only introduce the procedure on the condition that its own government had opposed the proposal.

REFERENCES AND BIBLIOGRAPHY

Belgian government (1995) 'Note de politique du gouvernement au parlement concernant la conférence intergouvernementale de 1996', *Synthèse, Bruxelles*, 'Beleidnota van de regering aan het parlement betreffende de intergouvernementele conferentie van 1996', *Systhèse, Brussels*, 28 July.

—— (1995) 'Note de politique du gouvernement au parlement concernant la conférence intergouvernementale de 1996', *Synthèse, Bruxelles*, 'Beleidnota van de regering aan het parlement betreffende de intergouvernementele conferentie van 1996', *Systhèse, Brussels*, 13 October.

'Belgian Memorandum on Institutional Relaunch' (1990) *Europe Documents*, no. 1608, 29 March.

CDU–CSU Fraktion des Deutschen Bundestages (1994) *Ueberlegungen zur europaeischen Politik*. Bonn, September.

Coolsaet, Rik (1987) *Buitenlandse Zaken*. Leuvwn, Kritak

Dehaene, Jean-Luc, Prime Minister of Belgium (1994) Speech before the Institut français des relations internationales, Paris, 26 October.

—— (1995) speech entitled 'European Union: Objective 1996', Brussels, 29 March.

—— (1995) 'Intergovernmental Conference of 1996 and the Future of Europe', address to the College of Europe, Bruges, 22 March.

—— (1995) 'My Vision on Europe', speech before the United Students for Europe, 21 February.

Derycke, Erik (1995) 'Discours du Ministre des Affaires étrangères Erik Derycke', Colloque: L'élargissement de l'Union européenne. Enjeux et implications politico-institutionnelles, Brussels, 13 October.

Dumoulin, Michel (ed.) (1987) *La Belgique et les débuts de la construction européenne*. s.1: Ciaco.

Dutch Ministry of Foreign Affairs (1994) 'Enlargement of the European Union: Possibilities and Problems'. The Hague, (First IGC 1996 Memorandum of the Dutch Government).

—— (1995) 'European Foreign, Security and Defence Policy: Towards Stronger External Action by the European Union'. The Hague, (Second IGC 1996 Memorandum of the Dutch Government).

Eppink, Derk Jan (1995) 'Buitenland blinde vlek bij partijen', *De Standaard*, 19 May.

'European Security Policy Towards 2000: Ways and Means to Establish Genuine Credibility' (1994). A report of a high-level group of experts for Commissioner Hans van den Broek. Brussels, 19 December.

'European Union. Report by Mr Leo Tindemans, Prime Minister of Belgium, to the European Council', *Bulletin of the European Communities*, Supplement 1/1976.

Flesch, Colette (1983) 'La diplomatie luxembourgeoise: nécessité, réalité et défi', in *Studia Diplomatica*, vol. 36, no. 2, pp.145–62.

Goerens, Charles. 'Le rôle des parlements dans l'Union européenne de demain,' Rapport à M Jean-Claude Junker, Premier Minstre.

Government of Luxembourg (1995) *Aide-mémoire du Gouvernement luxembourgeois sur la Conférence Intergouvernementale de 1996*. Luxembourg, 30 June.

van Hulten, Michiel (n.d.) 'The Short Life and Sudden Death of the Dutch Draft Treaty Towards European Union', mimeo.

Jansen, Max and De Vree, Johan K. (1985) *The Ordeal of Unity 1945–1985*. Bilthoven, Prime Press.

Kersten, A.E. and Boekestijn, A.J. (1994) in Postma, A. *et al. Benelux in de kijker. Gedenkboek ter gelegenheid van 50-jarig bestaan van de samenwerking tussen Belgie, Nederland en Luxemburg*. Tielt, Lannoo.

Keukeleire, Stephan (1995) 'Hervorming Europese Unie krijgt te weinig publieke aandacht', *De Standaard*, 2 October.

van Meerhaeghe, M.A.G. (ed.) (1992) *Belgium and EC Membership Evaluated*. London, Pinter Publishers and St. Martin's Press.

Pauly, Alexis (1994) 'Luxembourg and the ratification of the Maastricht Treaty', in Laursen, Finn and Vanhoonacker, Sophie (eds) *The Ratification of the Maastricht Treaty:*

Issues, Debates and Future Implications. Maastricht-Dordrecht, EIPA and Martinus Nijhoff Publishers, pp. 203–11.

Penders, Jean and Kwast, Marja (1992) 'The Netherlands and political union', in Pijpers, Alfred (ed.) *The European Community at the Crossroads*. Dordrecht, Martinus Nijhoff, pp. 253–70.

Pijpers, Alfred (1996) 'The Netherlands: The weakening pull of Atlanticism?' in Hill, Christopher (ed.) *The Actors in Europe's Foreign Policy*. London, Routledge.

Poos, Jacques (1995) Vice-Premier Ministre, Ministre des Affaires Etrangères du Commerce Extérieur et de la Coopération du Luxembourg, *Déclaration de politique étrangère à la Chambre des Députés*. Luxembourg, 16 February.

—— (1995) Vice-Premier Ministre, Ministre des Affaires Etrangères du Luxembourg. Intervention at the Institut Royal des Relations Internationales, Brussels, 3 April.

'Le rôle des belges et de la Belgique dans l'édification européenné' (1981) *Studia Diplomatica*, vol. 34, no. 1–4.

De Ruyt, Jean (1987) *L'Acte unique européen*. Brussels, Institut d'Etudes Européennes.

van Schendelen, M.P.C.M. (1995) *Gelijkhebben of Winnen: Nederlandse belangenbehartiging in de Europese Unie*. Amsterdam, Amsterdam University Press.

Tindemans, Leo (1976) *Report on European Union* (The Tindemans Report), *Bulletin of the ECs*, Supplement 1/76, Brussels, EC.

Trausch, Gilbert (1978) *J. Bech, un homme dans son siècle – Cinquante années d'histoire luxembourgeoise*. Luxembourg, Editions Saint Paul.

Vanhoonacker, Sophie (1992) 'Luxembourg and political union', in Laursen, Finn and Vanhoonacker, Sophie (eds) *The Ratification of the Maastricht Treaty: Issues, Debates and Future Implications*. Maastricht-Dordrecht, EIPA and Martinus Nijhoff Publishers, pp. 155–62.

—— (1994) 'Belgium and the ratification of the Maastricht Treaty', in Laursen, Finn and Vanhoonacker, Sophie (eds) *The Ratification of the Maastricht Treaty: Issues, Debates and Future Implications*. Maastricht-Dordrecht, EIPA and Martinus Nijhoff Publishers, pp.47–60.

Voorhoeve, J.J.C. (1979) *Peace, Profits, and Principles: A Study of Dutch Foreign Policy*. The Hague, Martinus Nijhoff.

Wallace, H. and Wallace, W. (1995) *Flying Together in a larger and more diverse European Union*. The Hague, Netherlands Scientific Council for Government Policy, Working Documents W87.

Werner, Pierre (1991) *Itinéraires européens et luxembourgeois. Evolution et souvenirs 1945–1985*. Luxembourg, Editions Saint Paul.

Wester, Robert (1992) 'The Netherlands', in Laursen, Finn and Vanhoonacker, Sophie (eds) *The Intergovernmental Conference on Political Union*. Maastricht, European Institute of Public Administration, pp.172–5.

de Wilde d'Estmael, Tanguy and Franck, Christian (1993) 'Du mémorandum belge au traité de Maastricht', in Franck, Christian, Roosens, Claude and de Wilde d'Estmael, Tanguy (eds) *Aux tournants de l'histoire. La politique extérieure de la Belgique au début de la décennie 90*. Brussels, De Boeck and Wesmael, pp. 41–65.

Wurth-Rentier, Jeannine (1981) 'Du Grand-Duché de Luxembourg et de la construction européenne', *Studia Diplomatica*, vol. 31, no. 1–4, pp. 87–109.

8

THE EU AND THE COMMON INTERESTS OF THE SOUTH

PANOS TSAKALOYANNIS

INTRODUCTION

The notion that the Southern member states of the European Union (EU) share certain basic common interests *vis-à-vis* their Northern brethren has a long pedigree, going back to the origins of the European Communities. In the earlier years of the EC, the affinity of interests between France and Italy stemmed from the fact that both had to undergo a process of modernization, especially of their Southern, mainly agricultural regions. Both had a Northern as well as a Southern dimension and a compelling need to bridge the economic, social and even political discrepancies between their South and North. The Community's structural funds, for example, were originally conceived as a means for catering for the less developed regions of these countries. Before the enlargement to the South, France and Italy absorbed the lion's share of the EC's funds. For example, in the second half of the 1970s they were recipients of £2.622 million in grants, and £3.383 million in loans from the European Investment Bank (EIB) (Blasksell 1984: 269).

There has, in addition, been a political convergence between France and Italy in the post-war period, mainly due to Italy's desire to keep some distance from Germany as well as from Britain, for different reasons related to her war experience. It is not accidental, therefore, that in the early post-war years, France and Italy took common initiatives at integration, one of them bearing the name of the still-born FRITALUX, before the launching of the Schuman Plan. The main reason for FRITALUX's failure was due to the fact that such union would have limited economic effects, given the low degree of overlap between the two economies. In other words the EC's very creation rested in part on the complementarity, economic and political, between the EC's North and South and a need to balance the interests of both sides.

Such affinity of interests, however, was largely confined to low-key coordination, mainly on economic and trade matters. Yet, occasionally, it spilled over into the political realm. For example, Italy was the only member which waited (in vain) on the ratification of the European Defence Community (EDC) Treaty by the French Parliament before beginning her own process of ratification. Similarly it was an Italian diplomat, Attilio Catanni, who replaced Christian Fouchet, in the aborted negotiations in the early 1960s for a rather different form of political integration. Finally, during the 1965 crisis, Italy tried to play the role of 'honest broker' between France and her EC partners to ensure that the crisis did not get out of hand. Such political affinity between Paris and Rome was, though, a rather limited affair. Gaullist France in its bid for leadership in Western Europe and recognition of equality of status in NATO, on a par with the USA and Britain differed in political perspective from Italy. On such issues of high politics Paris and Rome parted ways.

The Community's first enlargement towards the North in the early 1970s brought to the fore the question of taking complementary steps to strengthen its Mediterranean dimension. Yet, due to political, economic and social considerations this could only be confined to a patchwork of non-preferential trade and financial agreements between two grossly uneven sides, given the 'lack of economic and psychological balance' (Henig 1976: 306), separating the Nine, on the one hand, and the individual Mediterranean countries on the other. Needless to say, such agreements hardly deserved the adjective 'global' that was attached to them. But what is interesting to note, is that the Southern European countries were virtually absent from such agreements. In the case of Portugal, still under the Caetano regime, this was due to lack of interest (Portugal had become a part of the European Free Trade Area (EFTA) and to her preoccupation with her African colonies. Spain, still under Franco, applied for an association agreement in 1972 but was rebuffed on political grounds. Greece's Association Agreement with the EC had been put in cold storage after the colonels' coup in 1967. Only in the case of Turkey did political imperatives not stand in the way for an upgrading of relations with the signing of an Additional Protocol in the early 1970s. In other words, these agreements, by keeping the other Southern European countries at arm's length, underscored the distance dividing those *inside* the Community from those *outside* it. Bridging this gulf between insiders and outsiders was to play a prominent role in the EC's life for nearly fifteen years. Its accomplishment in the mid-1980s, by the accession of Greece, Portugal and Spain, represents one of its most remarkable achievements at that time.

The point to be underlined here is that this enlargement would perhaps not have come into full fruition had it not been for the EC's own metamorphosis in the mid-1980s. Greek accession posed limited economic problems, in contrast to the political difficulties which the then Nine were inclined to shun for a number of reasons – not least because of their desire to anchor Greece into the European fold. The fact that France, and to a lesser extent Italy, were earnest supporters of Greece's drive for accession to the EC was instrumental in overcoming doubts or objections by some Northern members, like Britain and Germany, and, indeed, the Commission, as to the wisdom of this policy.[1]

Yet, on the eve of Greece's accession to the EC, President Giscard d'Estaing was calling for 'a pause', as far as further enlargement was concerned on the grounds that the EC was not ready yet for such step (Tsoukalis 1981: 9). French and Italian calls for caution with regard to Southern enlargement stemmed from their concern that Spain's accession to the EC might jeopardize their agricultural and weak industrial sectors. At the same time, it was feared that it would suck EC resources, at a time when the EC was facing severe budgetary problems. In other words, the completion of the EC's Southern enlargement in the very early 1980s, appeared to be an almost impossible task as long as the Community was in the grips of a deep multiple crisis or 'Eurosclerosis'. The overcoming of such deep-seated problems in the EC was a prerequisite to solving the question of Southern enlargement.

The reforms initiated in the EC in early 1984 – with the resolution of the (British) budgetary problem, the elaboration of the White Paper for the completion of the single market by 1992, and the endorsement of the Single European Act (SEA), as well as a number of other sundry initiatives, such as the reactivation of the Western European Union (WEU) – radically transformed the climate in the Community and within a remarkably short time they led to its metamorphosis. The pertinent point here is that this new dynamism in the EC not only made possible the settlement of the question of enlargement, but also led to the creation of a Southern dimension in the EC. This was largely because the Southern enlargement was congruent with social and political developments in Southern Europe; i.e., it coincided with the ascendancy of new social and political forces in Spain, Greece and Portugal.

Such forces were epitomized in the ascendancy of Socialist Parties in all three countries in the early 1980s. Parties and governments then displayed a spirit of solidarity not only against their own domestic political opponents, but also vis-à-vis their Northern partners in the EC, who were lurching to the political Right. It is remarkable, therefore, especially in the face of earlier concerns lest Southern enlargement would have seriously upset, or retarded the EC's delicate political and economic balance, how smoothly the EC's transformation proved to be. The reason for this success was due to the fact that Southern enlargement became part and parcel of a wider process in the EC. Within this process the South was not only rehabilitated but it also forged its own identity.

It is remarkable, for example, with what ease the Socialist governments switched their economic policy from Keynesianism to free market principles. Even if the conversion represented a concession to economic pressures from the more powerful economies of the EC's North, it was also certainly lubricated by the provisions made in the SEA for transfers of Community funds to the EC's less developed regions. This was deemed necessary in order to sustain a more balanced development within the single market. Cohesion was, in effect, the price the more competitive economies of the North were asked to pay for the realization of its '1992' blueprint. This point was put most succinctly by Jacques Delors, then President of the Commission, in 1985; the SEA, he contended, was:

> a splendid opportunity for the Community to emerge from what it is at present – a free trade area, plus budgetary transfers … cohesion is a new idea, the idea that convergence of economic and social policies – and not merely budgetary transfers will in ten years' time enable every Member State, including the poorest, to say that all in all Community life has been of benefit. (quoted by Featherstone 1989: 196)

This was a common objective shared by all Southern EC members in the second half of the 1980s. They pursued it, with Mitterrand's France in the driver's seat. In other words, the EC's Southern members, as a matter of economic, political and social expediency, shared a common perspective and specific economic interests in a community in the process of transformation. As the 1980s drew to a close this affinity of interests grew in strength. Its image was also strengthened by conjunctural factors, such as the fact that at the close of the 1980s, the EC's Presidency was held successively by Greece, Spain and France, that is, at a time expectations of the EC were at a peak.[2] It also found expression in the apportioning of EC portfolios in the new Commission formed in January 1989, in which those related to aspects of cohesion, including Social Affairs, went to Southern members.

In short, on the eve of the historic changes in Central and Eastern Europe, the EC's Southern members appeared to share a common platform on the Community's future development. However, its focus was restricted to those issues related to the distribution of resources in the EC or to specific policies which were relevant to their own interests. In other words, the greatest convergence was on cohesion and on the development of a social dimension in the EC. On other Community issues, such as Economic and Monetary Union (EMU), views varied. France, Italy and Greece were in favour of the Commission proposals, submitted to the European Council in Madrid, in June 1989, on the realization of EMU in stages, whereas Portugal and Spain sided with the sceptics. Similarly, on political issues the threshold of consensus among the Southern members also lagged behind, in that their stance was determined, to a very large extent, by a host of specific considerations. Nevertheless, even here, the accession of Portugal and Spain to the WEU, in 1988, brought them into the inner security core of Western Europe. In this respect, Greece was the sole Southern member left in the cold, something which attested to the limits of convergence, on political security issues.

SOUTHERN RESPONSES TO NEW EXIGENCIES: FROM THE 1989 REVOLUTIONS TO THE TREATY ON EUROPEAN UNION

The rather idyllic climate for the Southern members of the EC in the late 1980s goes some way in explaining their consternation at the political changes in Central and Eastern Europe. This was also due to the fact that they were taken completely by surprise by the collapse of the Cold War order in Europe. This incredulity at the speed of events in Europe was not, of course, confined to the new members who had stood on the periphery of European politics; Italy and France were as much surprised as Greece, Portugal and Spain. And while each country varied in its reading of the new situation, they all shared certain concerns.

First, it seemed clear that the South would have to compete with Central and Eastern Europe for funds and resources. The question, as Bonvicini put it, was far from being rhetorical for three main reasons: first, because of the scarcity of international finance and resources which imposed rigid priorities; second as a result of the huge and urgent financial needs of the East, which might have been met by corresponding cuts to the resources available to the South; and last, because, in the short term at least, the South and the East would be competing for exports to the Community as their products were largely similar or comparable (Bonvicini 1992: 171).

Second, apprehension that the South would have to compete with the East also extended to the political and the security realm. It was widely felt that, with the liberation of Central and Eastern Europe, there would be a shift in the centre of gravity from the South-west to the East, with the South consequently marginalized. Such concerns were fed by fears that Germany might have been lured if not by the pull of *Mitteleuropa*, by a moral duty to reward the democratic forces in Central Europe whose support and solidarity had played a decisive role in toppling the Communist regimes and ending Europe's division. In other words, at a societal level there was a strong pull in Germany towards the peoples of Central Europe whose fate she had partly shared in the Cold War era (Garton Ash 1991).

Finally, the new security exigencies in Europe also implied a shift of emphasis from the South to the East. To begin with, the dissolution of the Warsaw Pact raised certain doubts about the future of NATO. The latter would have to find a niche in the much discussed new European architecture whose centrepiece was expected to be, in the euphoric days of 1989–90, the Conference on Security and Cooperation in Europe (CSCE). The talk about a new European architecture, hinged on the CSCE, made some Southern members in the EC feel somewhat neglected and apprehensive lest the new political and security exigencies in Europe were bound to play a decisive role in the EC's economic and security priorities.

Of course it would be naive to suggest that all Southern members shared such concerns in a uniform manner, or that they responded to the new situation in unison. It merely suggests that all of them felt that the changes in the autumn of 1989 marked a decisive turning point, not only for Europe as a whole, but also for the EC, whose priorities had to be adjusted to the new realities. Yet, it was easier to diagnose the problem than to come up with uniform and coherent responses. The changes in Europe in the autumn of 1989 put political coherence among the EC's Southern flank to the test. Although there were attempts to adopt a common stance, their responses hardly amounted to a comprehensive strategy on how the South could fit into the emerging picture in Europe. Such a strategy might well have been impossible given their heterogeneity and their different preoccupations stemming from the new realities in Europe. Their very involvement in the winding-up of the old order complicated the issue since it varied from that of France, who was a participant of the 'Two-plus Four' negotiations; to Italy, who appeared somewhat vexed at being excluded from them; to Spain and Portugal, who tried to draw attention to the security needs of their own backyard in Western Mediterranean; to Greece who, absorbed as she was by her domestic economic and political problems, was eager to demonstrate her EC credentials even if that implied certain aloofness from her Southern partners. It is impossible here to give a comprehensive account of individual responses of the five Southern countries to the new exigencies (see Laursen and Vanhoonacker 1992; Hill 1996). Suffice it to say that their responses tended to focus on taking initiatives aimed at making their presence felt and at enhancing their standing in the emerging order. The initiatives varied from Italy's overtures to the Danube region and the Balkans (the *Pentagonale* and the *Hexagonale*), France's calls in late 1989, early 1990, for the creation of a European confederation, and Spain's and Portugal's calls for the creation of a Mediterranean Conference on Security and Cooperation (CSCM) (for the last see Aliboni 1991). However, following the Dublin European Council meeting in April 1990, at which the idea for an IGC on Political Union was launched, such uncoordinated moves subsided as attention turned to the IGC.

What is interesting to note is that throughout the IGC there was not a single joint initiative by the Southern EC members. Most initiatives bore the stamp of France and Germany. But Italy, too, was highly active, either in submitting her own ideas, as happened in September 1990, when, in her capacity as President of the Council, she drew the outlines for a Common Foreign and Security Policy (CFSP), or by joining forces with Germany, as in April 1991, when they submitted a paper on institutional reform focusing mainly on the powers of the EP and the Commission in the EU, and with Britain in October 1991, in submitting common ideas on security. By contrast Spain focused in the IGC on defending the economic *acquis* of the South as well as in canvassing its social and dimension. On the CFSP, Spain sided with France and Italy, joining the Eurocorps in October 1991, whereas Portugal's position was closer to the minimalists, or the Atlanticists, headed by Britain and the Netherlands. Greece, for her part, kept a low profile though she backed Bonn's calls for a federal union. Her chief specific political objective in the IGC was to accede to the WEU, something which she accomplished, although with certain provisos, with the Petersberg Declaration of June 1992.

In short, the IGC in 1990–91 underscored the limits of convergence among the five Southern members of the EU. Above all, it showed that France was not in a position to provide the leadership that she had done in the 1980s. French priorities and concerns were now on a different track from those of her Southern partners. The ratification of the TEU demonstrated this gap between France and the rest. Only in France, among the Southern members of the EC, did the question of ratification turn into a major political controversy (Laursen and Vanhoonacker 1994). This was a manifestation of French anxieties about Maastricht and an early warning of a change of heart concerning Paris' commitment to European integration.

THE SOUTH AND THE CHALLENGE OF THE 1996 IGC

In view of this background the approach of the Southern members of the EU towards the 1996 IGC was problematic. There were doubts from the beginning about whether they could muster their collective energies and work out, if not a uniform strategy, at least a common platform for pursuing their objectives. The IGC posed some fairly fundamental questions about the degree of homogeneity among the EU's Southern members as well as about their leverage in the context of the IGC.

The convening of another IGC stemmed from two different requirements, one political and the other institutional. The latter is related to the Article N (2) of the TEU that which stipulates that an IGC should be convened in 1996 in order to examine those provisions of the Treaty for which revision is provided. The political imperative of the 1996 IGC lies in the fact that the 1991 IGC did not fully address the political issues for which it was convened. The Madrid European Council of December 1995 suggested that the EU's agenda over the next five years as well as that of the 1996 IGC would be even more dominated by political imperative than before, given the need to deal with the remaining adjustments to the TEU, make the transition to a single currency, prepare for and carry out enlargement negotiations, determine the financial perspective beyond 31 December 1999, contribute to establishing the new European security architecture and actively continue the policy of dialogue, cooperation and association with Russia, Ukraine, Turkey and the Mediterranean countries (Europe, Special Edition No 6629, 17 December 1995).[3] It is clear that the issues involved are mutually dependent and, therefore, that their solution requires comprehensive responses, instead of piecemeal *ad hoc* improvisation. For example, the realization of enlargement to Central and Eastern Europe, or a meaningful dialogue with Russia, Turkey and third Mediterranean countries depends on the Fifteen's capacity to sort out their domestic institutional, political–security and economic–monetary problems.

This would require the existence of a comprehensive strategy, if not a vision, on how to organize these elements, domestic and external, into a coherent and workable framework. To put it simply, the demands made of the 1996 IGC were far more taxing for the Fifteen than the previous IGC for the Twelve and thus would require greater leadership and sense of purpose. In the previous IGC such leadership and sense of direction came from France and Germany, who took the initiative, in April 1990, in convening the IGC. In this respect the EU's South could rest assured that its overall interests would not be shunned, as France, the leading member of the group was in the driving seat. In other words, the 1990–91 IGC could be perceived through the prism of the developments in the EC since the mid-1980s, in which the Mediterranean members had played an active part.

The situation today is rather different. One of its most interesting features is that France does not seem to be as keen as she was in 1990–91 on taking the lead. In effect it would not be an exaggeration to suggest that the only comprehensive proposals for the 1996 IGC were those of the CDU–CSU Papers, of September 1994 and June 1995. These Papers not only failed to command France's full endorsement, but, on institutional and political–security issues, appeared to be driving France closer to Britain. Despite, therefore, the attempts by Bonn and Paris, in the autumn of 1994, to regain the joint initiative in the EU, unambiguous evidence of such a common venture by France and Germany, concerning the 1996 IGC has, as yet, been missing. As Dominique Moïsi put it, since 1989, 'history is proving unfair to the French' as the net effects of political changes in Europe made them feel geographically marginalized and uncertain as to how to face the new challenges in the EU framework. As he concluded: 'France wants a strong Europe, but with weak institutions that will not underline its claim to Grand Nation. As long as France fails to resolve this fundamental contradiction, its policies towards Europe will be dogged by problems' (*Financial Times* 20 January, 1995; see also Tsakaloyannis 1996).

The effects of this development on the other Southern EU members, especially on their capacity to formulate individual or collective positions in the 1996 IGC have been considerable. France's distancing herself from her German partner has disoriented the other Southern members of the EU and has added to their difficulties in working out comprehensive proposals to the IGC. The problem is compounded by the fact that the 1995 elections brought about a change of guard in Paris and early indications suggested strongly that the Gaullist President Jacques Chirac was intent on reviewing the main premises of Mitterrand's foreign policy. Some of the decisions of the French government, like the resumption of nuclear tests in the Pacific, caused major dissentions and frictions with other member states, not least with Italy among those of the South.

The net effect of such developments has been disorientation and loss of confidence among the EU's South. This can be attested by the fact that their Presidencies of the Council during 1994–96 were marked by nervousness and sometimes a lack of inspiration, especially if compared to the robustness of the previous round in the late 1980s. This suggests that their positions to the 1996 IGC were determined with domestic, political, economic and security considerations in mind. In other words, present realities in the EU, as well as in the world at large, have not been as propitious as in the past in pursuing a collective Southern vision in earnest. This, of course, does not mean that the EU's Southern members would not coordinate their efforts to defend those interests they share in common. Rather, it suggests a more *ad hoc* basis for such coordination than in the late 1980s and that the pull for doing things together has been hindered by differences on a host of other issues. Last, but by no means least, it implies that France's distancing from her Southern brethren, especially if this is accompanied by policies with which some other Southern members strongly disapprove, might induce them to turn to the North, especially to Germany. The significance of these observations may become more apparent if one examines in more concrete terms individual positions by the EU's South, as far as they have been clearly articulated, to the 1996 IGC and beyond, at least on two of the most difficult issues: reform of the institutions, and the CFSP, especially the debate on the merger of the WEU with the EU, both of which need to be seen in the context of further enlargement (for the debate on the CFSP see EIPA 1995; and for the Spanish paper, *Europe* No 6483, 11 March 1995).[4]

Institutional reform

There are two inter-related aspects to institutional reform that warrant particular emphasis, namely the powers of the EP and the Commission and the question of decision-taking in the Council, including the subject of the extension of qualified majority voting (QMV), especially on issues related to CFSP. On the EP and the Commission, there is a broad consensus among the five EU Southern members that they should be vested with greater powers. However, this is tempered by two caveats, found in varied degrees and formulated in different ways in most national papers: first, the need to define more clearly their competencies as well as the principle of subsidiarity. This, in the case of the EP, means that all Southern members see a need for a greater involvement of national parliaments in EU affairs, especially in the realm of CFSP. However, most of them do not seem to have rendered their support to French calls, going back to the IGC of 1990–91, for the creation of a separate Chamber, formed by national representatives, which would supervise the Union's CFSP (Assembly of the WEU 22 May 1995). This became obvious in the Reflection Group's Report, whose conclusions indicate that the idea for a separate chamber was decisively turned down by nearly all other EU members (Reflection Group 1995: 26). On decision-taking in the Council, there is an overall consensus among the Southern members that QMV should be extended even into the realm of CFSP, provided vital national interests are taken into consideration. The consensus masks a good deal of ambiguity and contradictions. On the one hand, Greece, for example, makes a strong case for a security Community which would automatically guarantee the borders of the Union, yet she would like to preserve the national veto when vital interests are at stake. Spain, on the other hand, considers the veto be phased out except on 'super-sensitive' issues. Yet, the problem is how to define these issues. From Madrid's vantage point, such a category should include Spanish fishing rights off Morocco's coast, while for Athens, it covers the sovereignty of its rocky islets in the Eastern Aegean. In the same vein, the Spanish view to relegate future small members, like Cyprus and Malta, to the status of 'micro-states', which should not be accorded the same privileges as Luxembourg, a founding EC member, is also bound to cause raised eyebrows in other Southern capitals. It is questionable, however, whether these rather divisive positions will be defended in earnest. More likely, the spirit of solidarity will prevail and the Southern members would not be inclined, at least at present, to support more radical proposals for the phasing out of the veto even in the realm of CFSP.

The picture is somewhat more complicated on the question of introducing the population criterion in decisions taken in the Council by qualified majority. On this issue there is a three-way split, with Italy and Spain being strongly in favour, Greece and Portugal against, and France standing in the middle, being in principle in favour of a double criterion, but not resting solely on the population factor. The same split holds on the question of the Presidency, with Greece and Portugal being in favour of retaining the present practice of a rotating Presidency and the larger Southern members in favour of radical reforms which might end the current practice based on the principle of one country one Presidency. In a same vain, Italy, Spain and to a lesser extent France, are more in favour of a reduction in the number of EC Commissioners, even for a more radical streamlining, which would do away with the current practice whereby all EU members have at least one Commissioner.

In short, there is a discernible distancing between the South's larger members, not least Italy and Spain, from their smaller and geographically more peripheral neighbours. This stems not only from the obvious fact that their interests on some crucial issue coincide more with the other larger EU members, but also by the fact that, due to French aloofness and diminished interest in leading the group, Italy and Spain are exploring other options – not least how to adjust their positions to the Union's largest member, Germany. This is especially the case on issues which do not demand obvious, or immediate sacrifices, like the question of enlargement to the East, where one detects a softening in Spain's position, especially if compared to her tough stance on the previous enlargement. In this respect what needs to be stressed is that the question of enlargement to Central and Eastern Europe did not figure very prominently in the Papers elaborated by the Southern members of the EU in the run up to the 1996 IGC – perhaps because the political, security and economic complexities of the subject were increasingly seen as too much for the IGC despite the remit given to the Reflection Group. What needs to be said is that some Southern members, like Portugal and Spain, have toned down their strong reservations on enlargement *tout court*, in the late 1980s–early 1990s. This was partly due to the syndrome of newcomers feeling certain unease with new members joining the Club, as well as to an over-estimation of their capacity to control the pace of enlargement.

The Common Foreign and Security Policy (CFSP)

With regard to issues related to the Union's CFSP in the context of the 1996 IGC, the situation in the South is equally confounded. In this area more than perhaps in any other the strains in the Franco-German tandem have been particularly noticeable, especially after the publication of the CDU–CSU paper in September 1994 (*Europe Documents* No 1895/96, 7 September 1994). For the purposes of this essay what needs to be emphasized is the paper's invitation to France to join forces with Germany in forming an inner core, 'the core of the hard core', as it put it. In return, France is asked to make sacrifices as regards 'the unsurrenderable sovereignty of the "Etat nation"', which, in any case has long been 'an empty shell', according to the paper. This part of the CDU–CSU paper is particularly instructive for, instead of inducing France to join in such core of a core, the paper played a catalytic role in distancing her from her special partner in the EU. At the same time it produced some important side effects on the other two large members of the South, Italy and Spain. Both had felt, if not offended, at least somewhat neglected by the contents of the CDU–CSU paper. After all, both had shown interest in the Eurocorps since the late 1980s and were supposed to be part of the Union's political–security inner core. For Italy, a founding member of the EC and a professed supporter of a federal Community, to be left out from the Union's inner political–security core was particularly injurious. Hence their effort to redress the situation, made easier by French disinterest in joining such a core of a core. The net effect of such developments was that Italian and Spanish proposals related to the CFSP appeared to be inching towards German views. The process was further encouraged by the fact that the revised CDU–CSU paper of June 1995 dropped the notion of a core within a core (CDU–CSU 13 June 1995). In general, therefore, Italy and Spain, as well as Greece and to a limited extent Portugal, are prepared to support proposals which aim to infuse greater sense of purpose into the Union's CFSP. They agree, for example, on the idea of financing the Union's CFSP from the EC's budget, something to which the British and French have appeared hostile, largely because this would blur the line between the Union's separate pillars.

An issue of extreme importance that requires resolution is the relationship between the EU and the WEU. Of course, this is an old question going back to the latter's reactivation in 1984. Yet, the issue has now assumed a much greater urgency for two important reasons: first, because of the security situation in Europe; and second because the Brussels Treaty of the WEU expires in 1998. It would not be an exaggeration to suggest that for this factor alone the 1996 IGC has assumed historic proportions. This is because if it fails to produce tangible results there may be a temptation for some EU members to renounce the Brussels Treaty, as a means of cutting the Gordian knot, thus ending the current state of institutional overlapping. A warning was given to this effect by some unnamed members in the WEU and in the EU in 1995, which could not be dismissed lightly. As the Final Report of the Reflection Group stated, some of its members drew attention to the prospect of not renewing the Brussels Treaty, should they deem the results of the IGC inadequate. Should that happen the WEU would 'disappear and the present duplication of structures for security (CFSP) and for defense in the broad sense (WEU) would be eliminated' (Reflection Group 1995: 48).

There is no doubt, therefore, that the question of working out viable security structures is urgent, not least the vexed question of the merger of the WEU into the EU. Yet, as the Report of the WEU Council of November 1995, suggests views on how this relationship should be developed in the future differ considerably, ranging from those who would like to see the maintenance of full autonomy of the WEU to others calling for a full merger of the WEU with the EU in the short term, that is, even before the Brussels Treaty lapses. In between there are three intermediate positions: one calling for 'reinforced partnership'; a second for 'a greater role of the Union in the Petersberg tasks'; and a third for 'the gradual integration of the WEU into the EU' (WEU November 1995).

It would be hazardous to place the Southern EU members too precisely into this kaleidoscope. What is important to note is that none of them endorses the two extreme views, i.e., either the maintenance of full autonomy of the WEU from the EU or a full merger between the two within a short and fixed time. Having said that, however, there are some important differentiations among them. France, for example, seems to be less enthusiastic for a distinct European security pillar than she has been in the past. A clear sign of this was her re-entry into the military structure of NATO. On the other hand, Italy, Spain and Greece, seem to favour a gradual merger between the WEU with the EU, although not within a fixed timetable. However, should they be confronted with the stark dilemma of some other members, led by Germany, pulling out of the WEU and forming a distinct security arm in the framework of the EU, they might follow suit. Of course, while this may be an extreme case scenario, it cannot be totally ruled out.

THE 1996 IGC AND THE QUEST FOR A EURO-MEDITERRANEAN PARTNERSHIP

The launching of the 1996 IGC, at the Corfu European Council meeting, renewed interest among the EU's Southern members in the development of a comprehensive framework among the countries of the Mediterranean littoral. There had been a short lull following the signing of the TEU which coincided with the endorsement of the Final Document in early 1992, in Malaga, which called for the creation of a CSCM. However, developments in the Balkans and in the former Soviet Union, as well as in the EU itself, since early 1992, switched the focus of attention to other issues. In a sense, therefore, this renewed interest in a comprehensive Mediterranean partnership was spurred by a concern lest the South might be sidelined in the context of the 1996 IGC. For a number of reasons this concern is stronger today than in 1989–90, when the previous IGC was launched. One reason is that the internal balance in the EU in the mid-1990s has shifted to the North–East, with the enlargement from Twelve to Fifteen, as well as the prospect of further enlargement to the East.

At the same time, the political balance seems to have shifted as well, with Germany playing a more assertive role in the remoulding of the EU than she had in the previous IGC. This is reflected in the CDU–CSU paper on the 1996 IGC, released in September 1994. The paper's call for an inner core has already been discussed, but three other aspects of the paper need to be mentioned. First, it puts emphasis on the political–security necessity for the EU's enlargement to the East, which could not be eschewed by economic, institutional, or technical arguments. Second, and related to this, is the paper's reference to the inherent dangers in the EU of a 'South–West grouping, more inclined to protectionism and headed in a certain sense by France, drifting apart from a North–East grouping, more in favour of free trade and headed in a certain sense by Germany'. And third, a point which is derived by the above considerations, is the compelling need for a comprehensive strategy in the EU which should be mapped out by the 1996 IGC. This strategy, according to the CDU–CSU paper should cover both the Union's East as well as its South. In other words, as the paper explicitly states, 'a common policy in the Mediterranean, where stability is of fundamental concern not only to the littoral states but to Germany as well'. This is an additional challenge which the Southern members of the EU have had to take into account in the context of the 1996 IGC. In effect their renewed efforts to craft a Euro-Mediterranean Partnership stems not only from a desire to preserve some sort of a balance between East and South in the EU's priorities, but also from an implicit urge to show that the Southern members of the EU, or at least some of them, remain custodians of this region's interests. However, the pertinent question is whether the EU's Southern members could sustain this role under present circumstances. Is there enough cohesion and sense of purpose, to say nothing about material and political–security resources at their disposal to discharge effectively this role? Are conditions in the mid-1990s more propitious than in the early 1990s for the EU's South pursuing this vocation? Could there be a balancing act between the Union's Eastern and Southern agenda in the coming years? Are the problems and issues encountered comparable and subject to similar solutions?

Such a catalogue of questions could be multiplied almost *ad infinitum*. What needs to be noted for the purposes of this essay, is that the prospects for fulfilling this role successfully is far more remote today than in the past. In the past, there were a host of deep-seated problems and difficulties that the EU's Southern members encountered in discharging this Mediterranean vocation effectively – such as the high degree of cultural, social, political, and economic heterogeneity in the region – or, in other words, the hindrances posed by 'the logic of unevenness'. But new obstacles have been added recently. One is related to the additional problems posed by the disintegration of Yugoslavia and the Soviet Union, and their political, economic, security side-effects on the Mediterranean region. These effects have been multiple in that they have rendered the addressing of the Mediterranean issues not only more awesome but have also profoundly affected perceptions and priorities, not least of the Southern members of the EU themselves. Of course, the way member states have been affected varies considerably: France, who, in effect, has turned her attention to other more pressing issues, not least on how to preserve her status as a major power in the new international order; Greece, who feels the combined effects of the crises in the Balkans and in the former Soviet Union, as well as of the disintegration of the Cold War era; Italy, where the collapse of the ancient regime of the bi-polar era has spilled over to her domestic politics, with the collapse of the traditional political parties and a revival of regionalism and the extreme Right.

In other words, the effects of these historic events on each country have varied considerably, according to geographical, historical, political and other exigencies. The overall result has been to weaken the South's homogeneity, as well as its capacity to address the problems of the Mediterranean region in unison. It has also given rise to a certain estrangement among them, even to some friction. What is important to note here is that preoccupation with more pressing matters has led to a diminishing interest in Mediterranean initiatives. It is not perhaps coincidental that the country which has taken over the torch in championing the South's Mediterranean vocation is Spain, the one least affected by recent developments in the Balkans and in the former Soviet Union.

The net effect of recent efforts to infuse new dynamism to the Euro-Mediterranean notion was the Barcelona Declaration, adopted on 28 November, 1995, by the Fifteen EU members and the EU Commission, with eleven non-EU Mediterranean countries and the Palestinian Authority. Its purpose was to create among the participants a comprehensive partnership, 'the Euro-Mediterranean partnership, through strengthened political dialogue on a regular basis, the development of economic and financial cooperation and the greater emphasis on the social, cultural and human dimension' (*Europe Documents* No 1964, 6 December

1995). For the realization of these objectives, the Barcelona Declaration outlined a number of ideas for a political–security, economic and financial, and cultural and human affairs partnership between the two sides. Taken together they provide an impressive list of more than one hundred items covering a huge spectrum of activities. It remains to be seen, of course, whether this will be translated into tangible results, or whether it will add yet another set to the 'profusion of studies and ideas' on this subject going back to the early 1970s, with the global Mediterranean policy, the Euro-Arab dialogue, the proposal for a CSCM, etc. (*International Spectator* 1994 and 1993; Tsakaloyannis 1992). This scepticism does not stem only from the EU's record so far to cope with the challenges posed in the region, but also by economic and political constraints. For example, it is a moot point whether a meaningful economic and financial partnership can be created by a long list of generalities, like the 'acceleration of the pace of sustainable socio-economic development', or an 'improvement of the living conditions of their populations … and a reduction in the development gap in the Euro-Mediterranean region'. The gap between expectations and capabilities is even greater than in the past and it is hard to see how it could be filled in the coming years. It is doubtful, therefore, whether this bout of Euro-Mediterranean endeavour will prove to be more sustainable than previous exercises. As a problem-solving mechanism it lacks the resources, capabilities and the institutional mechanisms for making a lasting impression on the ground. In the crisis in the Aegean between Greece and Turkey, for example, in early 1996, which brought the two sides to the brink of armed conflict, the Euro-Mediterranean Partnership did not enter into the equation, in stark contrast to the US, the EU, especially German, Russia, or even Syria. The same could be said of its potential in other trouble spots in the region.

CONCLUSIONS AND PROSPECTS

The commencement of the 1996 IGC found the five members of the EU's South in a strikingly different situation to that of the previous IGC in early 1990. A chief feature in the current situation has been sagging confidence, a sense of disorientation and even a certain degree of alienation among the five members of the group. This is the result of a host of domestic and external developments a net effect of which has been the desertion of France, thus leaving the group orphaned and leaderless. At the same time there has been a growing asymmetry between the EU's North–East and its Southern flank. For in addition to the old problems the South was confronted with in the past there have been since the early 1990s a host of new huge problems in the Balkans and in south-west Asia, which create extra political, security, economic and demographic pressures. Besides, whereas Central and Eastern Europe enjoys the strong backing of Germany, the EU's most powerful member, who is unwaveringly pursuing the region's eventual accession to the EU, the South lacks a similar sponsor.

There has therefore been considerable ambiguity as to the objectives to be realized in the region and to the means for their fulfilment. At the same time, the threats to peace and security in the South are greater and more immediate than in Central Europe. The 1996 crisis in the Aegean between Greece and Turkey is the most telling example of the kind of problems the region faces, to say nothing about the crisis in former Yugoslavia, or the looming threats posed by economic, social and demographic pressures which induce ethnic conflict or the spread of Islamic fundamentalism, from Algeria to Turkey and Egypt.

And this is at a time some members of EU's South are becoming more inward-looking and preoccupied with other issues of a divisive nature. For instance, President Chirac's decision to resume French nuclear tests in the South Pacific, apart from the outcry it provoked from world public opinion, also impaired the EU's Southern coherence with effects that spilled over to the 1996 IGC itself. Chirac's warning to his EU partners of the dire consequences should they vote in favour of a UN resolution condeming nuclear tests in the Pacific did not deter Italy from doing just that (along with Portugal, while Greece abstained). Italy's action provoked the cancellation of an official visit by the French president to Rome, on the eve of the latter's assumption of the Presidency of the EU, a move unprecedented in the EC's history (*Le Monde* 19 November 1995), as well as his initial refusal of Prime Minister Dini's invitation to attend the opening ceremony in Turin on 29 March, to inaugurate the 1996 IGC at the European Council level.[5] While one should not over-dramatize the importance of such episodes, it would be equally misleading to brush them aside, and not to interpret them as indicative of the current state of affairs among the EU's Southern partners.

The analysis leads to two overall conclusions. First, that coherence among the EU's Southern members has been considerably eroded since the late 1980s. Their strategy for the 1996 IGC was therefore moulded more by domestic considerations. This, of course, does not imply that they will not pursue their common interests in common whenever this is demanded by the circumstances. It does mean, however, that such alliances will be on a more *ad hoc* basis and on a rather low threshold level. Second, it suggests that the problems facing the South are too large to be dealt with by the Southern member states on their own. As Lorenzo Natali, a former EC Commissioner with special responsibilities for the Mediterranean put it in the early 1980s:

> Geopolitical reasons in themselves make an impressive case for the necessity of a coherent European Community policy on the Mediterranean. A glance at the map proves it. Look first in the Balkans and the mouth of the Atlantic, take in the Dardanelles and the petrol producing region of the Near East: remember, too, that the Mediterranean is the inescapable North–South axis for links between Europe and Africa. We must question whether the Community could survive a serious disturbance in the Mediterranean region. (1982)

Needless to say, such a sobering assessment carries today far more weight than in the early 1980s. This makes more imperative the need for a comprehensive and purposeful attempt to tackle the problems in the Mediterranean region. This could be possible only if the EU itself settles its own domestic agenda and it acquires such capabilities which would enable it to map out a comprehensive, long-term strategy. This is why the 1996 IGC assumes such historic proportions for the region. For a failure to overcome existing problems in the course of the 1996 IGC would not only affect the Mediterranean region at large, but also the EU's Southern members who will find themselves more and more immersed by the problems of this region, thus falling behind their partners in the North.

NOTES

1. It should be noted that the negative Opinion of the Commission on Greek accession from Athens' point of view, released in early 1975, which called for a deferral of negotiations till an unspecified time in the future, was not subscribed by the French and Italian Commissioners.
2. Incidentally, the first pilot issue of *The European* appeared at the European Council meeting in Rhodes, in December 1988. This carried an interview by the late Robert Maxwell with Chancellor Kohl and President Mitterrand, under the heading 'We Have a Dream'. It was within this context that a Southern caucus took shape.
3. According to the Presidency's conclusions in Madrid, the EU in the next five years must accomplish the following objectives: carry out adjustments to the TEU; make the transition to a single currency; prepare for and carry out enlargement negotiations; determine, in parallel, the financial perspective beyond 31 December 1999; contribute to establishing the new European security architecture; and actively continue the policy of active dialogue, cooperation and association with Russia, Ukraine, Turkey and the Mediterranean countries. See 'Madrid Summit', *Europe, Special Edition*, No 6629, 17 December 1995.
4. I would like to thank Sally Haworth for translating into English the long (99 pages) Spanish Paper entitled 'La Conferencia Integuvernmental de 1996: Bases Para Una Reflection', of March 1995, a summary of which was published by *Europe*, no. 6438, 11 March 1995.
5. Felipe Gonzalez, the host of the Madrid European Council admitted that there had been 'a certain amount of Franco-Italian tension'. It is worth noting that the only other leader who refused Dini's invitation in Madrid to attend a summit meeting in Turin, on 29 March, 1996, was John Major. For details see *Europe, Special Edition: Madrid Summit* (15–16 December 1995) no. 6629, 17 December 1995.

REFERENCES AND BIBLIOGRAPHY

Aliboni, Roberto (1991) *European Security Across the Mediterranean*. Paris, Institute for Security Studies, WEU, Chaillot Paper 2.

Blasksell, Mark (1984) 'The European Community and the Mediterranean Region: two steps forward, one step back', in Williams, Allan (ed.) *Southern European Transformation: The Political and Economic Change in Greece, Italy, Portugal and Spain*. London, Harper and Row.

Bonvicini, Gianni (1992) 'The Mediterranean and Eastern Europe: two worlds in competition?' in Telo, Mario (ed.) *Towards a New Europe?* Brussels, Université Libre.

CDU–CSU (1995) 'Pressedienst, CDU/CSU Fraktion im Deutschen Bundestag', 13 June.

EIPA (1995) 'Common Foreign and Security Policy and the 1996 IGC: Positions of Main Actors', Maastricht, October.

Featherstone, Kevin (1989) 'The Mediterranean challenge: cohesion and external preferences', in Lodge, Juliet (ed.) *The European Community and the Challenge of the Future*. London, Pinter.

Garton Ash, Timothy (1991) *We the People: The Revolutions of '89 Witnessed in Warsaw, Budapest, Berlin and Prague*. London, Granta Books.

Henig, Stanley (1976) 'Mediterranean policy in the context of the external relations of the EC: 1958–73', in Shlaim, Avi and Yannopoulos, George (eds) *The EEC and the Mediterranean Countries*. Cambridge, Cambridge University Press.

Hill, C (ed.) (1996) *The Actors in Europe's Foreign Policy*. London, Routledge.

The *International Spectator* (1994) 'Cooperation and Stability in the Mediterranean: An Agenda for Partnership', vol. 29, no. 3.

The *International Spectator* (1993) 'Mediterranean: Risks and Challenges', vol. 28, no. 3.

Laursen, F. and Vanhoonacker, S. (eds) (1992) *The Intergovernmental Conference on Political Union*. Maastricht, European Institute of Public Administration.

—— (eds) (1994) *The Ratification of the Maastricht Treaty: Issues, Debates and Future Implications*. Maastricht-Dordrecht, EIPA and Martinus Nijhoff Publishers.

Natali, Lorenzo (1982) 'L' élargissement de la CE vers le sud', speech before the Konrad Adenauer Foundation. Brussels, 2–3 December.

'Reflection Group's Study: Second Part, an Annotated Agenda', SN 520/95 Reflex 21, 1995.

Tsakaloyannis, Panos (1992) 'The European Community and the Wider Europe: Risks and Opportunities in the East and South', in Pijpers, Alfred (ed.) *The European Community at the Crossroads*. Dordrecht, Martinus Nijhoff, pp. 253–70.

—— (1996) *The European Union as a Security Community: Problems and Prospects*. Baden-Baden, Nomos Verlag.

Tsoukalis, Loukas (1981) T*he European Community and Its Mediterranean Enlargement*. London, Allen and Unwin.

WEU (1995) 'National Parliaments, European Security and Defense and the Road to the 1996 IGC', Assembly of the WEU, Document 1459, 22 May.

—— (1995) 'WEU Contribution to the European Union: The IGC of 1996', WEU Press and Information Service, WEU Council of Ministers. Madrid, 14 November.

9

THE NORDIC TRIO
AND THE FUTURE OF THE EU

NIKOLAJ PETERSEN

INTRODUCTION

On 1 January 1995, the European Union (EU) acquired a genuine northern dimension, when Denmark, its lone Nordic member for more than two decades, was joined by Sweden and Finland. Even though this Nordic component was limited by the negative referendum on membership in Norway, the fact that there are now three Nordic members of the Union raises interesting questions about the prospects for the extension of Nordic cooperation into the politics of the Union.

The 1996 Intergovernmental Conference (IGC) provided an almost immediate opportunity to test that cooperation, if for no other reason than because the three countries shared a hesitant attitude towards it. To Denmark, the IGC raised the disturbing prospect of a repetition of the Maastricht process, in which the political establishment (government and parliament) was deeply embarrassed by the public's initial rejection of the Treaty on European Union (TEU). The IGC was also seen as threatening the exemptions from Maastricht which eventually allowed Denmark to sign the treaty after the 1993 referendum. Furthermore, Denmark has always been status quo-oriented in questions of institutional development, and few have seen the need for change. On the other hand, great importance has been attached to the Eastern enlargement of the Union, which is seen as the only really valid rationale for the 1996 IGC. In the Danish view this has compensated for some of the inconveniences of the conference, but does not remove the fears that it will challenge fundamental aspects of Denmark's position in the Union and threaten a fragile domestic consensus.

Sweden and Finland have not suffered from Denmark's 'Maastricht blues', nor have they had a long and sometimes troubled relationship with the Community before Maastricht. On the other hand, the two governments have reason to fear that the conference will reopen the difficult debates of 1994 on the pros and cons of membership. This has been especially the case in Sweden where support for the Union has dropped significantly since the referendum of November 1994, and where the pro-Europeans suffered a serious setback in the European Parliament (EP) elections of September 1995. A problem for both countries is a lack of experience of the Union and knowledge of how it actually functions. When the IGC opened, Sweden and Finland had been members for barely a year, a very short period in which to form considered opinions about the Union's deficiencies and the strategies necessary or possible to overcome them. On the positive side, both countries support Eastern enlargement, and are, at least in theory, prepared to pay concessions to the union process to facilitate it.

The prospects for Nordic cooperation in the EU are strengthened by the fact that the three countries share some basic attitudes on Europe, both towards institutional development and policy. All are inter-governmentalist rather than federalist in their approach; they share a political culture which emphasizes democratic participation and control; and they have a preference for pragmatic cooperation in areas of low-politics rather than for the grandiloquent planning of political utopia. And, as already mentioned, they share a common interest in the enlargement of the Union to the east.

A theoretical note

Mouritzen (1993) has sketched a general model for national strategies *vis-à-vis* regional integration, which distinguishes between strategies followed by *insiders* (EU members), *would-be insiders* (applicants), and *outsiders*, i.e. countries outside the integration process – whether by choice or otherwise. Being an insider, i.e., part of the centre, gives 'plenty of room for the influence of domestic factors ... but also for the role of ideology and historical factors' (Mouritzen 1993: 396). Insiders will therefore follow a balanced integration strategy, which seeks to balance out domestic interests and external demands.

Would-be insiders face a different situation. They abide by the rules and norms of the Union wherever relevant for the simple reason that they wish to appear as natural future insiders, as 'good Europeans'. They therefore tend to follow an acquiescent strategy. This leads to the hypothesis, that Finnish and Swedish attitudes to integration may have changed significantly with membership, and that they will now follow a more balanced mode, in which domestic preoccupations play a larger role than they did during the membership process.

With respect to Denmark's integration strategy, Mouritzen argues that prior to the 1992 referendum Danish politicians gave priority to offensive power, i.e., influence on EC developments, over defensive power or autonomy, but that subsequently autonomy concerns won over wishes for more offensive power. In this way 'we are back at the "classic" priorities that determined Danish EC policy from the inception of EC membership 1973 until about 1986 – the kind of posture that has been labelled "footdragging" by its critics' (ibid.: 380). Whether Sweden and Finland will choose to balance their relationship with the EU in a defensive or offensive mode remains to be seen.

NORDEN AND EUROPE: A SHORT HISTORY

Norden outside the community

Norden[1] has had a troubled relationship with European integration from its very beginning. While Finland, with its special relationship with the Soviet Union based on the 1948 Treaty of Friendship, Cooperation and Assistance, remained outside the integration process until 1961, Denmark, Norway and Sweden were involved in discussions over the future of Europe from the late 1940s. At that point they came down decisively on the side of inter-governmentalism and separate national development of the welfare state. As a result they resisted cooperation with the Six and tried instead to foster Nordic economic cooperation.[2] By the late 1950s the creation of the EEC increased the pressure on Norden, and especially Denmark, but, in the first instance, the three countries reacted by joining the British-sponsored European Free Trade Association (EFTA) in 1960. A year later, in 1961, Finland was associated with EFTA through the so-called FINEFTA agreement. When Britain applied for EEC membership in 1961 Denmark (and Norway) followed suit. They did so once again in 1967 and were joined this time by Sweden, who sent in an open-ended application which did not exclude membership. However, while the doors to Europe remained shut, another abortive attempt was made to create a Nordic Economic Union (NORDEK).

When the obstacles to EC membership were lifted in 1969, both Denmark and Norway negotiated accession treaties, but as the Norwegian deal was rejected by a referendum, only Denmark actually joined the Community (1973). Sweden had by this time decided against membership, mostly because it was seen as incompatible with its policy of non-alignment. Instead it signed a free trade agreement with the EC. Norway followed suit after its referendum, as did Finland after reassuring the Soviet Union by negotiating a similar agreement with Comecon. Thus the Nordic countries parted ways in 1973 with Denmark joining the EC, while the rest of Norden continued in EFTA with free trade agreements with the EC.

Denmark in the European Community

Denmark joined the EC on the basis of a clear mandate in the October 1972 referendum, in which 63 per cent voted in favour and 37 per cent against (Rüdiger 1995; Petersen 1995). Denmark's European honeymoon soon ended, however, when public support began to drop both as a reaction to the oil crisis and to the EC proponents' lavish promises during the referendum campaign. For more than a decade supporters and opponents of Denmark's membership were evenly balanced. In part as a result, Denmark's EC policy became cautious and 'footdragging', opposed to institutional changes, but not to pragmatic economic cooperation. Footdragging was most prominent in the Social Democratic Party which held power for most of the period, and whose rank and file remained deeply sceptical of the EC.

Matters came to a head over the Single European Act (SEA) in 1986. The governing non-Socialist government (1982–93) welcomed the Act, but was voted down in Parliament by a coalition of Social Democrats, Social Liberals and leftist parties. Instead of admitting defeat the government called a non-binding referendum, which sanctioned the SEA by 56 against 44 per cent, after which the Parliamentary opposition caved in.

This dramatic episode ushered in a more positive phase in Denmark's relationship with the EC, in which public debate was no longer dominated by the membership issue, but rather by the future development of the Community. This phase culminated in 1990 with the negotiation of a broadly based domestic platform for the Intergovernmental Conferences of 1991, which was characterized by a certain readiness to accept a deepening of European integration. Against this background, the Maastricht Treaty was received much more positively in the political establishment than the SEA had been. In May 1992 the *Folketing* approved the Treaty by 130 to 25, before sending it for confirmation in a referendum. The results of the June referendum showed that the political élite had seriously misjudged the public mood, as 50.7 per cent voted against the Treaty.

The political turmoil that was created coalesced after a few months in a so-called National Compromise in which the opposition of Social Democrats, Social Liberals and the Socialist People's Party in effect forced a reluctant government of Conservatives and Liberals to demand the negotiation of a number of exemptions from the Maastricht treaty as the price for Danish ratification. These exemptions concerned the EMU, the defence aspects of the Common Foreign and Security Policy (CFSP), Union citizenship and issues falling within the third pillar on Justice and Home Affairs (JHA). In addition, the National Compromise also put forward a number of demands concerning increasing openness, 'nearness' (the Danish for subsidiarity) and democracy in the Community.

These demands were largely accepted by the European Council at its December 1992 meeting in Edinburgh. It was agreed that Denmark would stay outside the third stage of EMU and would not take part in the defence aspects of the CFSP, i.e., Article J.4 of the TEU. Furthermore, the Danish interpretations of Union citizenship and the third pillar were implicitly accepted,[3] and the Danish position accommodated in the Edinburgh Conclusions with respect to increasing openness and nearness. The Maastricht Treaty now including the Edinburgh Agreement was then presented at a second referendum in May 1993, the political parties having expressly agreed that the four Edinburgh exemptions could only be lifted after a further referendum. On this basis the Treaty passed the referendum by 57 per cent – not a very convincing majority given the fact that seven out of eight political parties in the *Folketing* stood behind it.[4]

Sweden's accession to the Union

After Denmark joined the EC in 1973, Sweden gave up any thoughts of a formal relationship beyond the free trade agreement for almost 20 years. Broadly speaking three factors were responsible for this. First, Sweden's policy of non-alignment was seen as incompatible with membership of a Community which increasingly emphasized its ambition to become an international actor and which was clearly a part of the Cold War. Second, Sweden's strong economy created few incentives for membership as long as the free trade agreement functioned satisfactorily. Third, the dominant welfare state ideology required a high degree of political and economic autonomy.

Sweden's membership of the European Union from 1 January 1995, therefore represents a major change in Sweden's post-war foreign policy, made possible by a specific constellation of permissive and constraining factors. One permissive component was the end of the Cold War and the subsequent collapse of the Soviet Union. This permitted Sweden to relax its longstanding belief that taking part in European integration was incompatible with the official doctrine of non-alignment in peace and neutrality in war. After 1989 this argument lost its force. At the same time, two new constraints entered the picture to influence Swedish policy (Pedersen 1994). The first was the European scene as it appeared in the early 1990s with the EC seemingly destined to become the focal point of European politics with Germany as the leading power. By remaining on the sideline, Sweden risked being isolated from European politics, a much less agreeable position than the self-imposed isolation of the Cold War era. Then it had given Sweden a certain sense of security, but now the prevailing sense was one of influence foregone.

The second constraint was economic. By the late 1980s Swedish business circles had become increasingly nervous at the prospect of being excluded from the single European market. As a result, they stepped up their pleas for membership and, perhaps more effectively, started to divert their investments away from Sweden into the EC market. Economic pressures to join the EC grew in 1990 as Sweden slumped into deep and prolonged economic crisis, which called into question the very preservation of the welfare state, the 'People's Home'. Swedes suddenly realized that their unique societal experiment might have to retrench in order to save itself. The sobering effect of the welfare crisis was thus another permissive factor in the decision to join, which was reflected in a sudden pro-EC turn in public opinion and in the labour movement.

These developments soon eclipsed the efforts, initiated in 1989, at negotiating a European Economic Area (EEA) between the EC and the EFTA countries. When the EEA agreement was concluded in October 1991, the Swedish government and *Riksdag* (Parliament) had already decided to seek outright membership, the formal application having been handed in on 1 July 1991. As a modern and, despite recent setbacks, rich country Sweden had no difficulty in adjusting to the EC's internal market. After a drastic devaluation of the krona, Swedish industry started to regain its competitiveness, and there were few ailing industries or regions to protect during negotiations for membership, which were initiated in 1993. Sweden therefore had few problems with accepting the *acquis communautaire*.

The *acquis politique* presented more difficulties. Sweden accepted the Maastricht Treaty's CFSP without reservation, but also emphasized that formal neutrality would be upheld. Sweden subsequently opted for observer status in the WEU like Denmark. Any thoughts about joining NATO or even discussions on the possibility were firmly spurned by the government.[5]

Finland's accession to the Union

To Finland, membership of the EU represents an even more conspicuous rupture with foreign policy tradition than to Sweden. Finland's self-proclaimed neutrality during the Cold War had its special character by virtue of the 1948 Treaty of Friendship, Cooperation and Assistance with the Soviet Union and a European policy of equidistance – Finland could not have closer formal relations with the EC than with Comecon. In 1973 it had therefore had to sign similar agreements with the two highly dissimilar organizations (Pedersen 1994).

The end of the Cold War and the demise of the Soviet Union radically changed Finland's security environment by opening an opportunity, which Finnish politicians readily exploited, to strengthen Finland's Western links.[6] An important consideration in this about-turn was that, while Russia had ceased to be a security threat because of changing policies and external as well as internal weaknesses, it was wise to reorient policy before any possible turn for the worse in Russian policy. Thus, the main Finnish motivation for approaching Europe was security, the calculation being that 'Union membership will help Finland repel any military threats and prevent attempts to exert political pressure' (Security 1995: 59).

The security motive was supplemented by important economic considerations. In 1990–91 Finland ran into a serious economic crisis caused by, inter alia, the breakdown of its eastern trade; from 1989 to 1992 GDP dropped by 8 per cent (Väyrynen 1993: 68). The crisis, which led to a major devaluation of the markka and deep cuts in state expenditures, drastically strengthened perceptions of Finland's dependence on Western Europe and strongly encouraged following Sweden's example of applying to the EC. In any event, the so-called 'Swedish imperative', defined by Klaus Törnudd as early as 1969, as: 'Finland must not remain outside any preferential trade arrangement which includes Norway and Sweden together with any principal customer' (quoted in Väyrynen 1993: 64), would have served as a forceful factor for a policy change. The government handed in Finland's application to the EU in the spring of 1992.

Finland entered the EU on similar conditions as Sweden, i.e., wholesale acceptance of the acquis communautaire, though with extended special arrangements for agriculture and its less privileged regions. As to the acquis politique, Finland accepted the CFSP without formal reservations and has repeatedly pledged itself to contribute constructively to the development of a defence dimension. On membership, however, Finland made clear that, at least for the time being, it preferred to be only an observer with the WEU. Thus Finland formally stuck to neutrality, but redefined it 'in a minimal fashion consisting of two main elements; non-membership in military alliances, i.e. non-alignment, and the capacity for independent defence' (Väyrynen 1993: 73). The Finnish debate on the WEU and NATO has been less absolutist than in Sweden, suggesting a certain flexibility in this field.

DENMARK AND EUROPEAN UNION

Background factors

As the historical analysis has demonstrated, Denmark has a long and fairly traumatic relationship with European integration compared to Sweden or Finland.

Historically conditioned features therefore have an important impact on Danish integration policy together with structural factors, such as geographic position, economic structure, political system, political culture and the like.

The geographic factor has acquired a new significance with the enlargement of the Union. For 22 years Denmark was situated on the geographical margins of the Union – a Nordic outpost, so to speak, both geographically and culturally. During this period, Danes often felt estranged from what was perceived as the dominant élitist and idealistic political culture in the EU with its emphasis on 'southern', rather than 'northern' political and social values.[7] On the other hand, being the sole Nordic member also gave Denmark the status of the informal voice of the North.

EU enlargement to take in Sweden and Finland has eliminated this particular status, but has created new potential allies. Denmark is no longer on the periphery of the Union, whose geographical and political centre is moving to the north and east. Enlargement with the Visegrad and (especially) the Baltic countries will further increase the centrality of Denmark by turning the Baltic Sea into an EU lake. Enlargement may therefore in the long term weaken Danish political–cultural reservations to European integration and the reluctant, footdragging attitude, which has been its corollary. The political need to put the Union's house in order before further enlargement may also convince Danish politicians to give concessions to the integration process, which would otherwise not be given. On the other hand, the possibility of joint Nordic footdragging in the Union should not be discounted.

Economically, over the last decade Denmark has moved from having a weak, crisis-ridden economy to boasting one of the strongest economies in Europe. The Danish krone has regained its old ERM parity with the DM; inflation is low, and the Maastricht goals for public debt and budget deficits are within reach. Thus there are no economic reasons for Denmark not to join the third stage of the EMU. However, as part of the effort to gain public acceptance of the Maastricht Treaty after the aborted 1992 referendum the government pledged to stay outside the EMU's third stage unless mandated to enter by another referendum.

The most important flaw in Denmark's economic performance has been the continued high rate of unemployment, which has baffled government. Building on a long Danish EU tradition, the Social Democrat-led government that took over in 1993 after ten years of non-socialist governments, has argued that employment should be rated on a par with monetary stability within EMU, and that the Union in general should concentrate more on fighting unemployment and promoting economic growth. In the Danish view, pragmatic efforts to increase welfare are more important than institutional reform.

Politically, Parliament and the political parties play crucial roles in the making of Denmark's EU policy, because the country is usually governed by minority governments with a weak parliamentary base. This problem is mitigated by the formation of broad foreign policy coalitions, so that Danish EU policy is normally decided by a six-party coalition of pro-EU parties, with the Social Democrats in a commanding position.[8] Despite this, governments cannot expect automatic support in the *Folketing*.

As early as 1960 Parliament set up a Market Relations Committee to oversee Denmark's EC policy (Nehring 1992). The powers of the Committee, rechristened the Europe Committee in 1994, has gradually grown, especially after EC membership in 1973, the SEA in 1986, and the Maastricht Treaty in 1993. The Committee meets once a week to discuss current EU matters and is empowered to give the government a binding mandate in EU negotiations. Denmark's parliamentary control is generally viewed as the most effective in the Union.

Besides Parliament, public opinion has a significant impact on European policy because of a strong political convention that major changes in Denmark's formal relationship with the Union should be approved by a referendum. Article 20 of the 1953 Constitution stipulates that the delegation of sovereignty rights to international bodies can only be decided by a 5/6 majority of all members of Parliament, or – failing that – by a simple majority in Parliament followed by approval in a popular referendum. In theory, then, Parliament can decide, if there is a sufficient majority, or if no formal delegation of sovereignty is involved.[9] In terms of practical politics the situation is different. The four EU referendums so far (1972, 1986, 1992 and 1993) have established the convention that the people are the final arbiter of Denmark's EU policy. This convention was further strengthened when the political parties committed themselves to calling a referendum on future changes to the four Edinburgh exemptions. There is therefore a general expectation that the result of the 1996 IGC will also be subject to a referendum.

A further complication is that Danish opinion tends to be Euro-sceptical (Worre 1995). Between accession in 1973 and 1988 supporters and opponents of EC membership were fairly evenly balanced, though with opponents in the lead most of the time. Only in 1988 did an upward trend begin to manifest itself. This gradually removed membership as such from the political agenda with, instead, the focus falling on specific aspects of European integration.

Overall, the Danish public is significantly less supportive of European integration than most other European publics. In the early 1980s, Eurobarometer polls showed that strong opponents of European integration overshadowed supporters by a margin of 19 to 13 per cent (Eurobarometer 1991). Since then support for integration has increased, but the majority of Danes continue to prefer intergovernmental cooperation over supranational integration; in fact, less than one-fifth of the public has federalist sympathies.

This turned into a political problem when the Maastricht Treaty was narrowly rejected by the referendum in June 1992. Opposition was concentrated on the left; 92 per cent of the People's Socialists and (more seriously) 64 per cent of the Social Democrats voted 'no'. But there was also a majority of noes among the rightist-populist Progress Party's voters (55 per cent). The vote must be interpreted therefore as a rejection of the Union or federal perspective; there was opposition to the CFSP, to a common currency, to the social dimension and to joint citizenship (Siune et al. 1992; Worre 1995). Although the Maastricht Treaty was accepted in the second referendum, it was not very convincing. The public remained sceptical and sullen. Public attitudes to European integration have not changed much since then.[10] As a result, the political establishment has ample reasons to worry about the public reception of the 1996 IGC.

Denmark, the 1996 IGC and the future of European union

In view of this historical and cultural background, the approach of Danish policy-makers to the 1996 IGC, as well as to the development of the EU in general, has been extremely cautious. Besides the problem of public approval, the expected focus of IGC 1996 on institutional change was at odds with Danish preferences for pragmatic, functional cooperation on an intergovernmental basis. From the beginning therefore the government's secret preference was probably for results so small and insignificant that it could decently bypass the requirement of a ref-erendum. In fact, the Social Liberal Foreign Minister, Niels Helveg Petersen, has hinted that a referendum may not be necessary after all.

On the other hand, the government cannot count on such an outcome, and the cost might very well be high, namely to jeopardize the Eastern enlargement of the Union, which has topped the Danish EU agenda since 1993. At the Copenhagen Summit in June of that year the government gained general support for the prin-ciple of 'Europe' Agreements (and hence eventual membership) for the Baltic republics. The signing of such agreements in the summer of 1995 was seen as a major step toward Union membership for the three countries.

Against this background the government and political circles in Denmark have acknowledged the need for some institutional change in order to make a Union of perhaps 27 members as effective as the present one of fifteen and to avoid skew-ing the balance too far in favour of the small countries (Niels Helveg Petersen in *Berlingske Tidende* 1 October 1995). The problem is to find a proper balance between concessions to the Union process, the demands emanating from the domestic scene, and not least the defence of important policy bastions, such as the Edinburgh exemptions, the National Compromise and the intergovernmental character of the Union.

The preparatory phase

A popular theory holds that the 1992 referendum went wrong because the public debate did not start until after the Maastricht Treaty had been signed – though it had been under discussion at the political level for two years. Whether this analy-sis is right or not, it was given considerable credibility in political circles and flavoured the preparations for the IGC.

In preparation for the 1996 IGC, the government initiated the preparation process in 1994 by setting up an interdepartmental study group to analyse the likely agenda, and commissioning a report on Denmark's security policy, includ-ing the tricky issue of WEU membership. (As a consequence of the Edinburgh exemptions Denmark had rejected membership in the WEU and opted for observer status in 1994.) The report, published in May 1995 by the independent Commission on Security and Disarmament Affairs (SNU), argued for Danish membership of the WEU (SNU 1995). The Foreign Office's report on the

European Agenda (*Udenrigsministeriet* June 1995), while giving a factual report on the prospects for the IGC, also gave a judicious warning that some of the government's top priorities, such as the environment, consumer protection and the social dimension, were controversial issues in the EU and were not necessarily destined to be placed high on the IGC agenda.

During the first half of 1995 several political parties and interest organizations came out with recommendations for Denmark's future EU policy. The Liberals advocated revoking the Danish Edinburgh exemptions, a speedy enlargement of the Union, including necessary reforms of EU policies, the communitarization of most of the TEU's third pillar, the adoption of a '*Kompetenzkatalog*', a realistic balancing of small and large member states, and a strengthening of the EP with the eventual establishment of a two-chamber system based on Parliament and Council (Venstre 1995). The Conservatives released a less pro-European paper (Konservative 1995), which pointed to the need for clear limits to integration, for Eastern enlargement with the necessary structural changes, for a clear specification of the subsidiarity principle, for a repeal of the Edinburgh exemptions, for a limitation of the social dimension, and for some communitarization of third pillar issues.

The Social Democratic Party started to spell out its position in a 'grass roots' paper in December 1994 (Social Democratic Party 1994). It argued for 'a more Social Democratic Europe' catering to people's 'genuine needs', i.e., employment, protection of the environment, consumer protection and defence of the welfare state. It also recommended adherence to the Edinburgh reservations, EU enlargement, including changes in agricultural and structural policies, a strengthening of openness, subsidiarity and democracy in the EU, unchanged relations between large and small members, and a certain strengthening of the Parliament at the expense of the Commission. In September 1995 the Social Democratic Annual Conference adopted a programme on the same lines, but more cautious and less precise in its formulation (*Socialdemokratiet* 1995). Among its specific recommendations was to inscribe employment into the fundamental goals of the Treaty and to have more majority decisions in social and environmental policies. Concerning the WEU a small chink was opened with the remark that the party would want the organization to take on humanitarian and peace-keeping tasks for the UN and Organization of Security and Cooperation in Europe (OSCE). However, any re-evaluation of the Danish policy towards the WEU would have to wait until after the IGC. The other government party, the Social Liberals, also laid down their EU policy at a party conference in September 1995 by adopting a broadly phrased programme, which defended the retention of the Edinburgh exemptions, but which also gave the government great latitude to negotiate at the IGC.

On the anti-Unionist side, the Socialist People's Party conference in May 1995 adopted a programme on 'A Europe of Several Spaces', where each member state would decide for itself which projects it wanted to participate in, environmental policy and the social dimension being obligatory. While anti-Unionist the programme nonetheless advocated a major role for the EU as the spearhead of a new 'economic security policy' in Eastern Europe and the Mediterranean. The June

Movement, one of the anti-unionist movements, published a paper on 'Democratic Cooperation in Europe'. This proposed the dissolution of the Union and a broad all-European cooperation based on the Council of Europe, the OSCE and the UN. If the EU were to continue, Denmark should negotiate a withdrawal from its political part. The other anti-unionist movement, The Popular Movement against the European Union, being even more fundamentalist, urged a total break with the Union.

Among the social partners, the trade union movement is split over the Union. The Trade Union Congress (LO) and the Metal Workers' Union are pro-unionist and criticize the official policy of exemptions to the TEU, while the General Workers' Union (SiD) is openly Euro-sceptical. Most trade union interest focuses on strengthening the social dimension, including stronger EU employment policies. Industrial interests, in contrast, argue that the social dimension should be given less emphasis, but they agree with the trade unions that Eastern enlargement should include the whole *acquis*, including environmental and worker protection policies.

The original idea of the government was that these preparations should be followed by a public debate over the summer and autumn of 1995, which in turn would lead to the political decision phase. By November 1995, no such debate had taken off, a major factor being the difficulties of the government parties to give any clear signals. The government sees the need for public debate but at the same time dreads it, the result being a postponement. Popular interest in European affairs remains limited, a sign, perhaps, of Euro-fatigue after the referendums of 1992 and 1993 and the EP elections in 1994.

The outcome of this preparatory process was not clear, either. Consultations between the government and opposition parties started in October 1995, but were hampered by the government's inability to present an agreed platform. Earlier ambitions of a comprehensive statement of Danish preferences and positions at the IGC therefore gave way to more modest expectations of a short but general position paper designed to offend no one but allow the government greater leeway at the Conference.

The main issues

The issues in the Danish debate on the future of EU can be lumped together under four main headings: (i) the Edinburgh exemptions; (ii) democracy and openness; (iii) institutional development; and (iv) EU policies, including the Common Foreign and Security Policy. Added to these is the issue of enlargement but this is beyond partisan strife and is seen as a basic premise of all discussions on the future of the Union.

The Edinburgh exemptions are the touchiest of the issues involved and yet may turn out to be a non-issue in the short term since the subjects they relate to may not rank high on the IGC agenda. In the longer term, however, they are likely to present very difficult problems for Denmark's position in the Union. The reservation on the third stage of the EMU may not be directly relevant to the discussions on IGC 1996, but will pose a major problem if and when the third stage is initiated, because there are no economic reasons why Denmark should not join. The reservation concerning JHA will only be activated if the IGC decides to move policies from the third to the first pillar, but again in the longer run it may be an impediment to participation in the third pillar activities. And finally, the reservation concerning WEU membership and participation in the defence dimension of the CFSP will only become relevant, if the IGC decides to develop cooperation in the defence field. In that case, Denmark may either have to seek to modify its reservation to meet the new situation or give it up altogether. In the longer term, the reservation may have more serious consequences for Denmark's position in European security policy.

The Edinburgh exemptions are, however, mostly of a symbolic character. To their critics, who include most non-Socialist parties as well as a majority in the media and in academia, they are a symbol of Denmark's half-hearted participation in the Union, which seriously reduces Denmark's influence and should therefore be given up as soon as possible after the conference – no one believes in the possibility of removing them beforehand. Left-wingers and anti-unionists, on the other hand, have regarded the exemptions as important signposts of Denmark's resistance to a further unionist development and therefore wanted them inscribed in the government's negotiating posture for the IGC.

In between are those political groups, mainly the Social Democrats and Radicals, who sympathize somewhat with the contents of the reservations, but who also see them as a political embarrassment. The important consideration for the government parties, though, is public opinion and especially opinion in their respective hinterlands, which makes it very difficult for them to suggest a repeal of the exemptions. The Edinburgh exemptions are therefore likely to be the most prominent bastions which the present government will want to hold to in the Conference and beyond.

Openness, Nearness and Democracy have been very close to the top of the Danish EU agenda since 1990 and especially the 1992 referendum. There is a broad domestic consensus on the need to open up the closed EU system, and Denmark can be counted on to use every opportunity to press the issue. At the Edinburgh Summit in December 1992 the EU pledged to increase openness and transparency in its internal processes, and Denmark has, since then, sought to have these decisions implemented, though only with limited success. That pressure – to open up some meetings, at least, of the Council, and for the publication of voting records in the Council, and easier access to EU documents – will continue. 'Nearness' or subsidiarity has been seen exclusively as a decentralizing principle. In the Danish view the principle of subsidiarity has become a valuable reality in EU politics, resulting in fewer, but more effective and goal-directed initiatives on the part of the Commission. The government has noted, though, that the subsidiarity principle has been abused by certain governments in attempts to lower environmental and consumer protection standards. There is a broad consensus that these issues, together with protection of the work environment, should be decided at Union level.

Democracy in the Danish view usually refers to ensuring the influence of national parliaments rather than strengthening the EP. The EP has traditionally been much maligned by Danish politicians, but attitudes have perhaps begun to change somewhat. For instance, the EP is now seen as an important ally on environmental issues. Denmark is likely to concede the Parliament a right of initiative as well as an extension of the co-decision procedure to cover issues now governed by older forms of cooperation.

Institutional development in the EU, as far as most Danes are concerned, becomes necessary to the extent that the present decision-making procedures are regarded as unnecessarily complex. Danish politicians also acknowledge the need to tighten up the Union's decision-making in preparation for enlargement. In principle, therefore, the Danish government has been willing to envisage a number of changes and modifications, but, at the same time, has stuck to the long-standing policy of defending the existing balance between large and small member states and between the Union's institutions.

In the Danish view the balance between the institutions allows for some increase in the EP's powers, though not in a decisive way, but any increase in the Commission's power is out of the question. Rather, the Danes favour weakening the Commission – in clear contradistinction to other small EU members who see the Commission as the guardian of small power interests. Thus Denmark continues to see the Council (not the European Council, which is deemed too dominated by the big powers) as the central decision-making body. It opposes any overt push towards approaching the 'federal goal', as it did during the final Maastricht discussions.

While open in principle to adjustments, the problem is to find acceptable ones. There is no willingness to give up the right to have a national Commissioner, but a minor change in favour of the larger countries in the Council appears to be acceptable. There is also some sympathy for a double majority consisting of a qualified majority of member states with the added requirement that this majority should also represent a majority of populations. Foreign Minister Helveg Petersen has supported the notion of Presidency teams of three to four countries working together for one year (*Berlingske Tidende* 1 October 1995).

Any drastic changes with respect to rights and obligations in the future Union are less acceptable. The various concepts of a core-periphery Europe, which were aired during 1994–95 (see, for example, Chapter 2), have been rejected, if for no other reason than that Denmark would then risk being placed in the periphery. The official position taken by Foreign Minister Niels Helveg Petersen, has been that all members must share the same goals, but may approach them at different speeds. It has been pointed out that some variable geometry already exists in the Union, and that there should be some possibility for opt-outs – but not on essential issues. Europe à la carte has few supporters, except among People's Socialists. The Danish position is not very clear, though, because Denmark already has four opt-outs. Public opinion on this issue is unknown, but is probably less averse to Denmark being on the European periphery than the political establishment.

EU policies in the Danish view should primarily aim at providing practical solutions to concrete problems. In the context of the IGC this view has manifested itself in calls for a strengthening of the Treaty in the fields of environmental politics, the social dimension and consumer protection, even if through the introduction of more majority voting. The fight against fraud has also been high on the Danish EU agenda. Lack of success in the Conference, if such proposals could not muster winning coalitions at the conference, the government may run into problems with public opinion afterwards.

The strengthening of the CFSP is likely to remain one of the thorniest of problems beyond any outcome of the IGC. It has already been, and is only too likely to remain difficult for Danish governments to handle. In a review of the implementation of Maastricht, the government noted that the CFSP has not developed and performed as well as expected: only a few modest common actions have been initiated, and single countries (such as Greece over the former Yugoslavia) have been able to block initiatives on which the other member states agreed. It observed also that the coordination of decisions that touch on both the Community and CFSP frameworks had not been satisfactory, and that important financial problems have hampered the CFSP (*Udenrigsministeriet* 1995).

The Danish government has been firmly opposed to efforts to solve the problems of the CFSP by communitization. The CFSP may need strengthening but not by making it supranational. The Danish government has therefore rejected a role for the ECJ and has seen no need for an increased Commission role. The government has also opposed any application of qualified majority voting (QMV) in the CFSP, though it has been willing to discuss solutions like 'consensus minus one' and perhaps even 'consensus minus two'. The government has also seemed willing to accept opt-outs as long as loyalty towards the common policy is preserved. While the government has generally been sceptical of the idea of a Secretary General for CFSP matters, it has been sympathetic to strengthening the CFSP Secretariat.

The Edinburgh exemption from WEU membership has determined basic Danish attitudes towards any expansion of the defence dimension of the CFSP, the implication being that Denmark cannot participate very actively in the debate over the future relationship between the WEU and the EU. Its general position has been against integrating the WEU further into the Union and in favour of the *status quo*. However, the WEU issue is hotly debated in domestic politics, and a *rapprochement* with the WEU may occur after the IGC.

A final set of European issues concerns the third pillar. Except for transferring it, in part or *in toto*, to the first pillar, Denmark is in favour of expanding cooperation in justice and home affairs. Support has been expressed, for example, for instituting a joint immigration policy in the EU and for stepping up the common fight of international crime. This derives from the feeling that some countries, including Denmark, have carried too heavy a burden of immigrants and asylum-seekers, and that some burden-sharing should be instituted in the Union. Denmark also favoured a strengthening and simplification of the cumbersome decision-making procedures in this area, though remaining firmly intergovernmental.

Conclusion

In the early 1990s the basic Danish policy towards the Community could best be characterized as an active balancing policy, focused on 'offensive power' (Mouritzen 1993). At the 1991 IGC on Political Union Denmark put forward a number of concrete proposals for change and was committed to active participation in the negotiations. Demands were coupled with a certain readiness to accept further institutional development of the EC, as well as an insistence on certain policy bastions, i.e. positions to be held at (almost) any price. It was in essence a 'give and take' attitude, which corresponded well with the pro-European sentiment of the government of the day, and the personal activism of its Foreign Minister, Uffe Ellemann-Jensen (Liberal). Basically, Denmark wanted then to place itself unequivocally as a committed European core country after many years of footdragging.

In the aftermath of Maastricht this proved to have been a dangerous strategy in so far as it did not command sufficient public support. As a consequence, Danish European policy shifted gear into a more defensive mode, which emphasized autonomy and protection against the integration process rather than influence and concentrated on establishing and defending exemptions from the Treaty.

The Social Democrat-led government that entered into office in 1993 has represented a less pro-European approach than its predecessor and has had constantly to look over its shoulders to be certain of the support of its followers. The Social Democrats themselves have a particular problem as two-thirds of their voters opposed Maastricht in the first referendum and only one-half could be persuaded to vote 'yes' in the second. Consequently, the Social Democrats and the Radicals have been cautious and late in their final bids for changes before the IGC opened. It suggests the continuation of the autonomy-oriented approach to European politics in the future. In terms of actual strategy it means a rather low degree of commitment to the process of change, a limited capacity to accept concessions, a limitation of demands to domestically safe issues, and a concentration on the defence of the bastions of Danish European policy. The best outcome of IGC in the eyes of the government could therefore be one which is substantial enough not to be an outright failure and hence threaten enlargement, but thin enough to be uncontroversial domestically – perhaps so uncontroversial that a referendum is unnecessary. On the other hand, the worst-case outlook would be a serious questioning of one or several of the Edinburgh exemptions, a significant step towards the Union's 'federal goal', an increased great power dominance in the Union or the formal or informal formation of a European core from which Denmark would have to keep outside.

SWEDEN AND EUROPEAN UNION

Background factors

The newness of her affiliation with the EU is probably the most important determinant of Sweden's relationship with the Union and of its attitudes towards its revision. Prior to Sweden's membership, it was expected and sometimes feared in Denmark, that Sweden enter the Community and rapidly call the Nordic tune. It was also a widespread feeling in Sweden itself that Sweden would be an active participant in the Union, intent on making its influence felt over a broad sweep of issues. From the theoretical perspective suggested by Mouritzen (see pp. 160), Sweden would relinquish her acquiescent posture towards the Union as soon as she moved from 'would-be insider' to 'insider' status, and begin to pursue a more active and balanced policy, in which domestically generated demands were more prominent. For various reasons, these predictions have been only partially successful.

A fear of isolation and marginalization derived at least in part from its geography have been important determinants of Sweden's European policy and can be expected to continue to play a role. Expectations that Sweden would place itself in a central role in the Union by striking an informal alliance with Germany and opting for an active stance in the CFSP have not materialized – perhaps because Germany and the EU have not lived up to earlier expectations of becoming the core and motor of European politics. Geography has also been an active factor in leading Sweden to be a strong supporter of further enlargement, especially to the Baltic countries, which is widely seen as the prime argument for the IGC. For Denmark and Finland, enlargement would place Sweden closer to the geographic and political centre of the Union.

Although the Swedish economy has seen signs of recovery, EMU membership still seems a few years off. While Sweden has no formal reservations about EMU, it is not part of the present ERM system and prospects for joining are unclear (Reuters 21 June 1995). Its large public debt is the main obstacle, but it also falls short on most of the other convergence criteria. However, according to the governor of the National Bank, Urban Backstöm, Sweden stands a reasonable chance of complying with them by 1999 (Reuters 31 May 1995). Finance Minister Göran Persson has expressed himself even more optimistically (*Nordisk Kontakt* 1995/96: 64).

Sweden's political system differs from Denmark's in that majority governments are more frequent. This may imply a weaker parliamentary control over EU policy than in Denmark, even though the experience of the first year in the Union is too limited to judge what the real powers of the newly established Parliamentary Advisory Committee on European Union Affairs will be. The Committee meets before every Council meeting, and has already succeeded in widening its powers on the Danish model. The time-honoured tradition of administrative openness, which finds expression in Europe's most liberal information legislation, reinforces Swedish pressure for greater openness. The compatibility of the EU's closed and secretive practices with Swedish practices was a major complication during the accession negotiations, and Sweden can therefore be counted on to support any initiative to open the EU system to public scrutiny and make it more transparent.

The Social Democrats under Ingvar Carlsson led an atypical government when they entered office in 1994 in that it was a minority government and dependent on support for its domestic policy on the Euro-sceptic Left Party and the half-hearted Centre Party. In its European policy the government has been able to count on support from the more Euro-positive opposition parties to the right, but after the serious Social Democratic defeat in the September 1995 election for the EP and the victory of the EU-sceptics – including those within the Social Democrat party itself – the government has had to listen more carefully to their views. The Carlsson government is also special since it included ministers who advocated a 'no' in the referendum. In general it has been more cautious in its European policy than its non-Socialist predecessor.

The outcome of the first elections to the European Parliament on 17 September 1995 (before which, the 22 Swedish MEPs had been appointed by the *Riksdag* according to the results of the 1994 general elections) was a devastating setback for the pro-Union forces and especially for the Social Democratic Party. First, participation was an all-time low in Swedish politics: only 41.3 per cent as against 86.3 per cent in the parliamentary elections a year earlier. The deeply divided Social Democrats came out as the great losers with only 28.1 per cent of the vote against 45.3 per cent in 1994 and winning only 7 out of the 22 seats. Another loser was the pro-integrationist People's Party (Liberals) with only one MEP and 4.8 per cent of the vote (1994: 7.2 per cent). The big winners were the two anti-Union parties: the Greens more than trebled their share of the vote (from 5 to 17.2 per cent) and now has 4 MEPs in Strasbourg; the Left Party doubled its vote (from 6.2 to 12.9 per cent) and gained three seats. The Moderates (Conservatives) and the Centre Party held their turf with five and two seats, respectively, the Centre Party electing one EU supporter and one critic.

The openly anti-Unionist parties thus won nearly a third of the contested mandates, but as both the Social Democratic and Centre parties fielded and elected both pro- and anti-EU candidates, Sweden ended up sending a delegation to Strasbourg consisting of eleven for Swedish membership in the Union and eleven against. This 50–50 ration contrasts with the Danish 75–25 split between pro-Union and Union critics in the European Parliament.

The collapse of the Social Democratic vote reflected the deep split in the Social Democratic rank and file and the inability of the party leadership to enforce a joint party line. Officially the party takes a wait-and-see attitude to Sweden's participation in the EMU, is against membership in the WEU, but advocates some expansion of the CFSP with respect to peace-keeping. Split, too, was the Centre Party, which led its 1995 EP campaign under the ambivalent slogan of *'Nja till Europa'* ('Nyes to Europe') and which also fielded both supporters and opponents of Swedish EU membership. The party opposes participation in the EU's defence dimension as well as EMU

Among the other parties, the Moderates (Conservatives) and Liberals (People's

Party) are pro-Unionist and favour Sweden's participation in the EMU and the WEU. The Liberals are mildly pro-federalist and advocate a decisive strengthening of the EP. On the Left, both the Left Party (former Communists) and the Greens are opposed to Swedish membership in the Union and opposed to any strengthening of it, except in environmental politics.

Most explanations of the defeat of the pro-Unionists in the EP elections focus on people's disappointment with the immediate consequences (or lack of such) of membership. Food prices had not dropped very much since January 1995, nor had interest rates or unemployment. According to this theory the pro-Unionists over-sold membership in 1994 and now reap the bitter harvest. A somewhat deeper explanation focuses on Swedish political culture which for a long time has been dominated by political values that make for a sceptical view of European integration. The neutrality tradition has been immensely powerful and remains strong, and the same applies to the Social Democratic welfare ideology with its emphasis on autonomous national distribution policies. Stated somewhat pointedly, Swedish membership in the Union was made possible by the perhaps temporary weakening of these two powerful strands, but their hold on the public mind is strong and may be strengthened once again, when the particular political and economic constellation of the early 1990s no longer prevails.

Together with the EP election result, polls taken after membership indicate that Sweden may duplicate the experience of Denmark after 1973, i.e., with continuing public doubts as to the wisdom of joining. At the referendum in November 1994 a meagre majority of 52.3 per cent voted 'yes', while 47.7 per cent voted 'no'. However, polls taken during the first half of 1995 showed a declining support for EU membership, especially among the Social Democratic voters and among women. In an authoritative poll, published in early July 1995, 61 per cent would vote no to EU membership if a new referendum were held, and only one in four women would vote 'yes' (Reuters 3 July 1995).

This negative trend in public opinion is especially important as it is most prominent in the rank and file of the Social Democratic party. To be true, there is no constitutional requirement for referendums in Sweden, and the government need not subject the outcome of the IGC to public approval; in fact, Prime Minister Carlsson has clearly stated that he sees no need for a referendum if Sweden should join the EMU. However, it may be difficult to resist demands for a referendum after the IGC if a Danish referendum were invoked as an argument, and if vocal forces in the government party demanded it. Sweden may therefore confront the same problem as Denmark, that any constitutional change in the Union will imperil the very basis of participation in European integration. This prospect, together with the obvious strengthening of the Euro-sceptic forces, influenced the preparations of the Swedish politicians for the IGC and strengthened the low-key stance which Sweden had adopted in EU politics.

Sweden, the 1996 IGC, and the development of European union

SWEDISH PREPARATIONS FOR THE IGC

Sweden's lack of EU experience inevitably coloured its preparation for the IGC. It takes time to adapt to the intricacies of EU politics and to form considered opinions on the way the system functions and may be improved. Sweden, therefore, has been cautious and slow in its approach to the future development of the Union and has taken a flexible position on many issues.

Sweden started its preparations for the IGC in early 1995 when a Parliamentary Advisory Committee on European Union Affairs was set up. Another initiative was the creation of a so-called EU '96 Committee, consisting mainly of parliamentarians, but with affiliated experts. The Committee was charged with discussing questions likely to arise at the IGC, publishing reports (two factual reports were issued in the summer of 1995), arranging public hearings, and coming up with proposals. The basic object was to broaden the political debate, both at the parliamentary and the popular levels.

At the government level, the prevailing attitude was and remains 'wait-and-see'. According to Europe Minister Mats Hellström, Sweden has been in no hurry to lay down its position, and the Parliamentary Committee was expected to work not only during the whole of 1995, but into 1996 (*Nordisk Kontakt* 1995/2: 106–7). The aim was to come up with a general memo for the conference and then to concentrate on strategic inputs into the negotiations as they proceeded. A contributory factor to this relative sluggishness in preparing for the IGC was the exhaustion of Swedish politicians after the EU negotiations and the referendum campaign of 1994 and their unwillingness to open up once again the Pandora's box of European integration. However, the campaign before the September 1995 elections for the EP served to clarify the positions of the political parties, even if only somewhat.

THE MAIN ISSUES

The virtues of openness have clearly been a top concern, together with nearness and democracy. Easy access to EU documents somewhat on the lines of Sweden's own information legislation is a prominent demand. Besides that, Sweden has generally been in support of most efforts to democratize the Union.

In the Swedish view the national parliaments are the most important guarantors of democracy in the Union. Attitudes towards the EP have therefore been ambivalent. During the EP campaign of August–September 1995 the Parliament was generally lauded for its progressive stand on environmental and other affairs, but the general attitude to increasing its powers through a right of initiative or by an expansion of co-decision was sceptical and at best undecided.

On institutional development in the Union, Prime Minister Carlsson and Europe Minister Mats Hellström pointed out that Sweden does not want the Union to lose its decision-making capacity in the face of possible enlargement. At the same time, decision-making efficiency should not be driven so far as to reduce the influence of member states. Specifically, the ministers emphasized Sweden's basic view of the EU as a cooperation between states and the need to defend the interests of small and medium countries (Carlsson and Hellström 1995). Thus Sweden seems very firm in its rejection of a reform of voting powers in the Council, which would inevitably reduce Sweden's own weight. On the other hand, the Prime Minister has not been negative towards the idea of shared, regional Presidencies.

Generally, Sweden has been against tampering with the institutional balance in the Union; as in Denmark, the Commission is seen as a huge anonymous bureaucracy rather than the defender of small power interests. As a minimum, Sweden insists on retaining a national Commissioner. Sweden had no firm position on the core-periphery issue in the summer of 1995, except for a general negative feeling about the core concept. So, even though Sweden saw the need for institutional modifications in the light of hoped-for enlargement, practical readiness to compromise on the *status quo* has been quite small.

As far as Community policies have been concerned, the Swedish view has been that the Union should concentrate primarily on providing practical solutions to the everyday problems of ordinary people. Prominent among these is the fight against unemployment, which Sweden would like to have inscribed among the Treaty's main objectives. Other priority issues are environmental politics, the social dimension (worker protection) and consumer protection. Further sensitive issues in Sweden's EU relations are drugs, the protection of animals and veterinary policy. Finally, Sweden, as the Carlsson–Hellstrom article suggested, was likely to take up equality between the sexes as a separate goal to be adopted in the Treaty (ibid.).

Sweden's original high hopes for the CFSP have not been realized. In a speech in Brussels on 30 May 1995, Foreign Minister Lena Hjelm-Wallén declared that enlargement should be the decisive factor in shaping the efforts of member states at the IGC. The Conference should also take steps to strengthen the CFSP, in particular, she stressed, it needed to take 'a long, hard look' at the consensus requirement. Sweden would certainly not agree to be outvoted on vital issues, but was prepared to consider modifications of the principle in less vital areas. She also indicated Swedish support for a strengthening of the EU's capacity for planning and analysis in the foreign policy field. At the same time, she reiterated that Sweden would retain as 'the core of (its security) policy, the non-participation in military alliances' (Hjelm-Wallén 1995). Sweden also saw the need for a better coordination between the CFSP and the Union's economic, trade and development policies (*Försvarsdepartementet* 1995: 47).

Sweden has chosen to be a so-called 'active' observer in the WEU and generally views WEU cooperation in a favourable light. Thus she has sought close cooperation in the Union's joint actions, as in the Mostar operation, and will undoubtedly continue to do so, the limiting case being collective defence. Sweden is therefore basically *status quo*-oriented with respect to the future relationship between the Union and the WEU. As the 1995 Defence Report noted, the fact that the EU now includes several non-aligned countries and that the UK opposes any integration of the WEU into the EU, complicates the implementation of a common defence (*Försvarsdepartement* 1995: 47). On the other hand, the report expected an expansion of the so-called Petersberg actions, i.e. peace-keeping, humanitarian actions, crisis management etc., without indicating Sweden's likely response to such a development (ibid.).

Conclusion

Sweden's EU policies so far have been less activist than originally expected. This is certainly due to the unfinished process of adaptation to Union politics. But it also has deeper political–cultural roots, which were decisively strengthened in the EP elections of September 1995. Sweden's serious problems with public opinion has led the government to concentrate on low-cost demands in 'motherhood and apple-pie' issues, such as openness, environment, etc., combined with a conservative position on constitutional issues and issues of foreign and defence policy, including defence of policy bastions like non-alignment.

Unlike Denmark, Sweden has accepted the Maastricht Treaty wholesale, but its uncertain prospects for participation in the EMU and express reservations concerning defence cooperation place Sweden in a slightly 'off-centre' position in the Union. In the field of the CFSP, Sweden will probably be active in discussions of its political aspects, but reticent on the defence aspects. In constitutional matters Sweden has certainly proclaimed a policy of non-obstruction, i.e. Sweden will not prevent others in developing the Union, but constructive proposals have been few so far. Mouritzen's prediction that Sweden would move to a more balanced posture after membership seems certainly to have come true. However, indications are that Swedish policy will focus more on defensive power or autonomy than on offensive power, i.e. active influence in the Union. If this comes true, Sweden's EU policy concentrates relatively more on defending certain bastions than on effecting desired changes in the Union.

FINLAND AND EUROPEAN UNION

Background factors

In many respects Finland's relationship with the EU resembles that of Sweden, but there are some important differences. Prior expectations of a fairly high-profile participation in the Union, once Finland became an 'insider', have been met to a larger degree than in the case of Sweden, and Finland is often seen as the country which has adapted most easily to the EU of the three newcomers.

The geographic factor remains an all-important variable in Finnish foreign policy. Though Russia is a different neighbour than the old Soviet Union, it is unpredictable, and both worsening social and economic conditions and political radicalism there would once more create an acute security problem on Finland's 1200 km eastern border. Consequently, Finland firmly supports programmes which aim both at stabilizing Russia's immediate neighbours, the Baltic countries in particular, and at integrating Russia more into Europe, whether via the OSCE (Organization of Security and Cooperation in Europe), the Stability Pact, NATO's Partnership for Peace or especially, through the inclusion of the Baltic states in the EU and the promotion of close EU–Russian relations. At the same time, Finland is cautious not to provoke Russia by joining NATO or the WEU outright, even though the possibility of closer future relations is not ruled out.

After the economic crisis of the early 1990s, Finland's economy has been recovering once again. Export industries (metal and wood products, mainly) are booming, and public finances are improving. Though not yet part of the ERM, Finland's prospects for qualifying for the EMU by the late 1990s are generally deemed good by international bankers. According to Merrill Lynch, Finland will be already close to meeting the Maastricht convergence criteria on government deficit and gross debt by the end of 1996 (Reuters 5 July 1995). The government has indicated that ERM talks may then begin, and has declared as its official policy that Finland should be in the position to join the third stage of EMU from the very beginning if it so decides (Reuters 16 June 1995; Lipponen 1995).

Finland's political system is unique in Northern Europe in that it gives the President a central role in foreign affairs. The Presidential foreign policy prerogative normally works well as far as security policy is concerned, but threatens to complicate the formulation of Finnish EU policy, since it covers many issues normally the province of the Prime Minister. A struggle over Finland's representation in the European Council has provisionally been solved by both the President and Prime Minister taking part. This solution is fairly unproblematic in the present constellation of President Ahtisaari and Prime Minister Lipponen, as both are Social Democrats and active pro-Europeans, but it could create problems in the future with other constellations.

At the parliamentary level, Finland seems to approach a system where the Social Democrats and the Centre Party alternate as leader of broad government coalitions (Wilén 1995). In April 1995, Social Democrat Paavo Lipponen took over from Esko Aho (Centre Party) as leader of a Finnish 'rainbow coalition' of Social Democrats, the National Coalition Party (Conservatives), the Swedish People's Party, the Left-Wing Alliance and the Greens. Despite its heterogeneous character the government has appeared more pro-European than its predecessor, not least because foreign policy is firmly in the hands of pro-European Social Democrats. In the Finnish political spectrum Euro-scepticism is mainly confined to the agricultural wing of the Centre Party, the Left-Wing Alliance (former Communists) and part of the Greens (Kaiser *et al.* 1995).

In terms of political culture, pragmatism must be a dominant trait among Finns. This explains some of the ease with which they have adapted both to the constraints of the Cold War and the opportunities of the post-Cold War period. Support for Finnish accession to the EU was more broadly based than in Sweden, with 56.9 per cent voting for and 43.1 per cent against. And, again in contrast to Sweden, there has been no perceptible hangover since membership. In one poll 46 per cent professed to view membership as advantageous for Finland, while only 20 per cent were negative (Reuters 27 June 1995). In other words, within six months of joining the EU, Finland seemed to have adjusted faster to the EU than Sweden or Austria, both at the popular and élite level (Peter Ludlow in interview with Reuters 14 June 1995).

Finland, the 1996 IGC and the future of European union

PREPARATION FOR THE IGC
Like Sweden, Finland was handicapped in its preparations for the IGC by having been a member for only a short period. On the other hand, Finnish preparations were not hampered by an unstable public opinion or misgivings within the leading party of government, i.e., the Social Democrats. The basic attitude to the IGC has been that the Union's institutions and goals need undergo only minor change, and that the efficiency of the Union should be improved by better use of existing structures and programmes.

In May 1995, the Finnish government appointed former Defence Minister, Ingvar Melin, to the IGC Reflection Group and at the same time set up an interdepartmental working group to prepare Finland's stance at the IGC. The group consisted of three sub-groupings, on foreign and security policy, institutional and economic issues and enlargement (Reuters 5 May 1995). The group published its first report in September 1995, which gave a very comprehensive, but also very cautious account of the issues involved in the IGC (*Memorandum* 1995).

Also playing an important role in the government's preparations for the conference, was parliament's 'Great Committee'. Since Finnish membership, the Committee, which consists of leading parliamentarians, has become a *de facto* Europe Committee. It meets on a weekly basis with government representatives for the exchange of information and political viewpoints.

THE MAIN ISSUES
The Finns have been strong supporters of greater openness in decision-making and similar issues, having, for example, called for an improvement in access to documents for the public (Lipponen 1995; *Memorandum* 1995) and, reportedly, proposing a new transparency article in the Treaty (Reuters 22 June 1995). They might, though, be somewhat less insistent about such issues as Denmark and Sweden. Finland supports the principle of subsidiarity, but has also warned against it being misused to lower social and environmental standards.

In the Finnish view the Union's democratic deficit should primarily be solved by strengthening the national parliaments and their role in European integration (*Memorandum* 1995). The Finnish government appears not to foresee any increase in the powers of the EP, not even as a consequence of a simplification of decision-making structures, such as a wider use of the co-decision procedure (*Helsingin Sanomat* 31 August 1995). In September 1995 the interdepartmental working group suggested 'a cautious review' of the EP's position, but without changing the institutional balance or giving it a genuine right of initiative (*Memorandum* 1995).

There has also been some interest in the development of the concept of union citizenship and for strengthening the human rights component of the Treaty. On sexual equality, Finland has favoured inscribing the principle in the Treaty – as has Sweden (*Memorandum* 1995).

At a general level Finland's position on institutional development has been conservative. In February 1995 the then Prime Minister, Esko Aho, (Centre Party) told Parliament that Finland expected the basic character of the Union as a grouping of independent, sovereign states to remain. The government also emphasized that the Council of Ministers should remain the central decision-making body, and that the European Parliament could not replace national parliaments (*Nordisk Kontakt* 1995/2: 61–3). Although the Lipponen government usually expresses itself in more pro-European terms, it basically shares this attitude (Lipponen 1995). On specific issues there has been greater flexibility. Paavo Lipponen went on the record to declare that Finland should act pragmatically on any expansion of majority decision-making, on, for example, environmental issues, common economic questions and problems of employment (*Nordisk Kontakt* 1995/2: 63).

The Finnish view has been largely *status quo*-oriented as far as the Commission's powers are concerned, although there has been a certain openness with respect to its role in the third pillar. Finland has not been prepared to give up a nationally appointed Commissioner (*Memorandum* 1995). On the core-periphery question the Finnish position has insisted that all member states be formally equal with equal opportunities to act in all fields covered by the Union. Finland has therefore been clearly against permanent, unequal membership terms, but 'subject to clear, jointly-approved conditions, agreement may be reached in exceptional cases to allow a member state to follow a different timetable in the implementation of common goals' (Tapani Vaahtoranta in *Revision of Maastricht* 1995: 15). The interdepartmental report of September 1995 also recognized the importance 'that the Union remains a tool, which the major member states will use to solve common questions' (*Memorandum* 1995).

Finland's basic pragmatism has led it to emphasize functional cooperation in the EU, and especially cooperation that benefits (and is felt to do so) ordinary people. Like Denmark and Sweden, Finland has stressed the need to do more about employment, and also has supported, though perhaps less emphatically, the strengthening of the Union's environmental, social and consumer policies.

Moreover, while opinion was negative towards the communitarization of the CFSP, there has been an acceptance of the need for majority decision-making in the implementation of common decisions (*Revision of Maastricht* 1995: 38; *Memorandum* 1995). As the 1995 security report put it, 'in Finland's view, the key principle in developing the Union's common foreign and security policy is intergovernmentalism' (*Security* 1995: 61). In general, Finland attached great importance to the role of the CFSP in European politics and especially in furthering peace and stability, together with the OSCE and the UN. Finland shared the general disappointment with the CFSP, but has regarded the problem as one of a lack of political will rather than of institutional defects. Finland has therefore seen no need for substantial changes in the CFSP, but supported the strengthening of its analytic capabilities (*Memorandum* 1995).

Finland has chosen to be an observer with the WEU, and the question of membership has not been on the agenda, even though it has not excluded a change if NATO were to fade away, and the WEU or the EU evolved into a military alliance proper. In the meantime Finnish expectations are that the peace-keeping and crisis management functions of the EU–WEU should increase in importance, and, as a full member of the Union with no formal reservations to the CFSP, Finland has also expected as of right to take part in such operations whenever politically acceptable and practically possible. The exception, according to the Council of State's report was 'crisis management calling for peace enforcement or the use of military force against other states or parties involved in the conflict' (*Security* 1995: 37). Thus, 'in the new situation [after the Cold War] Finland's strategy is an active participation in international political and security cooperation for the prevention and resolution of security problems' (ibid.: 58). As far as the IGC was concerned, there was no expectation that Finland's formal military non-alignment would become a problem, because there was seen to be little likelihood that the conference would take up and decide the question of common defence (ibid.: 62).

The Finnish view of third pillar questions was also generally positive and pragmatic. There was a certain willingness to accept a larger Commission role in the third pillar, and Finland did not reject a transfer of questions from intergovernmental cooperation to the Community framework (*Memorandum* 1995).

Conclusion

Finland has probably been the Nordic EU country with the least to fear from the IGC's outcome and from the broader development of the EU. Public opinion has remained firmly behind the policy of membership, and the Finnish Social Democrats have not evinced the ambivalence of their Danish and Swedish sister-parties towards European integration. The domestic basis for participation in Union politics thus appears stronger than in the other Nordic countries – though an important caveat must be introduced concerning the slim temporal basis for this analysis.

Nor has Finland had to defend policy bastions of the same strength as Denmark and Sweden in the field of defence policy, even though her policy of non-alignment sets definite limits to how actively she can participate in the development of the defence dimension of the CFSP. Another important factor, which sets Finland somewhat apart from Denmark and Sweden, is the general cooperative spirit in which she approaches the Union. Part of it may be a reminiscence of 'would-be insider' attitudes, mixed with the insecurity of the newcomer. But it may also be a deeper reflection of a non-ideological pragmatism in the Finnish attitude, which contrasts with the more ideological approaches of Denmark and Sweden. If so, Finland can be expected to approach the political and institutional development of the Union in a flexible and undogmatic mind which is open to compromise and concessions, but also seeks to promote national goals whenever realistic.

TOWARDS A NORDIC BLOC IN THE UNION?

Differences in national style in relation to the EU among the three Nordic member states has presented problems for Nordic cooperation in Union politics, both in general and with respect to the 1996 IGC. As a matter of fact, Finland has indicated that she does not aim to form a Nordic bloc, neither in ordinary EU politics, nor at the IGC (Reuters 4 April 1995). This is probably not so much due to differing interests than to Finland's wish not to be associated too closely with nations, especially Denmark, with a footdragging image in the EU.

There are other arguments against a Nordic caucus in the EU as well. All three countries are well aware of the general disapproval of permanent coalitions in the EU (save the German–French tandem) and have repeatedly made clear that they do not envisage the building of a Nordic 'bloc', however desirable and natural Nordic cooperation is.[11] Nor should it be forgotten that the Nordic countries have different interests on important EU issues, such as agriculture, fisheries, and industry, just as they have their own particular sensitivities, expressed in different national policy bastions.

On the other hand, as this analysis has shown, there are important similarities in the views of the three countries on the EU and its future. They share a fundamental intergovernmental view of the Union and reject any federal goal for it. They also feel that the present balances between institutions and between large and small members are near-ideal and only in need of minor adjustment. In particular, they want to retain the Council of Ministers as the central decision-making body, which means that they are not willing to give significant concessions to the Parliament. In contrast to the Benelux countries, the Nordics do not see the Commission as the natural ally of the smaller member states, but rather as the embodiment of weakly legitimated power. In the field of institutional politics the three Nordic countries therefore share a conservative, *status quo*-oriented attitude even though their different experiences and history may result in diverging reactions to proposals in the field.

With respect to openness and democracy the three countries are in almost total agreement, although they may focus on slightly different aspects of it and put different accents to it. Initiatives to increase openness and transparency can be expected from all three countries, which are also likely to support each other strongly in this field. Another common Nordic characteristic is the view that the EU should concentrate on pragmatic problem-solving rather than on institution and state-building. The view, that the Union should be of visible benefit to ordinary people, is especially prevalent in Denmark and Sweden with their sceptic publics. The fight against unemployment is high on the three countries' EU agenda together with the environment, the social dimension, consumer protection, etc. This will be another field of concentration where the Nordics can be expected to work closely together in the Union.

In foreign and defence policy the Nordics seemingly take in similar positions: all three value the foreign policy component highly and share a frustration over its lack of efficiency so far. All three have their reservations to the defence component and have opted for observer status with the WEU (with Sweden's self-styled 'active' observer status being mainly cosmetic). The background, though, is different. Denmark is a member of NATO, and her difficulties with the WEU are rooted both in history and domestic politics, while Sweden's and Finland's relationship with the WEU are directly related to their continued policies of military non-alignment. Save for a general *status quo* orientation towards relations between the WEU and the Union, these differences hardly make for concerted Nordic action as far as the defence dimension of the CFSP is concerned. Chances are better in the field of foreign policy, i.e. the old European Political Cooperation (EPC). In general the three call for increased powers of action by increasing the analytical capabilities of CFSP, and they also show a certain readiness to envisage deviations from the consensus rule which all of them continue to consider the necessary and inevitable ground rule for CFSP.

By late 1995 Nordic cooperation in the preparation for the IGC was still limited and mainly confined to contacts between Danish and Swedish officials. As we have seen, there are distinct possibilities for cooperation, that are likely to be exploited in due course. But there are limiting factors as well, such as remaining concrete policy differences, differing policy styles, competition for Nordic leadership in the EU, and – not least – the fact that the Nordic countries to have any influence over outcomes will have to enter into broader-based coalitions with other EU members. To further their specific policy agenda the Nordics will have to convince all the other twelve members of its merits, as well as be willing to give concessions in turn. This may prove to be a tall order.

NOTES

1. In the three Scandinavian languages (Danish, Swedish and Norwegian) Norden denotes the five Nordic nations: Denmark, Finland, Iceland, Norway and Sweden. As there is no English equivalent to this concept, its Scandinavian form will be used in this chapter.
2. Among the results of early Nordic cooperation was the establishment of the (weak) Nordic Council (1952) and the creation of a Nordic Passport Union and a joint Nordic labour market (1954). However, attempts to create a Nordic customs union were abortive.
3. On citizenship, a Danish declaration spelled out the differences between state citizenship and union citizenship and called attention to the fact that future expansions of union citizenship would require unanimity in the Council as well as national ratification according to constitutional procedures. On the third pillar another Danish declaration pointed out that a decision to transfer parts of the third pillar to the first pillar would similarly require the agreement of all members as well as national ratification.
4. The right-wing Progress Party was the only party against. The problem with public opinion was illustrated by the fact that only half of the Social Democratic voters voted for (in 1992 it had only been one-third).
5. In the spring of 1995 the Conservative and Liberal members of the 1995 Defence Committee boycotted the Committee after their demand for an open-minded analysis of Sweden's NATO option had been rejected by the government (*Forsvarsdepartementet*

1995).
6. Finland has also approached NATO by becoming an observer in the North Atlantic Cooperation Council and full participant in the Partnership for Peace programme.
7. A leading Social Democratic spokesman on European Affairs, Mr Iver Nørgaard, used to talk contemptuously of 'lard Europeans' (flommeeuropæere) when referring to eloquent and lofty southern proponents of federalism, whom he contrasted with the pragmatic northern advocates for gradual reform and concrete policies.
8. Other participants in the EU coalition are the Conservatives, the Liberals, the Social Liberals, the Center Democrats, and the Christian People The Socialist People's Party joined the coalition after the 1992 referendum, which enabled it to claim substantial concessions, but will probably not be part of a new IGC 1996 platform.
9. The concept of sovereignty in the Danish Constitution is a rather technical one, as its defining characteristic is the exercise of direct authority over Danish citizens by foreign authorities.
10. In the elections for the EP in June 1994 the two anti-Unionist movements, the June Movement and the Popular Movement against the EU, together gained four out of Denmark's 16 seats.
11. A practical problem is the fact that with only ten votes in the Council the Nordic countries do not even make up a blocking minority in the EU, let alone a majority.

REFERENCES AND BIBLIOGRAPHY

Carlsson, Ingvar and Hellström, Mats (1995) 'Sakfrågorna styr EU-arbetet', *Sydsvenska Dagbladet*, 9 May.

Eurobarometer (various dates) *Public Opinion in the European Community*. Brussels: Commission of the European Communities.

Finnish Ministry for Foreign Affairs (1995) *Security in a Changing World. Guidelines for Finland's Security Policy*. Report by the Council of State to the Parliament, Helsinki, 6 June.

Finnish Ministry of Foreign Affairs (1995) *Memorandum concerning Finnish Points of View with Regard to the 1996 Intergovernmental Conference of the European Union*, Helsinki.

Försvarsdepartementet (1995) *Sverige i Europa och världen. Säkerhetspolitisk rapport från försvarsberedningen våren 1995*, Stockholm: Ds 1995:28.

Hansen, Peter (1974) 'Adaptive Behavior of Small States: The Case of Denmark and European Integration', *Sage International Yearbook of Foreign Policy Studies*, vol. 2, pp. 143–74.

Hjelm-Wallén, Lena (1995) *Towards a new European security order – a Swedish view*, address by the Minister for Foreign Affairs, Mrs Lena Hjelm-Wallén, at the Centre for European Policy Studies, Brussels, 30 May.

Istituto Affari Internazionali (1995) *Revision of Maastricht: Implementation and Proposals for Reform. A Survey of National Views*, Third Bulletin, Rome.

Jerneck, Magnus (1993) 'Sweden – the reluctant European?', in Tiilikainen, Teija and Damgaard Petersen, Ib (eds) *The Nordic Countries and the EC*. Copenhagen, Copenhagen Political Studies Press, pp. 23–42.

Kaiser, Wolfram, Visuri, Pekka, Malmström, Cecilia and Hjelseth, Arve (1995) 'Die EU-Volksabstimmungen in Österreich, Finnland, Schweden und Norwegen: Folgen für die Europäische Union', *Integration*, vol. 18 (February), pp. 76–87.

Konservative (1995) *Det konservative Folkepartis EU-politik*, Copenhagen.

Lipponen (1995) *Program för statsminister Paavo Lipponens regering*, 13 April.

Mouritzen, Hans (1988) *Finlandization: Towards a General Theory of Adaptive Politics.* Aldershot, Avebury.

— (1993) 'The two musterknaben and the naughty boy: Sweden, Finland and Denmark in the process of European integration', *Cooperation and Conflict,* vol. 28, pp. 373–402.

Nehring, Niels-Jørgen (1992) 'Parliamentary control of the executive', in Lyck, Lise (ed.) *Denmark and EC Membership Evaluated.* London, Pinter, pp. 76–81.

Pedersen, Thomas (1994). *European Union and the EFTA Countries. Enlargement and Integration.* London, Pinter.

Petersen, Nikolaj (1977) 'Adaptation as a Framework for the Analysis of Foreign Policy Behavior' *Cooperation and Conflict,* vol. 12, pp. 221–50.

— (1989) 'Mod en generel teori om adaptiv politik', *Politica,* vol. 21, pp. 174–88.

— (1993) '"Game, Set and Match": Denmark and the European Union from Maastricht to Edinburgh', in Tiilikainen, Teija and Damgaard Petersen, Ib (eds) *The Nordic Countries and the EC.* Copenhagen, Copenhagen Political Studies Press, pp. 79–106.

— (1995) 'Denmark and the European Community 1967–1985', in Due-Nielsen, Carsten and Petersen, Nikolaj (eds) *Adaptation and Activism. The Foreign Policy of Denmark 1967–1993.* Copenhagen, Dansk Udenrigspolitisk Institut and DJØF Publishing, pp. 189–225.

Rüdiger, Mogens (1995) 'Denmark and the European Community 1967–1985', in Due-Nielsen, Carsten and Petersen, Nikolaj (eds) *Adaptation and Activism. The Foreign Policy of Denmark 1967–1993.* Copenhagen, Dansk Udenrigspolitisk Institut and DJØF Publishing.

Rosenau, James (1970) *The Adaptation of National Societies: A Theory of Political Systems Behavior and Transformation.* New York, McCaleb-Seiler.

Siune, Karen, Svensson, Palle and Tonsgaard, Ole (1992) *– Det blev et nej.* Aarhus, Politica.

SNU (1995) *Dansk og europæisk sikkerhed.* Copenhagen: Det Sikkerheds- og Nedrustningspolitiske Udvalg. (English summary: Danish and European Security. Summary. Copenhagen, The Danish Commission on Security and Disarmament.)

Snyder, Glenn (1984) 'The security dilemma in alliance politics', *World Politics,* vol. 36, pp. 461–95.

Social Democratic Party (1994) Introductory paper for a debate by the Grass Roots Committee of the Danish Social Democratic Party on The Social Democratic Party and the European Challenge, Copenhagen.

Sundelius, Bengt (1994) 'Changing course: when neutral Sweden chose to join the European Community', in Carlsnaes, Walter and Smith, Steve (eds) *European Foreign Policy. The EC and Changing Perspectives in Europe.* London, Sage, pp. 177–201.

Udenrigsministeriet (1995). *Dagsorden for Europa. Regeringskonference 1966,* Copenhagen, Udenrigsministeriet.

Väyrynen, Raimo (1993) 'Finland on the way to the European Community', in Tiilikainen, T. and Damgaard Petersen, Ib (eds.) *The Nordic Countries and the EC.* Copenhagen, Copenhagen Political Studies Press, pp. 43–63.

Venstre (1995) *Den nye udfordring: Et helt Europa.* Venstres synspunkter og holdninger til Danmarks deltagelse i EU's regeringskonference i 1996. Copenhagen, Venstre.

Wilén, Henrik (1995) 'Finland under forandring', *Udenrigs,* 2/1995, pp. 51–7.

Worre, Torben (1995) 'First no, then yes: the Danish referendums on the Maastricht Treaty 1992 and 1993', *Journal of Common Market Studies,* vol. 33, pp. 235–57.

10
THE COMMISSION AND THE REFORM PROCESS

DESMOND DINAN

INTRODUCTION

Judging by its title, an intergovernmental conference (IGC) could be contrary to the Commission's interests. Being close to the supranational or federal end of the integration spectrum, the Commission would be forgiven for doubting the motives of member states' officials and ministers meeting regularly, over a period of several months, not only to discuss important issues on the Union's agenda, but specifically to revise the Union's constitution. As a method of treaty revision and reform, an intergovernmental conference seems analogous to a wedding without a best man.

Yet the IGC label is misleading, because the Commission has been fully involved in virtually all aspects of the conference. Both the Commission and the European Parliament (EP) participated in the work of the IGC's Reflection Group, though only the Commission has sat with national delegations around the IGC table – at the official, ministerial, and European Council levels. As in the 1991 IGC, the Commission makes proposals and suggestions, and attempts to broker agreement. In one decisive respect, however, IGCs are truly intergovernmental: national delegations alone have the power to veto proposals and, ultimately, to reject the entire package.

Although institutional and procedural issues have tended to dominate IGCs, the fundamental questions underlying the 1996 IGC's work could not be more important: how can a Union of twenty or more diverse member states best serve its citizens' interests? How can it enhance their welfare, security, and solidarity? How should it be structured? Is the Maastricht agenda any longer appropriate? Was it too modest or ambitious?

As both a product and an instigator of European integration, the Commission has more than a passing interest in helping to answer those questions. As developments in the late 1980s and the early 1990s proved rather painfully, even if at the centre of the Union's institutional structure, the Commission's position is nonetheless precarious. Moreover, IGCs present dangers as well as opportunities: they give member states a chance not only to speed up, but also to slow down, the pace of European integration. The peculiar circumstances of 1996 – an obligatory IGC taking place at a time of unprecedented public and political unease – were inauspicious for a Commission still coping with the legacy, both positive and negative, of Jacques Delors' presidency.

THE 1985 AND 1991 IGCs AND REFORM

The 1985 IGC and the Single European Act

Despite Andrew Moravcsik's exhaustive analysis of the Single European Act (SEA) solely as an intergovernmental bargain (Moravcsik 1991), most observers agree that the Commission, and especially its President, played a pivotal role in the events and negotiations that led to the 1986 treaty revision (Ross 1995; Grant 1994). The Commission had not pulled its '1992' proposals out of thin air, but had cleverly played the role of 'policy entrepreneur', identifying a demand (completion of the single market) and delivering a product (the White Paper). In addition, the Commission had played an active part in the work of the *ad hoc* Committee on Institutional Affairs (the Dooge Committee), whose report, together with the White Paper, formed the basis for the Milan European Council's decision to hold an IGC. Indeed, Delors helped to convince Council President Bettino Craxi to take the unprecedented step of calling for a vote at a European Council, on the contentious question of whether or not to convene the IGC. The result – seven in favour and three against – finally settled the issue.

The negotiations for what became the SEA were essentially two separate sets of negotiations, on treaty reform and on European Political Cooperation (EPC), which almost led to two separate acts. Because of the intergovernmental nature of political cooperation and of the Political Committee, which managed the procedure and debated its reform, the Commission was not in a good position to influence the EPC negotiations. By contrast, with respect to revising the existing treaties, the Commission submitted numerous proposals to strengthen Community decision-making and to increase the Community's competence. Perhaps the Commission's greatest achievement was to champion the cause of economic and social cohesion. The ensuing commitment in the SEA to a redistribution of wealth from north to south seemed insignificant at the time, but soon became critical for the Commission's and the Community's progress. Finally, at the December 1985 Luxembourg summit where most of the SEA was agreed upon, Delors played a key role of broker and facilitator.

The Commission emerged from the 1985 IGC not only with greater powers, but with a considerably enhanced authority and reputation. Nevertheless the negotiations had not gone entirely the Commission's way. Delors' biggest disappointment was his failure to include at least a rhetorical commitment in the SEA to Economic and Monetary Union (EMU). Other rejections or amendments of Commission proposals resulted in a much weaker SEA than Delors had hoped for, or than he thought necessary to invigorate European integration. Indeed, a despondent Delors wondered in early 1986 whether the SEA would suffice to bring about the internal market by 1992.

In another respect also the Commission had suffered a setback. As in the case of the Community's first enlargement, the Commission had linked the Community's Mediterranean enlargement to the need for both procedural reform – lest a larger Community become further mired in indecision – and a substantive deepening of European integration – lest wider mean weaker. In the early 1970s, the Commission failed completely to convince the member states of that link, and did so only to a limited extent in the mid-1980s. By that time the member states all wanted to complete the single market, and most were either eager or at least willing to go beyond that by reforming the Community's institutional structure and increasing the Community's competence. Mediterranean enlargement was an additional reason, but by no means the only reason, for doing so. Indeed, the Commission had unsuccessfully argued that the Treaty of Rome should be amended at the same time as the Treaty of Accession of Spain and Portugal was ratified (Commission 1986: point 4). Instead, the member states separated treaty reform from the accession negotiations, and tackled the former in an IGC that began even before Spain and Portugal became Community members.

The lessons of the IGC were clear for the Commission: to a considerable extent its success depended on a strong President who could:

- generate good ideas and proposals;
- focus on a manageable number of goals and objectives;
- judge with reasonable accuracy the member states' likely response to those goals and objectives;
- identify and seize opportunities which exist in large part because of the member states' predisposition to deeper integration;
- exploit policy networks such as the industrialists' influential lobby group, the European Round Table;
- excel in the highly personal setting of the European Council, and form alliances with key government leaders whose countries were well disposed toward the Commission and who regarded the Commission President as a peer but not as a threat; and
- extend the Paris–Bonn axis into a Paris–Bonn-Commission axis or, more precisely, extend the axis between the two countries' leaders into an axis involving also the Commission President.

The 1991 IGC and the Treaty on European Union

The voluntarist nature of Commission leadership was borne out in the prelude to, and the conduct of, the 1991 IGCs. One of the IGCs – on EMU – was to some extent an inevitable sequel to the single market programme. The title of the Commission's rationale for EMU – 'One Market, One Money' (Commission 1989) – implied an inevitable continuity between a single market and a single currency. The unofficial name of the document that formed the basis of the EMU negotiations – the Delors Report – even bore the President's name. As a reflection of his passionate interest in the subject, Delors became deeply involved in every aspect of the EMU negotiations. Although he lost the battle to establish the European Central Bank (ECB) at the beginning of Stage II rather than at the beginning of Stage III (launch of the single currency), the Commission won the more important arguments in favour of a timetable for the final stages of

EMU and against a formal two-tier structure. Yet Delors had been one of the first to propose an informal two-tier system when he suggested letting Stage III begin with less than a full complement of member states, and subsequently proposed an opt-out for any member state not wishing to join the currency union until a later date.

The generally favourable outcome – from the Commission's point of view – of the EMU negotiations contrasted with the Commission's and Delors' setbacks in the European Political Union (EPU) negotiations. The rejection by all but Belgium and The Netherlands of the first Dutch draft treaty, which replaced the Luxembourg draft's 'temple' with a unitary 'tree', was as much a humiliation for Delors as for the Dutch Presidency. Delors may have been correct in characterizing the three-pillar approach as 'organized schizophrenia' (European Parliament 3–411, November 1991: 126), but it was obvious early in the negotiations that a majority of member states opposed a single structure.

Delors' uncompromising support for the Dutch draft was symptomatic of a growing insensitivity to member state concerns. Even more than EMU, the Common Foreign and Security Policy (CFSP) – EPU's main plank – was highly contentious in national capitals. Together, the EMU and CFSP negotiations stirred latent public unease about the Community's encroachment on national sovereignty. The CFSP negotiations, to which Delors made a visible contribution, in the form of a highly publicized speech in March 1991 (Delors 1991) also alerted increasingly jealous governments to the extent of the Commission's pervasiveness and ambition. Inevitably, the politically charged nature of both EMU and CFSP put the Commission in an awkward position during the IGCs. On other issues under the heading of EPU, the Commission was also on the defensive, and found itself fighting a rear-guard action to protect some of its existing prerogatives. In particular, Delors had to fend off a strong attack on the Commission's exclusive right of initiative, and a move to permit the Council to amend Commission proposals by qualified majority instead of unanimity. Were the latter to happen, Delors told the EP in April 1991, the Commission would be reduced to 'a sort of Secretariat-General for the Council' (European Parliament 3–221 April 1991: 98).

The course and conduct of the 1991 IGCs confirmed, negatively, the lessons of the previous IGC for the Commission:

- external circumstances: despite the seeming inevitability of EMU and the impetus, because of German unification, for EPU, the political and economic environment in Europe was increasingly unfavourable to deeper integration;
- leadership: Delors was no longer simply a strong Commission President, but had become overbearing. His leadership and managerial styles were proving counterproductive for the projection of Commission influence;
- focus: Delors and the Commission could not focus exclusively on the IGCs, but were preoccupied also with the Commission's response to developments in Central and Eastern Europe and with the unfinished Uruguay Round of the GATT;

- interpersonal dynamics at the heads of government level: Delors' personal and political stature had risen enormously, to the extent that some government leaders may have resented his achievements and ambition;
- policy networks: there was no level or network of private sector support for the 1991 IGCs comparable to the 1985 IGC, which the Commission could exploit;
- the Paris–Bonn–Brussels axis: under strain in the aftermath of German unification, Franco-German relations suffered also from differing perspectives on many aspects of EMU and EPU. This lessened the prospects for a strong Franco-German-Commission alliance.

THE 1996 IGC

Background

The 1985 and the 1991 IGCs were markedly different from each other in scope, but not in origin. By contrast, the 1996 IGC may have the most limited scope of all, but its origin is unique. Whereas the previous IGCs came about because of a momentum toward deeper integration – fuelled in 1985 by the White Paper and in 1991 by the success of the single market programme and the unexpected achievement of German unification – the 1996 IGC is taking place simply because it is mandated under the terms of the Maastricht Treaty. Although there may have been pressing reasons to revise the Treaty based on the experience of implementing Maastricht and on the prospect of enlargement to the East, it is unlikely for either reason that the member states would have convened an IGC as early as 1996 unless obliged to do so. On the one hand, the Maastricht Treaty had been in operation only since November 1993. As the Council, Commission, and EP pointed out in their separate submissions to the Reflection Group, it was – is – still too soon to make an authoritative judgement about how badly or well it works (Reflection Group 1995). On the other hand, enlargement may be inevitable, but it is by no means imminent. Even if the IGC continues until late 1997, it may still take place too early to facilitate the kinds of changes necessary to make the Treaty more effective in light of the lessons of implementation and the pressures of enlargement.

The most striking difference between the 1996 and previous IGCs is the political environment surrounding them. The IGC on Political Union was a hasty response to dramatic changes in Eastern Europe and the Soviet Union whose impact was expected to be profound, but could not be accurately predicted. War in the disintegrating Yugoslavia broke out during the June 1991 Luxembourg summit, and the Soviet Union collapsed during the December 1991 Maastricht summit. The euphoria and optimism of 1989 and 1990 gave way in 1991 to apprehension about the configuration of the post-Cold War international system and its possible impact on stability in Central and Eastern Europe, the cohesiveness of the EC, and the future of trans-Atlantic relations.

Uncertainty about the international system, one of the worst economic recessions since the Second World War, and the far-reaching nature of EMU and EPU caused enormous public unease in 1992 and 1993, which manifested itself in the Maastricht Treaty ratification crisis. The crisis was not only about the terms of the Treaty itself, but was an expression of profound public uncertainty about employment, social welfare, democracy, security, and the future of the nation-state. Inevitably, the Commission fared badly during the crisis. Lacking direct democratic accountability and legitimacy, the Commission was vulnerable to charges of aloofness, authoritarianism, and élitism. Accordingly, the crisis greatly damaged the Commission's image, effectiveness, and internal morale.

One of the ironies of the ratification crisis was that, as early as 1985 during the SEA negotiations, the Commission had championed subsidiarity, which was formally written into the Maastricht Treaty and which some member states, during the ratification crisis, cited as a means of curbing Commission power. Another irony was that, by default, Delors had no choice but to defend a treaty which benefited the Commission relatively little, but which the public perceived as having greatly enhanced the Commission's power. Seemingly, the more Delors defended the treaty, the less the public (especially in Denmark) liked either him or it.

The legacy of the crisis, and its relevance for 1996, are compelling for the Commission. The majority CDU–CSU group in the German parliament may aspire to a new EU institutional balance in which the Commission 'will take on (the) features of a European government' (Europe Documents 1895/96, 7 September 1994: 4) and Belgium may be resolute in its support for the Brussels bureaucracy. Otherwise, the Commission has few influential allies and a number of avowed enemies (notably Britain and Denmark, and, to a lesser extent, France). One former supporter – Italy – has virtually disappeared as a major player in the Union, due to the domestic political upheaval that accompanied the end of the Cold War. Indeed, the crisis of political confidence in Europe since 1991 – manifested generally in public cynicism toward political institutions, the prevalence of weak governments, and weak political leadership – compounds the Commission's particular problems.

The Commission's pre-IGC approach

The IGC is a lens through which most of the Santer Commission's work can be filtered. The Commission recognized that its general performance in 1995 and early 1996 would be as important for the Commission's success at the IGC as its performance at the IGC itself. Specifically, the Commission needed to regain credibility with the Union's citizens and governments. The Commission's success determines, to a great extent, the seriousness with which other players take its proposals and respect its position. The Commission has sought to substitute its image of ambition and intrusiveness, personified by President Delors, with that of discretion and pragmatism, personified by President Santer. The key to Santer's and the Commission's success, both symbolically and substantively, is to make subsidiarity meaningful; consult and inform as widely as possible; encourage deregulation and competitiveness; buttress the single market; promote EMU; fight fraud in the Community; and put the Commission's house in order.

SUBSIDIARITY

This is the user-unfriendly term to describe the Commission's overall approach to legislative initiation and execution. In practice, as Santer told the EP in January 1995 in a phrase that he has used in many of his public speeches as Commission President, subsidiarity means 'less action, but better action' (Santer 7 January 1995). As a result of a comprehensive review, begun in 1993, the Commission has redrafted, simplified, and consolidated numerous pieces of legislation. Moreover, largely because of completion of the single market legislative programme, the number of proposals for principal legislation dropped sharply from over 180 in 1990 to over 100 in 1991, and thereafter dropped progressively to approximately 45 in 1994 (European Commission 1995b: Annex 9). In future, the Commission expects to introduce between 40 and 50 proposals annually.

The Commission's 1995 Social Action Programme (European Commission 1995a) is a striking example of a more modest and considered Commission approach to legislation at the European level. By relying less on legal instruments to protect and strengthen workers' rights, and more on discussion and concilia- tion, the Programme signals not only a shift in the direction of EU social policy, but also the Commission's increasing aversion of interventionism.

CONSULTATION

Although the Commission has always been susceptible to lobbying, it is more eager than ever to consult as broadly as possible on putative or pending legisla- tion. Thus the Commission has begun to publish not only its work programme, legislative programme, and some legislative proposals, but has also stepped up publication of Green and White Papers in an effort to ascertain the necessity for legislation and the form it should take. As a result, the Commission published six Green and White Papers in 1993, nine in 1994, and planned 23 in 1995 (European Commission 1995b: 32).

INFORMATION

At the same time, the Commission is trying to make documents more widely available, notably by entertaining requests for unpublished materials. Of the 238 requests acted upon by May 1995, the Commission had accepted over 50 per cent and rejected nearly 20 per cent (mostly for reasons of 'confidential discussions' and 'public interest'). The Commission deemed the remaining requests ineligible, largely because the documents were either already published or were from another institution (ibid.: Annex 13).

DEREGULATION AND COMPETITIVENESS

The Commission is involved in a number of initiatives to promote deregulation and competitiveness (*Business Europe* 22 May 1995). Foremost among these is the 'Molitor Group' established during Germany's 1994 Presidency, under the chairmanship of Dr Bernhard Molitor, a former senior official in Germany's Ministry for Economic Affairs. Although concerned at first that the Molitor Group was intended to circumvent it, the Commission subsequently became involved in the Group's work. Composed of independent experts, the Group is examining the impact of EU legislation on competitiveness and employment in four priority areas: social legislation, company law, environmental standards for machinery, and food hygiene.

A complementary committee 'for improving and simplifying the business environment' is part of the Commission's small and medium-sized enterprises programme. Consisting of representatives of member state departments or agencies responsible for administrative streamlining, and representatives of European business organizations, the 'simplification committee' is comparing national experience and considering its applicability to the EU. The initial focus of the committee was the problems involved in successfully launching small businesses.

A third body, the Competitiveness Advisory Council, takes a broader approach than the microeconomic perspectives of the Molitor Group and the simplification committee. Santer set up the Council in early 1995, inviting thirteen senior business people, trade unionists, and former politicians to submit six-monthly, independent reports to the European Council on general issues affecting European competitiveness.

THE SINGLE MARKET

Santer's personal emphasis on reinforcing the single market should be seen in the context of restoring the Commission's credibility and effectiveness, and making the Commission more relevant to ordinary Europeans. Apart from simplifying legislation, Santer's commitment to the single market includes the liberalization of energy and telecommunications, accelerating the transposition of directives into national law (if necessary by taking member states to court), and pursuing a vigorous competition policy. The information superhighway, on which the Commission hosted a G-7 conference in Brussels in February 1995, provides an ideal opportunity for the Commission to press for the rapid deregulation of telecommunications services and infrastructures, and to improve its stock with a private sector eager to exploit new technologies.

EMU

Based on his belief that a single currency will boost the Union economically and 'bring substantial benefits to people in their everyday lives' (Santer 1995), the Commission President has been adamant that the Commission will hold member states to the convergence criteria, thereby enhancing the credibility of both EMU and the Commission itself. The Commission's Green Paper on EMU provided a detailed blueprint for the move to a single currency by the end of the decade (European Commission 1995c). It also represented an important step in a lengthy campaign to convince European citizens, as well as their politicians and central bankers, that EMU is feasible and desirable.

FRAUD

One of the most visible and creditable ways in which the Commission believes it can redeem itself with the Union's citizens is by putting up a serious 'fight against fraud' (Santer 1995). The Commission is notorious both for lax financial management of Union policies and programmes, and for spendthrift habits. The Court of Auditors' 1993 report, for example, which was released in November 1994, was highly critical of the Commission, triggered an extensive debate in the EP, and received considerable publicity in the national media. The Commission's reaction was typical of its former defensiveness. Under Santer, by contrast, the Commission has put a far greater emphasis on openness and on financial responsibility. Erkki Liikanen, the Budget Commissioner, and Anita Gradin, Commissioner for Financial Control and Fraud Prevention, jointly spearhead the reform effort. Significantly, both Commissioners come from the new Scandinavian member states, which have a reputation for open government and bureaucratic integrity.

INSIDE THE COMMISSION

Liikanen's proposed reforms have important internal as well as external implications for the Commission, and go to the heart of Santer's determination finally to put the Commission's house in order. Reportedly with Santer's support, Liikanen organized a network of officials specializing in financial management, charged with tightening controls in their respective departments, and guaranteed rapid promotion. In future, Santer and Liikanen want all directors-general to have completed assignments as financial managers (*Financial Times* 4 April 1995). This would revolutionize promotion in the upper echelons of the Commission, which is currently dominated by patronage and an unofficial but rigid system of national quotas.

The problem of promotion, which is symptomatic of a long-standing and deep-seated managerial malaise, needs to be resolved not only to improve the Commission's morale and efficiency, but also to enhance the Commission's deplorable public image. It is easy to caricature the Commission as unwieldy and arcane, and Commission staff as pampered and overpaid, because there is a great deal of truth to those charges. The ugly Berlaymont building used to symbolize the Commission's technocratic character and centralizing tendencies; now the Commission's dispersal all over Brussels symbolizes the institution's disarray. As the Maastricht ratification crisis demonstrated, appearances and perceptions are important in the EUs' politics.

The Commission's structural and managerial problems are rooted in the member states' determination to retain as much influence as possible over the Commission, and have been compounded by successive enlargements, the proliferation of portfolios, and the excessive power of the Cabinets. Dirk Spierenburg identified those problems as early as 1979, but they have never been seriously tackled (Spierenburg 1979). Staff policy remains under used as a powerful instrument of internal reform, new management techniques have rarely been introduced, and the decentralization procedures adopted in 1989 and extended in

1991 and 1993 have had only mixed results.

It will be impossible for Santer suddenly to reform the Commission, and to change the member states' behaviour towards it. Nor is he responsible for the Berlaymont's architecture or asbestos. But his apparent seriousness about correcting the most egregious cases of Commission maladministration, and beginning a process that could ultimately result in far-reaching reform, are both symbolically and substantively important. Of course, public opinion may be less understanding, and may judge Santer solely by the results that he does or does not achieve. While introducing as many reforms as possible in his capacity as Commission President, however, Santer should attempt to educate public opinion about the stranglehold that member states have on key aspects of the Commission's structure and staff policy.

THE COMMISSION'S IGC STRATEGY AND PROSPECTS

Strategy involves setting goals and objectives, and taking steps to achieve them. In the prevailing political circumstances, it has not been surprising that the Commission's goals were constrained, that its means were relatively modest, and that its overall strategy has been unassuming. Santer is a federalist who declared in 1991, as a member of the European Council at the outset of the earlier IGC, that 'our target – not in five or ten years, but for the next generation – would perhaps be a federal United States of Europe' (Santer 1991). That ambitious objective has receded farther into the future, but, as Commission President, Santer undoubtedly remains committed to it. Not all his fellow Commissioners share Santer's federal vision (any more than they shared Delors'), but the Commission's ethos is integrationist, and collegiality serves to point Commissioners away from a nationalist – and toward a supranationalist – perspective on the Union's development.

More immediately, the Commission has argued for the Treaty's three pillars to be replaced by a unitary structure in which the Community decision-making model would prevail, and would like at least to become centrally involved in a revamped and more effective Pillars II (CFSP) and III (Justice and Home Affairs, JHA). Given the political climate and popular backlash against supranationalism, however, the Commission realized the political and public relations danger of making proposals for which there was insufficient support in national capitals. Thus, although Santer claims that the present Commission is politically influential because it contains more than the usual number of former senior ministers (including prime ministers), it has been wary of making the kinds of demands or launching the kinds of initiatives at the 1996 IGC that characterized the Delors Commission's contributions to either the 1985 or the 1991 IGCs. The Commission has neither expected nor advocated a great leap forward with the 1996 IGC, and has sought enhanced powers neither for the Union nor for itself.

The ideal as far as the Commission was concerned was for the 1996 IGC to provide an opportunity for the Commission to do what it has tried to do during previous enlargements: leverage an impending accession in an effort to promote deeper European integration. As the European Council pointed out in June 1994, the link between the IGC and enlargement is obvious. The exceptionally small size of the two Mediterranean applicants and the varying sizes of the Central and Eastern European potential members, as well as their relatively low levels of economic development, have clear implications for the future functioning of the Union's institutions and policies. The Union needs a workable institutional system and a durable policy framework in order to function with twenty-some members, and the IGC was seen as a fortuitous chance to make the necessary adjustments. Indeed, the December 1994 European Council endorsed a pre-accession strategy for the prospective new members 'in the knowledge that the institutional conditions for ensuring the proper functioning of the Union must be examined at the 1996 IGC, which for that reason must take place before accession negotiations begin' (*EC Bulletin* 12–1994: point 1.13).

The Commission has played a key part in the Union's pre-accession strategy, and produced an influential White Paper on integrating the countries of Central and Eastern Europe into the single market. Arguably, the Commission could have used its indispensable role in the enlargement process to strengthen its tenuous position *vis-a-vis* the member states in the run up to the IGC. But the Commission was in no position to go beyond that and advocate radical Treaty reform on the basis of impending enlargement. Apart from the lack of synchronization between the IGC and enlargement, the political circumstances were unpropitious for such a strategy.

Instead of setting ambitious goals for the IGC, therefore, the Commission has approached the negotiations in a pragmatic way, emphasizing the overarching principles of greater legitimacy, accountability, transparency, and efficiency. The Commission's specific objectives seem mostly defensive or reactionary, but have been geared both to completing the Maastricht agenda and to positioning the Union to meet the challenges of enlargement. They include: retaining the single institutional structure and maintaining the institutional balance; improving the effectiveness of the second and third pillars; simplifying the Treaty and its procedures; reforming the Commission's composition and selection;

The single institutional structure and institutional balance

One of the consolations for the Commission in 1991 was that, despite the introduction of two intergovernmental pillars to prop up the new Union, the Treaty maintained a single institutional structure. This by no means ensures consistency between the Union's different pillars, policies, and procedures, but at least provides a framework for coherence. The Commission is not always involved as fully as it would like to be, but it participates to some degree or other in all the Union's activities.

The Maastricht Treaty introduced two important institutional innovations with potentially profound consequences for the future of the EU: the social chapter set a dangerous precedent for à la carte integration; and EMU formalized the prac-

tice of a two-speed Europe. As the Union enlarges, and as the interests and economic levels of its member states diversify further, the tendency toward differentiated integration will increase. As the social chapter demonstrates, an à la carte
arrangement threatens the Union's institutional and political coherence, and
could give rise to major legal complications. A two- or multi-speed Europe, by
contrast, is not only politically and institutionally practicable, but is even desirable
if the Union is to make any headway with an increasingly diversified membership.
Like the member states – except the member state in question – the Commission
would like the IGC to have reopened the social policy debate with a view to ending Britain's self-exclusion and bringing the Social Chapter back into the Treaty.
At the same time, while preferring a joint approach, the Commission will not
object to suggestions for further integration along the lines of EMU, as long as the
single institutional structure is maintained.

Although guaranteeing against institutional exclusion from a field of Union
policy, the single structure does not ensure a perpetuation of the inter-institutional
balance that is essential for the Union's progress. The triangular relationship
between the Council, Commission, and Parliament is dynamic and constantly
changing. Its success, and that of the Union, depends on a fundamental balance
based on the unique roles and responsibilities, the activism, and the independence
of each institution. The Commission may have fared less well at the 1991 IGC
than Parliament or the Council Secretariat, but the Maastricht Treaty did not
undermine the Commission's institutional position. Whatever the degree of its
involvement in the activities of the Union's three pillars, the Commission remains
independent of, yet fully associated with, the Council's work (Piris 1995).
Similarly, the synchronization of the Commission's and the Parliament's terms of
office, and the new appointment procedure, will increase the Commission's
democratic legitimacy without eroding its independence of Parliament
(Fitzmaurice 1994: 183).

The greatest threat to the institutional balance in 1991 came from efforts to
end the Commission's exclusive right to initiate Community legislation. The
Commission's success in educating member states at that time to the value of its
unique role as a defender of the Community interest and as a neutral source of
draft legislation, together with the EP's acquisition of the right to suggest legislative initiatives, has meant that there was no serious onslaught on the Commission
in the IGC or attempts to remove its right to amend or withdraw proposals during the legislative process.

The Commission's right of initiative is crucial not only for formal, but also for
informal, agenda setting in the Union. Having the exclusive right – and responsibility – to introduce legislative proposals inculcates a culture of initiative and leadership in the Commission. Speaking at the height of his power as Commission
President, and in response to the British backlash against him and his institution,
Delors remarked that:

> it is above all in exercising its right of initiative that the Commission shoulders its
> responsibilities ... everyone gives it credit for having defined goals and proposed ways

and means of revitalizing European integration. The Commission intends to retain this dynamic approach, assuming [that] it can come up with new ideas and options. (Delors 1989)

The Commission has been eager to extend the scope of qualified majority voting both to increase decision-making efficiency, and to enhance its own ability to broker compromises and agreements. Yet there is one area in which the Commission cherishes unanimity: the Council's ability to amend a Commission proposal. Just as it wants the opportunity to nudge draft legislation along by helping member states to overcome a possible blocking minority (instead of a national veto), the Commission does not want member states to be able to change one of its proposals by adopting a qualified majority (instead of a unanimous position).

There was, however, one threat to the Union's institutional balance, and to the Commission's very existence, in a proposal by the British government to 'unbundle' the Commission's powers. Calls to curb drastically the Commission's role and responsibilities emanate mostly from right-wing British Euro-sceptics, notably the Fresh Start Group, the European Foundation, and the pan-European (but British-dominated) European Research Group, which published a manifesto in February 1995 urging, among other things, that the Commission be reduced to 'a civil service carrying out the will of elected ministers' (European Research Group 1995: 34). But a much more thoughtful, and potentially more damaging, critique of the Commission comes from an influential British conservative think-tank, the European Policy Forum, and especially from the work of its director, Frank Vibert. The main thrust of Vibert's proposals is to rob the Commission of any political role, end its exclusive right of initiative, and restructure its managerial responsibilities by establishing separate agencies. Thus, the Commission would be 'unbundled' into a single market commission (to manage the internal market), a treasury board (to oversee expenditure), a trade commission (to manage external commercial policy), and a competition authority (to implement competition policy) (Vibert 1994 and 1995; European Policy Forum 1994).

Although ideologically inspired and seemingly far-fetched, Vibert's recommendations are not without merit. The Commission may have assumed too many responsibilities, and the line between political opportunism and managerial ability may have become unacceptably blurred. Merger control – for which, above a certain threshold, the Commission has sole responsibility – is particularly vulnerable to such charges. A number of member states are known to be sympathetic to the idea of establishing an independent EU cartel office, along the lines of the *Bundeskartellamt*. Claus-Dieter Ehlermann, the formidable former head of the Commission's competition directorate-general (DG IV), accepts the idea in principle, but argues that it should not be implemented until the EU's political development made it more likely that such an office could be fully independent – or at least manifestly more independent than DG IV currently is (Ehlermann 1995).

Hiving-off the Commission's responsibilities and establishing separate agencies is a recipe for decentralization rather than for better management and, especially, control. The Union already has a plethora of specialized agencies – ranging from service-providers to think-tanks – whose status and accountability are uncertain. In many cases the rationale for establishing those agencies was to satisfy national sensitivities, not to meet legitimate demands. Practical problems – such as recruitment procedures and remuneration for agency employees – and political problems – such as adequate supervision – remain unresolved. Given the Union's record to date, the proliferation of specialized agencies is not necessarily in the interests of efficiency, transparency, and accountability – objectives that Vibert's proposals seek to achieve.

Improving Pillars II and III

COMMON FOREIGN AND SECURITY POLICY (CFSP)

So far, the Union's CFSP has not amounted to much. Neither its common positions nor joint actions have reflected the Union's potential international impact or influence. The problem lies largely with the intergovernmental nature of CFSP. Member states were used to cooperating in EPC, but have been unwilling to go beyond that and avail themselves of the CFSP's provisions for majority voting. Accordingly, as Santer told the EP, the CFSP 'is still too much of a continuation of the old political cooperation arrangements with a more attractive name' (Santer 17 January 1995). The separation of foreign and security policy from the other components of external relations means that the Union lacks a coherent approach to political, economic, and development issues.

Procedural problems within the Council – the ongoing dispute between the Brussels-based Committee of Permanent Representatives and the national capitals-based Political Committee – and within the Council secretariat – with mutual suspicion between officials seconded from national foreign ministries and the secretariat's own officials – are minor by comparison with the problems of involving the Commission fully in CFSP. The Commission is supposed to be associated with all aspects of CFSP and, together with the member states, has the right to make proposals. In 1992, shortly after the Maastricht Treaty was negotiated, the Commission transformed its small staff dealing with EPC into a new Directorate-General (DG 1A) for External Political Relations. Partly for personal reasons (rivalry between Leon Brittan and Hans van den Broek) and partly for practical reasons (the Commission lacks competence for CFSP), DG 1A has had a troubled history. It was restructured when Santer reorganized external relations in the Commission along geographical lines, nonetheless allowing van den Broek to retain responsibility for CFSP, but under the President's overall supervision.

Yet the Commission does not have competence for CFSP; therefore van den Broek's 'responsibility' for it is nominal (although, because international affairs are glamorous, van den Broek's portfolio is prestigious). A majority of member states, and the Council secretariat, do not want the Commission (or the Parliament) to be involved in CFSP, except when it comes to operational expenditure, which may be charged to the Community budget. Indeed, the demarcation between Pillars I and II is far from clear not only with regard to funding, but also to certain decision-making procedures. In the Commission's view: 'the complexity of the present system gives rise to procedural debates instead of debates of substance' (European Commission 1995b: 23).

Notwithstanding these problems, few member states seem enthusiastic about involving the Commission fully in CFSP, let alone in a possible Union defence policy. According to Niels Ersboll (who, as a former secretary-general of the Council Secretariat, has not been particularly keen on the Commission): 'if anything, resistance to a Community-type [CFSP] practice, with regard to the roles of the Commission and the Parliament, has grown since Maastricht' (Ersboll 1994: 416). Indeed, to some extent van den Broek, DG 1A, and the EP's committee on Foreign Affairs inhabit a fantasy world. For instance, the Committee spent considerable time at van den Broek's investiture hearing in January 1995 questioning the Commissioner-designate about Chechnya and Bosnia, as if he or the Commission had much influence over events in either place.

No one can doubt the importance of foreign, security, and defence policy for the Union, not least because of diminishing US military involvement in Western Europe, the perpetuation of the Bosnian conflict, uncertainty about Russia's future, and increasing instability in North Africa. The Commission could play an important part by providing the analysis and planning necessary for an effective CFSP, for which the Council lacks sufficient resources. The widespread use of qualified majority voting in CFSP would also allow the Commission to play the role of instigator and broker that characterizes its contribution to Community decision-making. It became increasingly clear that the member states were reluctant to approve such changes in the 1996 IGC. At best, greater experience with the present procedures, and public impatience with CFSP's inadequacies, may result in more relevant and effective common positions and joint actions. It is conceivable that a small group of member states, dissatisfied with the situation, will press ahead by themselves with greater integration in the realm of foreign, security, and defence policy.

JUSTICE AND HOME AFFAIRS (JHA)

Progress on justice and home affairs has proved even more disappointing than on CFSP. Pillar III has amounted to little more than a continuation of earlier intergovernmental efforts to cooperate on issues such as immigration and international crime. The Council has made little use of the Maastricht Treaty's new JHA instruments, preferring instead to use the pre-existing, and relatively meaningless, recommendations, resolutions, and conclusions. The problem lies squarely with the fact that unanimity is required for all JHA areas, thereby making it impossible to reach decisions over the objections of even one member state.

As part of his effort to make the Union more relevant for its citizens, Santer has stressed the importance of progress on such highly visible issues as the fight against drugs and organized crime. Indeed, the Commission has even used its right of initiative in JHA, but to no avail. Justice ministers have little tolerance for the Commission, and none for qualified majority voting. Although Santer identified 'concrete improvements to the [JHA's] decision-making procedures' as a priority for the IGC (Santer 17 January 1995), little progress was actually expected.

Simplifying the Treaty and its procedures

As anyone who teaches courses on the Union knows, the Union's structure, treaties, and procedures are obscure. Even the most enthusiastic students – let alone the Union's ordinary citizens – have difficulty grasping them. As part of an effort to bring the Union closer to its citizens, the Commission would like to merge the three Communities and the Union into a single entity, and fuse the respective Treaties into a single document. Moreover, the member states agreed at Maastricht in 1991 to review the classification of Community acts at the 1996 IGC with a view to establishing an appropriate 'hierarchy' between them. In other words, the idea is that there should be a clear distinction between genuinely legislative measures, which need to be decided upon by the Council and (in some cases) Parliament, and other rule-making acts which may be adopted by the Commission (as the Union's executive). This was closely related to two other issues on the IGC's agenda: the scope of co-decision, and comitology. All are linked, in turn, to subsidiarity. Thus, some of the most incomprehensible terms in the Union's lexicon (hierarchy of norms, comitology, and subsidiarity) were put high on the IGC's agenda in an effort to make the Union more comprehensible to its citizens.

Simplification is undoubtedly desirable, but not necessarily possible. Current procedural and institutional complexities reflect the complexity of European integration itself. As the Commission wrote, with unusual eloquence: 'the complexity of European integration, the fruit of layer upon layer of hesitant advances and compromises, is reflected in the complexity of its legal instruments' (European Commission 1995b: 34). The 1991 IGC is a classic case in point. Because the negotiators: 'were not able to come to a clear decision, either towards more integration or towards more intergovernmental cooperation, they were led to increase the complexity and the lack of transparency of the system' (Piris 1995: 19). It is ahistorical to imagine that, in the 1996 IGC, the negotiators could simply wave a magic wand and produce a short, simple, consolidated text that eradicated over 40 years of bureaucratic battles, procedural wrangles, and tortuous negotiations.

Moreover, apart from the unique history of European integration, there is no governmental system in the world fully understood by its subjects. Americans are no more familiar with the Congressional committee system than Europeans are with the EP's committee system. This is not to dismiss the importance of clarity and comprehension, or to deny an onus on the EU, precisely because of its history and supranational nature, to make a special effort to close the incomprehension gap. But there are limits to how simple a system of governance can be, and there are limits to the citizens' interest in understanding how the system works.

Ideally, Parliament would like the Union to have a single decision-making procedure: a revised form of co-decision. This has a direct bearing on the arcane debate about comitology (the committee system built around the Commission's implementing powers) currently raging in the corridors of the Council Secretariat and the EP. Until the EP acquired co-decision powers under the Maastricht Treaty, it had relatively little involvement in comitology, which was a bone of contention primarily between the Council and the Commission.

Since the Community's earliest days, the Commission pressed the Council for the fullest and freest powers to implementing legislation arising out of Community acts. In that way, the Commission would truly become the Community's executive. The Council was generally reluctant to concede too much because the Commission sometimes altered the Council's acts with its implementing legislation, and member states wanted to retain as much executive autonomy as possible. The Commission scored a victory during the SEA negotiations in 1985 when the member states agreed to change the Treaty to make it a general rule to give the Commission implementing powers, and asked the Council to stipulate, before the SEA came into force, how such powers should be exercised. In response, the Commission proposed three 'tried and tested procedures': the advisory committee, the management committee, and the regulatory committee. But the Council added two variants on the regulatory committee and a safeguard clause procedure (Commission of the European Communities 1988: point 4; Docksey and Williams 1994). Thus, with the exception of the advisory committee, which gave the Commission virtual autonomy, the committee system constrained the Commission by guaranteeing, to some degree or other, the Council's involvement in implementation.

Since 1987, when the Council adopted the rules for exercising implementing powers, the Council and Commission have sparred over the appropriate procedure for each legislative act. Yet the Council-Commission dispute was more ritualistic than real. In effect, the Commission enjoyed a considerable degree of autonomy, the culture of the Commission in any case stressed the importance of legislative initiation rather than implementation, and the efficiency of the various procedures was never an issue (although the variety of procedures available often leads to protracted and theoretical discussions about which one to use, thereby slowing down the legislative process). Thus, the Commission reached the logical, but politically surprising, conclusion in its report for the Reflection Group that, with one exception: 'the implementing procedures operate satisfactorily and present no major obstacles to actual implementation.' The Commission also provided compelling statistics: of the more than 200 comitology committees in existence, only 30 are the kind that can block decisions; and of the thousands of decisions taken by the comitology committees since 1992, only six were referred back to the Council, which then made a decision in each case (European Commission 1995b: 22).

If comitology were still restricted to Council-Commission relations, the controversy about it would erupt only in the lifeless pages of the *Official Journal* and the Commission's *General Report*. But co-decision, which gave Parliament real legislative powers, introduced a new element to an already controversial issue. Because it championed the Commission's implementing powers and wished, in turn, to control the executive, Parliament always took a keen interest in comitology. Until implementation of the Maastricht Treaty, however, Parliament lacked direct involvement. Now the EP argues that it should have equal rights with the Council to control implementation by the Commission of legislation enacted through co-decision. In response, member states claim that the Council's and Parliament's roles are not comparable in that respect.

Parliament's intensity of feeling about comitology was evident in President Haensch's inaugural address, when he warned the Council: 'not to try to use comitology to deprive Parliament of co-decision rights [which] it is entitled to under the Maastricht Treaty' (European Parliament 19–22 July 1994: 13). Haensch's point was brought home with a vengeance when Parliament's insistence on involvement in comitology (in legislation on voice telephony) caused the conciliation phase to fail for the first time under the co-decision procedure.

Parliament's assertiveness with respect to comitology threatened to paralyse co-decision and poison relations between Parliament and the Council. An interinstitutional agreement in December 1994 resulted in a truce, but committed the parties to settle the matter definitively at the IGC. The scope of co-decision has a bearing on the comitology question. The Commission has been in favour of an extension of co-decision to new areas in order to extend Parliament's legislative role. As for the relationship between co-decision and comitology, however, the Commission has merely looked for the simplest procedures that allow the minimum amount of interference either from the Council or Parliament.

The Commission's composition and selection

The number of Commission members and the method of their selection and appointment is crucial for the Commission's credibility and legitimacy. The Maastricht Treaty procedure for appointing the Commission was applied for the first time in 1994. However, it was marred by the controversy surrounding Santer's nomination which, ironically, had nothing to do with the new procedure, but was part of the pre-existing arrangement by which the heads of state and government had to agree unanimously on their choice of Commission President-designate. Santer was not the first ever Commission President-designate to be the European Council's second choice (Delors was also a compromise candidate), but the high degree of public interest in the selection of Delors' successor, Britain's humiliating veto of Dehaene, and the Franco-German stranglehold on the appointment process reflected badly on the European Council and – indirectly – on Santer. It also cast the new appointment procedure, which began after Santer's nomination, in a poor light.

Opinion in the EP in July 1994 differed on Santer's qualifications and suitability for the job, and also on the appropriateness of endorsing a candidate selected (according to the leader of the Socialist Group) in such a 'squalid, shabby, and ill-judged way (ibid.: 79). Many MEPs felt that Parliament should reject Santer in order to pressure the European Council to choose another candidate more on the basis of merit than expediency (although there was no reason to believe that the European Council would have acted any differently a third time round). MEPs especially resented the member states' warnings that Parliament would be responsible for the crisis that would follow Santer's rejection, and their pressure on MEPs to vote in Santer's favour. In the event, Santer's narrow endorsement averted a public relations disaster but further weakened the President-designate's stature.

The remainder of the appointment procedure – the nomination of Commissioners' and Parliament's vote on them – included well-publicized, but hardly insightful, individual hearings for each Commissioner-designate (something not expressly provided for in the Treaty). Parliament's approval of the College by a large majority undoubtedly enhanced the Commission's legitimacy, although both Parliament and the Commission have a long way to go before winning widespread public support. Moreover, the entire appointment procedure took too long (beginning with the debate on Santer's nomination in July 1994 and ending with Parliament's vote on the Commissioners-designate in January 1995, the process lasted nearly seven months in all).

The appointment procedure can be fine-tuned outside the IGC in order to synchronize more closely the beginning of a new EP and the approval by it of a new Commission. As the Santer case demonstrated, however, a major weakness lies in the selection of a President-designate by the European Council. Santer himself hopes that, in future, Parliament will elect the Commission President from a list chosen by the European Council (ibid.: 85). This could have far-reaching consequences for the Commission and Parliament: it could improve Parliament's importance in the eyes of its electorate, thereby increasing voter turn-out in Euro-elections, and it could result in a 'parliamentary' Commission, more responsive to the majority opinion in Strasbourg (Fitzmaurice 1994: 183). The danger with such a system, of course, is that the Commission would move from sycophancy to subservience in its formal dealings with Parliament.

Whatever the advantages or disadvantages of the Commission President's election by MEPs, what about the procedure for, and consequences of, candidate selection by the European Council? Would the heads of government vote on a slate of candidates to go before Parliament? What would be their criteria for choosing candidates? The unseemly dumping of Dehaene and selection of Santer demonstrated how contentious these questions can be, but also showed that, despite their disagreement over Dehaene (a disagreement due to domestic British politics), the heads of government have no intention of giving up their prerogative to select the President-designate, subject only to the possibility that Parliament could reject their choice.

The number and selection of other Commissioners is a closely related issue. Although the question of the Commission's size could easily consume a lot of time and energy at the IGC, radical reform is not necessarily in the Commission's interest. Arguably, it is more important for the member states, their citizens, and the Commission to have direct, high-level channels of communication via 'national' Commissioners, than to go through the politically painful and essentially unrewarding exercise of drastically reducing the Commission's size. Indeed, the fact that each member state has at least one of its senior officials or politicians on the Commission 'undoubtedly contributes to ... general confidence in the Commission and the acceptance of its wide powers' (Ersbøll 1994: 417).

Despite dire warnings about the unmanageableness of a college of more than the existing number of Commissioners (or even with the existing number of Commissioners), and imaginative ideas to limit the college to ten or twelve members, governments have been reluctant to surrender their right to appoint one Commissioner each. Confident that they will not be asked to make such a sacrifice, large member states have generally been silent on the issue. By contrast, many small member states have stated unequivocally that they were not about to forego 'their' Commissioner. The Netherlands have even been fearful of formalizing the Benelux caucus in the Union, 'because a formalized Benelux role could tempt other countries to lump us together in discussing such things as the size of the Commission (van den Berg 1994: 15). Portugal similarly opposes the possibility of regional representation on the Commission. 'Although today it has excellent relations with Spain,' Portugal's Foreign Minister remarked in October 1994, 'Portugal will never feel itself to be represented (on the Commission) by a Spaniard' (*Agence Europe* 5 October 1994).

In the end, with the exception of tiny Cyprus and Malta, which may agree not to appoint a Commissioner, and the large member states, which may also agree to give up their second Commissioners, the current system of selecting Commissioners-designate might well remain the same. Thus, in a Union of twenty member states (the existing members plus Cyprus, Malta, and the Visegrad Three), the Commission would have eighteen members – two fewer than at present, and only one more than the highly successful first Delors Commission. Even with more than twenty members, the Commission would function much as it now does, with a group of undeclared but easily identifiable 'core' Commissioners, supported by strong cabinets, setting the Commission's agenda, and launching major initiatives.

APPLYING THE LESSONS OF PREVIOUS IGCs

The lessons of previous IGCs cannot be applied straightforwardly to the radically changed circumstances of 1996. On the other hand, IGC procedures remain largely the same. Although more open to public scrutiny, the meetings at senior official, ministerial, and European Council levels follow the same format that they did in 1985 and 1991. The high public and political stakes in 1996 means that the role of the heads of government is even more prominent than it was in the past. Certainly it was expected that, in between their regularly scheduled summits, and any extraordinary summits called to discuss the IGC, the heads of government – and the Commission President – would hold numerous bilateral and multilateral meetings to assess the strength of each other's positions, make deals, strike bargains, and form coalitions on IGC issues. The high degree of personal politicking that characterized previous IGCs was regarded as likely to be an even more striking feature of the 1996 IGC.

Some of the lessons of previous IGCs, which in the Commission's case pointed to Delors' decisive role, therefore seem especially apt with reference to 1996.

LEADERSHIP

Through no fault of his own – except that he accepted a nomination knowing it to be controversial – Santer's pre-presidency got off to a bad start. Although the approval procedure is intended to strengthen the President's legitimacy and political primacy, the fractious parliamentary debate and narrow vote of approval of July 1994 did little to enhance Santer's authority. Some MEPs based their 'no' vote on the assumption that the nature of Santer's appointment would irretrievably weaken his presidency. As one MEP opined: 'better to have a crisis lasting two months now [as a result of a parliamentary rejection of Santer] than a crisis which will drag on for five years [the span of a Santer presidency]' (European Parliament 1994: 84). Yet the impact of the bruising appointment procedure seemed surprisingly short lived. Santer acquitted himself well both before and during the debate, steadily winning over waverers. Not least because he won, he appeared to bear no ill-will toward those who voted against him. Since then, his dealings with Parliament, and especially with the dominant Socialist Group which opposed his candidacy, have been cordial and constructive. Nor does it seem that his parliamentary ordeal damaged Santer's public standing.

During the debate, Santer expressed his wish 'to become a strong President at the head of a strong, coherent, determined Commission' (ibid.: 78). In the wake of the Maastricht crisis, the European Council was unlikely to nominate a Commission President in the mould of Jacques Delors; yet three of the leading candidates – Lubbers, Dehaene, and Santer – were experienced prime ministers with the potential to become reasonably forceful Presidents. Some MEPs complained that, because he had been a prime minister for more than ten years, Santer would never become independent of his fellow heads of government; as Piet Dankert put it: 'I would like to call on the European Council to extend the field of candidates beyond "one of us"' (ibid.: 76).

It has perhaps been hard for Santer to keep his distance not so much from the heads of government in general, but from Chancellor Kohl in particular. Not only is Santer friendly with Kohl, but he owes his appointment as Commission President to him. Moreover, as well as being the most influential member state, Germany has one of the most Commission-friendly governments in the Union. Santer used the allocation of portfolios in October 1994 to demonstrate his distance from one head of government: John Major. During his visits to member state capitals before assigning portfolios, Santer made the statements expected of a President-designate about imperviousness to national lobbying. In the event, he allocated portfolios according to most member states' wishes, with the exception of reducing the scope of Leon Brittan's responsibilities for external economic relations. Thus, with one relatively easy act, he curbed a potential rival in the Commission and sent a signal to the least Commission-friendly government.

Santer was quick to point out during and after the appointment debate that coming from the Union's smallest member state would not preclude him from becoming a strong President. Yet coming from one of the Union's largest and most influential member states, where he was seen as a potential President of the Republic, was one of Delors' greatest assets, especially at meetings of the

European Council and when representing the Community internationally. Being a Luxembourger puts definite limits on Santer's leadership, but not necessarily in the context of the IGC.

Santer's long experience as a prime minister could not only be to the Commission's benefit, but his prime ministership during Luxembourg's two IGC Presidencies (in late 1985 and early 1991) is an invaluable advantage. In close collaboration with Delors, Santer helped to fashion the SEA at the December 1985 Luxembourg summit. Six years later, he and Delors disagreed about the structure of the Union, but their difference was one of means rather than ends. Both were Euro-federalists, but Santer had a shrewder understanding of what the member states would accept in the Maastricht Treaty. That shrewdness, knowledge of the IGC process, and experience of past negotiations may well assist the Commission greatly in 1996.

Ultimately, Santer's leadership at the IGC will derive not only from his official position, experience, independence, and country of origin, but also from his achievements and record within the Commission. Santer is a consolidator and a conciliator, skills that are sorely needed in his dealings with the 'barons' who remain in his Commission from Delors' days, and some of the ex-ministers (including ex-prime ministers) who are new to the Commission. Santer's grouping of portfolios along thematic lines and, in the most sensitive areas, under his direct responsibility, is an effective way to improve coordination, communication, and collegiality, while blunting the unilateralist tendencies of some of his high-profile colleagues.

POLICY NETWORKS

Apart from a general focus on deregulation and competitiveness, and the opportunity provided by the information superhighway to replicate the Davignon-European manufacturers, collaboration of the early 1980s, the issues on the IGC's agenda have not lent themselves to the kind of lobbying and Commission-private sector cooperation that preceded the White Paper and the SEA (but see Mazey and Richardson in this volume). Santer has not had as much opportunity to use groups such as the ERT to bolster the Commission's position.

FOCUS

Santer in particular, and the Commission in general, focused early on the IGC. As the discussion of the Commission's pre-IGC strategy indicates, the Commission's work has been conducted with a view toward strengthening the Commission's position during the negotiations. In addition, Santer's assignment to Marcelino Oreja of responsibility for institutional relations and preparation for the IGC, was astute. As a former Spanish foreign minister, and a former chairman of the EP's Institutional Affairs Committee, Oreja has the weight within the Commission, and with Parliament and the member states, to push IGC issues to the top of the agenda. Oreja's influence was also important during the Spanish Presidency in late 1995, when the Reflection Group (under Spanish chairmanship) conducted its work.

FRANCO-GERMAN-COMMISSION RELATIONS

The Franco–German relationship remains pivotal for the Union, but is no longer predictable. The relationship always required work to overcome the inevitable differences of policy and perspective between both countries, but was invariably buttressed by a shared commitment to the fundamental principles of European integration. The relationship waxed and waned under particular leaders, and at particular times during their leadership. Since the end of the Cold War and the Maastricht crisis, however, that shared commitment cannot be taken for granted (see Chapter 5). The strength and utility of the Franco-German relationship is one of the imponderables at the IGC. Without doubt, however, the Commission will be unable to intrude on it. On a personal level, Santer may be a friend of Kohl's, but he cannot aspire to the near-equality of the Delors–Kohl relationship, let alone hope to establish a Santer–Kohl–Chirac triumvirate – not least because of Chirac's unpredictability and distrust of the Commission.

CONCLUSION

IGCs tend to assume lives of their own, and their outcomes are notoriously diffi-cult to predict. The 1996 IGC has presented additional challenges, because of Europe's – and the EU's – uncertainty in the post-Cold War, post-Maastricht period. There is no inevitability about the Union's progress, or immutability about its institutional structure. The Commission has been marginalized in the past, and may be marginalized again at some point in the future. Nevertheless Treaty revisions have generally benefited the Commission, and it is unlikely in 1996 that the member states will deliberately reduce the Commission's role.

At the IGC, however, the Commission has had to look out not only for its own institutional interests, but also for the interests of the Union as a whole. As Oreja told the EP during his approval hearing:

> the Commission is there to represent the Community interest. It should defend this interest and present proposals to Member States identifying problems and suggesting solutions ... the Commission must, at all events, defend and promote the Union's past achievements and fundamental principles. It must also prevent any gulf from develop-ing between the national governments. (European Parliament January 1995: 4)

With its emphasis under Santer on efficiency and effectiveness, the Commission is bolstering its otherwise weak position. As a multi-functional organization in a fluid system of governance, the Commission is striving to become more flexible and adaptable in order to meet the political and bureaucratic demands placed upon it. Despite a manifestly unfavourable climate, and low expectations for the conference's outcome, the Commission has been attempting to play its character-istic role of instigator, arbitrator, and broker, and constantly reminding the mem-ber states of its unique attributes as the Union's conscience, institutional memory, pace-setter, policy entrepreneur, think-tank, and guardian.

REFERENCES AND BIBLIOGRAPHY

Commission of the European Communities (1986) *Nineteenth General Report.* Luxembourg, Office of Official Publications. (Before 1993 publications by the Commission come under the title Commission of the European Communities).

—— (1988) *Twenty-first General Report.* Luxembourg, Office of Official Publications.

—— (1989) *One Market, One Money: An Evaluation of the Potential Benefits and Costs of Forming an Economic and Monetary Union in the European Community.* Luxembourg, Office of Official Publications.

Delors, Jacques (1989) Speech at the College of Europe, Bruges, 17th October.

—— (1991) 'European integration and security', *Survival* vol. 33, no. 2 (March/April), pp. 99–109

Docksey, Christopher and Williams, Karen (1994) 'The Commission and the execution of Community policy', in Edwards, Geoffrey and Spence, David (eds) *The European Commission.* Harlow, Longman/Cartermill.

Ehlermann, Claus-Dieter (1995) 'Case for a Cartel Body', *Financial Times* (7 March).

Ersbøll, Niels (1994) 'The European Union: The immediate priorities', *International Affairs No. 3, Vol. 70*, pp. 413–19.

Europe Documents (1994) 'Document of the CDU/CSU Parliamentary Group in the German Parliament on the Future of European Unification', 1895/96, 7 September.

European Commission (1995a) *Medium Term Social Action Program 1995–97.* COM(95)134 final, Brussels, Office of Official Publications, 12 April.

—— (1995b) *Report on the TEU for the IGC Reflection Group.* Luxembourg, Office of Official Publications.

—— (1995c) *Green Paper on EMU.* Luxembourg, Office of Official Publications.

European Parliament (1991) 'Debates of the European Parliament', *Official Journal, Annex* 3–221 (April).

—— (1991) 'Debates of the European Parliament', *Official Journal, Annex* 3–411 (November).

—— (1994) 'Debates of the European Parliament', *Official Journal, Annex* 4–449 (19–22 July).

European Policy Forum (1994) *A Proposal for a European Constitution: The Report of the European Constitutional Group.* London.

Fitzmaurice, John (1994) 'The European Commission', in Duff, Andrew, Pinder, John and Price, Roy (eds) *Maastricht and Beyond.* London, Routledge.

European Research Group (1995) *A Europe of Nations.* London.

Grant, Charles. (1994) *Delors: Inside the House That Jacques Built.* London, Nicholas Brealey Publishing.

Moravcsik, Andrew (1991) 'Negotiating the SEA', *International Organization*, vol. 45 (winter), pp. 19–56.

Piris, Jean Claud (1995) 'After Maastricht: Are the Community Institutions More Efficacious, More Democratic, And More Transparent'. Brussels, unpublished paper.

Reflection Group (24 August 1995), progress report on the 1996 Intergovernmental Conference.

Ross, George (1995) *Jacques Delors and European Integration.* New York, Oxford University Press.

Santer, Jacques (1995) 'Inaugural Address to the European Parliament', *Europa*, 7 January (Home Page of the European Commission on the World Wide Web).

—— (1991) *Europe Magazine*, Washington DC, January.

Spierenberg, Dirk (chairman) (1979) *Proposals for Reform of the Commission of the European Communities and its Services.* Brussels, European Commission.

van den Berg, Dirk (1994) 'The Netherlands and Luxembourg: Small countries in an ever larger Europe' *EIPA News*, Summer, p. 15.

Vibert, Frank (1995) 'The case for "unbundling" the Commission', in Davignon, Etienne *et al. What future for the European Commission*, Brussels, The Philip Morris Institute for Public Policy Research, pp. 72–85

11
PRESSURE FROM THE
EUROPEAN PARLIAMENT

PIET DANKERT

INTRODUCTION

There is no union like the European Union (EU); there is no parliament like the European Parliament (EP). Before 1979, when its members were elected by universal suffrage for the first time, the EP functioned as a consultative assembly for national parliamentarians interested in European union. Although they were members of political groups within the EP, they remained in essence national parliamentarians. Their influence, and particularly their monitoring role with regard to European policy, tended largely to be felt in the national sphere.

Since, in 1979, there was still a very large number of directly elected Members of European Parliament (MEPs) who combined a European with a national mandate, the far-reaching significance of the direct election of MEPs became apparent only gradually. The relationship with national parliaments, which had provided the EP's membership, gradually became a competitive one. The relationship with the Council of Ministers, characterized up to 1979 by what were often close contacts between national ministers and national MEPs, became mainly one of considerable distance. And, in order to survive as a directly elected parliament, the EP was forced, more than it had ever been prior to 1979, to seek competencies and powers in inter-institutional relations and recognition, or at least familiarity, among the electorate.

This has been no easy task in an essentially intergovernmental structure such as that of the EU. Its intergovernmental nature was moderated by a number of factors, not least the replacement of national parliaments' right of assent, by the right – as it was originally conceived – of the EP to advise, but also by the possibility of majority decision-making, by the European Commission's proprietorial right of initiative and the jurisdiction of the Court of Justice. But the EP's task would seem well-nigh impossible, especially given the EU's re-emphasis on the purely intergovernmental nature of policy-making in the fields of foreign affairs and security, and justice and home affairs, and given the greater and formalized role played by the European Council. Only a parliament that can counterbalance the power of the European Council and national parliaments can rise to such a challenge. Powers alone are not sufficient for a task of this kind.

The member states certainly never intended direct elections to cause the EP to grow into a force to be reckoned with, or to give European integration a democratic legitimacy through the EP. At best, direct elections have created the semblance of democratization. That it is no more than a semblance is evident from the fact that the decision to give the European Council of heads of state and government a fixed place in the European process was directly connected to the decision to introduce direct elections. The Maastricht Treaty confirms the role of the European Council as the source of 'the necessary impetus for [the] development [of the Union]' and as the organ that defines the Union's 'general political guidelines'. The European Council has become the symbol of the intergovernmental nature of the Union.

REFORM AND CONTINUING CONSTRAINTS

Since the first direct elections there has, nevertheless, been some development in the EP's powers. The budgetary powers obtained in the early 1970s – a first step being taken in 1970 and an important second step in 1975 – combined with the financing of the EC budget from the EC's own resources made a major contribution in this respect. The right to have the last word on 'non-compulsory' expenditure – in other words, non-European Agricultural Guidance and Guarantee (EAGGF) funds – and the right to reject the budget in its entirety very much aided the Parliament in its efforts to reinforce its own position in the institutional triangle Commission–Council–Parliament. The rapid growth of non-compulsory expenditure was a further important factor. The way in which the EP exercised its budgetary powers contributed towards its development into an equal partner of the other arm of the budgetary authority, the Council.

Initial moves were made in the Single European Act (SEA) of 1987 to secure legislative powers for the EP. However, the cooperation procedure set up for this purpose gives the European Commission, which plays a central role in the procedure, and the Council, which can in practice opt out of the procedure too easily, too much leeway to be able to speak of significant progress. Progress was, however, achieved in the shape of the parliamentary assent procedure laid down in the SEA. This means that agreements on the enlargement of the EU require the assent of an absolute majority of MEPs. Association agreements, other agreements establishing a specific institutional framework by organizing cooperation procedures, agreements having important budgetary implications for the Community and agreements entailing amendment of an act adopted under the procedure referred to in Article 189(b) require the assent of a simple majority in the EP of those voting. The heads of state and of government, apparently convinced, erroneously, that this procedure was less potentially harmful than the co-decision procedure, decided in their wisdom at Maastricht also to subject the tasks, priority objectives and the organization of the structural funds to the assent procedure.

The satisfactory functioning of the cooperation procedure, and the dissatisfaction experienced by a number of member states over the lack of democratic legitimacy in EC decision-making procedures, led in Maastricht to the introduction of the co-decision procedure in Article 189(b). This gives the EP limited co-legislative status. But it only covers a small percentage of the decisions taken by the Council of Ministers with a qualified majority. Agricultural legislation does not fall within its domain, for instance, whereas much of the legislation relating to the internal market and flanking policies does. It is sometimes difficult to fathom quite what the reasoning of the treaty drafters was on co-decision. In its cultural chapter, the 1991 IGC stated that the co-decision procedure was applicable, but at the same time adopted the unanimity principle in Council decision-making which invalidated co-decision.

Although the EP has become a much more significant Community institution through the assignment of these powers, and the use it has made of them, it remains relatively weak compared to most national parliaments. Too weak, perhaps, to be able to justify direct elections much longer? The gradual decline in electoral turnout between 1979 and 1994, with a dramatic decrease in countries such as The Netherlands, gives grounds for serious concern. Can this reduction be explained by the fact that the EU, as a 'process of creating an ever closer union among the peoples of Europe, in which decisions are taken as closely as possible to the citizen', is still too far away from that citizen? Is it because there is a lack of clarity concerning the EP's role in bringing the European process to the citizen? It certainly can. The fact that the European institutional structure deviates sharply from national structures, particularly in terms of the relationship between Parliament and the Council of Ministers, creates considerable confusion. Both the Council and the EP moreover remain unfamiliar bodies, as long as the European mass media continue to bring to their readers or viewers, not the considerations of *the* Council or *the* Parliament, but the views of their own minister or, every now and then, of their own national MEPs. This system works out much more in favour of the minister, as a member of a national government, than it does for the European parliamentarian, who as the member of a European institution that takes decisions by simple majorities must seek the backing of the national electorate. Moreover, even those members of the national electorate who seek to understand the division of competencies between the Council and the Commission will find it impossible to get a clear picture of their powers, obscured as they are by a forest of complex decision-making procedures. They cannot, furthermore, be blamed for judging the situation by analogy with national institutions and laying the responsibility for policy implementation, including fraud and irregularities, at the door of the Commission, or even of Parliament, unaware that the member states have delegated a great many implementary tasks to the national level, i.e., to themselves.

This sort of problem existed before the Treaty on European Union (TEU) was ratified. That Treaty has just made things much more complex. The Union, for example, has 'a single institutional framework which shall ensure the consistency and the continuity of the activities carried out in order to attain its objectives while respecting and building upon the *acquis communautaire*' (Article C). But, since the Treaty also allowed the roles of the institutions to vary in each of the pillars, one is forced more and more to wonder whether Article C is not increasingly at odds with reality. Perhaps it is all clear for a very small group of experts. As far as the average individual is concerned, the Union has gradually become such a labyrinth that he or she no longer even tries to find the exit. Why should they make the effort, anyway, aware as they are that its institutional and procedural structure impedes decision-making on the major issues which confront the Union, and which it appeared to wish to tackle at Maastricht, not least the former Yugoslavia (within the framework of the Common Foreign and Security Policy (CFSP), the free movement of persons or the elimination of transborder crime (within the Justice and Home Affairs Pillar (JHA))? Worse still, the need for European decisions has greatly increased as Europe struggles with a new role following the collapse of the Soviet empire. In view of the slow pace of decision-making within the various pillars and the reluctance of some member states, there is a growing danger that EU members who seek to take on these new challenges will find themselves forced to draft policy outside Union structures, or, in anticipation of EU decisions, to form their own core group in order to assume responsibilities emanating from the TEU. The European presence in the contact group on former Yugoslavia and the continuation of the Schengen Agreement following the entry into force of the internal market are the most striking examples. They are also examples of the erosion of the Union's credibility, including that of the Parliament, which had already largely been forced onto the sidelines as a result of the pillar structure.

STRATEGIC CHOICES?

Is federalization the solution? The TEU represents a step away from, rather than towards that scenario. This can be seen, as suggested above, in the role of the European Council and the pillar structure for the CFSP and JHA. But even the Council of Ministers has not escaped unscathed from the trend of further intergovernmentalization. Although Article G (43) of the TEU does not appear in the official publication of the Treaty, it was that Article, according to the footnote to Article 146, that caused the Council to lose its independence. In 1987 the Council still had decision-making powers, as laid down in Article 145 of the SEA. In the new Article 146 this has become: 'The Council shall consist of a representative of each Member State at ministerial level, authorized to commit the government of that Member State.' The use of the phrase 'authorized to' means that the text offers no scope for any hopes raised by the direct election of the EP: Council members need not so much be in Brussels and Luxembourg as in national capitals, where Euro-parliamentarians, too, were largely to be found before 1979.

Is this turning into a plea for a return to that situation? Not yet. The final answer to the question of whether the EP has a right to exist as a directly elected parliament depends on two factors: when it becomes clear to what extent the EP can develop into a Union institution of similar standing to the Council; and whether the equality of the two institutions would be recognized by public opinion. That means that in the years ahead, the EP will have to fight for its position as an institution of equivalent status to the Council on the basis of its electoral mandate, both in the legislative process and, perhaps predominantly, as the monitor of policy laid down by the Council but implemented by the Council, member states and Commission. This requires the further reinforcement of the EP's position in the legislative process; it also requires considerable strengthening of the Commission's capacity and powers regarding the administration of the Union, and the EP's willingness to act as watchdog. At the same time, efforts must be made to bring about a more transparent EU decision-making process and open government.

The majority decisions reached by the Council behind closed doors have contributed significantly to the growth of the EP's powers. Such decisions were made a formal possibility by the SEA of 1987 and have increasingly become a practical reality. To a certain extent, this was the price that had to be paid for direct elections and national parliaments did not appear unduly troubled by the development. National control of European policy does not amount to much in most member states, both because agreement usually exists between the minister deputized to the Council and his or her broad parliamentary majority, and because it is an area that rarely tends to create media interest of a kind sought by parliamentarians. Moreover, the scope for genuine control is limited. National parliamentarians are dependent, in most cases at least, on the communications made by their own Council member during press conferences or in national documents. In a growing number of instances these can now be supplemented by explanations of vote and voting patterns. However, none of this affects the Council decision. It does not help for a national parliament to provide a minister with authorization before he or she travels to a European Council meeting. That would simply block an already laborious decision-making process, or lead to the relevant member state being isolated from negotiations if its involvement were not necessary in order to reach a qualified majority.

It is only by involving the EP more closely in the legislative process and by creating closer ties between European and national parliamentarians that a chance remains of realizing the provision laid down in the EU treaty that 'the systems of government [of its member states] are founded on the principles of democracy'. Up to now this has been not been achieved because of the limited scope of the co-decision procedure laid down in Article 189(b) of the Treaty establishing the European Community. Moreover, the significance of this procedure is very much lessened by the fact that the legislation to which Article 189(b) largely relates, i.e. that concerning the internal market, is largely complete. Now that the initial fear, in Council circles, that Article 189(b) would further impede and delay the legislative process has proved unfounded, the IGC has no grounds on that score for trying to prevent an expansion of the EP's co-legislative powers.

And yet, as was discovered at Maastricht, this is no easy task. It was therefore agreed that a practical approach would be sought by means of a hierarchy of different categories of act, to be developed at a later stage, at the 1996 IGC. It was not possible to do this at Maastricht due to the lack of preparation time.

However, the European Community needs such a hierarchy, because within it, every decision laid down in a directive or regulation has the formal status of an act, and must accordingly be treated as such. If the EP's powers of co-decision-making were to extend to all the legislation resulting from Council decisions reached by a qualified majority, this would not only completely overload the parliamentary agenda, it would also reinforce the EP's image as a cog in a technocratic and bureaucratic machine which produces a never-ending stream of regulations. Even if it were possible to demonstrate that many European regulations replace fifteen not quite overlapping sets of national rules, it would still be impossible to convince the man in the street that Europe has a right to interfere with the curvature of bananas, that it is up to Brussels to decide how and where a farm tractor's roll bar should be attached, or that it is for the EP to pronounce on the proposal for a council Regulation establishing a pilot observer scheme applicable to Community vessels operating in the regulatory area of the Northwest Atlantic Fisheries Organization.

The notion of a hierarchy of categories of act will not solve all these problems. However, if it is sensibly developed, it will have a positive effect on the EP's image as co-legislator. One of the models which lends itself for adoption is the Dutch system, which in addition to acts of parliament, has orders in council and decree orders based on those statutes. Orders in council only have to pass through parliament if the national parliament deems it necessary.

A decision to introduce such a system by treaty amendment would be of considerably greater political benefit to the EP if it incorporated implementary legislation, which is currently the preserve of comitology. The regulatory comitology – now primarily the domain of national civil servants and the Commission – is hard to reconcile with the need, regularly expressed by the Council, for greater transparency in the decision-making process. Moreover, it may well lead to the erosion of the EP's co-legislative powers.

The introduction of co-legislative powers and, earlier, of the cooperation procedure, seem to have pushed the notorious budgetary conflicts between the Council and the EP in the early years of its directly elected existence into the background. Thanks to the agreement reached in 1988 between the Council and Parliament on a multi-year *Financial Perspectives*, a degree of peace seems indeed to have been restored on the budgetary front. This does not alter the fact that the EP's powers are gradually increasing. In 1995 an agreement was reached with the Council, whereby multi-year financing, in the sense of 'maximum amount', can in principle only be laid down as binding in legislation if the EP possesses co-legislative powers in that sector. If not, the budgetary procedure will prevail. In the field of agricultural expenditure (classed as 'compulsory' expenditure), *ad hoc* consultations now take place with the Council before the latter decides on the draft budget at the first reading. However, that lack of competence *vis-à-vis* agricultural expenditure, which is increasingly shedding its 'compulsory' character as a result of the McSharry and other reforms, continues to constitute a bone of contention. This also applies, of course, to the fact that the EP is not permitted any powers with regard to Community income – its 'own resources' – a state of affairs that gravely threatens the EP's development into a parliament of serious stature.

It is not the only threat that relates to a lack of power. The decisions taken at Maastricht concerning the role of the European Council in directing cooperation in the fields of foreign and security policy and justice and home affairs have the potential in the long term to undermine the EP's position as the Union's parliament. It is clear that national sensitivities led to the unrestrainedly intergovernmental character of those pillars and that such sensitivities are not confined to governments. Many a national parliament shows a lack of enthusiasm about transferring powers in these fields to the EP and the Court of Justice.

A parliament of the Union whose real powers are confined to a part of that Union finds it difficult to live up to its status as *the* parliament of the Union. That task is made even more difficult by the fact that the Community which is so crucial to the functioning of the EP is being further undermined by the second and third pillars of Maastricht. This is partly due to the TEU itself, which, for instance, left the free movement of persons as an area of Community competence, but which at the same time provided that the establishment of such free movement should fall under decision-making in the intergovernmental framework of the justice pillar. It is also partly due to a move, initiated by the political directors in the Political Committee and parts of the Council secretariat, to give the CFSP pillar some standing by eroding Community competence with regard to external policy, notably by dipping into the till. The funding of the Palestine Liberation Front's police force as a result of agreement within CFSP may serve as an example of this. But even where the Council operates within the powers laid down in the EU treaty, decisions are being sloppily handled. The Mostar operation, for instance, whereby the EU has attempted to reconstruct civil administration in that city, was set up in a way which contravened financial rules, and the scheme continued to be implemented in conflict with those rules. Similar claims can be made with regard to the JHA pillar, which shows a tendency to take over areas of competence previously belonging to the Community. It is a process which already affects efforts to combat fraud, and it threatens to affect drug-related issues, where the public health side is expressly a matter of Community competence. Moreover, in today's climate it is hard to imagine that Council of Economic and Finance Ministers (ECOFIN), which is directly interested in countering money-laundering, would retain its competence to decide on the money-laundering directive. Ministers of JHA, now meeting as the Council of the third pillar, will regard this as their prerogative, irrespective of whether it is one with which they can cope.

The EP's competence with regard to the pillars is minimal. In the second pillar, the TEU (Article J.7) is not open to misinterpretation: 'The Presidency ... shall ensure that the views of the European Parliament are duly taken into consideration.' In Council practice this means, at most, that an EP resolution has to be invoked by a member state in a minority position in order to modify a Council standpoint. But this is a very rare occurrence. An annual debate on the subject of 'progress in implementing the common foreign and security policy' (J.7) is a fairly pointless occupation as long as the European Council has not yet proved itself able to 'define the principles ... and general guidelines' (J.8) of that policy.

Things are no better as far as the JHA pillar is concerned. There is perhaps some hope of improvement through Article K.9 of the TEU which allows scope for transferring certain essential policy fields relating to the free movement of persons to Article 100(c) of the EC Treaty. However, the heated debate in the Cannes European Council in June 1995 on the involvement of the Court of Justice in decisions affecting the people of Europe in the third pillar does not give rise to great expectations on this score. This leaves budgetary powers. Both J.11 and K.8 provide scope for funding policy expenditure from the Community budget or from national funds in accordance with a scale to be subsequently established. As far as the CFSP is concerned, the possibility of national funding has already been ruled out. This leaves funding from the Community budget, subject to the relevant procedures. Since this is not classified as compulsory expenditure, the EP can, if it wishes, get its foot firmly in the door here.

Powers and their intelligent use are crucial if the EP is to consolidate its position among EU institutions. Greater powers do not automatically lead to a greater involvement of the electorate in the EP, especially if those powers do not relate to subjects that concern the electorate, such as immigration and asylum policy or, for instance, the EU's policy on former Yugoslavia. There were few indications that the 1996 IGC was going to be able to do much to reinforce the EP's involvement in this sort of issue. In fact, indications of policy intentions in the capitals of the member states during the preparatory period pointed in the opposite direction.

It is not easy to correlate the turnout figures for European elections and the significance that the electorate attaches to the EP. Domestic policy considerations play an important role in many EU member states at European elections, and such elections are primarily seen as national opinion polls. In other countries, compulsory voting makes evaluations difficult. However, it has been established that since 1979 the turnout for member states as a whole has gone down, though not very greatly (63 per cent turnout in 1979, 56.8 per cent in 1994). In a country like The Netherlands, where in 1994 European elections took place shortly after the elections for the national parliament, the decline since 1979 (then 57.8 per cent) has been greater, and the result in 1994 (36 per cent) was catastrophic.

Although low turnout in a member state does not necessarily raise the question of the EP's legitimacy (and this is particularly true of the UK), where there has been a continued decline the question can no longer be wholly ignored. It is sometimes said that the EP need not concern itself too much about winning sufficient electoral support as long as the EU continues to prosper. In the light of the IGC, the third stage of EMU, the review of Community funding and the next round of enlargement, it is hard to gauge what the response of each national public will be. Even at this stage, prior to any great debate on these issues, which touch at the very heart of integration, nationalist trends have been reviving, and are affecting the moderate forces to the left and right of centre. The EP provides little counterweight here; indeed, it too seems to have been infected by the nationalist virus. This makes it more difficult to wage the battle with national parliaments to place European priorities above immediate national interests. And yet this is the battle which looms on the horizon.

There is another threat that needs to be taken seriously, and which reinforces those outlined above. It is that of the frontrunners or core groups and of 'variable geometry'. Account needs to be taken of the fact that if the engine of integration is to be kept ticking over in an expanding Union, this sort of development cannot be avoided. The question then arises, however, as to the extent to which such trends are compatible with the objective of democratization, to which a number of member states still attach great importance. Must this lead to re-nationalization of parliamentary control, at least in areas affected by such frontrunner or core group cooperation? Will the situation arise in which ten or more national parliaments, like the Dutch parliament *vis-à-vis* Schengen and the JHA pillar, must approve decisions before they can be taken? The Dutch assent procedure, as required in the legislation ratifying the TEU, was intended as a stop-gap solution pending European control. The development seems to be leading towards national parliamentary rather than European control. Would it then still be possible to speak in terms of European decision-making, even in frontrunner or core group circles?

In short, the future of the EP is far from assured. The development of its position in terms of EC inter-institutional relations might be reasonably encouraging, but in the wake of Maastricht there is little positive news to report, either in terms of powers or relationship with the electorate. And what about the future? That looks anything but rosy.

THE EP: GROWING ITSELF INTO AN EARLY GRAVE?

For the first time since the genesis of the EEC in 1958, the vast majority of member state governments appear to wish to make the relationship between Europe and its citizens a central political theme. Up until Maastricht, leaving aside Denmark and the UK, this did not seem particularly necessary. Europe may then have been a long way off for its citizens, but the negative feedback was less pronounced (not counting farmers and others directly affected by European legislation) because those citizens were also a long way off from Europe. The Maastricht Treaty, which resulted in European powers in fields directly affecting the general public such as currency, internal security and – notably as a result of the war in former Yugoslavia – foreign and security policy, radically changed all this. The results of the Danish and French referendums showed that stronger public support was a necessary precondition for further integration. The *Bundesverfassungsgerichtshof* in Karlsruhe added to this the criterion of democracy. It is therefore understandable that the Cannes European Council in June 1995 gave the Reflection Group preparing the 1996 IGC as its main task 'the strengthening of public support for the process of European integration by meeting the need for a form of democracy which is closer to the citizens of Europe'. However, in doing so it is far from certain that the European Council was primarily thinking of the EP.

That is itself, of course, not so very surprising. Each head of government has a national parliament. That national parliament has a far greater affinity with the position adopted by its own prime minister in the European Council than with the compromises achieved by the European Council as a whole. It tends to set itself up as an ally of its own representative in the European Council, rather than judging whether that Council's conclusions are beneficial or prejudicial to the progress of European unification.

At the same time it is apparent that national parliaments, influenced by trends such as Europeanization and regionalization, but even more by the relinquishing of powers to 'the market', are losing some of their stature and are wary of ceding more power, in this instance, to the EP. It was therefore an adroit move, on the part of the authors of the Cannes text, to use the weakness of public support for the EU which became apparent after Maastricht as an argument to create room for greater involvement of national parliaments in the European process. The EP will need to keep a sharp eye on competition from national parliaments in the years ahead, in order to prevent policy presently subject only to democratic control at European level from becoming controlled, in the near future, at fifteen or more national levels. Such a development would not only harm the quality of democracy, it might also, if it amounts to more than the retroactive rubber-stamping of decisions which have already been taken, impede the drafting of policy necessary to keep the process of unification in motion.

Since this has already been acknowledged by the majority of member states, the debate has gone back to the stage which it had reached prior to December 1991 in Paris, i.e., to the notion of establishing a European organ of national parliamentarians to supplement and to a certain extent to replace a stronger EP. This will not help to make Europe more comprehensible to its citizens, or to bring it closer to them. Nor is it a way of increasing the involvement of national parliaments in European integration. This can still best be achieved by combining certain national and European mandates. It is, however, a very effective way of completely demolishing the fragile electoral support so far gained for the EP.

What the EP therefore needs to do is to seek allies among those member states that take the question of democratic control of European policy seriously. Moreover, the EP will have to take measures of its own to ensure that it cannot easily be elbowed aside.

In addition to the development of powers for the EP, member states who seek to give shape to parliamentary democracy in the European union primarily via that parliament will first have to turn their attention to its size. The reason for this is that the EP is on the verge of falling victim to its own growth. It started in 1979 with 400 members; these have meanwhile increased to 626. On the basis of present forecasts regarding future Union membership, this number may swell to over 800 members. The increase in the number of parliamentarians is a serious problem; the rapid increase in the number of countries from which they originate – from nine in 1979 to fifteen in 1995 – coupled with the increase in the number of languages – from six to eleven – and very differing parliamentary traditions, amounts to a virtually insoluble dilemma.

It is evident that it will be difficult to reduce, rather than further increase, the number of members. This is mainly due to the comparative overrepresentation – in terms of size of population – of the small member states. At the same time their representatives tend to be too few in number to make organizing separate European elections worthwhile. The fact that Luxembourgish, Portuguese or Irish delegates, despite often being members of large multi-national parties, are still seen as national representatives makes it difficult to create a feeling in such small countries that the EP is also their parliament. They therefore neither seek to expand its powers nor, in the interests of its effectiveness, do they envisage a reduction in their number of delegates, even though this would reinforce the position of the remaining Irish or Luxembourgish members within the Parliament.

And yet reducing the number of members is urgently needed. The Parliament is sinking under its own weight. The plenary debates, influenced by the national media's need for access to recognizable national spokespeople and the strong tendency of parliamentarians to make almost all decisions during plenary sessions, are increasingly turning into unilateral statements dealt with in the space of one or two minutes. As a result, the real debate takes place within the special parliamentary committees. Some of these, too, have meanwhile become too large for this to be feasible. Moreover, the central role of the specialized committees means that the EP finds itself increasingly unable to coordinate and integrate policy fields which often span a number of committees. The two largest political groups suffer from the same defect, and are thus incapable of using the instrument of group meetings as a steering mechanism.

The lack of coordination and integration of policy also reinforces the problem of the informal exercise of power within and on behalf of the EP. Although this is not a phenomenon unknown to national parliaments, it is one likely to be far more damaging to the EP, in the light both of the nationality problem and of the fact that 'Europe' already has a reputation for opaqueness, technocracy and bureaucracy. The EP's powers of co-decision in areas of European legislation, the constant need experienced by the Council and the Commission, but above all by the EP, for interinstitutional agreements on policy procedures, negotiations on financial issues: all this has gradually led to the creation of a process of negotiation largely beyond political control. That control, though, is of great significance for the position of the EP alongside the Council and Commission. It is an underground circuit that operates behind closed doors. It is, moreover, a circuit that suits the Council, which prefers to offload its negotiating tasks onto the Committee of Permanent Representatives (COREPER). Of course, the Council Presidency tends to ensure that it is chaired by a political functionary. However, in practice it boils down to COREPER negotiating with EP representatives of equal but political standing. It is the almost inevitable consequence of the EP's new position in the European decision-making process. Probably this is the only way in which it can function satisfactorily. At the same time, it serves as a warning that as long as the Council refuses to conduct such negotiations in complete openness, the EP threatens to become sucked into the Council system. In other words, it runs the risk of turning into an institution that only needs parliamentarians to bestow their imprimatur on decisions taken by experts – although, in this instance, experts who tend to be parliamentarians. It is a development that is stimulated by the considerable growth in the EP's powers. In order to appreciate the pernicious trend of that development, however, one must look once again at the difficulties experienced by a multinational parliament with 626 members that seeks to be both effective and transparent.

The Martin–Bourlanges report produced in the spring of 1995 – actually the mandate for the two EP representatives in the Reflection Group preparing the IGC – proposed that under no circumstances should EP members exceed 700 in number. From the point of view of getting it through the IGC it was a realistic proposal; that does not, however, make it a good proposal. A further increase in the number of parliamentarians will exacerbate the existing shortcomings of the EP if it is not matched by the creation of truly European political parties and the organization of genuinely European elections based on a uniform electoral system and European party lists. Since there is still no such thing as a European citizen, let alone a European people, it would seem that such a development can be ruled out, at least in the foreseeable future. If anything, further re-nationalization seems more likely. Under those circumstances it is essential that the EP is reduced to a size that makes integration in political parties necessary – in short which provides work for all – and can ensure a unity of policy. The lessons that have been learnt since 1979 show that, to this end, the number of parliamentarians should not exceed 400, or 450 at most. They also show that the Council would not be prepared to countenance such a step – which would be tantamount to cutting the numbers predicted for the 21st century by half.

A similar obstinacy exists with regards to the issue of the Parliament's seat, which has dragged on for many years. During the Edinburgh European Council, France did not find it very difficult to secure a guarantee of twelve parliamentary sessions a year in Strasbourg, while Belgium, without a quid pro quo, got the short plenary and committee meetings, and Luxembourg kept the library (200 km away from the parliamentarians' session chambers) and the rest of the Parliament's general secretariat. The average citizen, unfamiliar with the ins and outs of such decisions, will ultimately hold the EP accountable for the resultant wastage of resources and debating chambers. The EP is left with the job of determining how best to comply with legally enforceable decisions while maintaining a modicum of efficiency and, at the same time, making advances down the difficult path of bringing Europe to the citizen.

The limitations referred to above make a great deal impossible. There is, though, some light at the end of the tunnel. Now that Jacques Delors has left the European Commission, for instance, there is certainly scope for the Parliament to get a comprehensive debate going on the IGC, EMU, funding and enlargement. It must also be possible, by restricting the more technical questions on the parliamentary agenda and by lengthening session times in Brussels, to turn the present system of debate from a series of 'explanations of vote' into politically meaningful debates with a speaking time of at least five minutes. Even if much of the implementation of European policy has been delegated to the member states, the EP will still have to make a greater effort to get a grip on this process. It can call the political representatives of the Commission and the Council to account or require them to provide information more often than it does now. In order to do this, especially to do it well, it will have to reorganize itself. Its present poor state of organization might be deduced from the fact that of all the parliaments in Europe – and one of the least competent at that – it spends the greatest number of weeks a year in session.

NEW POWERS

It was always unlikely that there would be a consensus at the IGC on reducing the EP to a workable size. Resistance, notably from the smaller member states, was always predicted. On the other hand, the EP has entertained higher hopes with regard to the development of its powers. But new or extended powers will not automatically reinforce the relationship between the Parliament and the European citizen. It is at least equally important that present criticism of policy's lack of effectiveness dies down, that member states keep Community agreements, and that the EP is accepted by the national parliaments as the central parliamentary organ for the democratic control of European policy.

For more clarity, greater openness is needed. The much-used term 'transparency' may contribute toward such clarity, but it will not be enough in itself. Openness is particularly necessary in the legislative process. Steps taken thus far by the Council, such as the publication of voting records or of explanations of vote, are insufficient if the process of compromise which European legislation actually amounts to is to be followed and understood. The documents which underlie such compromise, as well as the Council minutes, should be made publicly accessible. Unfortunately, even maximum openness is not going to make the proverbial man on the Clapham omnibus much more familiar with the European decision-making process – a process which is not always clear to many a Council member. It must therefore be simplified. There are just too many decision-making procedures. Martin and Bourlanges counted twenty. In principle, they feel that these should be reduced to three: consultation, co-decision and assent. These are procedures with which Council and Parliament are familiar and which function reasonably well, although the co-decision procedure might usefully be simplified. The parliamentary rapporteurs seek also to apply these procedures, possibly at some later stage, to the CFSP and JHA pillars. They advocate integration of the pillars in the EC; in short, the restoration of the Community structure. Although it is by now abundantly clear that the pillars do not produce policy, especially not the type of policies that are needed to respond to the proliferation of internal and external challenges that have

223

followed the collapse of the Soviet Union, it was over-optimistic to expect the 1996 negotiators to achieve what could not be achieved in 1991. In point of fact, they are likely to achieve even less.

In the present pillar structure, the EP does not play a significant role. At the same time it cannot escape the fact that the EU's declaration of competence with regard to foreign and security policy, asylum, immigration and transborder crime has raised expectations among the general public which also extend, whether or not fairly, to the EP. An EP that does not pronounce on former Yugoslavia, the drugs issue or Schengen would lose contact with public opinion. And yet, all these pronouncements, unsustained as they are by any powers, are so noncommittal that the public's trust in the Parliament can easily be undermined as a result.

There is also the threat that the intergovernmental structure of the CFSP and JHA pillars will allow national parliaments to strengthen their scope for national control by calling their Council representatives to account both before and after decision-making, or by giving them the authority to take a decision only after sanction has been given at national level. This situation already exists in The Netherlands with regard to the JHA pillar, the intergovernmental pillar for which the greatest amount of legislation was predicted. From the point of view of the workings of parliamentary democracy, a solution of this kind is preferable to no solution at all. However, if fifteen national parliaments opt for this approach, the question naturally arises as to whether the JHA pillar will be able to continue to function even if that is the wish of the various governments.

Meanwhile, a debate has been initiated on majority decision-making within the pillars. Although it is not easy to estimate how beneficial such majority decision-making would be to the development of policy, it is of potential interest to the EP in that the effect would be to reinforce its position in relation to national parliaments. In the Union's present political climate, it is unlikely that the EP's position will be strengthened *vis-à-vis* the pillars. And yet it is crucial to the EP's future that its activities extend beyond the texts of non-binding resolutions when it pronounces on internal or external security. The Maastricht Treaty does offer toeholds in this respect. The scope it provides for the 'communitarization' of JHA pillar issues relating to the internal market may serve as example. If, for instance, the policy on asylum and immigration is transferred from the JHA pillar to Article 100(c)(EC) – an option provided for in the Treaty – and if the IGC reached agreement on majority decision-making in respect of the same article, the EP has a future. Things are even simpler in the case of the CFSP. No consensus has been reached on the national funding of CFSP policy. This leaves the alternative referred to in the TEU, i.e. Community funding. The EP's rights in the budgetary procedure have gradually acquired sufficient stature to enable it to use that budget, too, to exact a reasonable amount of involvement in policy. All this, of course, does not alter the fact that full integration of the pillar structure in the Community, majority decision-making and co-decision is considerably more attractive for the EP. The thinking is, though, that the EP is not doomed if it ends up with less. At the same time, that 'less' would appear to be a minimum requirement.

Since the SEA and the TEU, the position of the EP has been considerably strengthened in the Community pillar. The cooperation and co-decision procedures have enabled it to exert real influence on the legislative process. However, the scope of co-decision, in particular – which endows the Parliament with co-legislative status – is too limited. Moreover, the field to which co-decision largely applies, the internal market, is in less and less need of legislation.

The EP's desire to apply the co-decision procedure in all cases in which the Council acts by a majority vote is logical, given, among other things, the impossibility of sufficient national parliamentary control if the national minister can be outvoted. At the same time, it can only be put into effect if the IGC carries out the Maastricht undertaking to establish an appropriate hierarchy between different categories of act. Only by drawing a sharper distinction between legislation in the true sense and the implementary decisions resulting from it, will it be possible to extend the co-decision procedure so as to encompass, for instance, the field of agricultural policy. Such a distinction would make it possible to subject the decision-making for which the regulatory committees are now responsible to the scrutiny of both Council *and* Parliament, for instance by agreeing that legislation of this type is adopted if it is not amended or rejected within a certain timespan by the Council and the Parliament. This would relieve the tension that now exists between the powers of co-decision invested in Council and Parliament and the regulatory comitology of the Council.

It is, furthermore, important to use the IGC to seek ways of simplifying existing procedures. Both the budgetary and co-decision procedures would benefit from simplification.

Up to now the EP has done far too little in terms of scrutinizing the implementation of policy. This, of course, has largely been because much of the implementation has actually been delegated to the member states. The annual reports and special reports submitted by the European Court of Auditors show all too frequently that in many respects implementation is flawed. The importance attached by the EP to legislation and the securing of policy funding means that controls on implementation often take a back seat. The Commission fosters this trend by its tendency to neglect the field of supervision, and to focus on legislation and funding above all else.

It seems likely that much of the criticism of the Community's functioning derives from a conviction that the above attitude is outmoded. Now that the internal market has been created through the harmonization of legislation, it is necessary for that market to be properly administered and directed. One cannot leave a common visa policy to the mercies of what will soon be more than twenty member states, operating in isolation. A digital super highway is not a super highway if it suddenly peters out at the internal borders of the member states. Measures to combat fraud will not be effective if one member state's efforts are disproportionate to another's.

In addition to its understandable wish to develop fully fledged co-legislative status, the EP will therefore also have to focus on the need for European management and administration. All the more reason to turn the floodlights on the present shortcomings that result from the delegated implementation of policy. New powers? In addition to expanding its present competencies, the EP certainly does need new powers. Above all, however, Europe needs a parliament that makes use of instruments such as the right of inquiry and high-grade research capacity to take up new challenges, thus helping to ensure that in 50 years time the EU will still be relevant to the European citizen.

12
Agenda Setting, Lobbying and the 1996 IGC*

Sonia Mazey and Jeremy Richardson

THE IGC AS A 'DECISION SITUATION': IDEAS, INTERESTS, AND GARBAGE CANS

In discussing the process by which political agendas are set, one needs to recognize that all actors may be subject to influences and trends which are seemingly beyond any one actor's control. Thus, not only do institutions structure debate, determine access to decision-making and constrain policy choices but also, problems themselves and the development of ideas for their solution are significant constraints on the degree of choice which policy actors possess. As Kingdon argued, the 'inexorable march of problems' (Kingdon 1984) cannot be ignored by policy-makers. Thus, policy-makers occupying 'official' positions must generate solutions to problems which are thrust before them, whether they like it or not. In looking for solutions they, of course, face an array of ideas and policy solutions, backed by a complex pattern of interest group representation, from which choices must be made. Even the interest groups themselves are constrained by the prevailing climate of opinion, by the existing knowledge base, and by the sometimes overbearing weight of conventional wisdom.

Thus, one needs to exercise caution in perceiving an intergovernmental conference such as the 1996 IGC, as a situation of free choice for the various policy actors involved. Much has gone before, there are enormous ambiguities and (the focus of this chapter) a rather well-organized and rapidly maturing Euro-level interest group system. Rather than seeing the IGC as a discreet 'choice situation', it might be more useful, therefore, to view policy-making in the IGC in terms of a process of learning in some kind of collective problem-solving. 'Learning' in the policy process is a concept which emphasizes the importance of collective decisions within an unending enquiry, rather than simply conflict resolution (Radaelli 1995: 165–73). When we examine the behaviour of different actors in a problem-solving situation such as an IGC, we need to know more about how they came to 'frame' problems. As Radaelli suggests (drawing on Rein and Schön 1991), 'when faced with problematic situations, actors tend to rely on "frames", in which values, social science models and interests are integrated. Framing is an activity of selection, organization and interpretation of a complex reality' (Radaelli 1995: 168). As defined by Rein and Schön, 'a frame is a perspective from which an amorphous ill-defined situation can be made sense of and acted upon' (Rein and

226

Schön 1991: 262). Much of the activity in the lead up to the 1996 IGC was, in fact, about the attempts by different actors to 'frame' the problems which the member states face on the IGC's agenda. By 'framing' problems in particular ways, policy choices are restricted and particular policy outcomes become more likely. This process bears a close resemblance to the 'garbage can' model of decision-making developed by Cohen *et al.* in 1972 and elaborated by Kingdon (Cohen *et al.* 1972; Kingdon 1984). The central feature of the original garbage can model is that 'decision situations' (or what Cohen *et al.* termed 'organized anarchies') are characterized by three general properties. First, there are *problematic preferences*. The organization operates on the basis of a variety of inconsistent and ill-defined preferences (Cohen *et al.* 1972: 1). Their description of organizational life fits well what we already know about the 1996 IGC – namely that 'it (the organization) can be described better as a loose collection of ideas than as a coherent structure, it discovers preferences through action more than it acts on the basis of preferences' (Cohen *et al.* 1972: 1). The second characteristic of decision situations is *unclear technology*. Thus, 'although the organization manages to survive and even produce, its own processes are not understood by its members. It operates on the basis of simple trial-and-error procedures, the residue of learning from the incident of past experience, and pragmatic inventions of necessity' (Cohen *et al.* 1972: 1). Finally, there is *'fluid participation'* in that participants vary in the amount of time and effort they devote to different domains. Again, the characterization seems to fit the IGC 1996 rather well in that it has attracted a vast range of political activity, but different actors commit different levels of resources and time to trying to influence the IGC, depending upon their expected payoffs. (This is as true for member states as it is for interest groups, of course). In practice, it is useful to view an organization as *'a collection of choices looking for problems, issues and feelings looking for decision situations in which they might be aired, solutions looking for issues to which they might be the answer, and decision-makers looking for work* (Cohen *et al.* 1972: 2).

If one accepts the garbage can analogy for the 1996 IGC, then it follows that, above all, the IGC is a *fluid and unpredictable* decision situation in which all actors are operating under an unusual degree of uncertainty. A second important characteristic, therefore, is that all actors are engaged in a complex multi-level, multi-arena or 'nested game' (Tsebelis 1990), the outcome of which is unknowable to any one actor or set of actors. However, different sets of actors may have different identifiable preferences. By its very nature the IGC is about *intergovernmental* bargaining and, therefore, the interests of states as actors are enormously important. In terms of economic policy and international negotiations, for example, Katzenstein has argued that 'the main purpose of all strategies of foreign economic policy is to make domestic policies compatible with the international political economy' (Katzenstein 1978: 4). Yet, as Putnam argues, some of the work in the 'state centric' genre represents a unitary actor model run amok (Putnam 1993: 435). Thus, a more adequate account of domestic determinants of foreign policy and international relations, Putnam argues, 'must stress *politics*: parties, social classes, interest groups (both economic and non-economic), legislators, and even public opinion and elections, not simply executive officials and institutional arrangements' (Putnam 1993: 435). As we have argued elsewhere (Mazey and Richardson 1995) a complicating factor for states as policy actors at the EU level is that interest groups, in particular, may have Euro-level objectives (and, therefore, Euro-lobbying strategies) which are different from and incompatible with state interests. Even where the interests of the state and those of private interest groups coincide, the ability of states to secure a 'policy win' at the Euro-level is highly unpredictable. As Héritier has demonstrated, much of the explanation for the great variety of types of regulation at the Euro-level (what she terms a 'regulatory patchwork') is that no one state *consistently* wins in the battle to get its favoured regulatory framework adopted at the Euro-level. In her terminology, the ability of any one state to secure a 'home run' is limited as other states move quickly to thwart it (Héritier 1996).

If we take the British case as an example, it is clear that the British government (representing the British state) has some very specific party and electoral considerations which have influenced its approach to the IGC (see Chapter 6). There is no doubt that these considerations are often inimical to the interests of many domestic interest groups (ranging from environmentalists, consumers, and trade unions, to banks, financial institutions, companies and industrial federations and confederations). Not only do objectives and strategies differ on particular policy issues which may come up in the IGC, but the domestic interest group system has to calculate the consequences of 'loyalty' to a particular actor – in this case the Conservative Government of Mr John Major – which may not even last beyond the life of the IGC itself. As one respondent, representing a leading British business organization put it to us, 'the British government is a joke in Europe. That presents major problems to us'. Moreover, interest groups have become used to developing independent Euro-lobbying strategies in the normal day-to-day business of Euro policy-making, outside IGC and European Council meetings. National interest groups are embedded in the 'low politics' of the bulk of EU policy-making and are becoming increasingly embedded in cross-national policy networks of various kinds. Clearly, there will be cross-national differences in the degree of cleavage between state and interest group policy objectives, but even in those states where these objectives have either tended to coincide or where states were hitherto able to maintain a *dirigiste* relationship with their domestic interest group systems, there is a growing realization by interest groups that they must develop their own independent lobbying positions (Mazey and Richardson 1993). For example, in her Anglo-French comparison of the relevance of domestic policy networks to European negotiations, Josselin's evidence suggested that domestic policy networks 'in which private actors retained relative autonomy fuelled in part by distrust and the need for information, appeared to be better suited to the pursuit of multiple [lobbying] targets; conversely, vertical, state-dominated structures would not encourage the development of active strategies of transnational linkages on the part of non-governmental organizations' (Josselin 1996). Thus, British sectoral actors, who were 'less tied to a strict policy structure than the French, were better able to exploit the multi-access lobbying system of the EU' (ibid.).

A central feature of the lobbying strategies of member states and interest groups is that partners in the 'policy game' are all unreliable – in the sense that no single actor can control the game and deliver the desired pay-off. Even in such areas as monetary union, where conventional wisdom might suggest that the German state, and especially the *Bundesbank*, have enough 'state strength' (Krasner 1978: 55) to secure their desired pay-offs, the policy process seems much more messy and complex. Indeed, in his excellent analysis of the process of economic and monetary union in Europe, Dyson borrows a term suggested by Heinz *et al.* – the 'hollow core'. Thus 'there is little evidence that a single actor – whether the Commission or Ecofin or the Bundesbank – occupies the central policy-brokering role within the EMU process in any continuous sense, capable in a more or less autonomous way of promoting compromise or imposing settlements. In this sense, the EMU policy process has a "hollow core"' (Dyson 1994: 332). Again, parallels with the IGC system are clear. Just as even EMU – with obvious key players such as the German state and the *Bundesbank* – does not illustrate dominance of one actor, then so we might expect the IGC, confronted with a range of controversial issues to discuss, to be something of a 'hollow core', surrounded by a *mélange* of players and with action taking place in a number of venues distant from the IGC itself. This, inevitably, lends support to Putnam's notion of a two-level game for the analysis of international interactions. Drawing on Walton and McKersie's 'behaviourial theory of social negotiations' (Walton and McKersie 1965), he stresses that the unitary-actor assumption does not accord with what we know about the reality of international negotiations. In a crucial passage, he argues that:

> the politics of many international negotiations can usefully be conceived as a two-level game. At the national level, domestic groups pursue their interest by pressuring the government to adopt favorable policies, and politicians seek power by constructing coalitions among those groups. At the international level, national governments seek to maximize their own ability to satisfy domestic pressures, while minimizing the adverse consequences of foreign developments. (Putnam 1993: 436)

He goes on to analyse the strategic situation facing actors in these two level games. Thus 'the unusual complexity of this two level game is that moves that are rational for a player at one board may be impolitic for the same player at another board'. The complexities of this two level game are, he suggests, staggering. Yet, if we see the EU policy process, and specifically the IGC process, as a policy game, it becomes even more complex to model. More than two levels are involved in the sense that, in terms suggested by Baumgartner and Jones (1991, 1993) there are several 'venues' where players may try to engage their preferences. Hence, the notion of 'nested games' suggested by Tsebelis (1990) is probably more appropriate. Trying to understand the behaviour of different actors (whether state or non-state) in relation to the IGC 1996 is inherently difficult because each of the actors is involved in a series of nested games.

If we take the leadership of the Confederation of British Industry (CBI) as one example, in developing its Euro-policy stances it has to manage a complex internal decision-making procedure which must produce an effective consensus between large and small firms. This in itself is a difficult task as the costs and benefits of further Europeanization (essentially further Euro-regulation) are quite different between, say, large British multinationals such as ICI or BP and medium or small manufacturers in, say, the food processing industry. Indeed, as the CBI's own survey on monetary union demonstrated, attitudes to a single currency correlated with size of firm. For example, companies with more than 100 employees (53 per cent positive) and those in the wholesale, retail and service sectors (56 and 53 per cent positive respectively) are proportionately more likely to support joining a single currency than are smaller companies. Similarly, on the broader question of membership of the EU, only 2 per cent of companies with over 500 employees were strongly in favour of the UK not remaining in the EU, yet 12 per cent of companies employing fewer than 50 employees would prefer Britain to leave the EU (CBI 1995). 'Broad church' representative organizations like the CBI have inherent difficulties in formulating clear policy positions. A second 'game' in which the CBI is involved is, of course, with 'its' national government. This is an especially delicate game in view of the Conservative Government's increasingly cautious Euro stance, forced by the need to avoid further party disunity from the Right 'Euro-sceptic' wing of the party. The CBI has to take a broader and longer-term view of the interests of its members, a high proportion of whom take a much more positive view of European integration. A third game in which the CBI is involved is, of course, at the Euro-level, as it is an important member of the Euro-level association, UNICE (see pp. 238–9. Here, it has to maintain some influence in an organization which contains members who are more enthusiastic about further Europeanization and it has to be part of UNICE's consensus building processes.

Other actors wishing to influence the IGC face similar complexities. This is even more so for Euro-level groups, which have to deal with up to fifteen member states, the European Parliament (EP) and the Commission, and which participate in many transnational policy networks and policy communities – all these present opportunities for influencing the Euro-policy process in some way. Moreover, the number of coalition-building possibilities is further increased by the fact that different coalitions can be constructed in different policy areas, with partners on one issue, such as strengthening the EP, being opponents on others, such as subsidiarity. Thus, 'lobbying the IGC' as a policy game could not get underway properly until positions became clearer, especially as the Report of the Reflection Group left many issues open and unresolved, or even unaddressed.

If the characteristics of the decision situation presented by the 1996 IGC are essentially garbage-can-like, and if the many players are embedded in a series of nested games, the likelihood of a clear set of consistent winners emerging may be low. This is similar to the paradox of lobbying at the national level found by Heinz *et al.* in their study of the US lobbying system. They concluded that 'although greater numbers of organizations of all types actively monitor and participate in the making of national policy, and although the scope and intensity of their efforts has increased significantly, the returns on these efforts are not at all clear (Heinz *et al.* 1993: 369). Of particular relevance to our study, they concluded that 'no single category of interest group proved more successful than others in achieving policy objectives in the events we analysed from 1978 to 1982. Nor did any group unambiguously seize control of the agenda for policy-making in this period' (Heinz *et al.* 1993: 369). One reason for the lack of dominance of one interest, identified in their study, was that interest groups have tried to reinforce their control over their 'agents'. But, 'by creating structures to control or adapt to uncertainty, they have contributed to the development of a more complex and rapidly changing policy environment' (Heinz *et al.* 1993: 371). In the IGC case, for example, literally hundreds of organizations responded to the EP's Institutional Affairs Committee's invitation to participate in its hearings prior to the IGC. A further complication is that it is not wise to assume that interest groups always hold clear and relatively *unchanging* preferences. As Heinz *et al.* suggest, 'changes in the political situation may require the balance of political risk and advantage to be recalculated thus, uncertainty is likely to beget more uncertainty' (Heinz *et al.* 1993: 391–2).

This (US centred) view of the lobbying process is rather close to the empirical evidence which emerged from our series of interviews with a range of interest groups active in trying to influence the IGC process. Many interviewees remarked that it was difficult to define their position clearly in advance of the IGC. There were several reasons for this. First, there was the purely tactical consideration of not revealing one's hand too early in what is expected to be a long drawn-out game. Second, and more importantly, they wished to see how the early stages of the game unfolded and wanted to reserve judgement on how best to 'position' their organizations in the ensuing debate. Thus, there is an element of Samuel Beckett's play *Waiting for Godot* in the early stages with much talk of Godot's arrival but no-one knowing who he was or what he looked like! Third, there was a clear recognition that the game might entail a process of complex coalition building over time, involving some complex cross-sectoral trade-offs. This realization created a reluctance to 'close' options in advance of the IGC by coming out too clearly in favour of or against particular policy ideas. In leading up to the IGC 1996, therefore, everyone was in a position of trying to guess which of the many policy ideas floating around might gain good currency by the start of the IGC or, indeed, might by then have become conventional wisdom.

The more sophisticated players recognized the importance of the long term and the need to 'frame' the future in a particular way. Thus, for them, the IGC was of some importance – in that it could produce 'wrong' decisions – but they had more important long-term objectives, based on a clear notion of the kind of world, and of Europe's place within it, which their organizational interest demanded. To those players, the game is more about the politics of ideas than about specific reforms which might or might not emerge from the IGC. Thus some of the large multinational corporations, though concerned that the IGC should not derail monetary union, have longer-term objectives – such as a common European defence policy or an EU–North American free trade area. They see their task as gradually planting these ideas in the minds of leading politicians in a gradual 'framing' exercise. This is often done in entirely private meet-ings, say in hosted dinners, with prime ministers, presidents and other élite politi-cians and civil servants. 'Policy framing' takes place after dessert! Just as institu-tions *do* matter, so do ideas. As Reich suggests, public policy outcomes are often derived from perceptions of the public interest rather than simply the result of individuals or organizations pursuing their self-interest. Public preferences and support for policies grows and changes 'as people have come to understand and engage with the ideas underlying them' (Reich 1988: 4). Ideas are important for public policy-makers, too. As Reich also argues, 'the most accomplished govern-ment leaders have explicitly and purposefully crafted public visions of what is desirable and possible for society to do' (Reich 1988: 4). This is a key observation helpful to understanding the history of the EU and the continued process of European integration. Just as US scholars have noted the crucial role of ideas in the 'framing' of public policy problems, so the history of European integration has been characterized by political leaders seizing upon the 'big idea' and driving this forward in terms of a series of public policy decisions. Thus, it was the vision of the founders of the EU which proved the spark for the process of European inte-gration (Mazey 1992). By and large these founding ideas were not business driven, compared with the very considerable business influence over European leaders today (see *Waiting for Godot*). Thus, over time, intellectual fashions, so important in the policy process at both the national and supranational level, do change. They are of crucial importance in influencing preference formation, even of the member states.

When analysing the US policy process, Reich and his colleagues were 'struck by how much the initial definitions of problems and choices influences the subse-quent design and execution of public policies' (Reich 1988: 5). The core activity of the 1996 IGC is probably as much about the definition of problems and choices as it is about discrete policy decisions. Essentially, the IGC process is an example of what Majone identified as a key aspect of modern democracies – namely, that they were not simply concerned with problem-solving, but were as concerned with debate and persuasion (Majone 1989). Those non-governmental policy actors engaged in this process (and for the 1996 IGC it has been a vast array of actors) were centrally concerned with trying to 'frame' policy problems in the minds of governmental leaders, prior to the Conference's actual opening. Hence, if we are to understand the IGC process – or indeed to really understand the intergovernmental aspects of the EU policy process more generally – we need to be conscious of the crucial role that 'framing' plays in the policy process. Before turning to the specific attempts by key interest groups to frame problems before the IGC 1996 we, therefore, need to address briefly the question of whether, because the IGC is, by definition, both *intergovernmental* and concerned with *high politics*, interest groups can hope to play any part in it at all?

'CONDITIONED INTERGOVERNMENTALISM' OR WHO DECIDES WHAT HIGH POLITICS IS ABOUT?

In a seminal paper 30 years ago, Stanley Hoffmann suggested the distinction between high and low politics (Hoffmann 1966). The essence of the distinction was that 'high politics' issues were those that concerned or threatened the very existence of the state – such as defence, foreign policy, law and order, etc. The implication was that the behaviour of the state in relation to other actors might well be different when high and low politics issues were at stake. Thus, as suggested by Theordore Lowi a few years before (Lowi 1964), there was an assumption that different policies produce different politics. Yet one needs to be cautious in treating the high politics issues as 'given' and then merely analysing how these issues are processed via interaction between sovereign states. Following Schattschneider, we believe that determining what politics is about (both high and low politics) is the supreme instrument of political power (Schattschneider 1960). Especially in garbage can decision situations, as described earlier, focusing on the behaviour of the set of policy actors taking the final decision may be misleading. One needs to know why are they deciding at all and from which options do they choose? Here, informal power is important. As Tsebelis has suggested in his sophisticated analysis of the EP, it is possible to construct quite misleading models of who has power, especially over agenda setting in the EU (Tsebelis 1994, 1995). He sees the EP as potentially (and in some cases actually) much more powerful as an agenda setter – a *conditional* agenda setter in his terms – than do many other observers of the EU policy process (Tsebelis 1995). If we borrow (loosely) Tsebelis' notion of conditional agenda setting, might it be that notions of intergovernmentalism need to be qualified when one considers the importance of 'framing', as we suggested above?

The classic statement of the intergovernmental position is relatively unambiguous. In his study of the negotiations surrounding the Single European Act (SEA), Moravcsik concludes that, 'although supranational institutions have an important role in cementing existing interstate bargains as the foundation for renewed integration 'the primary source of integration lies in the interests of the states themselves and the relative power that each brings to Brussels' (Moravcsik 1991: 75). In a subsequent work he re-iterated the view that key decisions (presumably 'high politics' in Hoffmann's terminology) were the result of interstate bargaining on the intergovernmental model. Thus, his basic claim was that 'the EC can be analysed as a successful intergovernmental regime designed to manage economic interdependence through negotiated co-ordination' (Moravcsik 1993: 474). He went on to claim that:

> intergovernmentalist theory seeks to analyse the EC as a result of strategies pursued by national governments acting in the basis of their preferences and power. The major agenda-setting decisions in the history of the EC, in which common policies are created or refined, are negotiated intergovernmentally. (Moravcsik 1993: 496)

In a crucial passage for our analysis of the role of non-state actors in the 1996 IGC, Moravcsik went on to state that 'the unique institutional structure of the EC is acceptable to national governments only insofar as it strengthens, rather than weakens, their control over domestic affairs, permitting them to attain goals otherwise unachievable' (ibid.: 507). Essentially, the thrust of his argument was that EC institutions strengthen the power of national governments.

There are two major weaknesses in this analysis. First, it is possible to argue that the unique institutional structure of the EU, far from 'strengthening the autonomy of national leaders *vis-à-vis* particularistic social groups within their domestic polity' (ibid.: 507), is, logically, just as likely to undermine it. This is because, in the context of multi-level, multi-arena and nested games, *the uncertainty principle* is of enormous importance, as we argued earlier. States might well be rational actors (though state politicians may act rationally in their own interests rather than those of the state), but so are domestic and (increasingly) transnational interest groups. If they, too, act rationally, they will know that the ability of any one state to influence, let alone control, the EU policy process – especially at the agenda setting stage – is extremely limited. Hence, it is rational for them also to seek supranational solutions, in their own right. The Europeanization of policy-making, i.e. transference of decision-making power to a supranational level – although one in which the states have a very clear formal role – has done as much to weaken states as policy actors as to strengthen them. As Bulmer suggests, 'an investigation below the surface suggests that national governments are in many cases prisoners of domestic and international circumstances' (Bulmer 1983: 360). The British government is a case in point. In its review of the implementation of EC law and of ways in which Britain might increase its influence over European policy-making, it has openly conceded that it can no longer 'deliver' to its domestic interest groups. Thus, it recognizes that qualified majority voting (QMV) has introduced very different decision-rules and has suggested that 'ministers and officials should therefore have the confidence to be open about the difficulties they sometimes face in Brussels, and should be prepared to make use of business contacts and networks in reinforcing the UK negotiation position' (DTI 1993). Tellingly, it noted that 'the requirement to reach agreement by recognizing the needs and fears of others, by trading concessions and identifying common interests, is as pressing in the board room as it is in the Council of Ministers' (DTI 1993). In essence this was 'civil service speak' to business that Her Majesty's Government could not be relied upon in European negotiations!

The transnational activities of domestic interests (and the increasing emergence of genuinely European interests who do not frame problems in national terms) has been noted by others as weakening the intergovernmentalist stance. This is especially so in those very policy areas which Moravcsik claims support for the intergovernmentalist thesis. Thus, Sandholtz and Zysman (1989) suggest that the 1992 project owed much to the close collaboration of business and the Commission (as well as, they readily concede, to national governments whose policies and perspectives changed). Thus, they argue that 'European business and the Commission may be said to have together bypassed national governmental processes and shaped the agenda that compelled attention' (Sandholtz and Zysman 1989: 116). Based on a more detailed analysis of the agenda setting

234

process leading to the 1992 project, Maria Green Cowles reaches similar conclusions. Thus, she argues that the European Round Table (ERT) 'played a leading role in setting the agenda and providing policy alternatives for the 1992 programme'. Indeed, she goes on to suggest that the 'agenda for the single market programme was set by economic interests' (Green Cowles 1995: 522). As Caporaso and Keeler interpret her data 'by the time state leaders came to the bargaining table, a substantial amount of work had been accomplished' (Caporaso and Keeler 1995: 45). Thus, one needs to ask from where do national leaders acquire the 'intellectual baggage' which they take to international negotiations? To whom did leaders such as Margaret Thatcher talk? Other studies indicate the links between business leaders, operating transnationally, and national political leaders. Thus, Sandholtz and Zysman's interviews confirmed that the ERT became a powerful lobby *vis-à-vis* the national governments. They quote one member of the Delors Cabinet as declaring 'these men are very powerful and dynamic when necessary they can ring up their own prime minister and make their case' (Sandholtz and Zysman 1989: 117, citing van Tulder and Junne).

It is in this way that 'mood changes', shifts in 'climates of opinion' and new 'policy fashions' which become 'conventional wisdoms' emerge. Just as epistemic communities are turned to by international and national policy-makers in times of uncertainty (Haas 1992, Adler and Haas 1992), then so political leaders also listen to business and financial leaders, particularly when faced by economic problems and uncertainties. As Sandholtz and Zysman suggest, the 1992 movement was characterized by uncertainty – 'neither the pay-off from nor preferences for any strategy were or are yet clear' (Sandholtz and Zysman 1989: 107). If as, they suggest, 'with 1992, decision-makers do not possess the intellectual means to foresee alternative outcomes, much less rank them', it is not surprising that business interest groups mobilized to 'solve' the problem for them! Our own interviews with a wide range of non-governmental actors, concerning their lobbying activities in the run-up to the 1996 IGC, suggest that the success of the business lobby in the 1992 project has been noted and acted upon. As in the US cases analysed by Heinz *et al.*, the problem for interest groups lobbying the 1996 IGC is that, dealing with uncertainty by increasing one's lobbying efforts can make matters worse, as all other interest groups do the same. In the approach to the IGC 1996 this produced a more crowded, and therefore more uncertain, policy environment for everyone, on the classic garbage can model. A common response from many (though not all) of our interviewees was that their lobbying activities relating to previous IGCs had been minimal or non-existent, but that they saw clear risks, in the run-up to 1996, in allowing events to unfold without their participation. Hence, there has been a 'cacophony' of interest group activity, all designed to 'condition' the IGC deliberations – in other words, to determine in advance what the 'high politics' of the IGC should be about. There has developed an intense market for the 'framing' of policy problems. It is to the nature of this market that we now turn.

Waiting for Godot? Competitive Framing of Problems and Opportunities Prior to the IGC

There was a strong sense among non-governmental actors, in the lead-up to the 1996 IGC, that the process was altogether more open and that public policy-makers were more willing to see how the various interests saw the future of European integration and to see if some consensus could emerge than had been the case with previous IGCs. There seem to have been two more reasons for the rather different character of the policy formulation process. First, there was a common awareness that the Maastricht process was a near disaster for those in favour of European integration. It was a clear case of public decision-makers moving too far ahead of 'public opinion' and caused a setback to the impetus which produced the SEA and the 1992 project. As one key European industrial-ist put it to us, 'the public opposition to Maastricht really shocked European busi-ness leaders. In marketing terms it was a complete disaster. We must ensure that the politicians do not make the same mistake again'.

Somehow, opinion needs to be mobilized to support any major further changes which might result from the IGC 1996. In a sense, public decision-makers and those private interest group leaders favourable to further European integration (the vast majority of interest groups, we believe), have recognized that any political system must mobilize widespread support if it is to remain stable. But how can sup-port for a supranational institution such as the EU be mobilized? In the absence of Euro-level parties and the absence of a Euro-level media, interest groups seem a key channel in testing the degree of support for reform. Therefore, more opportu-nities seem to have arisen for interest group mobilization for the 1996 IGC com-pared with its predecessors. For example, the EP Institutional Affairs Committee held a public hearing in October 1995 to sound out the opinions of non-govern-ment organizations (NGOs). Representatives of nearly 100 interested NGOs and lobbies took part in this hearing. (The first hearing covered citizenship and funda-mental rights, social, environmental, and consumer questions.) The range of inter-est groups represented was considerable and included such groups as the Euro-group for Animal Welfare, the European Disability Forum, the Commission of the Bishops' Conferences of the Member States of the EU, the Jewish Information Centre, and even the National Board of Italian Psychologists (who wanted, for example, an improved fight against organized crime and standardized policy enlistment and cooperation) (Challenge 96, Belmont: 14).

Second, the current lobbying seems to be a classic example of David Truman's notion of potential groups (Truman 1951). His theory was that if any one group, or set of groups, became too successful, this would provoke the emergence of countervailing groups who would mobilize to regain lost ground or prevent fur-ther successes by the dominant group(s). There is now a widespread belief that business groups have dominated both the high and the low politics of European integration from the mid-1980s (as, probably, business has at the national level too). As one respondent put it to us 'the 1992 process was a business agenda and the politicians delivered on it'. He went on to argue that the 1992 process was essentially legislative driven, i.e. very much concerned with the technical legislation needed to create the 1992 project. The process was now becoming more concerned with 'high-politics' again – such issues as the balance between economic and social stability, the linkages between monetary union and political change, and the type of European union that should emerge in the future. Thus, many policy actors whom we interviewed would have been surprised by Andrew Moravcsik's analysis of the emergence of the SEA, as this did not accord with their own experience of events. As another respondent put it, there was a very effective business 'Mafia' at work, which 'captured' leading European politicians and convinced them that something like the SEA and 1992 was needed. In political science terms, the existence and behaviour of this advocacy coalition (Sabatier 1988) helps to explain the missing link in understanding the behaviour of national governments in ceding their sovereignty under the 1992 project. There was skilled cross-national coordination of national preference formation. 'Village life' in Brussels is such that there is an effective process whereby the many policy actors come to learn, reputationally, who gets what. Among the non-business groups there was, therefore, an awareness of the major policy gains which business had made since the mid-1980s, and a belief that some counter moves were needed in order to influence the 'framing' of policy problems in 1996.

Many non-business groups recognize that there are some very strong 'policy fashions" which favour business interests. Their strategy is, therefore, to recognize the current strength of this fashion, but to try to secure concessions, or 'side payments', as the price for maintaining the momentum of European integration and as a means of re-mobilizing public support for the European project. This represents a classic case of interest groups 'lobbying with the grain', a tactic which was to some degree successfully employed by the trade unions in the Maastricht process. The increased group mobilization for 1996 made the IGC even more garbage-can like, in that special interests attempted to attach their own pet issues onto the whole process, whether or not these issues were directly relevant to the main functions of the IGC. Hence, 'piggy-backing' (or free-riding) of issues was regarded as a likely characteristic of the lobbying process once the IGC unfolded. Within the more sophisticated sections of the business community too, there was also an awareness that, even though 'business is still back in fashion', businesses had to recognize that concessions have to be made and trade-offs agreed, just as was the case at Maastricht with the social and environmental provisions. They felt this because they recognized that the process of European integration would stall (again) if those who had lost out since the mid-1980s did not receive at least some side payments for their continued support. For example, businesses that support majority voting for taxation issues may have to accept that eco-taxes might also emerge from such a system. In fact, business currently seems to be the best organized of the various interest groups, in a number of senses.

First, with some exceptions, European business interests appear to be singing from the same hymn sheet. Moreover, they have a very catchy tune – 'competitiveness' – to sing to. These interests, therefore, have a 'meta policy' issue which they are pressing on all national and Euro-level institutions. Clearly, this theme builds on the philosophy of the SEA and the 1992 project and seeks to carry that policy fashion forward into newer policy areas. The aim has been to make 'competitiveness' the big mobilizing idea, a bench mark against which other policy initiatives (and other policy problems) must be judged. The power of the idea rests on the argument that Europe as a whole is falling behind the US, Japan, and the so-called 'tiger economies' of the Far East. If Europe's competitiveness is not increased, so the argument runs, other desirable policy goals, espoused by the vast array of non-business interests (e.g. full employment, equal rights for women, effective environmental protection) are not attainable. Thus, UNICE's preliminary contribution to the preparations for the IGC stressed the centrality of 'competitiveness': 'If the EU is not competitive in the widest sense of this word, it will be incapable of achieving its main objective which is economic growth and job creation.' (UNICE 1995: 2) Hence, one of business's central objectives was to see the IGC upgrade competitiveness to the status of an 'objective' on a par with economic and social progress and to include it in Title 1, Article B, of the TEU. Business also wanted the preservation of competitiveness to be mentioned as a requirement in Article 2.2 of the Agreement attached to the Protocol on Social Policy (UNICE 1995: 2). A very similar argument was put forward by the ERT. For example, the chairman of the ERT (who is also chairman of the Compagnie Lyonnaise des Eaux) argued in early 1995, that 'Europe will be able to hold a central place in the world economy only if it adjusts to the revolutionary changes of the past few years. If it stumbles into the next century with the rules and attitudes of the last, Europe will be doomed' (*Financial Times* 10 April 1995). In fact the ERT and UNICE had been pressing the competitiveness issue for some time. The ERT published its *European Competitiveness: The Way to Growth and Jobs*, in 1994 (ERT 1994) and in its preliminary paper for the IGC it concentrated on those IGC issues that were 'linked directly and indirectly *with competitiveness, the ERT's main concern*' (ERT 1995: 2, emphasis in original document). Similarly, UNICE had published a major interim report in 1993, *Making Europe More Competitive: Towards World Class Performance* (UNICE 1993). It contained a number of indications of Europe's declining competitiveness, for example, the EC's share of world trade, the relative importance of the EC as a base for inward foreign direct investment, the low number of jobs created in Europe, etc. Its final report in 1994 recommended a range of policy options, very familiar to policy analysts at the national level in any member state. These included a more flexible labour market, new methods of production and new forms of work organizations, a smaller and more efficient public sector, an improved climate for entrepreneurs, reduction of the costs of employing people (particularly non-wage costs), reduction of minimum wage levels at national and at sectoral levels, and so on (UNICE 1994).

The advantage of 'competitiveness' as an idea is that it is a good example of a solution looking for problems on the Cohen *et al.* model discussed earlier. Thus, the business lobby is able to hang a number of specific policy proposals on this general 'solution'. For example, UNICE's proposals addressed key IGC issues such as QMV, subsidiarity, the role of the institutions, social policy, and trade policy. Thus, on the question of QMV, it held that very few actions deemed to be essential for completion of the single market should require a unanimous vote

(UNICE 1995: 5). On subsidiarity, however, its position possibly reflected a more general problem for the business lobbies, notwithstanding their current lead position in the agenda setting process. Business interests want a stronger and more effective Europe (especially monetary union) yet espouse the current policy fashion for deregulation and a generally reduced regulatory burden on firms. At a practical policy level, there may be some contradictions that are difficult to resolve. In the case of subsidiarity, UNICE was apparently strongly in favour of the principle. Thus, it argued, all proposals:

> for action at EU level should be accompanied by a detailed justification explaining why action at EU level is considered appropriate. It must be possible to challenge EU legislative proposals on subsidarity grounds before the European Court of Justice. *Nevertheless, Unice is clearly opposed to use being made of subsidiarity as a pretext to hinder necessary progress towards completion of the Single Market, or achievement of other agreed EU objectives.* (UNICE 1995: 3, emphasis added)

On the role of the institutions, UNICE (and the ERT and many other business organizations such as CEFIC, representing the chemical industry), pressed very strongly for a more 'efficient' decision-making process. In particular, over twenty different means of passing Euro-legislation were thought to be far too cumbersome and inefficient. Hence, an important business lobbying objective has been to secure a more 'efficient' Euro-policy process. In practice, UNICE has come out clearly in favour of a 'strong, effective, and well co-ordinated Commission', retaining its right of initiative and its responsibility for the execution of EU decisions. For the Council of Ministers, it argued that not only should QMV be the norm on single market issues but that, also, in a Union of 25–30 members, 'more extensive use of QMV is inevitable and unanimity should be retained only when strictly necessary for grave and objective reasons'. On the EP, business groups tend to be agnostic, perhaps recognizing the dangers of being portrayed as against addressing the democratic deficit issue. Thus, UNICE confined itself to calling for a simplification of parliamentary procedures (especially regarding co-decision) and for greater power for the EP to control spending and curb fraud. The theme of greater decision-making efficiency was also evident in UNICE's views on the European Court of Justice (ECJ) – namely, that procedures should be speeded up (UNICE 1995: 6).

Interestingly, in terms of our focus on the agenda setting process, UNICE illustrated an unusual, but central, aspect of the business lobbies' objectives for the 1996 IGC – namely, an attempt to keep a major issue *off* the agenda. Having won a major victory in persuading Europe's political leaders (more or less) to opt for monetary union, business was anxious that this particular decision-process should *not* be re-opened. UNICE's submission stated bluntly, 'UNICE reiterates strong support for the process of EMU as set out in the Treaty on European Union. The IGC should not re-open discussion on this issue' (UNICE 1995: 6). Similarly, the ERT's Chairman has argued that a single currency 'is critical because it will simplify industrialists' operations and raise their profitability. The cost of changing money alone amounts to Ecu 15bn a year' (Monod 1995). Similarly, Helmut Werner, President of Mercedes Benz, has argued that 'today, more than ever, Europe needs a strong single currency' and that 'there is an urgent need, therefore, for more strenuous efforts to convince decision-makers in those EU economies now benefiting from the depreciation of their currencies that such benefits are strictly short term' (Werner 1995). The EU Committee of the American Chamber of Commerce in Belgium (generally regarded as one of the most effective lobbying organizations in Brussels) also placed the considerable weight of US companies in Europe behind further economic, monetary and political integration (see letter from William Seddon-Brown to Mr Jean-Louis Bourlanes, MEP 19 April 1996). In a similar letter to David Martin, Vice-President of the EP, Mr Seddon-Brown urged that monetary union and a single currency should be achieved as soon as possible. While endorsing the EP's draft report for the IGC, he nevertheless urged that a fifth objective should be added to it, namely 'a Union which promotes the economic and social progress of its peoples by enhancing the competitiveness of European industry (letter 10 May 1995). Again, we see competitiveness emerging as a key theme from the business lobby, building on its success in getting the EU to set up a Competitiveness Advisory Group after the Essen European Council. (The Group consists of six business representatives, three trade union representatives, two academics, and various others. It is charged with reporting to the European Council and to the President of the Commission.) To some degree, therefore, the business lobby's key agenda item has already been institutionalized into the EU policy process. Similarly, the so-called Molitor Group, set up by the Commission at the request of the Council of Ministers of Economic and Financial Affairs (at its meeting in June 1994) might also be seen as the institutionalization of the business agenda. The group, chaired by Dr Bernhard Molitor, former Head of the Economic Policy Department at the German Ministry of Economy, was charged with 'examining the state of Community and national legislation and taking account of economic and social considerations in order to identify the real obstacles to the creation of jobs and competitivity – the excesses, weaknesses in application or deficiencies – how this might be alleviated and simplified, especially for small- and medium-sized enterprises'. (Terms of reference of the Group of Independent Experts for Legislative and Administrative Simplifications – see also Chapter 10.)

If – as seems probable – competitiveness (and its associated 'cascade' of specific policy issues such as deregulation) has achieved the status of a policy fashion or conventional wisdom, is there still space for other issues – and is there a rival meta-idea around which other advocacy coalitions might coalesce? As we suggested earlier, the IGC prompted very large numbers of national and Euro-level interests to produce policy position papers and to engage in the type of lobbying that has become absolutely routine in the EU policy process (i.e. lobbying national governments, lobbying the EU institutions, constructing policy networks, alliances, coalitions etc.). The institutional arrangements for preparing for the IGC 1996 provided a new and specific 'target' for interest group (and national government) lobbying, that is, the Reflection Group. Interest groups naturally saw the Reflection Group as a target and papers were formally directed to the Group, with some groups having direct meetings with the Chairman, Carlos Westendorp and with individual members of the Group. (The fact that the Group had a fairly broad membership opened up several 'access points' for interest groups, depending on their existing lobbying contacts. By the same token, it probably ensured that the Report would have to reflect the diversity of the Group's membership.) The Spanish Presidency was also the target of lobbying, as a new Presidency always is. However, the fact that the Reflection Group was reporting during the Spanish Presidency, added extra significance to lobbying the Presidency on this occasion.

Space does not permit a detailed review of the total 'map' of demands that emerged as the IGC opened. However, at least one rival advocacy coalition to the business lobby emerged and showed signs of being well organized – namely, the environmental lobby. Long practised at agenda setting (Mazey and Richardson 1993), the environmentalists appeared to be the only rival coalition with a tune which could prove as attractive as the tune to which the business lobby was singing. Thus, the notions of *sustainable development* and *participatory democracy* began to 'mobilize' ideas which could be difficult to resist openly, bearing in mind the continued high level of public support for environmental issues and the widespread concern (including within the business community) to raise the level of public support for European integration, after the Maastricht fiasco. While, as we suggested earlier, it is reasonable to suggest that the business agenda has tended to colour the high politics of the EC–EU since the mid-1980s (as it has at the national level), the environmental lobby has, nevertheless, a long track record in pushing its issues onto the agenda and in securing favourable policy outcomes. This was true even at Maastricht, when the European Environmental Bureau (EEB), Friends of the Earth (FOE) and World Wide Fund for Nature (WWF) were extremely successful in lobbying the IGC to strengthen the environmental dimensions of the Treaty of Rome via their paper *Greening the Treaty* (November 1990). They can justifiably claim that the Maastricht Treaty incorporated a number of their proposals in a clearly recognizable form.

For the 1996 IGC, the environmentalists constructed a broader advocacy coalition, on the Sabatier model (Sabatier 1988). Thus, six environmental organizations, Climate Network Europe, EEB, European Federation of Transport and Environment (T&E), Friends of the Earth Europe (FOEE), Greenpeace International – European Unit, and WWF in May 1995, jointly produced a very detailed document – *Greening the Treaty II: Sustainable Development on a Democratic Union. Proposals for the 1996 Intergovernmental Conference.* This was far more detailed than the UNICE paper, for example, and ran to some 44 pages, including a whole series of specific draft amendments to the Treaty. While it would be wrong to suggest that the environmental lobby is a completely unified body of policy actors, it is clear that the environmentalists find it easier to formulate detailed policy proposals than, say, UNICE, which has a more diverse set of interests to represent. The latter also has more cumbersome (a unanimity rule, for example) internal policy-making procedures. The themes of the environmental advocacy coalition were clear – 'the EU must seize the opportunity provided by the upcoming Intergovernmental Conference on Treaty Revision to confirm its commitment to a healthy environment and anchor the principles of sustainable development and participatory democracy firmly in the Treaty' (WWF *et al.* 1995: 1). The environmentalists demanded three changes. First, sustainable development should be the paramount objective of the TEU. Second, environmental considerations should be integrated into other policy areas of the EU. Third, in the interests of environmental protection, the democratic deficit in the EU's institutional structure should be reduced. Some of the more specific proposals – such as the proposal that the enforceability of environmental legislation must be strengthened, or that harmonization of legislation should not block more environmentally protective measures of the individual member states – were not seen as likely to win support from the business lobby. However, the possibility of the eventual emergence of a broader advocacy coalition on institutional reform was not unrealistic. Thus, the environmentalists wanted more transparency in the Council and better access to information from all EU institutions – proposals similar to those put forward by UNICE, which also stressed the need for more openness and consultation in the Euro-policy process. Even the environmentalists' plea for more use of QMV (though also with co-decision) on environmental matters was not inconsistent with the business lobby's general support for QMV as a decision-making process.

In fact, issues such as greater transparency, more consultation, extension of QMV cut across the wide range of groups trying to influence the IGC. For example, the trade unions – surely the interest group which has lost most power and influence at both the national and European level since the mid-1980s – also declared themselves in favour of reform on these issues. Thus, the European Trade Union Confederation (ETUC) argued that 'to prevent any unilateral obstruction of Union internal policies within the Council of Ministers, and prevent the use of the veto, the scope of qualified majority voting must be extended and become the general rule in social and environmental matters' (ETUC 1995: 4). Similarly, 'democratizing and bringing the Union closer to citizens also requires simpler, open, and more transparent decision-making in all institutions, especially the Council of Ministers'. ETUC's demand that 'Union initiatives must also be preceded by wide consultation of the representative organizations concerned' was also very close to UNICE's demand that 'the Treaty must put the Commission under the obligation to consult all parties affected by the measures it is proposing. Consultation must be genuine, and must be conducted within realistic deadlines' and that 'the Council, when legislating, must be put under the obligation to do so openly and transparently' (UNICE 1995: 3). Even on the defining issues of European high politics there was little divergence between the unions and business. Thus, the ETUC argued that European integration was 'now more essential than ever to confront the challenges of a profoundly transformed Europe in a radically changing world' and that there must be 'an ever closer union supported by its citizens' (ETUC 1995: 3). Similarly, UNICE argued that 'only a strong, confident and cohesive union is capable, over the long term, of guaranteeing peace and stability in our continent and of giving Europe the

242

political and economic structure to act as equal partner with giants on the world stage' (letter from the President of UNICE to Carlos Westendorp, 6 June 1995). The key area of difference between the unions and business has, of course, been social policy. Thus the ETUC has again laid great emphasis on issues such as employment, social rights, equal treatment and the environment. Essentially, the unions have been trying to ensure that economic and monetary union (which they support) is not at the expense of employment and welfare, etc. Hence, the ETUC is demanding that a real Social Union should be constructed and that the EU should 'build up an economic and fiscal policy and a strategy for full employment to restore the *balance* to Economic and Monetary Union' (ETUC 1995: 4, emphasis added). The emphasis on 'balance' in economic and monetary union was a clear plea for 'side payments' to emerge from the IGC process, as at Maastricht. The links between the unions and political parties at the national level could be an important factor in determining their degree of success. The price for support from the unions for an agenda which business holds dear is that the social aspects of the process of European integration need to be addressed.

On some of the specific demands which ETUC has made, consensus with the business community was always going to be difficult to achieve. For example, business leaders were unlikely to support ETUC's view that 'if undercutting of social standards between Member States is to be avoided, the Treaty's objectives must include a strategy for attaining convergence of labour law and social protection objectives while maintaining the improvements made' (ETUC 1995: 5). Yet the more thoughtful business leaders, whom we interviewed, privately recognized the need to keep the unions on board and were ultimately prepared to make concessions if that was needed to restore the momentum of European integration – their primary policy objective. Even British companies, generally thought to be the most hostile to European social policy, have not been united in their opposition. Thus, the CBI's own survey indicated that 21 per cent of UK businesses actually disagreed with the UK's opt out of the Social Chapter (CBI 1995). Indeed, several British companies have set up European Works Councils, contrary to the opt out. In terms of institutional reform, the unions have exhibited a classic interest group strategy – they wished to see a strengthening of the role of those institutions which they see as more likely to favour their future lobbying activities, namely the EP and the (so far weak) Economic and Social Committee (ETUC 1995: 4). These institutions are likely to be important in the trade union's defence of past policy gains. For example, the trade unions (and many, many, other interest groups representing women, environmentalists, consumers, the disabled, etc.) will form strong advocacy coalitions in order to resist the pressure for deregulation from industrialists. The constant pressure for further deregulation is illustrated by the Anglo-German Deregulation Group, set up by the Anglo-German Summit in April 1994 and which reported to the two governments at the 1995 Summit. This has made a very clear plea for the repeal of much Euro-regulation (*Deregulation Now* 1995). As at the national level, these moves will be resisted by those interests who benefit from such legislation. As we have seen with environmental legislation, the EP, for example, will be a key 'venue' where interests defend their previous policy gains.

If we see business interests, the environmentalists, and the trade unions as the key interest group players, does this mean that the hundreds of other interest groups concerned to enter the IGC 'garbage can' have been without influence? This is difficult to assess until the IGC is concluded and the complex process of restructuring successful advocacy coalitions can be clearly seen. These coalitions will include national governments, of course, interest groups, representatives of the EU institutions themselves and, no doubt, rather shadowy policy entrepreneurs, on the garbage can model. As these coalitions emerge around specific issues, groups such as consumers, women, local and regional governments, could emerge as significant policy actors. For example, BEUC (Bureau Européen des Unions de Consommateurs) has added its weight to the need to bring citizens closer to the European decision-making process, and this has been consistent with the views of many other groups. Like the environmentalists, it has been engaging in special pleading. Specifically it has sought to strengthen the existing Treaty Articles on Consumer Policy in order 'to consolidate and reinforce consumer policy as a priority for the European Union and as an autonomous EU policy, which is fully integrated with other EU policies' (Letter from BEUC to all MEPs, 15 May 1995). As with the ETUC, BEUC sees particular institutional arrangements as being to its advantage – for example, it has benefited from the introduction of the co-decision procedure. In fact BEUC is a good illustration of the potential for coalitions to emerge within the framework of the IGC. Superficially, it might be thought that consumers and business interests would always be in rival camps. This is not so. On previous occasions BEUC has, for example, formed a coalition with insurance companies and independent motor spare parts manufacturers against the car manufacturers, on the issue of legislation governing the production of spare parts for motor cars. In the approach to the IGC BEUC was aware that as yet unknown coalition possibilities could emerge, depending upon the positions taken up by other interest groups. Similarly, the local and regional authority interests might see opportunities on such issues as subsidiarity, for building alliances in the IGC process. The position of the local government and regional interests is obviously designed to protect the position of local and regional government in the face of increased supranationalism. Thus, they have sought a clear definition of the principle of subsidiarity to be included in the Treaty, the creation of a legal base for the principle of local self-government, an enhanced role for the Committee of the Regions and a revision of the powers of the EU in the fields of local authority competence to ensure that any necessary European promotion and regulation in those fields is undertaken in partnership with local government, etc. (LGIB 1995). Whether issues such as this, and the demands from less powerful interests such as women's groups and others, has successfully entered the 'log-rolling' process at the IGC remains to be seen.

CONCLUSION: EUROPEAN INTEGRATION WILL CONTINUE AS EXPECTED

We began by suggesting that the IGC was best characterized as a 'garbage can' into which problems and solutions were pitched and from which outcomes were difficult to predict. Moreover, we have stressed that the process itself is likely to see a shifting array of advocacy coalitions of considerable complexity and unpredictability. Can one, therefore, say anything useful in advance of the process itself? Our necessarily brief and unsystematic review of the positioning of interest groups does suggest some broad predictions, despite the 'policy mess' that the IGC might appear to be. Thus, there is clearly a very considerable weight of interest group support for the continuation of the process of European integration itself. While Euro-sceptics such as the British government under John Major (particularly the Euro-sceptic wing of the Conservative Party) may seek to halt, or even reverse, some aspects of the process of integration, there is very little evidence of significant interest group support for this stance. As the Report from the Reflection Group demonstrated, the British government is often in a minority of one or two on key issues, despite its more recent success in forming successful Euro-sceptic advocacy coalitions on some specific policy issues (George 1996 and Chapter 6). The broad thrust of lobbying from non-governmental organizations is that European integration must continue. The real debate, therefore, is about what type of integration is to take place. This concerns such questions as whether the EP should be strengthened, what deepening should take place and where, the pace and scope of enlargement, the pace and extent of deregulation, and the degree to which social questions can be addressed. Our guess is that many of these issues are bargainable and tradable between competing advocacy coalitions. Also, there is scope for bargaining and compromise over more specific policy issues such as sustainable development. For example, the chemical industry has published a position paper supporting the concept of sustainable development, possibly reflecting its realization that the environmentalists have hit on a rather catchy issue (ICA 1996). Thus, from out of the garbage can we can expect more, rather than less, European integration to emerge. Moreover, the whole process is now much more geared to encouraging participation, debate, persuasion, and consensus building. In this process, what Sebinius terms 'the zone of possible agreement' (Sebinius 1992: 333) may be quite broad, excluding only those member states and interests who are seemingly ideologically opposed to further integration at all. Those actors (Britain especially) who hope to halt the European train may find that even their policy successes in fact depend on a strengthening of the 'European state'. Thus, if the process of deregulation (e.g. in airlines, insurance, telecoms) is to be pushed forward, this will probably require a *stronger* European policy, not a weaker one. As Mrs Thatcher found in Britain post-1979, reducing the role of the state is not easy and often results in a more, not a less, intrusive state (Richardson 1994). Deregulation is likely to require a *dirigiste* state at the European level as it has at the national level. It is quite wrong to assume that the general business support for deregulated markets can be easily translated into policy at the national level. At this level, there are strong distributional coalitions in place which many national governments are reluctant to attack (airline deregulation being a current case). For action to be taken will need a strong Euro-level policy to force national governments to act. Thus, we conclude by suggesting that even the many side payments that will be needed to bring the IGC to a successful conclusion may in some way further the process of European integration.

NOTE

* This chapter was completed before the start of the 1996 IGC .

REFERENCES AND BIBLIOGRAPHY

Adler, Emmanuel and Haas, Peter (1992) 'Conclusion: epistemic communities, world order and the creation of a reflective research programme', *International Organization*, vol. 46, pp. 367–90.

Anglo–German Deregulation Group (1995) *Deregulation Now*. London, DTI, and Bonn, Federal Ministry of Economics.

Baumgartner, F.R. and Jones, B.D. (1991) 'Agenda dynamics and policy subsystems', *Journal of Politics*, vol. 53, no. 4, pp. 1044–74.

—— (1993) *Agendas and Instability in American Politics*. Chicago, Chicago University Press.

Bulmer, Simon (1983) 'Domestic politics and European Community policy-making', *Journal of Common Market Studies*, vol. 31, no. 4, pp. 349–63.

Caporaso, James, A. and Keeler, John, S.T. (1995) 'The European Union and integration theory', in Rhodes, Carolyn and Mazey, Sonia (eds) *The State of the European Union. Vol 3. Building a European Polity?* Boulder, Lynne Rienner/Longman.

CBI (1995) (in conjunction with Association of British Chambers of Commerce), *Business in Europe*. London, CBI/ABCC.

Challenge '96, IGC, Intelligence Service. Brussels, Belmont European Policy Centre.

Cohen, Michael, March, James and Olsen, Johan P. (1972) 'A garbage can model of organizational choice', *Administrative Sciences Quarterly*, vol. 17, pp. 1–25.

DTI (1993) *Review of the Implementation and Enforcement of EC Law in the UK*. London, DTI.

Dyson, Kenneth (1994) *Elusive Union. The Process of Economic and Monetary Union in Europe*. London, Longman.

ERT (1994) *European Competitiveness: The Way to Growth and Jobs*. Brussels, ERT.

—— (1995) *A New Architecture for Europe for the 21st Century. Preliminary Reflections on Priorities for the 1996 IGC from the Business Perspective*. Brussels, ERT.

ETUC (1995) *For a Strong, Democratic and Open Union Built on Solidarity*. Brussels, ETUC.

Green Cowles, Maria (1995) 'Setting the agenda for the new Europe: the ERT and EC 1992', *Journal of Common Market Studies*, vol. 33, no. 4, pp. 501–26.

George, Stephen (1996) 'The approach of the British government to the 1996 Intergovernmental Conference of the European Union', *Journal of European Public Policy*, vol. 3, no. 1, pp. 45–62.

Haas, Peter (1992) 'Introduction: epistemic communities and international policy co-ordination', *International Organization*, vol. 46, no. 1, pp. 1–35.

Heinz, John P., Laumann, Edward O., Nelson, Robert L. and Salisbury, Robert H. (1993) *The Hollow Core*. Cambridge, MA, Harvard University Press.

Héritier, Adrienne (1996) 'The accommodation of diversity in European policy-making:

regulatory policy as patchwork', *Journal of European Public Policy*, vol. 3, no. 2, pp. 149–67.

Hoffmann, Stanley (1966) 'Obstinate or Obsolete: The Fate of the Nation State and the Case of Western Europe', *Daedalus*, vol. 95, no. 3, pp. 862–915.

ICA (International Council of the Chemical Associations) (1996) 'Position Paper on Sustainable Development and the Chemical Industry.' Brussels, CEFIC.

Josselin, Daphne (1996) 'Domestic policy networks and European negotiations: evidence from British and French financial services,' *Journal of European Public Policy*, vol. 3 (1), pp. 297–317.

Katzenstein, Peter, J. (ed.) (1978) *Between Power and Plenty: Foreign Economic Policies and Advanced Industrial States.* Madison, University of Wisconsin Press.

Kingdon, John, W. (1984) *Agendas, Alternatives and Public Policies.* New York, HarperCollins.

Krasner, Stephen D. (1978) 'United States commercial and monetary policy: unravelling the paradox of external strength and internal weakness', in Katzenstein, Peter (ed.) *Between Power and Plenty. Foreign Economic Politics of Advanced Industrial States.* Madison, University of Wisconsin Press, pp. 51–87.

Local Government International Bureau (LGIB) (1995) *1996–The Local Government Agenda. For a Local Europe – Diverse, Democratic, and Decentralised.*

Lowi, T. (1964) 'American business, public policy, case studies, and political theory', *World Politics*, vol. 16, pp. 677–715.

Majone, Giandomenico (1989) *Evidence, Argument, and Persuasion in the Policy Process.* New Haven, Yale University Press.

Mazey, Sonia (1992) 'Conception and evaluation of the high authority's administrative services (1952–56); from supranational principles to multinational practices', in Morgan, R. and Wright, V. (eds) *The Administrative Origins of the European Community.* Baden, Nomos.

Mazey, Sonia and Richardson, Jeremy (1992) 'Environmental groups in the EC: challenges and opportunities', *Environmental Politics*, vol. 1, no. 4, pp. 111–28.

—— (eds) (1993) *Lobbying in the EC.* Oxford, Oxford University Press.

—— (1995) 'Promiscuous policymaking: the European policy style', in Rhodes, Carolyn and Mazey, Sonia (eds) *The State of the European Union: Building a European Polity?* Boulder, Lynne Rienner/Longman.

Monod, Jerome (1995) 'Help Needed For Take Off', *Financial Times.* 11 September 1995.

Moravcsik, Andrew (1991) 'Negotiating the Single European Act', in Hoffmann, Stanely and Keohane, Robert E. (eds) *The New European Community: Decision-making and Institutional Change.* Boulder, Westview Press.

—— (1993) 'Preferences and power in the European Community: a liberal intergovernmentalist approach', *Journal of Common Market Studies*, vol. 3, no. 4, pp. 473–524.

Putnam, Robert D. (1993) 'Diplomacy and domestic politics: the logic of two level games', reprinted in Evans, Peter B., Jacobsen, Harold K., and Putnam, Robert D. (eds) *Double Edged Diplomacy: International Bargaining and Domestic Politics.* Berkeley, University of California Press.

Radaelli, Claudio (1995) 'The role of knowledge in the policy process,' *Journal of European Public Policy*, vol. 2, no. 2, pp. 159–83.

Rein, H., and Schön, D. (1991) 'Frame-reflective policy discourse', in Wagner, P., Weiss, C. H., Wittrock, B. and Wollman, H. (eds) *Social Sciences Modern States: National Experiences and Theoretical Crossroad.* Cambridge, Cambridge University Press, pp. 262–89.

Reich, Robert, B. (ed.) (1988) *The Power of Public Ideas.* Cambridge, MA, Harvard University Press.

Richardson, Jeremy (1994) 'Doing less by doing more: British government 1979–93', *West European Politics*, vol. 17, no. 3, pp. 178–97.

Sabatier, Paul (1988) 'An advocacy framework of policy change and the role of policy-orientated learning therein', *Policy Sciences*, vol. 21, pp. 128–68.

Sandholtz, Wayne and Zysman, John (1989) 'Recasting the European bargain', *World Politics*, vol. 42, pp. 95–128.

Schattschneider, E.E. (1960) *The Semi-sovereign People: A Realist's View of Democracy on America*. New York, Holt.

Sebinius, James K. (1992) 'Challenging conventional explanations of international co-operation: negotiation analysis and the case of epistemic communities', *International Organization*, vol. 46, no. 1, pp. 323–65.

Truman, David (1951) *The Governmental Process: Political Interests and Public Opinion*. New York, Knopf.

Tsebelis, George (1990) *Nested Games: Rational Choice in Comparative Politics*. Berkeley, University of California Press.

—— (1994) 'The power of the European Parliament as a conditional agenda setter', *American Political Science Review*. vol. 88, pp. 128–42.

—— (1995) 'Conditional agenda-setting and decision-making inside the European Parliament', *Journal of Legislative Studies*, vol. 1, no. 1, pp. 65–93.

UNICE (1993) *Making Europe More Competitive: Towards World Class Performance. An Interim Report by UNICE*. Brussels, UNICE.

—— (1994) *Making Europe Competitive: Towards World Class Performance. The UNICE Competitiveness Report*. Brussels, UNICE.

—— (1995) *Preliminary UNICE Contribution to Preparation of the 1996 Intergovernmental Conference (IGC)*. Brussels, UNICE.

Walton, R.E. and McKersie, R.B. (1965) *A Behavorial Theory of Labour Negotiations*. New York, McGraw Hill.

Werner, Helmut (1995) 'Why Europe Needs a Single Currency', *Financial Times*, 26 May 1995.

WWF (1995) *Greening the Treaty II: Sustainable Development in a Democratic Union: Proposals for the 1996 Intergovernmental Conference*. Brussels, WWF.

Wincott, Daniel (1995) 'Institutional interaction and European integration: towards an everyday critique of liberal intergovernmentalism', *Journal of Common Market Studies*, vol. 33, no. 3, pp. 597–609.

THE AGENDA AND BEYOND

13

LEGITIMACY AND DEMOCRACY OF UNION GOVERNANCE

J. H. H. WEILER[1]

INTRODUCTION

Though legitimacy and democracy are often treated as part and parcel of the same set of problems, my plan in this essay is to treat them separately in two distinct parts. In relation to both I propose to be both descriptive – outlining the main debates concerning legitimacy and democracy in European governance – and prescriptive: suggesting ways in which I think this debate can and should develop, what I think ought to be the agenda of 1996 and beyond.

THREE FACES OF LEGITIMACY/ILLEGITIMACY

Legitimacy and illegitimacy are notoriously elusive concepts in political theory – suggestive rather than analytically rigorous – overreaching and under specified. One defining characteristic of legitimacy/illegitimacy discourse – in its multiple applications – is its appeal to foundations. Legitimacy and illegitimacy pertain to roots rather than foliage; to deep structure rather than surface. The following examples, turning on different situations in which appeals to 'legitimacy' or 'illegitimacy' are frequently made, are meant not simply to illustrate the foundational appeal of legitimacy discourse, but to create a (non-exhaustive) categorization and taxonomy which will make the elusive concept more usable.

Legitimacy/illegitimacy as a category of formal legal validity

I can, for example, be wholeheartedly and fundamentally opposed to the programme of, or the laws enacted by, a government, but not deny their legal validity and hence legitimacy. At the time of writing, the Conservative Government in Great Britain is thought to be very unpopular. It may be defeated in the next election but its legality and the legitimacy of its enactments are not challenged in a foundational sense. In this example, legitimacy appeals to some deeper validating legal Rules of Recognition (rules about rules) and not to programmatic content or specific enactment.

Legitimacy/illegitimacy by reference to deontological (non-legal) discourse

Notions of legitimacy and illegitimacy can extend beyond issues of legal validity. Thus, to give another example, I can acknowledge the perfect legality and formal validity of a programme or a law enacted by the government in terms of its self-referential positive rules but deny the very legitimacy of those rules. Even though legal I could still claim: 'They are illegitimate.' In this case I will be appealing to a deeper normative invalidating 'rule'. This invalidating rule may pertain to some normative political theory which sets out conditions for 'legitimate' *government* – democracy, for example. It may also pertain to ethics and morality as providing a deeper order of legitimacy against which even formally valid acts of *governance* must be checked.

Legitimacy/illegitimacy by reference to foundational myths

There is one additional aspect of legitimacy/illegitimacy in relation to governance which goes beyond formal validity and/or deontological discourse. Let us assume that we would posit today that democratic government and governance would be necessary conditions for an objective determination of the legitimacy of a polity. There would, however, be a condition precedent to such legitimacy – namely, the existence of a *demos* for which and by whom the democratic structure and process is to take place. In defining the *demos* one has to abandon the categories of formal validity or normative rationality.

The existence of the *demos* depends mostly on the subjective feelings of its members. Even to the extent that formal categories can exist, it has been cogently argued, by Böckenförder for example, that different nationalisms define differently the condition for their membership, which in turn become the ultimate referent for subjective, social legitimacy since the very understanding of the self, individual and collective, depends on it. The definition of *demos* is intricately connected to the definition of the *telos* of the polity, a telos the furtherance of which is the ultimate legitimating referent of the polity. It is to this stratum of legitimation then, rooted in the constitutive myths of the polity itself, that an appeal is made, and the explanation is given, for legitimacy of governance which transcends the normativity of the system of governance. This analysis explains not only social legitimation but also social illegitimation, i.e., the possibility of observing a polity which, on the surface is deontologically legitimate but to claim that beneath the surface there is a legitimacy problem gnawing at its roots. The Weimar Republic, for example, was legal and democratic. But it was felt to be betraying the 'destiny', the 'honour' etc. of the German nation and hence thought by many to be illegitimate.

Legitimacy/illegitimacy as a social and political category

This last category leads us to a final distinction in legitimacy/illegitimacy discourse. Formal validity and the deontological criteria, subject, of course, to the usual problems of epistemological uncertainty and moral relativity, are supposedly objective categories providing yardsticks for the legitimacy of a regime independently of its acceptance or otherwise by the governed. The fact, for example, that National Socialism was a hugely popular regime almost until its defeat, would be irrelevant to a determination of its legitimacy by reference to deontological criteria.

But the existence of myths going to the very foundation of the *demos* is clearly a matter which in large part goes to an empirically observable social reality. Social acceptance is a different face of legitimacy/illegitimacy discourse. The foundational nature of legitimacy/illegitimacy remains intact also in relation to this social-empirical dimension of the concept. When the claim is made that a regime is illegitimate in the empirical–social sense, more than mere unpopularity is implied. The extreme religious right in Israel, in its rejection of the Rabin–Peres peace plan, do not deny the formal validity of its government or its democratic nature. The policies, and the government which promotes them, are illegitimate since, through their eyes, they strike at some foundational understandings of the Jewish–Israeli Nation-State. The Separatists in Quebec, say, are not opposed to the federal government simply or primarily because of specific policies but because its very authority over Quebec is an affront to their self-understanding as an autonomous people.

There is no necessary connection between the objective strands of legitimacy/illegitimacy and its social manifestations. National Socialism had scarce legal validity and would require considerable contortions to justify its programme and acts under conventional normative theories – though, of course, apologists who used their intelligence to provide the contortions were not in short supply. Its considerable popular appeal and deep legitimacy in German society did not result from the consistency or otherwise of National Socialism with normative rationality. Legitimacy was acquired by an appeal to deeper strata in the human psyche where profound existential needs for meaning and belonging were met with captivating national myths.

THE RELATIONS BETWEEN THE CATEGORIES OF LEGITIMACY/ILLEGITIMACY

In one sense there is a clear division between formal and normative-deontological concepts of legitimacy/illegitimacy and its social manifestations. The pretense of the first two categories is to be able to pronounce on the legitimacy/illegitimacy of governance without reference to its social reality, in that it is like most normative judgements which are supposedly meant to be detached from their objects.

But the categories of legitimacy/illegitimacy are by no means watertight. How could it be otherwise? Surely the structure and process of government and the legality of its acts of governance will contribute to its legitimacy empirically defined? Supposedly in the liberal West there is meant to be a high degree of consonance between normative-deontological legitimacy/illegitimacy and its empirical manifestations. Supposedly, a non-democratic regime would enjoy low empirical legitimacy, or none at all, i.e., that normative legitimacy would be at least a necessary condition for social legitimacy and vice versa. Supposedly, a similar measure of consonance exists between formal legitimacy and its other manifestations.

Reality is, as usual, more complex than any modelling. The European Union (EU) itself, in certain periods, will provide an example of a cleavage between low normative legitimacy and high social legitimacy.

One interesting feature of legitimacy/illegitimacy discourse, despite its vagueness and under-specificity, is its relative prominence in academia as well as everyday politics. The foundational nature of the discourse and interplay between the normative and the empirical may account for this popularity. First, we note that legitimacy or illegitimacy are applied not only to outcomes (laws and programmes) but also to institutions, processes and, at times, the whole polity. For the academic to make a claim about illegitimacy, because of the foundational quality, is, in the first place to be consequential. If there is a problem of legitimacy, there is a legitimacy crisis. Crisis is important. Second, to make a claim about illegitimacy is also to be deep, because definitionally it is a statement about something that goes beyond the surface, that pertains to the foundations. It enables us to search for, and talk about, legitimating myths and narratives. It is also appealing because legitimacy legitimates the introduction, in broad daylight, of normative and moral discourse into 'scientific' observation and analysis. Finally, it is appealing since the inbuilt 'softness' of the components of the concept create a wonderfully broad area in which it is hard, perhaps impossible, to 'prove' either in normative or empirical terms the legitimacy or illegitimacy of outcomes, institutions, processes or polities. The discourse of legitimacy has the attraction of speculation.

THE DISCOURSE OF LEGITIMACY/ILLEGITIMACY IN THE EVOLUTION OF EUROPEAN CONSTITUTIONALISM

European constitutionalism provides a useful prism through which to understand the legitimacy/illegitimacy discourse of the Community since it intersects both the legal structure and the political process of European integration. The evolution of European constitutionalism has brought into play, in different ways, the different faces of legitimacy/illegitimacy.

Legal doubts and political legitimacy

The first legitimacy/illegitimacy issue was associated with what could be considered the most orthodox version of European constitutionalism which finds expression in some key legal doctrines, developed in the 1960s and early 1970s, which determined the relationship between the Community and member states. So much has been written about these so as to obviate any need for recapitulation. Simple codes will suffice: direct effect, supremacy, implied powers and European *judicial Kompetenz-Kompetenz* define the hierarchy of norms between the two orders. The combination of these legal doctrines positions European law, in its self-defined sphere of competences, as the 'supreme law of the land' – a position of practical as well as symbolic significance given the extraordinary system of judicial enforcement and compliance. From this legal perspective Europe obtained a place in the premier league of constitutional orders such as the USA, Germany and Italy by the most formalist definitions of constitutionalism which require the presence of a 'higher Law', judicial review as well as some material elements such as protection of fundamental human rights. These doctrines, it is said, are what differentiate the Community and Union from 'normal' international organizations and from the classical framework of international law.

Constitutionalism thus understood is very much a creature of legal discourse. It was, however, in many ways a far-reaching discourse, surprising in its reach and, arguably at least, pushing to the boundaries of the accepted canons of legal construction. The legitimacy/illegitimacy issues turn thus on the validity of the juridical constructs adopted in the legal community especially by the European Court of Justice (ECJ). Rasmussen, most famously, in his 1986 book *On Law and Policy in the European Court of Justice* challenges the legitimacy of the EC constitutionalism in terms of their legal validity as measured by hermeneutical norms. It is not the place here to rehearse this debate but simply to note that in objective terms the challenge was far from specious.

The relationship in this discussion between normative and social legitimacy is fascinating. Despite the legally problematic nature of the emerging constitutional structure of the Community, the most striking feature of the first phase of European constitutionalism was its acceptance by a series of member state interlocutors – an acceptance which, at first blush, may have seemed counter-intuitive since, prima facie European constitutionalism places shackles of member state legal and political freedoms under less constitutionalized transnational regimes. To explain how a radical constitutional construct, with, at best, fragile legal validity could generate such a high measure of empirical legitimacy by national polit-

Table 13.1 The evolving debate on EU constitutional legitimacy

	Normative – deontological issue	Empirical–social responses
First debate	Formal validity: the legitimacy of ECJ constitutionalizing legal discourse	Acceptance by national political interlocutors
Second debate	Deontological concerns: the democracy deficit	Social acceptance
Current debate	Foundational myths: issues of European identity and demos	Social scepticism

ical institutions is an integral part of that legitimacy/illegitimacy debate.[2]

The democratic deficiencies and social legitimacy

The second issue of legitimacy/illegitimacy relating to European constitutional-ism may seem even more intriguing. It is hardly contested in both the political and academic worlds that the Community, especially in the period leading up to Maastricht has suffered from serious democratic deficiencies in its mode of gov-ernment – often referred to as the Community democratic deficit. Here, too, the transparent democratic deficiencies did not simply prevent an acquiescence by national political institutions in the new constitutional architecture but also a gen-erally supportive public opinion which reached certain crescendo, almost a transnational psychosis, in the celebration of the 1992 plan and the Single European Act (SEA). This cleavage between normative-deontological legitimacy and its social counterpart is probably even more poignant than the cleavage between formal legal legitimacy and political acceptance.[3]

Challenging the foundational myths of the Union

Since Maastricht, the legitimacy/illegitimacy debate has changed considerably. First, it is evident that general public opinion has taken a much more sceptical and critical approach towards the European construct. Measurement of empiri-cal illegitimacy is difficult. Whether the serious erosion in public support for the European construct could be construed as a veritable legitimacy crisis is moot. This is certainly the spirit which imbues the 1996 IGC Reflection Group's Report.

Why this erosion has occurred has been the subject of considerable specula-tion but of greater interest is the emergence of a new discussion which goes to the fundamental myths of the Community or Union calling into question the very foundations of European constitutionalism. In explaining the contours of this new legitimacy/illegitimacy challenge (a challenge to which I am not indifferent), I propose to offer some ways of thinking and even responding to it (see Table 13.1).

THE ILLEGITIMACY OF DEMOS AND TELOS IN THE UNION

Here is one way of introducing this issue. For decades lawyers have been speaking loosely about the 'constitutionalization' of the Treaties establishing the European Community and Union. In part this has meant the emergence of European law as constitutionally 'higher law' with immediate effect within the 'legal space' of the Community. Thankfully, the political science of European integration, which had lagged somewhat in noticing the phenomenon and understanding its impor-tance, has in recent times been addressing it. But so far most searching, and illu-minating, analysis has been on constitutionalization as an element in understanding governance with most attention given to the newly discovered

actors (for example, the European Court and national courts), to the myriad factors which explain the emergence and acceptance of the new constitutional architecture, to the constraints, real or imaginary, which constitutionalism places on
political and economic actors and to the dynamics of interaction between the various actors and between legal integration and other forms of integration. In very
large measure all these phenomena have been discussed in positivist terms, posi-
tivism as understood both in political science and law.

There is an underlying issue which, so far has received too little attention: by
what authority, if any – understood in the vocabulary of normative political
theory – can the claim of European law to be both constitutionally superior and
with immediate effect in the polity be sustained. Why should the subjects of
European law in the Union, individuals, courts, governments, etc. feel bound to
observe the law of the Union as higher law, in the same way that their counter-
parts in, say, the USA are bound, to and by, American federal law? It is a dramatic
question since constitutionalization has formally taken place and to give a negative answer would be very subversive. This is partly why the critique of European
democracy is often conflicted. One can, it seems, proclaim a profound democracy
deficit and yet insist at the same time on the importance of accepting the
supremacy of Union law.

One of the most trenchant critiques of authority to emerge recently has come
from a certain strand of German constitutional theory and can be entitled the
'no-demos' thesis. Interestingly, it found powerful expression in the so-called
Maastricht decision of the German Federal Constitutional Court. The decision,
formally unanimous, contains conflicting strands. We shall present the robust version culled from decision and constitutional writing. I should add that this is but
a German version of deep strand in both the political self-understanding and the
theory of the European nation-state.

The 'no-demos' thesis

The following is a composite version of the 'no-demos' thesis culled from the decision of the Court itself and some of the principal exponents of this thesis.

The people of a polity, the Volk, its demos, is a concept which has a subjective
– socio-psychological – component which is rooted in objective, organic conditions. Both the subjective and objective can be observed empirically in a way
which would enable us, on the basis of observation and analysis, to determine
that, for example, there is no European *Volk*.

The subjective manifestations of peoplehood, of the *demos*, are to be found in a
sense of social cohesion, shared destiny and collective self-identity which, in turn,
result in (and deserve) loyalty. These subjective manifestations have thus both a
descriptive and also a normative element.

The subjective manifestations are a result of, but are also conditioned on, some,
though not necessarily all, of the following objective elements: common language,
common history, common cultural habits and sensibilities and – this is dealt with
more discretely since the twelve years of National-Socialism – common ethnic

255

origin, common religion. All these factors do not alone capture the essence of *Volk* – one will always find allusions to some spiritual, even mystic, element as well. Whereas different writers may throw a different mix of elements into the pot, an insistence on a relatively high degree of homogeneity, measured by these ethno-cultural criteria, is typically an important, indeed critical element of the discourse. Here rests, of course, the most delicate aspect of the theory since the insistence on homogeneity is what conditions in its statal operationalization the rules for inclusion and exclusion. When, say, Jews were excluded from full membership in many European nation-states as equal citizens it was often on the theory that being a Christian was essential to the homogeneity of the people.

The 'organic' nature of the *Volk* is a delicate matter. We call 'organic' those parts of the discourse which make, to a greater or lesser degree, one or more of the following claims: the *Volk* pre-dates historically, and precedes politically the modern state. Germany could emerge as a modern nation-state because there was already a German *Volk*. The 'nation' is simply a modern appellation, in the context of modernist political theory and international law, of the pre-existing Volk and the state is its political expression. It is on this view that the compelling case for German (re)unification rested. One could split the German state but not the German nation. Hence, maybe unification of the state but certainly only reunification of the people. Anthropologically, this understanding of, say, being German, which means being part of the German *Volk*, is 'organic' in the following sense: it has, first, an almost natural connotation. You are born German the way you are born male or female – though you can, with only somewhat greater ease, change your national identity (even then you will remain an 'ex-German') and to the extent that ethnicity continues to play a role – muted to be sure – in this discourse of the *Volk*, ethnicity is even more immutable than gender – there is no operation which can change one's ethnicity. The implication of this is that one's nationality as a form of identity is almost primordial according to this view, taking precedence over other forms of consciousness and membership. I may have solidarity with fellow Christians elsewhere, fellow workers elsewhere, fellow women elsewhere. This would make me a Christian German, a socialist German, a feminist German or, at most, a German Christian, a German socialist, a German feminist. I cannot escape my '*Volk*ish', national identity.

No one today argues that the 'organic' is absolute. One can, after all, 'naturalize', acquire membership in a new nation – but even here, doesn't the word 'naturalization' speak volumes? And one can, more as an hypothesis than a reality, imagine that should the objective conditions sufficiently change, and a measure of homogeneity in language, culture, shared historical experience develop, a subjective consciousness could follow and a new *Volk*/nation emerge. But, realistically, these mutations are possible in a 'geological' time frame – epochal, not generational.

Volk fits into modern political theory easily enough. The German Constitution may have constituted the post-War German state, but it did not constitute the German people except, perhaps, in some narrow legal sense. The *Volk*, the nation, understood in this national, ethno-cultural sense are the basis for the modern state. They are the basis in an older, self-determination sense of political independence in statehood. Only nations 'may have' states. The state belongs to the nation – its *Volk*, and the nation (the *Volk*) 'belong' to the state.

Critically, *Volk*/nation are also the basis for the modern democratic state: the nation and its members, the *Volk*, constitute the polity for the purposes of accepting the discipline of democratic, majoritarian governance. Both descriptively and prescriptively (how it is and how it ought to be) a minority will/should accept the legitimacy of a majority decision because both majority and minority are part of the same *Volk*, belong to the nation. That is an integral part of what rule-by-the-people, democracy, means on this reading. Thus, nationality constitutes the state (hence nation-state) which in turn constitutes its political boundary, an idea which runs from Schmitt to Kirchhof. The significance of the political boundary is not only to the older notion of political independence and territorial integrity, but also to the very democratic nature of the polity. A Parliament is, on this view, an institution of democracy not only because it provides a mechanism for representation and majority voting, but because it represents the *Volk*, the nation, the demos from which derive the authority and legitimacy of its decisions. To drive this point home, imagine an *anschluss* between Germany and Denmark. Try and tell the Danes that they should not worry since they will have full representation in the *Bundestag*. Their screams of grief will be shrill not simply because they will be condemned, as Danes, to permanent minorityship (that may be true for the German Greens too), but because the way nationality, in this way of thinking, enmeshes with democracy is that even majority rule is only legitimate within a demos, when Danes rule Danes. Demos, thus, is a condition of democracy. By contrast, when democrats like Alfred Verdross argued for a Greater Germany this was clearly not motivated by some proto-fascist design but by a belief that the German speaking 'peoples' were in fact one people in terms of this very understanding of peoplehood.

Turning to Europe, it is argued as a matter of empirical observation, based on these ethno-cultural criteria, that there is no European demos – not a people not a nation. Neither the subjective element (the sense of shared collective identity and loyalty) nor the objective conditions which could produce these (the kind of homogeneity of the ethno-national conditions on which peoplehood depend) exist. Long-term peaceful relations with thickening economic and social intercourse should not be confused with the bonds of peoplehood and nationality forged by language, history, ethnicity and all the rest. At this point we detect two versions to the 'no-demos' thesis. The 'soft' version of the Court itself is the *not yet* version: although there is no demos now the possibility for the future is not precluded a priori. If and when a European demos emerges, then, and only then, will the basic political premises of the decision have to be reviewed. This is unlikely in the foreseeable future. The 'hard' version does not only dismiss that possibility as objectively unrealistic but also as undesirable: it is argued (correctly in my view) that integration is not about creating a European nation or people, but about the ever closer Union among the peoples of Europe. However, what the 'soft' and 'hard' version share is the same understanding of peoplehood, its characteristics and manifestations.

Soft version or hard, the consequences of the 'no-demos' thesis for the European construct are interesting. The rigorous implication of this view would be that absent a demos, there cannot, by definition, be a democracy or democratization at the European level. This is not a semantic proposition. On this reading, European democracy (meaning a minimum binding majoritarian decision-making at the European level) without a demos is no different from the German–Danish *anschluss* example above, except on a larger scale. Giving the Danes a vote in the *Bundestag* is, as argued, ice cold comfort. Giving them a vote in the European Parliament (EP) or Council is, conceptually, no different. This would be true for every nation-state. European integration, on this view, may have involved a certain transfer of state functions to the Union but this has not been accompanied by a redrawing of political boundaries which can occur only if, and can be ascertained only when, a European *Volk* can be said to exist. Since this, it is claimed, has not occurred, the Union and its institutions can have neither the authority nor the legitimacy of a 'demos-cratic' state. Empowering the EP is no solution and could – to the extent that it weakens the Council (the voice of the member states) – actually exacerbate the legitimacy problem of the Community. On this view, a parliament without a demos is conceptually impossible, practically despotic. If the EP is not the representative of *a* people, if the territorial boundaries of the EU do not correspond to its political boundaries, then the writ of such a parliament has only slightly more legitimacy then the writ of an emperor.

What, however, if the interests of the nation-state would be served by functional cooperation with other nation-states? The 'no-demos' thesis has an implicit and traditional solution: cooperation through international treaties, freely entered into by high contracting parties, preferably of a contractual nature (meaning no open-ended commitments) capable of denunciation, covering well-circumscribed subjects. Historically, such treaties were concluded by heads of state embodying the sovereignty of the nation-state. In the more modern version, such treaties are concluded by a government answerable to a national parliament often requiring parliamentary approval and subject to the material conditions of the national democratic constitution. Democracy is safeguarded in that way.

Democracy and membership

There is much that is puzzling in the reasoning of the German Court. For example: if the concern of the German Court was to safeguard the democratic character of the European construct in its future developments, and if its explicit and implicit thesis that in the absence of a European demos, democracy can be guaranteed only through member state mechanisms, it is hard to see how, employing the same sensibilities, it could have given a democratic seal of approval to the existing EC and EU. Whatever the original intentions of the high contracting parties, the Treaties establishing the EC and EU have become like no other international parallel, and national procedures to ensure democratic control over international treaties of the state are clearly ill-suited and woefully inadequate to address the problems posited by the EU.

One could suggest, explicitly or implicitly, that the current situation of the Union has been democratically legitimated by national processes – for example the successive approvals of the Community by the various national parliaments. But this is problematic and somewhat embarrassing, too. First, even if the current Union has been democratically approved by successive approvals of Treaty amendments (such as the SEA and the various acts of accession of new member states) this takes a very formal view of democratic legitimation. Is it not just a little bit like the Weimar elections which democratically approved a non-democratic regime? Is it not the task of a constitutional court to be a counter-balance to such self-defeating democratization? Member state mediation does have a powerful impact on the social and formal legitimacy of the European construct but it has done only little to address the problems of deficient democratic structures and processes. If the current democratic malaise of the Union can be said to have been cured by the simple fact that national parliaments have endorsed the package deal in one way or another, the Court would have engaged, at worst, in another form of fiction about the reality of the Union and the democratizing power of national structures and institutions. At best, it would seem to have adopted a formal and impoverished sense of what it takes to ensure democracy in the polity.

The Court could have adopted an alternative construct: highlight, embarrassing as this may have been, the democratic failings of the Community, uncured by Maastricht and in which all European and member state institutions (including courts) connived. Since, despite these failings, the Union was formally legitimated the Court could have approved the Treaty but insisted that the existing gap between formal legitimation and material democratic deficiency must be regarded as temporary and could not be accepted in the medium and long term. In this way the *Bundesverfassungsgericht* would have thrown its formidable power behind the pressure for democratization. For all its talk about democracy, the Court, by adopting the view it has on *Volk*, *Staat* and *Staatsangehörigkeit* has boxed itself into a further untenable situation. Stated briefly: if the judges who subscribed to the decision truly believe that a polity enjoying democratic authority and legitimate rule-making power must be based on the conflation of *Volk*, *Staat* and *Staatsangehörigkeit*, that the only way to conceive of the demos of such a polity is in thickly homogeneous ethno-cultural terms, then, whether one admits it or not, the future of European integration poses a huge threat. The problem is not that there is not now a European demos; the problem is that there might one day be one. And why is that a problem? Because the emergence of a European demos in a European polity enjoying legitimate democratic authority would signify – on this understanding of polity and demos – the replacement of the various member state demoi, including the German *Volk*. This, we would agree, would be a price too high to pay for European integration. But since on their reading there is only a binary option – either a European State (one European *Volk*) or a Union of States (with the preservation of all European *Völker*, including Germans), their fear is inevitable.

This view is based on one, and perhaps two profound misconceptions with unfortunate consequences both for Germany itself and for Europe. Our challenge, note, is *not* to the ethno-cultural, homogeneous concept of *Volk* as such. It is, instead, to the view which insists that the *only* way to think of a demos, bestowing legitimate rule-making and democratic authority on a polity, is in these *Volkish* terms. We also challenge the concomitant notion that the *only* way to think of a polity, enjoying legitimate rule-making and democratic authority, is in statal terms. Finally, we challenge the implicit view in the decision that the only way to imagine the Union is in some statal form: *Staat, Staatenbund, Bundesstaat, Staatenverbund.* Noteworthy is not only the 'enslavement' to the notion of State, but also, as we shall see, the inability to contemplate an entity with a simultaneous multiple identity. Polycentric thinking is, apparently, unacceptable.

I shall construct the critique step-by-step beginning with Demos-as-*Volk* first. I want to raise three possible objections to the Court's version of the 'no-demos' thesis and its implications. The first objection has two strands. One, less compelling, would argue that the thesis simply misreads the European anthropological map. That, in fact, there is a European sense of social cohesion, shared identity and collective self which, in turn, results in (and deserves) loyalty and which bestows potential authority and democratic legitimacy on European institutions. In short that there is, want it or not, a European people on the terms stipulated by the 'no-demos' thesis and that the only problem of democracy in the Community relates to the deficient processes, such as the weakness of the EP, but not the deep structural absence of a demos. Though there is no common European language, that cannot in itself be a *conditio sine qua non* as the case of, say, Switzerland would illustrate. And there is a sufficient measure of shared history and cultural habits to sustain this construct. The problem is that this construct simply does not ring true. For most Europeans, any sense of European identity defined in ethno-cultural or ethno-national terms would be extremely weak.

Although I do not wish to pursue this critique as such, there is one strand worth picking up from this first objection. One can argue that peoplehood and national identity have, at certain critical moments of transition, a far larger degree of artificiality, of social constructionism and even social engineering than the organic, *Volkish* view would concede. As such they are far more fluid, potentially unstable and capable of change. They decidedly can be constructed as a conscious decision and not only be a reflection of an already pre-existing consciousness. Indeed, how could one ever imagine political unification taking place if it has strictly to follow the sense of peoplehood? In the creation of European states involving political unification such as, yes, Germany and Italy, the act of formal unification preceded full and universal shift of consciousness. Although conceptually the nation is the condition for the state, historically, it has often been the state which constituted the nation by imposing a language and/or prioritizing a dialect and/or privileging a certain historical narrative and/or creating symbols and myths. This would, often, have to be the order in the process of unification. Think, say, of Prussia and Austria. Is it so fanciful to imagine a different historical path in which Prussia went its own way, privileging a particularized read of its history, symbols, cultural habits and myths and developing a sense of *Volk* and nation which would emphasize that which separates it from other German-speaking nations and that Austria, in this would-be history, could have just become another part of a unified Germany?

I take no position here on the desirability or otherwise of European unification driven by the notion of nation and peoplehood (though, as will transpire, I oppose it). But to insist on the emergence of a pre-existing European demos defined in ethno-cultural terms as a precondition for constitutional unification or, more minimally, a re-drawing of political boundaries, is to ensure that this will never happen. The 'no-demos' thesis which is presented by its advocates as rooted in empirical and objective observation barely conceals a pre-determined outcome.

The second objection is more central and is concerned with the notion of membership implicit in the 'no-demos' thesis. Who, we may ask, are the members of, say, the German polity? The answer would seem obvious: the German *Volk*, those who have German nationality. They are Germany's demos. Germany is the state of the Germans defined in the familiar ethno-national terms. By contrast, to say that there is no European demos is equivalent to saying that there is no European nation. I should immediately add that I agree: there is no European nation or *Volk* in the sense that these words are understood by the German Court and the constitutionalists on which it relies.

But that is not the point. The real point is the following: is it mandated that demos in general and the European demos in particular be understood exclusively in the ethno-cultural homogeneous terms which the German Federal Constitutional Court has adopted in its own self-understanding? Can there not be other understandings of demos which might lead to different conceptualizations and potentialities for Europe?

I have, so far, studiously avoided using the concept of citizen and citizenship. Can we not define membership of a polity in civic, non-ethno-cultural terms? Can we not separate ethnos from demos? And can we not imagine a polity whose demos is defined, understood and accepted in civic, non-ethno-cultural terms, and would have legitimate rule-making democratic authority on that basis? To be sure, there is a German constitutional tradition from which the 'no-demos' thesis arises which masks these possibilities since historically, at least from the time of the *Kaiserreich* or so there has been such a strong current which insists on the unity of *Volk*-Nation-State-Citizenship. A German citizen is, save for some exceptions, a German national, primarily one who belongs to the *Volk*. Belonging to the *Volk* is normally the condition for citizenship. And, in turn, citizenship in this tradition can only be understood in statal terms. Here the very language reflects the conflation: the concept of state is built into the very term of *Staatsangehöriger*. If there is citizenship, statehood is premised. If there is statehood, citizenship is premised. This is not simply a matter of constitutional and political theory. It finds its reflection in positive law. That is why naturalization in Germany – other than through marriage, adoption and some other exceptions – is an act which implies not simply accepting civic obligations of citizenship and loyalty to the state but of embracing German national identity understood in this thick cultural sense, a true cultural assimilation and a demand for an obliteration of other *Volk*ish loyalties and identification. Thus, for example, emancipation of the Jews in Germany was premised on a consignment of Jewishness and Judaism to the realm of religion and a refusal to accept Jewish peoplehood. To be a German citizen, under this conception, you have to be part of the *Volk*. And Germany as a state, is the state of the Germans understood in these terms.

Likewise, until very recently, you may have been a third generation resident of Germany and be denied citizenship because you are unable or unwilling to become 'German' in a cultural and identification sense. With few exceptions, the law specifically denies naturalization to residents who would wish to embrace the duties of citizenship but retain an alternative national identity. Multiple citizenship is permitted in peculiar circumstances but is frowned upon. By contrast, if you are an ethnically defined German national even if a third generation citizen and resident of some far flung country you would still be a member of the *Volk* and hence have a privileged position in applying for citizenship. On this view, the legal 'passport' of membership in the polity is citizenship: citizenship is what defines you as a member of the polity with full political and civil rights and duties. But that, in turn, is conflated with nationality, with being a member of the *Volk* in the ethno-cultural sense. And, since demos is defined in national terms, the only demos conceivable is one the members of which are citizen-nationals – hence the state.

I should point out again that Germany is not the only state in Europe or elsewhere whose membership philosophy is so conceived. In some measure that is the philosophy of the nation-state. But it does offer a rather extreme example of the conflation of state, *Volk*-nation and citizenship.

Be that as it may, this conflation is neither necessary conceptually, nor practised universally, nor, perhaps, is it even desirable. There are quite a few states where, for example, mere birth in the state creates actual citizenship or an entitlement to citizenship without any pretense that you thus become a national in an ethno-cultural sense. There are states where citizenship, as a commitment to the constitutional values and the civic duties of the polity, is the condition of naturalization whereas nationality, in an ethno-cultural sense is regarded, like religion, a matter of individual preference. There are states, like Germany, with a strong ethno-cultural identity, which, nonetheless, allow citizenship not only to individuals with other nationalities, who do not belong to the majority *Volk*, but to minorities with strong, even competing, ethno-cultural identities. It is, I suppose, a matter for the Germans to decide whether the unity of *Volk*, *Staat*, and *Staatsangehörigkeit* continues to be the best way in which to conceive of their state, nation and citizenry.

Embedded, however, in the decision of the *Bundesverfassungsgericht* is an understanding not only of German polity and demos but of Europe too, notably in its 'not yet' formulation. When the German Court tells us that there is not yet a European demos, it implicitly invites us to think of Europe, its future and its very telos in ethno-national terms. It implicitly construes Europe in some sort of 'pre-state' stage, as yet underdeveloped and hence lacking in its own legitimate rule-making and democratic authority. It is this (mis)understanding which produces the either–or zero sum relationship between Europe and member state. If demos is *Volk* and citizenship can only be conceived as ***Staat****sangehörigkeit*, then European demos and citizenship can only come at the expense of the parallel German terms.

What is inconceivable in this view is a decoupling of nationality (understood its *Volk*ish ethno-cultural sense) and citizenship. Also inconceivable is a demos understood in non-organic civic terms, a coming together on the basis not of shared ethnos and/or organic culture, but a coming together on the basis of shared values, a shared understanding of rights and societal duties and shared rational, intellectual culture which transcend ethno-national differences. Equally inconceivable in this view is the notion of a polity enjoying rule-making and democratic authority whose demos, and hence the polity itself, is not statal in character and is understood differently from the German self-understanding. Finally, and critically, what is also inconceivable on this view is that a member state like Germany may have its own understanding of demos for itself (for example, its relatively extreme form of state = people = citizens) but be part of a broader polity with a different understanding of demos.

At the root of the 'no-demos' thesis is ultimately a world view which is enslaved to the concepts of *Volk*, *Staat* and *Staatsangehöriger* and cannot perceive the Community or Union in anything other than those terms. This is another reason why the Union may appear so threatening since the statal vision can only construe it in oppositional terms to the member state. But that is to impose on the Community or Union an external vision and not an attempt to understand (or define it) in its own unique terms. It is a failure to grasp the meaning and potentialities of supranationalism.

Before returning, then, to the potentialities of decoupling nationality and citizenship, it is worth discussing the broader relationship between Union, nation and state within the European construct encapsulated in the term supranationalism. It will appear that supranationalism and nationalism are not truly oppositional.

SUPRANATIONALISM: COMMUNITY, NATION AND STATE

How, then, should we understand – or construe – the notion of supranationalism in this context? A word of caution would be necessary here. There is no fixed meaning to the term supranationalism. Indeed, from its inception there seems to have been two competing visions of its realization through the Community: a unity or statal vision – encapsulated in those who favoured a United States of Europe – and a more attenuated Community vision. The two strands (which, of course, overlap) have continued to co-exist. But it is our reading of the historical map – the rejection of the European Defence Community and the European Political Community in the 1950s and the articulation of supranationalism in, especially, the Treaty of Rome and its practices – that the Community vision prevailed in the formative years of the EC.

In trying to explain the ways in which the Community is, or has become, supranational, most discussion over the years has tended, interestingly, to focus on its relation to the 'state' rather than the 'nation'. This conflation of nation-state is not always helpful. Supranationalism relates in specific and discreet ways to nationhood and to statehood. Indeed, in my understanding and construction of supranationalism its value system is, surprisingly actually wrapped up with the value system of European ethno-national liberalism of the nineteenth century and, as such, can offer great comfort to those concerned to preserve the values and virtues of the nation-state.

With all the talk about *Volk* and nation and with all our obsessions about the dangers of nationalism and chauvinism and even racism, which are often said to derive from these concepts, what can be said about them in normative terms? What values can they be said to uphold and vindicate? I will talk about nationhood but this could, in most respects, capture *Volk* and peoplehood, too. It seems to us that, at least in its nineteenth-century liberal conception, two deep human values are said to find expression in nationhood: belongingness and originality. (It should immediately be stated that nationhood is not the only social form in which these values may find expression.)

Belongingness is inherent in nationhood, nationhood is a form of belonging. Nationhood is not an instrument to obtain belongingness, it is it. Form and substance here conflate, the way they do, say, in a love sonnet by Shakespeare: the value of the sonnet does not lie in, say, its message of love; we do not think of the sonnet as an instrument for the conveyance of the idea. Take away the form and the message is banal. What gives the sonnet its timeless value is the inextricable way in which the substance and the form were woven together by Shakespeare.

What are the values embedded in belonging, in national belonging, beyond the widely shared view that belonging is pleasant, is good? We can readily understand a certain basic appeal to our human species which is, arguably, inherently social: the appeal that family and tribe have, too. Part of the appeal is, simply, the provision of a framework for social interaction. But surely one has to go beyond that: after all, much looser social constructs than nationhood, let alone tribe and family, could provide that framework. Belonging means, of course, more than that. It means a place, a social home.

The belonging of nationhood is both like and unlike the bonds of blood in family and tribe and, in both this likeness and unlikeness, we may find a clue to some of its underlying values. It is like the 'bonds of blood' in family and tribe in that those who are of the nation have their place, are accepted, belong, independently of their achievements – by just being – and herein lies the powerful appeal (and terrible danger) of belonging of this type – it is a shield against existential aloneness. In, for example, the tradition of the Jewish nation, a tradition worthy of some consideration given the continuity of Jewish national survival for over three millennia, we find a normative expression to this form of belonging: 'even though he has sinned, he remains Israel.' The power of this belongingness may be understood by the drama and awesomeness of its opposites: isolation, seclusion, excommunication.

But nationhood transcends the family and tribe, and maybe here lurks an even more tantalizing value: nationhood not only offers a place to the familyless, to the tribeless, but in transcending family and tribe it calls for loyalty – the largest coin in the realm of national feeling – towards others which go beyond the immediate 'natural' (blood) or self-interested social unit. And, indeed, belongingness of this type is a two way street. It is not only a passive value: to be accepted. It is also active: to accept. Loyalty is one of those virtues which, if not abused, benefits both those on the giving and receiving ends.

The other core value of nationhood, in some ways also an instrument for national demarcation, is the claim about originality. On this reading, the Tower of Babel was not a sin against God but a sin against human potentiality; and the dispersal that came in its aftermath, not punishment, but divine blessing. The nation, with its endlessly rich specificities, coexisting alongside other nations, is, in this view, the vehicle for realizing human potentialities in original ways, ways which humanity as a whole would be the poorer for not cultivating. (How one decides the self which qualifies as a nation is a tantalizing issue which is not necessary to explore here.)

It is here that one may turn from the nation to the modern state. It is worth remembering at the outset that national existence, and even national vibrancy, do not in and of themselves require statehood, though statehood can offer the nation advantages, both intrinsic as well as advantages resulting from the current organization of international life which gives such huge benefits to statehood. I would argue that in the modern notion of the European ethno-national nation-state, the state is to be seen principally as an instrument, the organizational framework within which the nation is to realize its potentialities. It is within the statal framework that governance, with its most important functions of securing welfare and security, is situated. The well-being and integrity of the state must, thus, be secured so that these functions may be attained. That is not a meagre value in itself. But to the extent that the state may claim, say, a loyalty which is more than pragmatic, it is because it is at the service of the nation with its values of belongingness and originality. (This conceptualization underscores, perhaps exaggerates, the difference with the American truly radical alternative liberal project of the non-ethno-national polity, and of a state, the Republic, the organization of which, and the norms of citizenship behaviour within, were central to its value system.)

It is evident, however, that in the European project, boundaries become a very central feature of the nation-state. There are, obviously, boundaries in the legal-geographical sense of separating one nation-state from another. But there are also internal, cognitive boundaries by which society (the nation) and individuals come to think of themselves in the world.

At a societal level, nationhood involves the drawing of boundaries by which the nation will be defined and separated from others. The categories of boundary-drawing are myriad: linguistic, ethnic, geographic, religious etc. The *drawing* of the boundaries is exactly that: a constitutive act, which decides that certain boundaries are meaningful both for the sense of belonging and for the original contribution of the nation. This constitutive element is particularly apparent at the moment of 'nation building' when histories are rewritten, languages revived etc. Of course, with time, the boundaries, especially the non-geographical ones, write themselves on collective and individual consciousness with such intensity that they appear as natural – consider the virtual interchangeability of the word international with universal and global. It is hard not to think, in the social sphere, of the world as a whole without the category of nation (as in international).

Finally, at an individual level, belonging implies a boundary: you belong because others do not.

As evident as the notion of boundaries is to the nation-state enterprise, so is the high potential for abuse of boundaries. The abuse may take place in relation to the three principal boundaries: the external boundary of the state; the boundary between nation and state; and the internal consciousness boundary of those making up the nation.

The most egregious form of abuse of the external boundary of the state would be physical or other forms of aggression towards other states.

The abuse of the boundary between nation and state is most egregious when the state comes to be seen not as instrumental for individuals and society to realize their potentials but as an end in itself. Less egregiously, the state might induce a 'laziness' in the nation – banal statal symbols and instrumentalities becoming a substitute for truly original national expression. This may also have consequences for the sense of belongingness whereby the apparatus of the state becomes a substitute to a meaningful sense of belonging. An allegiance to the state can replace human affinity, empathy, loyalty and sense of shared fate with the people of the state.

There can be, too, an abuse of the internal boundary which defines belongingness. The most typical abuse here is to move from a boundary which defines a sense of belonging to one which induces a sense of superiority and a concomitant sense of condescension or contempt for the other. A sense of collective national identity implies an other. It should not imply an inferior other.

The manifestations of these abuses are a living part of the history of the European nation-state which are so well known as to obviate discussion. A central plank of the project of European integration may be seen, then, as an attempt to control the excesses of the modern nation-state in Europe, especially, but not only, its propensity to violent conflict and the inability of the international system to constrain that propensity. The European Community was to be an antidote to the negative features of the state and statal intercourse; its establishment in 1951 was seen as the beginning of a process that would bring about the elimination of these excesses.

Historically there have, as mentioned above, always been those two competing visions of European integration. While no one has seriously envisioned a Jacobin-type centralized Europe, it is clear that one vision, to which I have referred as the unity vision, the United States of Europe vision, has really posited as its ideal type, as its aspiration, a statal Europe, albeit of a federal kind. Tomorrow's Europe in this form would indeed constitute the final demise of member state nationalism replacing or placing the hitherto warring member states within a political union of federal governance.

It is easy to see some of the faults of this vision. It would be more than ironic if a polity set up as a means to counter the excesses of statism ended up coming round full circle and transforming itself into a (super) state. It would be equally ironic if the ethos which rejected the boundary abuse of the nation-state, gave birth to a polity with the same potential for abuse. The problem with this unity vision is that its very realization entails its negation.

The alternative vision, the one that historically has prevailed, is the supranational vision, the community vision. At one level aspirations here are both modest compared to the union model and reactionary: supranationalism, the notion of community rather than unity, is about affirming the values of the liberal nation-state by policing the boundaries against abuse. Another way of saying this would be that supranationalism aspires to keep the values of the nation-state pure and uncorrupted by the abuses I described above.

At another level, the supranational community project is far more ambitious than the unity one and far more radical. It is more ambitious since, unlike the unity project, which simply wishes to redraw the actual political boundaries of the polity within the existing nation-state conceptual framework, albeit federal, the supranational project seeks to redefine the very notion of boundaries of the state, between the nation and state, and within the nation itself. It is more radical since it involves more complex demands and greater constraints on the actors.

How, then, does supranationalism, expressed in the community project of European integration, affect the excesses of the nation-state, the abuse of boundaries discussed above? At the pure statal level supranationalism replaces the 'liberal' premise of international society with a community one. The classical model of international law is a replication at the international level of a liberal theory of the state. The state is implicitly treated as the analogue, on the international level, to the individual within a domestic situation. In this conception, international legal notions such as self-determination, sovereignty, independence, and consent have their obvious analogy in theories of the individual within the state. In the supranational vision, the community as a transnational regime will not simply be a neutral arena in which states will seek to pursue the national interest and maximize their benefits, but will create a tension between the state and the community of states. Crucially, the community idea is not meant to eliminate the national state but to create a regime which seeks to tame the national interest with a new discipline. The challenge is to control at societal level the uncontrolled reflexes of national interest in the international sphere.

Turning to the boundary between nation and state, supranationalism is meant to prevent abuses here, too. The supranational project recognizes that at an intergroup level nationalism is an expression of cultural (political and/or other) specificity underscoring differentiation, the uniqueness of a group as positioned *vis-à-vis* other groups, calling for respect and justifying the maintenance of intergroup boundaries. At an intra-group level nationalism is an expression of cultural (political and/or other) specificity underscoring commonality, the 'sharedness' of the group *vis-à-vis* itself, calling for loyalty and justifying elimination of intra-group boundaries.

But, crucially, nationality is not the thing itself – it is its expression, an artefact.

It is a highly stylized artefact, with an entire apparatus of norms and habits; above all it is not a spontaneous expression of that which it signifies but a code of what it is meant to give expression to, frequently even translated into legal constructs. Nationality is inextricably linked to citizenship, citizenship not simply as the code for group identity, but also as a package of legal rights and duties, and of social attitudes.

Supranationalism does not seek to negate as such the interplay of differentiation and commonality, of inclusion and exclusion and their potential value. But it is a challenge to the codified expressions in nationality. Since, in the supranational construct with its free movement provisions, which do not allow exclusion through statal means of other national cultural influences and with its strict prohibition on nationality–citizenship-based discrimination, national differentiation cannot rest so easily on the artificial boundaries provided by the state. At inter-group level, then, it pushes for cultural differences to express themselves in their authentic, spontaneous form, rather than the codified statal legal forms. At the intra-group level it attempts to strip the false consciousness which nationalism may create instead of belongingness derived from a non-formal sense of sharedness. This, perhaps, is the first Kantian strand in this conceptualization of supranationalism. Kantian moral philosophy grounds morality and moral obligation on the ability of humans not simply to follow ethical norms, but, as rational creatures to determine for themselves the laws of their own acting and to act out of internal choice according to these norms. Supranationalism on our view favours national culture when, indeed, it is authentic, internalized, a true part of identity.

Supranationalism at the societal and individual, rather than the statal level, embodies, then, an ideal which diminishes the importance of the statal aspects of nationality – probably the most powerful contemporary expression of groupness – as the principal referent for transnational human intercourse. That is the value side of non-discrimination on grounds of nationality, of free movement provisions and the like. Hermann Cohen, the great neo-Kantian, in his *Religion der Vernunft aus den Quellen des Judentums*, tries to explain the meaning of the Mosaic law which call for non-oppression of the stranger. In his vision, the alien is to be protected, not because he was a member of one's family, clan, religious community or people, but because he was a human being. In the alien, therefore, man discovered the idea of humanity.

We see through this exquisite exegesis that in the curtailment of the totalistic claim of the nation-state and the reduction of nationality as the principle referent for human intercourse, the community ideal of supranationalism is evocative of, and resonates with, Enlightenment ideas, with the privileging of the individual, with a different aspect of liberalism which has as its progeny today in liberal notions of human rights. In this respect the community ideal is heir to Enlightenment liberalism. Supranationalism assumes a new, additional meaning which refers not to the relations among nations but to the ability of the individual to rise above his or her national closet.

Between state citizenship and union membership

What, must now be asked, is the nature of membership in such a construct of Community and member states? Does that construct have a demos? Can it have a demos? How is it possible, it may be asked by those to whom *Volk* is the demos, and this demos is the basis for legitimate authority in a statal structure, other than in a formalistic and semantic sense to decouple peoplehood from citizenship? Do not *Volk* and nationality with their ethno-cultural grounding create in the individual member a sense of closeness, in the national community a sense of social cohesion, which are both necessary for the sense of duty and loyalty which are and should be conditions for citizenship?

There may be strength in this argument. The critique of it is not that it is necessarily wrong, but that it is a world view which may be seen as more or less attractive. It is certainly far from compelling.

At the level of the state, the reasons for being suspicious of this view include: first, the impoverished view of the individual and human dignity involved in the *Volk*-state-citizenship equation. Is it really not possible for an individual to have very strong and deep cultural, religious and ethnic affiliations which differ from the dominant ethno-cultural group in a country, and yet in truth accept full rights and duties of citizenship and acquit oneself honourably? And to look at the other, societal, side of this coin: is it necessary for the state to make such a deep claim on the soul of the individual, reminiscent of the days when Christianity was a condition for full membership of civic society and full citizenship rights – including the right to have citizenship duties?

Note, too, that the view that would decouple *Volk* from demos and demos from state, in whole or in part, does not require a denigration of the virtues of nationality – the belongingness, the social cohesion the cultural and human richness which may be found in exploring and developing the national ethos. It simply questions whether nationality, in this ethno-cultural sense must be the exclusive condition of full political and civic membership of the polity. Let us not mince our words: to reject this construct as impossible and/or undesirable is to adopt a world view which informs ethnic cleansing, though I am not suggesting, of course, that the German Court and its judges feel anything but abhorrence to that particular solution.

Be all this as it may at the level of state and nation, the conflating of *Volk* with demos and demos with state, is clearly unnecessary as a model for Europe. In fact such a model would deflect Europe from its supranational civilizing telos and ethos. There is no reason for the European demos to be defined in terms identical to the demos of its member states or vice versa.

Consider the Maastricht citizenship provisions, which, under Article 8, declare: 'Citizenship of the Union is hereby established. Every person holding the nationality of a Member State shall be a citizen of the Union.' The introduction of citizenship to the conceptual world of the Union could be seen as just another step in the drive towards a statal, unity vision of Europe, especially if citizenship is understood as being premised on statehood.

But there is another more radical way of understanding the provision, namely as the very conceptual decoupling of nationality–*Volk* from citizenship and as the conception of a polity, the demos of which, its membership, is understood in civic rather than ethno-cultural terms. On this view, the Union belongs to, is composed of, citizens who by definition do not share the same nationality. The substance of membership (and thus of the demos) is in a commitment to the shared values of the Union as expressed in its constituent documents, a commitment to the duties and rights of a civic society covering discrete areas of public life, a commitment to membership in a polity which privileges exactly the opposites of classic ethno-nationalism – those human features which transcend the differences of organic ethno-culturalism. What is special in this concept is that it invites individuals to see themselves as belonging simultaneously to two demoi, albeit based on different subjective factors of identification. I am, say, a German national in the in far-reaching sense of ethno-cultural identification and sense of belongingness. I am simultaneously a European citizen in terms of my European transnational affinities to shared values which transcend the ethno-national diversity. So much so, that in a range of areas of public life, I am willing to accept the legitimacy and authority of decisions adopted by my fellow European citizens in the realization that in these areas we have given preference to choices made by my out-reaching demos, rather than by my in-reaching demos.

The Treaties on this reading would have to be seen not only as an agreement among states (a Union of States) but as a 'social contract' among the nationals of those states – ratified in accordance with the constitutional requirements in all member states – that they will in the areas covered by the Treaty regard themselves as associating as citizens in this civic society. This would be fully consistent with, say, Habermas's notion of Constitutional Patriotism. But we can go even further. In this polity, and to this demos, one cardinal value is precisely that there will not be a drive towards, or an acceptance of, an overarching ethno-cultural national identity displacing those of the member states. Nationals of the member states are European citizens, not the other way around. Europe is 'not yet' a demos in the ethno-cultural sense and should never become one.

One should not get carried away with this construct. Note first that the Maastricht formula does not imply a full decoupling: member states are free to define their own conditions of membership and these may continue to be defined in *Volk*ish terms. (But then we know that the conditions of nationality and citizenship differ quite markedly from one member state to another.) Moreover, the gateway to European citizenship passes through member state nationality. More critically, even this construct of the European demos, like the *Volk*ish construct, depends on a shift of consciousness. Individuals must think of themselves in this way before such a demos could have full legitimate democratic authority. The key for a shift in political boundaries is the sense of feeling that the boundaries surround one's own polity. That is not to claim that this shift has already occurred or make any claims about the translation of this vision into institutional and constitutional arrangements. I am, however, claiming the following: (a) we don't know about public consciousness of a civic polity-based demos because the question has to be framed in this way in order to get a meaningful response; (b) this shift will not happen if one insists that the only way to understand demos is in *Volk*ish ways; (c) that this understanding of demos makes the need for democratization of Europe even more pressing. A demos which coheres around values must live those values.

There is one final issue which touches, perhaps, the deepest stratum of the 'no-demos' thesis. It is one thing to say, as Maastricht does, that nationals of member states are citizens of the Union. But are not those nationals also citizens of their member state? Even if one accepts that one can decouple citizenship and nationality and that one can imagine a demos based on citizenship rather than on nationality, can one be a citizen of both polities? Can one be a member of not one but also a second demos? We have already noted the great aversion of this strand of German constitutionalism to multiple citizenship.

And yet it is a fairly widespread practice of states to allow double or even multiple citizenship with relative equanimity. For the most part, as a matter of civic duties and rights this does not create many problems. This is so also in the Community. It is true that in time of war, say, the holder of multiple citizenship may be in an untenable situation. But cannot even the EU create a construct which assumes that war among its constituent member states is not only materially impossible but unthinkable? The sentiment against multiple citizenship is not, I think, rooted in practical considerations.

Instead, at a deeper level, the issue of double citizenship evokes the spectre of double loyalty. The view which denies the status of demos to Europe may derive thus from a resistance to the idea of double loyalty. The resistance to double loyalty could be rooted in the fear that some flattened non-descript unauthentic and artificial 'Euro-culture' would come to replace the deep, well-articulated, authentic and genuine national version of the same. It could also be rooted in the belief that double loyalty must mean that either one or both loyalties have to be compromised.

On the first point, I do not believe that any of the European ethno-cultural identities is so weak or fragile as to be risked by the spectre of a simultaneous civic loyalty to Europe. I have already argued that the opposite is also likely. Unable to rest on the formal structures of the state, national culture and identity has to find truly authentic expressions to enlist loyalty which can bring about real internally found generation. What is more, the existential condition of fractured self, of living in two or more worlds can result not in a flattening of one's cultural achievement but in its sharpening and deepening. Can anyone who has read Heine, or Kafka, or Canetti doubt this? (It might in fact be threatened far more by the simple economic Europe of the single market and the like. One cannot overestimate the profound impact of the market on low and high culture.)

But what about the political aversion to double loyalty? This, paradoxically, is most problematic especially in a polity which cherishes ethno-cultural homogeneity as a condition of membership. It is hard to see why, other than for some mystical or truly 'blood thicker than water' rationale, a British citizen, say, who thinks of herself as British (and who forever will speak with an English accent) but who is settled in, say, Germany and wishes to assume all the duties and rights of German citizenship, could not be trusted in today's Europe loyally to do so? Moreover, we have already seen that European citizenship would have a very different meaning than German citizenship. The two identities would not be competing directly 'on the same turf'. It seems that the aversion to double loyalty, like the aversion to multiple citizenship itself, is not rooted primarily in practical considerations. It lies, I think, in a normative view which wants national self-identity to rest very deep in the soul, in a place which hitherto was occupied by religion. The imagery of this position is occasionally evocative of those sentiments. Religion, with greater legitimacy, occupies itself with these deeper recesses of the human spirit and, consequently makes these claims for exclusivity. The mixing of state loyalty and religion risks, in our view, idolatry from a religious perspective and can be highly dangerous from a political one. Historically, it seems as if *Volk* and *Staat* did indeed come to occupy these deepest parts of the human spirit to the point of being accepted *über alles* with terrifying consequences. Our view of the matter is not that the very idea of *Volk* and *Staat* was murderous nor even evil though, as is clear from this essay, my preference is for multiple loyalties, even demoi within the polity. It is the primordial position which *Volk* and *Staat* occupied, instilling uncritical citizenship which allowed evil, even murderous designs to be executed by dulling critical faculties, legitimating extreme positions, subduing transcendent human values and debasing one of the common strands of the three monotheistic religions that human beings, all of them, were created in the image of God.

How then do we achieve 'critical citizenship'? The European construct I have put forward, which allows for a European civic, value-driven demos co-existing side-by-side with a national ethno-cultural one (for those nation-states which want it), could be seen as a rather moderate contribution to this noble goal. Maybe in the realm of the political, the special virtue of contemporaneous membership in a national ethno-cultural demos and in a supranational civic, value-driven demos is in the effect which such double membership may have on taming the great appeal, even craving, for belonging in this world which nationalism continues to offer but which can so easily degenerate to intolerance and xenophobia. Maybe the national in-reaching ethno-cultural demos and the out-reaching supranational civic demos by continuously keeping each other in check offer a structured model of critical citizenship. Maybe we should celebrate, rather than reject with aversion, the politically fractured self and double identity which dual membership involves which can be seen as conditioning us not to consider any polity claiming our loyalty to be *über alles*. This understanding of the European demos could also constitute an understanding of its deepest telos.

THE ILLEGITIMACY OF THE DECISIONAL PROCESS IN THE UNION – THE DEFICIENCIES OF DEMOCRACY

As we have seen, the nexus between democracy and legitimacy is not without its problems. There are and have been regimes aplenty which have enjoyed high levels of social legitimacy while rejecting democracy. We want to believe that in the liberal West, democracy would be at least a necessary if not a sufficient condition for social legitimacy. (Sadly, the Union itself, might give lie to that hope.)

My claim here is that the nature of the democratic problem has been, in at least some respects, misconceived. Understanding the misconception will help (others) develop the remedies. Let us first acknowledge that the governance of Europe suffers from considerable democratic deficiencies. Here is a little summary of the traditional literature on the subject.

European integration has seen many, and increasingly important, government functions transferred to 'Brussels' and brought within the exclusive or concurrent responsibility of the Community and Union. This is problematic in a variety of ways.

Though the formal political boundaries of the State have remained intact, in the transferred areas the functional boundaries of the polity have been effectively re-drawn. If critical public policy choices about, say, international trade, or environmental protection, or immigration come exclusively or predominantly within Community responsibility, for those matters the locus of decision-making is no longer the state but the Union. Even if the Union were to replicate in its system of governance the very same institutional set-up found in its constituent states, there would be a diminution in the political weight and level of control of each individual within the redrawn political boundaries. That is, *arguendo*, an inevitable result from enlarging the membership of the functional polity (when a company issues new voting shares, the value of each share is reduced) and from adding a tier of government thereby distancing it further from its ultimate subjects in whose name and for whom democratic government is supposed to operate. This could be called 'inverted regionalism'; all the real and supposed virtues of regionalism are here inverted.

Inverted regionalism does not simply diminish democracy in the sense of individual disempowerment, it also fuels the separate and distinct phenomenon of delegitimation. Democracy and legitimacy are not co-terminus: polities with arguably democratic structures but shaky political legitimacy have been replaced, democratically, with dictatorships; polities with egregiously undemocratic governmental structures have, nonetheless, enjoyed or enjoy high levels of legitimacy. Inverted regionalism, to the extent that it diminishes democracy or to the extent that it is thought to have that effect, will, to a greater or lesser extent, undermine the legitimacy of the Union.

The perniciousness of inverted regionalism and its delegitimation effect are enhanced by three factors. First, the reach of the Community or Union into areas which are, or are thought to be, classical symbolic 'state' functions in relation to which 'foreigners' should not be telling 'us' how to run our lives. These areas, socially constructed and culturally bound, are not fixed but can range from the ridiculous (the British pint) to the sublime (the right-to-life of the Irish abortion saga). Second, the reach of the Community or Union into areas which are, or are thought to be, matters left to individuals or local communities and in relation to which 'government' should not be telling 'us' (the people) how to run their lives. Third, the perception, whether or not rooted in reality, that there is no effective limit and/or check on the ability of the Community or Union to reach into areas previously thought to be the preserve of the state or of the individual.

Inverted regionalism is only one feature of the alleged democratic malaise of European integration. The Union, of course, does not replicate domestic democratic arrangements. A feature of the democratic process within the member states, with many variations, is that government, the executive branch, is, at least formally, subject to parliamentary accountability. In particular, when policy requires legislation, parliamentary approval is needed. In addition, national parliaments fulfil a 'public forum' function described variously as information, communication, legitimation, etc. The argument is that Community and Union governance and Community institutions have a perverse effect on these principal democratic processes within the member states and within the Union itself.

Community and Union governance perverts the balance between the executive and legislative organs of the state. The executive branch, government ministers, are reconstituted in the Community as the principal legislative organ with, as noted above, an ever widening jurisdiction over increasing areas of public policy. The volume, complexity and timing of the Community decisional process makes national parliamentary control, especially in large member states, more an illusion than a reality. When decisions are taken by a majority vote, the power of national parliaments to affect outcomes in the Council of Ministers is further reduced. The EP does not offer an effective substitution. Even after Maastricht the powers of the EP in the legislative process leave formal and formidable gaps in parliamentary control. Union governance therefore results in a net empowerment of the executive branch of the states.

The EP is debilitated not only by its formal absence of certain powers but also by its structural remoteness. The technical ability of MEPs to link and represent actual constituents to the Community process is seriously compromised in the larger member states by simple reasons of size. Its abstract representation function of 'the people' – its public forum function – is also compromised, by a combination of its ineffective powers (the real decisions do not happen there), by its mode of operation (time and place), by its language 'problem', and by the difficulty (and disinterest) of media coverage. It is evocative that over the years one has seen a gradual increase in the formal powers of the EP and a decrease in the turnout to European elections. And when they turn out, these elections are dominated by a national political agenda, a mid-term signal to the national party in power. The non-emergence of true trans-European political parties is another expression

of the phenomenon. Critically, there is no real sense in which the European political process allows the electorate 'to throw the scoundrels out', to take what is
often the only ultimate power left to the people which is to replace one set of 'gov-
ernors' by another. In its present state, no one who votes in the European elections has much sense of affecting critical policy choices at the European level and
certainly not of confirming or rejecting European governance.

Community governance might have a distorting effect also if one takes a neo-corporatist view of the European polity, whereby the executive and legislative
branches of government do not monopolize policy-making but are actors, important actors, in a broader arena involving public and private parties. The importance of parliament under this model is to give voice and power to diffuse and
fragmented interests whose principal political clout derives from a combination of
their electoral power and the re-election drive of politicians. Other actors, such as
big industry or organized labour, whose 'membership' is far less diffuse and fragmented, exercise influence through different channels and by different means,
including political contributions, control of party organization, and direct lobbying of the administration. When policy areas are transferred to Europe there is
inevitably a weakening of the diffuse and fragmented national interests because of
the greater difficulty they experience in organizing themselves at the transnational
level compared to, say, a more compact body of large manufacturers (e.g. the
tobacco industry). In addition, the structural weakness of the EP has a corresponding effect on these interests even if organized. Electoral power simply carries less weight in Euro-politics.

Since the outcome of the Community legislative process becomes the supreme
law of the land, so national judicial control of primary legislation – in those systems which have such control (as in Italy or Germany) – is compromised. The
ECJ, like the EP, does not, *arguendo*, offer an effective substitution since, inevitably,
it is informed by different judicial sensibilities, in particular in relation to interpreting the limits of Community competences. Since the governments of the
member states are not only the most decisive legislative organ of the Community,
but also fulfil the most important executive function (they, much more than the
Commission, are responsible for the implementation and execution of
Community law and policy) they escape both national parliamentary (typically
weak) and national judicial (typically stronger) control of large chunks of their
administrative functions.

Domestic preferences are, arguably, perverted in a substantive sense, too. A
member state may elect a centre-right government and yet might be subject to
centre-left policies if centre-left governments dominate the Council. Conversely, a
majority of centre-left governments in the Council could find themselves thwarted
by a single centre-right government where the rules provide for unanimity. Both
in Council and in the EP the principle of proportional representation is compromised: enhanced voice is accorded to citizens of small states, notably

Luxembourg, and, arguably, inadequate voice accorded citizens of the larger states, notably Germany.

Last, a feature which is said to pervade all Community governance and negatively affect the democratic process, is its overall lack of transparency. This is not just a result of the added layer of governance and its increased remoteness. The process itself is notoriously prolix, extremely divergent when one moves from one policy area to another and in part kept secret. 'Comitology' is an apt neologism – a phenomenon which requires its very own science which no single person has mastered.

Such an account has been put forward countless times.

But consider two hidden assumptions in the description: first about the nature of the polity – the EU the democratic deficiencies of which we decry; and second about the kind of democracy we wish to have.

The nature of the polity

A description and analysis of European governance will depend today in large measure on the literature one chooses to study. Three approaches have become prominent – for convenience we may call them the international (intergovernmental), supranational and infranational. There is an inevitable correlation between the disciplinary background of the literatures and their respective focus on governance. The international approach, typified by the work of, say, Andrew Moravcsik, has its intellectual roots and sensibilities in international relations. The supranational approach, typified by the work of Weiler and others has its roots and sensibilities in public law and comparative constitutionalism. The infranational approach, typified by the work of Giandomenico Majone and his Florence associates, stems from a background in domestic policy studies and the regulatory state. This is not, however, a case of disciplinary entrenchment. All approaches are mindful of the need to weave together the political, and social, the legal and economic. Nor is it yet another simplistic instance of the proverbial 'blind men and the elephant'. The three approaches are aware of the others but choose to 'privilege' what, given the disciplinary background, seems most important to explain and understand in Union governance. More importantly the approaches, in our view, reflect a reality. In some crucial spheres Union governance is international; in other spheres it is supranational; in yet others it is infranational. How the SEA was negotiated is not simply an example of the IR approach; it is an example of the Community at a high international or intergovernmental moment. Instances of supranational decision-making would be the adoption of the big framework harmonization directives such as banking or video rental rights or, at a lover level, the Tobacco Labelling Directive and, no less interestingly, the rejection of the Tobacco Advertising Directive. The infranational approach is characterized by the relative *unimportance* of the national element in the decision-making. Technical expertise, economic and social interests, administrative turf

276

battles shape the process and outcome rather than 'national interest'. Infranational decision-making is typified by the miasma of, say, health and safety standard setting, telecommunications harmonization policy, international trade rules-of-origin.

Table 13.2 Internationalism, supranationalism and infranationalism – static (structural) elements

Arena	International	Supranational	Infranational
Disciplinary background of observers	International relations	Law (typically public law)	Policy studies; sociology
Typical issues of governance	Fundamental system rules; issues with immediate political and electoral resonance; international 'high politics'; issues *dehors* treaty	The primary legislative agenda of the community; enabling-legislation; principal harmonization measures	Implementing and executive measures; standard setting;
Principal players	Member states	Union/ Community and member states	[Union/ Community is policy-making context]
Principal actors	Governments (cabinets-executive branch)	Governments, community institutions: Commission, Council, Parliament	Second level organs of governance (Com. Directorate, Committee, Government departments etc.); certain corporate and social-industrial NGOs.
Level of institutionalization	Low to medium	High	Medium to low
Mode of political process	Diplomatic negotiation	Legislative process bargaining	Administrative process, 'networking'
Type/style of intercourse	Informal procedures; low level of process rules	Formal procedures; high level of process rules	Informal procedures; low level of process rules
Visibility/ transparency	High actor and event visibility; low transparency of process	Medium to low actor and event visibility and medium to low transparency of process	Low actor and event visibility and low transparency of process

It is not, then, that the observational standpoint and the sensibility of the observer defines the phenomenon. On our reading, certain objective aspects of the phenomenon attract the attention of different observers. There are three approaches but also three modes of governance. Likewise, it would be facile, based on the above examples, to conclude, *simpliciter*, that intergovernmental deals with 'important' issues, supranational with 'middle range' issues and infranational with trivia. The commonsensical wisdom of Parkinson may well apply in this area too: huge diplomatic effort may be invested in this or that provision of, say, the SEA; enormous resources may be invested in shepherding a harmonization measure through the ever more complex Commission–Council–Parliament procedures; and yet the reality of important aspects of the single market may have a lot more to do with the details of implementation, with the actual standards set by committees and the like.

For the international approach states are the key players and governments the principal actors. As a mode of governance, the Union, on this perspective, is seen as an inter-national arena or regime in which governments (primarily the executive branch) are the privileged power holders. The Union is principally a context, a framework within which states/governments interact. In the supranational approach states are privileged players but the Community/Union is not only or primarily a framework but a principal player as well. The privileged actors are state governments and Community institutions. State governments here is understood to include the main branches – legislative and judicial though not necessarily with equal weight. But here, too, the executive branch is the key state player. The Commission, Council and increasingly the EP, are critical actors and fora of decision-making. The infranational approach is distinct in that it downplays both the Community and the member states as principal players and likewise the role of primary state and Community institutions. It is like the international approach in that the Union is primarily a context, a framework within which actors interact. The actors, however, at both Union and member state levels tend to be administrations, departments, private and public associations, and certain, mainly corporate, interest groups.

In the international mode the focus is on negotiation, intergovernmental bargaining and diplomacy. There is a relatively low level of institutionalization and a premium on informal and unstructured interaction. Formal sovereign equality (including a formal veto) and the loose reflexes of international law prevail which, of course, should not be understood as leading to full equalization of power among the actors. The *materia* is often – though clearly not always – constitutional (in a non-technical sense). The *modus operandi* of the supranational mode is more structured, formal and rule bound. Bargaining and negotiation are far more akin to a domestic legislative process of coalition building, vote counting and rule manipulation. The *materia* is, frequently, primary legislation. Infranationalism is mostly about regulatory governance and management. There is a medium to low level of institutionalization and informal networking between 'government' and corporate players abound.

The international mode is characterized typically by high actor visibility and medium to low process visibility. Supranationalism is characterized by medium (aspiring to high!) actor visibility and medium to low process visibility. Infranationalism has both low actor and process visibility. See Table 13.2

The inter–supra–infra trichotomy enables us to build a better picture of the disbursement of power and accountability in the Union. Critical in building this picture is to understand not only the different modes of empowerment of, and desert to, various actors according to the mode of governance but also the fluidity and hence dynamics of allocation of issues to the different forms of decision-making. The stakes as to arena, *where* (in this scheme) issues get decided, is as important as *what* gets decided – since the where impacts, indeed determines the what. For lawyers, the ERTA decision or Opinion 1/76 was not about content but about forum and mode of decision-making: a bid by the Commission to transfer the treaty negotiation from the international to supranational arena. The Maastricht three-pillar structure is also about arena, and the various positions of the EP in the ongoing Community debate should be partly understood as bids about mode rather than content of policy-making. Since the SEA which saw the strengthening of both the legal framework of supranational decision-making and the relative empowerment of the Commission and Parliament, we have seen considerable political battles concerning fora rather than outcome. Comitology becomes a live issue in exactly the same period.

The static model already suggested 'inbuilt' empowerment of certain actors: state government in the international mode, state government and Community institutions in the supranational mode, administrations (national and Community) and certain corporate actors in the infranational mode. But this is only a starting point. Examine the three modes from the perspective of non-governmental public and private actors. Actors which have privileged access to national government (e.g. government or political parties) could have an interest in international decision making. An opposition party may, by contrast, prefer supranational decision-making, if the Community balance of power favours its position. A coalition of member states may opt for transfer (or maintenance) of an issue in the supranational arena where majorities have more weight and are more legitimate. A minority or individual member state may press for transfer to the international arena (such as France over the Blair House Agreement) where by definition the weight of each member state is higher.

Control and accountability are also critical variables in understanding the implication of the three modes. The international mode will favour domestic arenas of accountability (national parliaments, national press). The supranational mode suffers from all the defects which the standard version tends to highlight. Infranationalism has an all-round low level of accountability. By contrast, judicial review tends to be more substantive in the supranational arena, procedural in the infranational arena and scant in the international arena. When judicial review is perceived as a threat we may expect to find arena battles.

This section only hints at a research agenda; but it is suggestive of the need for a differentiated approach in understanding the democratic problems of European integration.

The nature of democracy

Whatever insight the study of the three arenas may eventually yield regarding the disbursement and accountability of power, it will not, in and of itself, point to 'democratic' deficiencies or solutions. One key problem is that democratic theory, and democratic sensibilities, have developed almost exclusively in statal contexts. One enterprise would be to fashion a tailor-made democratic theory for the Community. Here, however, let us use simply off-the-peg democratic wares, though bearing in mind that, as in the discussion of demos and of governance, one must handle the transferability of statal concepts to the European context with care. What is needed, perhaps, are different garments for the different arenas and modes of Union governance.

I shall only take a first step in this essay to explore possible 'fits' between various democratic models and Union modes of governance with a view to a better understanding of the problems of democratic governance in the Union.

International governance and the consociational model

Consociational theory emerged to fill a gap in traditional democratic theory. One of the principle tasks of democratic theory was to explain the functionality and stability of pluralistic democratic political systems, given that, by definition of pluralist democracy, such systems would be divided by competing political forces. The classical explanation given by democratic theory to this basic paradox of functional stability in a competitive pluralistic society was by reference to the notion of cross-cutting cleavages. Cross-cutting cleavages, for reasons which do not interest us here, have the effect of leading both to stability and functionality.

By contrast, when social cleavages reinforce each other (Catholic–Protestant; poor–rich; urban–agrarian etc.), when the social policy is deeply fragmented, society becomes conflict-laden which (while democracy is preserved) leads in turn to immobilism in policy-making and erosion of stability.

And yet, historically, several smaller countries in Europe – Holland, Austria, Switzerland, and Belgium up to a point – were socially 'cleavaged' in just that way and yet managed to display in certain periods the functionality and stability of the centripetal explanation until the 1960s (Daalder, a Dutchman, and one of the fathers of consociational theory, recalls how he was told by a leading political scientist: 'you know, your country theoretically cannot exist'). Consociational theory tries to explain the functionality and stability of these countries. Its basic explanatory device has been the behaviour of political élites which control/lead the fragmented social segments.

Crucial to consociational theory is the existence of sharply segmented societal sectors. Consociational theory is not interested in the reasons for segmentation (the content of the cleavages), but in their empirical existence. At this level, then, the model seems to correspond to the international dimension of Union governance: a transnational polity sharply segmented by its member states and, indeed, displaying the expected characteristics of immobilism – and yet somehow creating structures which manage to transcend these immobilistic tendencies.

Of course, the very creation of structures and institutions for the international mode, like the two non-Community Maastricht pillars, like the European Council, may be said to indicate a higher level of commonality than that to which consociationalism is designed to respond. The commonality is in the desire to have a common policy but substantive policy fragmentation is acute in relation to several of the contexts in which the international mode operates. Indeed, the very lack of substantive commonality is what pushed the member states to insist on this form of governance in this area.

The essential characteristic of consociational democracy is not so much any particular institutional arrangement as the deliberate joint effort by the élites to render the system functional and stable. The key element is what Dahrendorf has termed a cartel of élites. Consociational theorists seek to show how in all successful consociational democracies, normal traditional political fora were bypassed, and substituted by fora in which the leaders of all social segments participated, and compacts were arrived at, disregarding the principle of majority rule and using instead consensual politics. Competitive features are removed and cooperation sought. Worth noting is that the alternative fora might in themselves become institutionalized and rather formal. Typically consociationalism works on the basis of consensus, package deals and other features characteristic of élite bargaining. The élites, representing their respective segments, realize that the game is not zero sum nor is it a winner take all.

The two basic requirements for success according to consociational theory would be that élites share a commitment to the maintenance of the system and to the improvement of its cohesion, functionality and stability; and that élites understand the perils of political fragmentation. Élites must also be able to 'deliver' their constituents (and compliance) to deals thus struck. This, of course, begs some questions. In traditional consociational theory this commitment will come out of the loyalty of élites to their country and society. Our claim is that the formal extension in Maastricht of Union governance to areas hitherto dealt with informally or, at best, within European Political Cooperation, demonstrates a degree of commitment to the European polity which, however, is not matched by sufficient degree of trust in supranational governance – hence consociationalism as a model.

But consociational theorists suggest it is possible in addition to identify several further features which will be conducive to the success of consociationalism. These include the length of time a consociational democracy has been in operation; the existence of external threats to the polity; the existence of a multiple balance of power; a relatively low total load on the decision-making apparatus. All these features are characteristic of the Union international mode of governance, too.

Beyond the behaviour of the élites themselves, consociational theory stipulates two further conditions for successful functioning: the élites must be able to carry their own segments along; and there should be widespread approval of the principle of government by élite cartel.

In looking at past practice there do seem to be several points of contact between the consociational model and the international practice of the Union. There is the existence of a structure composed of highly sharp segments (the member states) which display a tendency to immobilism (which classical theory would predict) but which manages, nonetheless, to score a measure of functionality and stability (which consociational theory tries to explain). The key factor of consociationalism élite behaviour (in our case governments), also seems confirmed in the international mode.

The pay-off of consociationalism seems to be the achievement of stability in the face of high degree of social fragmentation which normal pluralist models cannot achieve. There are, naturally, implications for self-understanding of democracy in the polity. The democratic justification of consociationalism begins from the acceptance of deep and permanent fragmentation in the polity. Even in traditional constitutional pluralist democracies there is an acceptance that certain 'high stake' decisions, such as constitutional amendments, require 'super majorities' or other mechanisms which would be more inclusive of minorities. Consociationalism rejects the democratic legitimacy of permanent minorityship which is possible, even likely, for a fragmented polity operating a pluralist, majoritarian election and voting system. Consociationalism seems, thus, to enhance legitimacy in its inclusiveness and the broadening of ultimate consent to government. Theoretically, there is a strong case to be made for a consociational type of inclusiveness also in relation to at least certain areas of Union governance. If the international mode is, in fact, consociational, this would be a justification not from an efficiency and stability perspective but from a normative representational one as well.

The democratic problems of consociationalism and hence of the Union when operating in the international mode are no less grave. First, the democratic gaze must shift to the constituent units of the consociational model – in this case to the member states. It will often be discovered that some élites, within the consociational cartel of élites, have very deficient internal democratic structures of control and accountability. Even a facile comparison among the structures of the various member states designed to control their governments is sufficient to illustrate this point. Even more troubling: consociationalism might actually act as a retardant to internal democratization because the 'external' context both empowers the representing élite (executive branch of government) and may even create a mobilizing ethos of, say, the 'national interest' which justifies sacrificing calls for transparency and accountability. These calls can be, and usually are, presented as 'weakening' the effective representation of the élite in the external context.

Secondly, consociational power-sharing is favourable to 'status' social forces, those whose élites participate in the cartel. It excludes social forces which are not so recognized. 'New' minorities are typically disfavoured by consociational regimes. The corollary of this in the Union would be 'new' minorities within the member states whose voices are not vindicated by the government and are those doubly disfavoured both at national and Union levels. Consociationalism can be seen as weakening true representative and responsive government.

Finally, consociational politics typically favour the social status quo and, while mediating the problems of deeply fragmented societies are also instrumental in maintaining those very fragments. This can be highly problematic for some conceptions of European integration. Given that the consociational fragments in this context are the member states themselves, the international mode understood in consociational terms is not only about ensuring the inclusion of all member state voices in certain critical areas. It is also about actually sustaining the member states and their governments and retarding the formation of transnational coalitions of interests that, in the areas of the international mode, would and could have no impact in a process privileging states and their governments.

Supranationalism, pluralism and competitive élitism

The supranational mode of governance is the closest to a state model and thus, paradoxically perhaps, less needs to be said about it. It can be analysed most profitably in our view either with insights from Weberian or Schumpeterian competitive élites model of democracy or, aspirationally at least, to a statal, federal version of pluralist democracy.

Infranationalism and the neo-corporatist model of governance and democracy

It is not our claim that infranationalism is the Union variety of neo-corporatism. But it does share some common features and hence the conjunction of both may help us identify some of the democratic problems with infranationalism. Classical neo-corporatism identified a privileging of government, industry and labour in an attempt to avoid a confrontational mode of governance and reach a politics of accommodation which would resolve economic problems in both periods of expansion and stagnation. The focus was on macroeconomic policy as defining the central public choices confronting the polity. Neo-corporatism was a technocratic view which believed in management, distrusted markets to some extent, and favoured stability and predictability. It is not surprising that its political instincts also favoured governance through negotiation with highly organized interests having representational monopoly. In some respects neo-corporatism is a technocratic version of consociationalism. Neo-corporatism does not replace parliament and other institutions and processes of pluralist democratic government, but simply side-steps them in reaching the fundamental public choices of the polity. Inevitably there is an erosion in the substantive power and status of parliamentary bodies parties and the like. Pre-Second World War corporatism was aimed at undermining those aspects of pluralist democracy in the name of efficiency and stability. Its post-war version did not have that objective but had some similar institutional frameworks.

The infranational arena is no neo-corporatist model. Its reach extends well beyond macro-economic policy and the concerns of managing the business cycles which dominated politics of the 1960s and 1970s. It is decidedly not a tripartite relationship between government, business and labour. But it has some evocatively similar features: (i) the underlying ethos of infranationalism is managerial and technocratic; the belief that a rational management and regulatory solutions can be found by an employment of technocratic expertise; (ii) there is an underlying premise which puts a premium on stability and growth and is suspicious of strongly re-distributive policies and, more generally, on ideology and 'politics'; (iii) infranationalism has a strong push toward representational monopolies and the creation of structures which will channel organized functional interests into the policy-making and management procedures (CEN, CENLEC and the like); (iv) infranationalism, because of its managerial, functional and technocratic bias operates outside parliamentary channels, outside party politics. There is nothing sinister or conspiratorial in infranationalism, but its processes typically lack transparency and may have low procedural and legal guarantees. It seeks its legitimation in results rather than process.

As we would expect, in some respects infranationalism overcomes some of the problems of the international mode. It is both an expression of, and instrumental in, the decline of the state and its main organs as the principal vehicle for vindicating interest in the European polity. Infranationalism is about transnational interest groups, governance without (state) government, empowerment beyond national boundaries and the like. But it suffers too from many of the problems of neo-corporatism and some problems of its own, in particular the following: (a) the technocratic and managerial solutions often mask ideological choices which are not debated and subject to public scrutiny beyond the immediate interests related to the regulatory or management area; (b) participation in the process is limited to those privileged by the process; fragmented and diffuse interests, other public voices are often excluded; (c) as in the consociational model, the process itself might distort power relationships and democracy within the groups represented in the process; (d) the process itself not only lacks transparency but is also typically of low procedural formality and does not therefore ensure the real equality of voice of those who actually take part in the process. Judicial review is scant and tends to insist on basic rights to be heard rather than fairness of outcome; (e) in general, the classical instruments of control and public accountability are ill-suited to the practices of infranationalism. They are little affected by elections, change in government and the new instruments introduced by, say, Maastricht.

A resolution of the democratic deficiencies of the Union will depend, in part, on an acceptance of its polycentric decision-making structure as well as on an understanding of the different modalities of democratic governance and their fit with the specificities of EU.

NOTES

1. I have preserved the free style of an essay and have thus avoided footnotes and references as far as possible. The bibliography acknowledges the numerous intellectual debts I owe in the writing of this essay.
2. I have tried to answer this question in 'Journey to an Unknown Destination: a

Retrospective and Prospective of the European Court of Justice in the Arena of Political Integration', *Journal of Common Market Studies*, vol. 31, no. 4, 1993.
3. I attempted to explore the aspect of legitimacy/illegitimacy in 'Parlement européen, intégration européene, démocratie et légitimité' in Louis & Waelbrook 1988.
4. SN 520/95 (Reflex 21) 5 December 1995 at pp. 1 *et passim*.

REFERENCES AND BIBLIOGRAPHY

On legitimacy in general

Connolly, W. (1984) *Legitimacy and the State*. New York, New York University Press.
Franck, T. (1990) *The Power of Legitimacy Among Nations*. Oxford, Oxford University Press.
Habermas, J. (1975) *Legitimation Crisis*. Cambridge, Polity.
Hyde, A. (1983) 'The Concept of Legitimation in the Sociology of Law', *Wisconsin Law Review*, no. 2, pp. 379–426.
McAuslan, P. and McEldowney, J. F. (eds) (1985) *Law, Legitimacy and the Constitution*. London, Sweet and Maxwell.
Weatherford, M.S. (1992) 'Measuring Political Legitimacy', *American Political Science Review*, vol. 86, no. 1, pp. 149–66.
Weber, M. (1979) *Economy and Society: An Outline of Interpretive Sociology*, edited by Roth G. and Wittich, C.W., Berkeley, University of California Press.

On legitimacy and democracy in the context of European integration

Lodge, J. (1994) 'Transparency and Democratic Legitimacy', *Journal of Common Market Studies*, vol. 32, no. 3, pp. 343–68.
Katz, R.S. *The Problem of Legitimacy in the European Community*. Mimeo, On file at the European University Institute.
Neunreither, K-H. (1994) 'The Democracy Deficit of the European Union', *Government and Opposition*, vol. 29, no. 3, pp. 299–314.
Telò, M. (ed.) (1995) *Démocratie et construction européenne*. Bruxelles, Bruylant.

Additional sources are cited in Weiler, J.H.H. (1988) 'Parlement européen, intégration européenne, démocratie et légitimité', in Louis, J-V. and Waelbroek D. (eds) *Le Parlement Européen dans l'évolution instituionelle*. Brussels, Etudes Européenes.

On European constitutionalism, its actors and its evolution

Curtin, D. (1993) 'The Constitutional Structure of the European Union: A Europe of Bits and Pieces', *Common Market Law Review*, vol. 30, no. 1, pp. 17–69.
Dehousse, R. (1994) 'Community Competences: Are There Limits to Growth?', in Denhousse, R. (ed.) *Europe After Maastricht – An Ever Closer Union?* Munich, Law Books in Europe.
Kramer, L. and Weiler, J.H.H. (1994) 'Theorie and Praxis des amerikanischen Föderalismus: Vorbild oder Kontrastmodell für Europa?', in Schneider, H. and Wessels, W. (eds) *Föderale Union: Europas Zukunft?*, Munich, Beck.
Lenarts, R. (1990) ' Constitutionalism and the many faces of federalism', *American Journal*

of Comparative Law, vol. 38, no. 2, pp. 595–614.

Mancini, G.F. (1989) 'The Making of a Constitution for Europe', *Common Market Law Review*, vol. 26, no. 4, pp. 239–78.

Rasmussen, H. (1986) *On Law and Policy in the European Court of Justice*. Dordrecht, Nijhoff.

Scharpf, F.W. (1988) 'The Joint-Decision Trap: Lessons From German Federalism and European Integration', *Public Administration*, vol. 66, no. 3, pp. 239–78.

Additional sources are cited in Weiler, J.H.H, (1991) 'The Transformation of Europe', *Yale Law Journal*, vol. 100, no. 8, pp. 2403–83.

On demos and national / European identity

Böckenförde, E-W. (1995) 'Die Nation: Identität in Differenz', *Politische Wissenschaft*. 974.

Bogdandy, A. von (ed.) (1993) *Die Europäische Option*. Baden-Baden, Nomos.

Habermas, J. (1990) *Staatsbürgerschaft und nationale Identität*, in (1992) *Faktizität und Geltung. Beiträge zur Diskurstheorie des Rechts und des demokratischen Rechtsstaats.* Frankfurt am Main, Suhrkamp.

Meehan, E. (1993) *Citizenship and the European Community*. London, Sage.

Soledad, G. (ed.) (1993) *European Identity and the Search for Legitimacy.* London, Pinter.

Weiler, J.H.H. (1993) 'Europe After Maastricht – Do the New Clothes Have an Emperor?', in *Democratic and Legal Problems in the European Community*, IUSSEF No. 12.

Additional sources are to be found in Weiler, J.H.H, (1995) 'The State "über alles": Demos, Telos, and the German Maastricht Decision', in Due, O. *et al.* (eds) *Festschrift für Ulrich Everling*.

On modes of democratic governance in the Union

See sources cited in Weiler, J.H.H, Haltern, U.R, and Mayer, F.C, (1995) 'European Democracy and Its Critique', *West European Politics*, vol. 18, no. 3, pp. 4–39.

Infranationalism

Dehousse, R., Joerges, C., Majone, G. and Snyder, F., (1992) *Europe After 1992: New Regulatory Strategies*, EUI Working Paper, Law No. 92/31.

Majone, G. (1993) *The European Community: An 'Independent Fourth Branch of Government?'* EUI Working Paper SPS No. 93/9.

—— (1989) 'Regulating Europe: Problems and Prospects', in Ellwein, T. *et al.* (eds) *Jahrbuch zur Staats-und Verwaltungswissenschaft.*

—— (1994) *Understanding Regulatory Growth in the EC*, EUI Working Paper SPS No. 94/17.

Intergovernmentalism

Moravcsik, A. (1991) 'Negotiating the Single European Act', in Keohane, R.O. and Hoffmann, S. (eds) *The New European Community: Decisionmaking and Institutional Change.* Boulder Colorado, Westview.

—— (1994) 'Preference and Power in the European Community: A Liberal Intergovernmentalist Approach', in Bulmer, S. and Scott, A. (eds) *Economic and Political Integration in Europe: Internal Dynamics and Global Context.* Oxford, Blackwell.

— (1994) *Why the European Community Strengthens the State: Domestic Politics and International Cooperation*, Harvard University CES Working Paper Series No. 52.

Putnam, R.D. (1988) 'Diplomacy and Domestic Politics: The Login of Two-Level Games', *International Organization*, vol. 42, no. 3, pp. 427–60.

Supranationalism

Weiler, J.H.H. (1985) *Il Sistema Comunitario Europeo*. Bologna, Il Molino.

For additional sources on supranationalism see Weiler, J.H.H, (1991) 'The Transformation of Europe', *Yale Law Journal*, vol. 100, no. 8, pp. 2403–83.

On models of democracy

Dahl, R. (1989) *Democracy and Its Critics*. New Haven, Yale University Press.

Held, D. (1987) *Models of Democracy*. Cambridge, Polity

March, J.G. and Olson, J.P. (1995) *Democratic Governance*, NY, Free Press.

Putnam, R.D. (1993) *Making Democracy Work*. Princeton, Princeton University Press.

On new institutional thinking of the Union

Bulmer, S. J. (1994) 'The Governance of the European Union: A New Institutionalist Approach', *Journal of Public Policy*, vol. 13.

—— (1994) 'Institutions and Policy Change in the European Communities: The Case of Merger Control', *Public Administration*, vol. 72, no. 3, pp. 432–44.

14

THE IGC AND INSTITUTIONAL REFORM OF THE UNION

BRIGID LAFFAN

INTRODUCTION

The importance of institutions to the European project is undeniable. Debate about the political and economic reach of the Union is always bound up with questions of how it should go about its business. Although the Union operates on the basis of a 'federal principle', the EU cannot be equated to any existing federation at this stage of its development. Because the goal of integration is heavily contested and different visions of the European project abound, there is no accepted model for the governance of the Union nor any agreement of what kind of polity is emerging or should emerge from the iterative process of constitution building. Institutional integration in the Union is characterized by the creation of a novel set of common institutions and the enmeshing of national and European levels of governance. Monnet identified the centrality of institutions when writing his memoirs in the following terms: 'nothing is possible without men; nothing is lasting without institutions' (Monnet 1978: 304).

The centrality of institutions in structuring political life is receiving increased attention in political science (March and Olsen 1989). What is called the 'new institutionalism' rests on the premise that a polity is 'constituted by its basic institutions-shared practices, rules, moral and causal ideas and meanings, and distributions of resources' (Olsen 1995: 8). Institutions provide order and continuity but also have an inherent dynamic element. Change in a political order flows from the interaction of and tensions between 'institutional practices, ordering principles and dynamics' (Olsen 1995: 9).

'Institutions matter' to the European project in a number of important ways. First, the Union's collective action and policy-making in its institutions bear the burden of creating a polity and 'ever closer union' among the peoples of Europe. Second, common institutions provide vital channels for collective action and law-making between the member states. Third, the intense pattern of transgovernmental interaction which characterizes EU governance is shaped and moulded by the unique context provided by EU institutions. The existence of EU institutions with a measure of autonomy from the constituent member states is critical if the Union is to represent something akin to a collective European interest. Common institutions reduce the transaction costs of cooperation, provide an information rich environment, structure channels of communication and in the long term shape the preferences pursued by national governments and their agents. However, the existence and development of collective institutions disturbs the institutional patterns of once dominant nation-states. Hence the unstable nature of the EU governance and the continuing tension between the EU and the national levels of governance. The development of EU institutions, a multiplicity of Brussels-level policy networks and the mobilization of interests in transnational and transgovernmental patterns may transform, if not transcend, the nation-state as the key institution structuring political order in Europe. The debate on the future development of EU institutions, although technical and esoteric in nature, personifies nothing less than a struggle about the exercise of political authority and the structuring of political order in Europe.

The evolution of the Union's governance capacity and the role of individual institutions within those governance structures is moulded by formal constitutional development, relevant judgements of the European Court of Justice (ECJ), the interplay of inter-institutional relations and informal politics. Institution building in the Union has been largely pragmatic, incremental and *ad hoc* once the original blueprint was established in the European Coal and Steel Community (ECSC). That said, there have been significant developments in each of the major institutions and in relations between them. The purpose of this paper is to analyse institutional reform in the context of the 1996 Intergovernmental Conference (IGC). The first important point to make is that unlike the Single European Act (SEA) which was driven by the 1992 project and the Treaty on European Union (TEU) which was predicated on Economic and Monetary Union (EMU) and issues of political union, the 1996 IGC lacks the big policy imperative. This reform, unlike previous ones, is predominantly about questions of *constitutional design* and *institutional balance*. It is about the effectiveness and legitimacy of the Union's governance structures and their capacity to accommodate a continental enlargement. The imperatives are political rather than policy-driven. The Commission report to the Reflection Group identified two main challenges for the 1996 IGC: that the Union must act democratically, transparently and in a way people can understand; and that the Union must act effectively, consistently and in solidarity (European Commission 1995: Preamble).

The need to ensure that the Union's governance structures are both effective and democratic runs through all discussions of the European project. Effectiveness is influenced not just by formal constitutional rules but by the interplay of the national and European arenas of policy-making and inter-institutional relations at EU level. Paradoxically, integration demands more rather than less of national governments as they are intimately involved in all phases of the EU policy process, especially at the implementation stage (Metcalfe 1993). The administrative and political capacity of the member states which is very uneven matters a great deal to the effectiveness of EU policy. The quest for effective governance structures in the Union is highly problematic because of the scale of the Union and a membership of diverse states. The challenge within the Union is 'time and time again, to fashion structures and procedures of governance that

Table 14.1 Sources of the IGC agenda

TEU provisions
- The Pillar Structure of the Treaty: Article B of the Common Provisions
- Widening the scope of co-decision: Article 189b
- The defence policy provisions of article J4 re. WEU
- Other cooperation on CFSP: Article J4
- Hierarchy of Community acts: declaration 16 TEU

European Council at Corfu
- Weighting of votes
- Threshold for qualified majority decisions
- Number of members of the Commission and other measures deemed necessary to facilitate the work of the institutions and guarantee their effective operation in the perspective of enlargement

Inter-institutional agreement
- Council agreed to take part in a conference with the EP on the system of own resources in preparation for the 1996 IGC as part of the 1993 Interinstitutional Agreement on the budget.

facilitate the accommodation of European policy with contrasting national policies, institutions and practices' (Hooghe 1995).

Although the rhetoric of integration has a strong normative element, the workings of EU institutions have been predominantly technocratic, and deliberately so. Pascal Lamy, Jacques Delors' *chef de cabinet*, described the Monnet method as 'St Simonian', whereby 'the people weren't ready to agree to integration, so you had to get on without telling them too much about what was happening' (quoted in Ross 1994: 194). Integration would be justified on the basis of its contribution to securing economic prosperity. This accords with the Humean view of legitimacy which suggests that legitimacy is sired from habit out of successful performance (Weale 1994). While effectiveness is undoubtedly an important element in rendering institutions legitimate, the Lockean notion that legitimacy must be secured by the consent of the governed should not be forgotten (Weale 1994). It could be argued that given the politicization of European integration in the member states during the TEU ratification process and the strain of ratification in many national polities, the Lockean imperative of consent has more salience at this juncture in the integration process.

THE CONTEXT OF INSTITUTIONAL REFORM

The debate on institutional reform in the EU is moulded by the legacy of the TEU, the prospect of a continental enlargement of the Union and the balance between the representation of small and large states. The 1996 IGC is the fourth formal process of constitution building since 1985 – and only the sixth since 1950 – which highlights the intensity of treaty change in the Union since the relaunch of formal integration in 1985 (see table 14.1). The legacy of the TEU is threefold. First, a number of articles in the TEU explicitly made provision for a revision of

---

Box 14.1: Preparations for the Intergovernmental Conference

The Corfu European Council in June 1994 agreed to the establishment of a *'Reflection Group'* to prepare the work of the IGC. The member states were represented by a representative of the Foreign Minister. Two members of the EP participated. The Council invited the institutions to submit reports on the functioning to date of the TEU. The *Reflection Group* is asked to enter into a dialogue with all Union institutions and organs. The *Reflection Group* began its work under the Spanish Presidency during the latter half of 1995 and submitted its report to the Madrid European Council in December 1995.

The most important section of the Conclusions states that the:

> Reflection Group will examine and elaborate ideas relating to the provisions of the Treaty on European Union for which a revision is foreseen and other possible improvements in a spirit of democracy and openness, on the basis of the evaluation of the functioning of the Treaty as set out in the reports. It will also elaborate options in the perspective of the future enlargement of the Union on the institutional questions set out in the conclusions of the European Council in Brussels and in the Ioannina Agreement (weighting of votes, the threshold for qualified majority decisions, number of members of the Commission, and any other measure deemed necessary to facilitate the work of the Institutions and guarantee their effective operation in the perspective of enlargement. (CORFU European Council June 1994)

---

the Treaty in 1996. In other words, the unfinished business of the Maastricht negotiations must be revisited. In Article B of the Common Provisions dealing with the objectives of the Union, the member states agree to:

> maintain in full the *acquis communautaire* and build on it with a view to considering, through the procedure referred to in Article N(2), to what extent the policies and forms of co-operation introduced by this Treaty may need to be revised with the aim of ensuring the effectiveness [emphasis added] of the mechanisms and the institutions of the Community. (Article B, Common provisions, TEU – the procedure referred to in Article N is the convening of an IGC in 1996)

The second legacy of the TEU is that the starting point of the negotiations was to be an assessment of the operation of the TEU in practice. The Corfu European Council established a Reflection Group to prepare for the IGC during the latter half of 1995. The European Council requested each institution to prepare a report on the functioning of the TEU for the Reflection Group. Third, the ratification crisis of the TEU politicized the European project in the member states and alerted national parliaments to the Europeanization of governance in Europe. The crisis highlighted the weakness of democracy in the EU system and its remoteness from the mass publics (see Box 14.1).

The politicization of the European project and the intensity of constitution building in the Union over the last ten years has mobilized considerable interest in the process of constitution building in the Union. There have been a plethora of proposals on the future of the Union, some debating alternative visions of integration, others advocating detailed constitutional blueprints for the Union, yet others attempting to come to terms with the problem of stretching the West European model of integration eastwards. The proposals originate in research institutes, political parties, individual politicians, political advisers, national parliaments, interest groups, the EP and academic analyses. The battle about 'more Europe', 'less Europe' or 'whose Europe' is on. The debate has echoes of older debates between intergovernmentalists and integrationists about institution building in the Union. The tension between those who see the need to enhance the political authority of the Union by strengthening its capacity for collective action and those who wish to maintain the status quo or even retreat from the existing system is evident. A cursory reading of the German CDU–CSU paper (CDU–CSU Fraktion 1994) and the British prime minister' s speech in Leiden in September 1994 (Major 1994) illustrates just how far apart positions are on Europe' s political order.

Enlargement provides the external context for discussion of institutional reform. The decision to proceed with the EFTA enlargement on the basis of a mechanical adjustment to the existing institutional rules meant that critical issues arising from a larger Union were left to future consideration. The quest for effectiveness is highly problematic in a Union of 20 to 25 states. Continental enlargement brings with it difficult dilemmas about representation, the balance between large and small states, languages and the problem of overload.

The legacy of the TEU

The provisions of the TEU came into operation on 1 November 1993 and were thus in operation for a relatively short period before preparations began for the 1996 IGC, making it difficult to reach any definite conclusions about its major provisions. The Treaty itself was the outcome of considerable disagreement among the member states about constitutional matters. It was an attempt both to accelerate economic integration and to respond to the challenges of the 'New Europe'. Whereas the SEA was narrow and limited in focus, the TEU touched on

Table 14.2 Distribution of EP's legislative work by Procedure – 8

May 1995

Simple consultation	Cooperation	Assent	Co-decision
214	48	19	104

Source: Millar G, 'Post-Maastricht Legislative Procedures: Is the Council Institutionally Challenged?' Paper presented to ECSA Conference, Charleston, South Carolina, May 1995.

broader and more sensitive political terrain. The Treaty bears all of the signs of difficult and contentious negotiations among the member states. The TEU contains no clear-cut relationship between policy goals and institutional provisions. It increased the complexity of the Union's decision-making process and reinforced its segmented nature. This is reflected in the structure of the Treaty which introduced the pillar concept (Community pillar, Common Foreign and Security Policy (CFSP), Justice and Home Affairs (JHA)) that operate on the basis of different decision rules and institutional prerogatives. Although the Union was to be served by a single institutional framework (Article C, TEU), it has proved difficult to integrate the second and third pillars into the traditional Council machinery. The desire by some member states to insulate the intergovernmental pillars from the traditional Community method comes face-to-face with the problem of financing joint actions particularly in the second pillar and the determination of the EP to enhance its role in the pillar system. The continuing struggle about financing the second pillar actions added to the teething problems experienced with the CFSP.

The Commission, in its report to the Reflection Group was not unexpectedly critical of the pillar system which it defined as a structural weakness. It argued that the multiplicity of procedures detract from the effectiveness of decision-making, makes the Treaty difficult to understand and makes it unclear who is responsible for what (European Commission 1995). The Commission reserved its most critical comments for the activities of the second and third pillars, the latter being described as having serious inadequacies. Although the Council Report was more neutral in tone, it, too, acknowledged that the procedures in the second pillar were at an early stage and needed to be improved. The difficulty of integrating the traditional EPC machinery into the Council was acknowledged and the growing burden on the Presidency and troika identified. The problems in the third pillar were regarded as even more acute as there had been little attempt to use the new instruments provided for in the TEU (joint actions), there were difficult lines of demarcation between the EC and JHA provisions in a number of areas and the third pillar procedures had proved very cumbersome (European Commission 1995; Council of the EU 1995). Inter-institutional conflicts (particularly between the EP and the Council) are particularly acute on second and third pillar matters.

The TEU, by introducing the new co-decision procedure, provisions on EMU and the social policy opt out for the UK, added to the number of different decision-making procedures in the Union (see Table 14.2). Problems of transparency, accountability and effectiveness were clearly exacerbated by the myriad of decision rules. The Council's report to the Reflection Group lists eleven legislative procedures, two budgetary procedures, three procedures for international agreements, two procedures under Titles V and VI, three EMU procedures, and two procedures for the appointment of members of the EU institutions making 23 in all (Council 1995: Annex 5). The Commission report lists 22 decision-making procedures under the EC Treaty, four in the second pillar and three in the third pillar (European Commission 1995).

The provision on *co-decision* was one of the most novel elements of the TEU as it significantly reinforced the role of the EP in legislation. An EP official concluded that:

> co-decision is fundamentally different in nature from the co-operation procedures: it involves a common act of the Council and Parliament. Throughout the procedure leading to the adoption of the act, the two institutions are on an equal footing. (Miller 1995: 30)

Co-decision allows for a conciliation phase between the Council and the EP in cases where the Council does not accept the amendments made by the EP on its second reading. In addition, Article 189b provides for the possibility that the EP may ultimately reject the act passed by the Council. The operation of Article 189b necessitated the creation of a new inter-institutional organ the 'Conciliation Committee' consisting of fifteen representatives each of the Council and EP. Since the entry into force of the TEU, 136 acts for co-decision have entered the legislative process and 30 proposals have been completed (Millar 1995: 10). The Commission's Reflection Group Report concluded that: 'the new co-decision procedure has proved operational and effective, in conjunction with qualified majority voting in the Council. It contains the principle ingredients of a balanced legislative regime' (European Commission 1995). The Council report was more nuanced in its assessment of co-decision. Apart from identifying the start-up problems in the procedure it suggested that inter-institutional relationships were complicated by:

Table 14.3 Majority voting in the Council of Ministers

Policy area	Total acts adopted	Negative votes cast	Abstentions only
Agriculture	114	17	10
Fisheries	51	4	7
Internal market	50	11	6
Environment	9	4	1
Transport	8	-	3
Social affairs	3	-	2
Research	27	1	1
Education	4	-	1
European citizenship	2	-	1
Consumer protection	1	1	-
Transparency	2	2	-
Other	12	-	-
Total	283	40	32

Source: Council Report on the functioning of the TEU, April 1995.

- the links established by the EP between conciliation and other issues particularly comitology (as on the packaging waste directive or the motor bikes directive), and the financial aspects of proposed legislation;
- the inherent complexity of the Article 189b procedures;
- the relationship between the Conciliation Committee and the EP meeting in plenary (as in the rejection of the biotech directive after the conciliation procedure) (Council 1995).

The EP, for its part, wants to expand co-decision to most legislative acts so that its legislative role equals that of the Council. Paradoxically, the Conciliation Committee may exacerbate problems of transparency in the Union as it essentially involves negotiations between representatives of the Council and the Parliament. In other words, the Parliament is now engaged in the negotiating practices of the Council rather than the Council becoming exposed to the accountability of Parliament.

The TEU extension of qualified majority voting (QMV) in Council built on the experience of the SEA. The main purpose of weighted voting is to increase the efficiency and capacity of the decision-making process by counteracting the blocking potential of individual states. Consensus remains the procedural norm in the Council as there is an inbuilt desire to bring all delegations along. Between December 1993 and March 1995, votes were cast on 40 occasions and abstentions registered on 32 other occasions out of a total of 283 legislative acts. These figures tend to downplay the impact of majority voting on the efficiency of the Council. The prospect of a vote is often the spur for further compromise which would not be forthcoming without the pressure of a vote. That said unanimity is still required for 62 different articles or aspects of articles of the Treaty (see Table 14.3).

The TEU represents an unstable compromise between different institutional models of integration and highlights the fluidity of inter-institutional relations in the Union over the last decade. The Commission has had to cope with an expanding policy remit, the introduction of the principle of subsidiarity, public scepticism about integration and the growing complexity of EP–Council relations. The Council and its Presidency have been faced with a growing international agenda, the incorporation of other forms of cooperation into its machinery and the enhanced role of the EP. The EP for its part is seeking to further embed itself in the legislative process and to use all of its powers to alter the Council–EP balance. Consequently the Parliament establishes negotiating links between legislative and budgetary power and between comitology and agreement on individual texts. Policy-making in the Union has not settled down into stable and agreed routines since the TEU came into operation.

Table 14.4 Institutional matters to be addressed regarding enlargement

Council of Ministers
- Blanket extension of QMV?
- Votes per member state
- Threshold for a qualified majority
- Duration of the Presidency
- Rotation of the Presidency
- Working languages
- Co-ordination of the Council system/pillars

Commission
- Should all states be represented?
- Should role of the President be enhanced?
- Junior/senior Commissioners
- Languages

European Parliament
- Common electoral system
- Size and distribution of seats
- Relationship with the Commission
- Role in legislation

Court of Justice/Court of Auditors and other organs
- Representation and working methods

Enlargement

Enlargement is by definition a dynamic process which alters the Union's boundaries, disturbs the existing *acquis* and potentially its institutional balance. Enlargement alters the dynamic of representation in the EU system by bringing in additional voices, interests and problems. Moreover, the issues raised by future enlargements are qualitatively different to those of the past because of the nature of the challenges facing the former communist states and the continuing uncertainty about the capacity of the Union to manage forthcoming enlargements without undermining the Union itself. Without institutional adaptation the Union 'would begin to degenerate into a kind of Council of Europe type organization rather than a more cohesive, effective and integrated organization' (House of Lords 1992: point 68).

From the outset the Union adopted a highly differentiated approach to the states of the former Soviet bloc. It offered Europe Agreements and PHARE to potential member states and Cooperation Agreements and TACIS to those that are considered beyond the Union and not likely to be members. Notwithstanding extreme caution at the beginning, the Union has gradually accepted that it will have to enlarge to the East and South within a reasonable timeframe. The Copenhagen European Council agreed that: 'the associated countries in Central and Eastern Europe that so desire shall become members of the European Union' (European Council June 1993). Since then the Union has been working on an accession strategy for the applicant states which was further elaborated at Essen in December 1994. The Essen conclusions explicitly state that: 'the institutional conditions for ensuring the proper functioning of the Union must be created at the 1996 Intergovernmental Conference, which for that reason must take place before accession negotiations begin' (European Council December 1994; see Table 14.4). Enlargement challenges the capacity of the Union' s institutions by increasing the range and diversity of interests that have to be accommodated and by altering the size of individual institutions. Enlargement raises a set of difficult and complex issues largely to do with representation and the capacity of the institutions to act. The issue of representation is essentially a large state/small state issue and is thus dealt with separately.

Large and small states in the Union

The EU is a delicate balance between large and small states. So far, the Union has successfully managed to expand its membership without undermining this balance. The Union accommodates Germany, on the one hand, and its tiny neighbour Luxembourg, on the other. Only five of the existing fifteen member states have populations of over 15 million or 5 per cent of the population. Eight out of the ten countries of Central and Eastern Europe have populations of 10 million or less and five of them have 5 million or less. The pool of candidate countries consists in large measure of small or micro states as only Poland and Turkey have sizeable populations. Size has little bearing on national approaches to substantive policy issues and small states are not likely to band together against the 'large states' in negotiations; their interests just like those of the larger states diverge. The coalition pattern in the Council always consists of a mix of large and small states on particular policy issues. Small states do, however, have a combined interest in the institutional balance, the 'rules of the game' and their representation within the system. Small states tend to favour multilateral frameworks based on law and procedural correctness. The Dutch government argued in 1990 during its preparations for the TEU negotiations that:

> the interests of small countries are best served by international co-operation based on legal structures with open decision-making processes. Large countries, on the other hand, also pursue structured negotiations but endeavour to protect their interests mainly by exploiting their position of power. (Dutch White Paper on the 1990 IGC June 1990: 3).

Small states have a vested interest in protecting the autonomous sources of power in the Union' s institutional framework.

A fundamental principle of the Community, now Union, is the formal equality of the member states under the Treaties and the adjustment of this principle to take account of size, especially population. The principle of equality is evident in the presence of nationals of each member state in the Union's institutions, the rotating Presidency, and on matters requiring unanimity under the Treaties. The adjustment of this principle to the realities of power and size allow for weighted voting, additional representation in the Commission and the EP. The larger states accepted from the outset the principle that small states would have a disproportionate presence in the Union' s institutions. Thus small states have equal representation in the Council of Ministers, although not of voting power, equal membership of the Court of Justice, one Commissioner and disproportionate representation in the Parliament and the Union's other organs. The balance between formal equality in the Council coupled with additional voting power for the larger states is a common feature of federal systems which must balance territorial representation with population size. In federal systems, the smaller units tend to be over-represented in central institutions. It could be argued that small states must be compensated for their size as formal representation is more important to them than to larger states. However, the EFTA enlargement and the prospect of future enlargements has led the large states to look carefully at the institutional balance and the level of representation accorded to small states. They are fearful of the voting and blocking power of small states.

Institutional reform

COMPETENCES AND PROCEDURES

The three main issues affecting EU institutions relate to the assignment of power between the national and the EU levels of governance, the links between the three TEU pillars, and the simplification of decision-making procedures. The inclusion of the principle of subsidiarity in the TEU and its adoption as an operating principle by the institutions reflected the need to balance national and European competence given the expansion of the Union' s policy remit. Subsidiarity was a response to fears (largely British and Danish) of a centralizing, over-powerful Union, to the need to tackle the impact of integration on intergovernmental relations within states (especially German federalism) and to a perception that the Union should not exceed its reach in terms of effective policy integration. Despite serious misgivings the Commission has adopted subsidiarity as an operating norm. The debate on subsidiarity continues with demands for further clarification of shared competence. A clear listing of the respective competencies which was already proposed in the d'Estaing report to the EP in 1990 resurfaced as a *Kompetenzkatalog* in the Wedenfield proposals (EP 1990; Wiedenfeld *et al.* 1994). The Reflection Group was opposed to any catalogue of powers at this stage of the Union's development largely because the system is still developing. However, the representatives of some member states want to exercise more effective control over the application of the principle of subsidiarity by advocating political supervision by national parliaments or new procedures for appealing to the Court (Reflection Group 1995).

The pillar structure of the TEU is a major subject of debate and disagreement. The pillars do not just connote three different strands of policy cooperation but also involve variegated methods of decision-making. Decision-making in the Community pillar conforms to the traditional Community method whereas the second and third pillars are essentially intergovernmental in so far as the

Community's legal system has no remit and the roles of the Commission and the EP are restricted. The TEU did, however, bring these areas of cooperation closer to the traditional Community method, somewhat like a half-way house between intergovernmentalism and supranationalism (Luxembourg Presidency June 1991). The debate has increasingly concentrated on issues of clarity and simplicity with some governments and institutions arguing that the pillar system be abolished. Although this maximalist position is unlikely to predominate, the debate on the pillars will have to deal with difficult questions about links between the three arenas of activity and the need for greater coherence in the Union' s external profile. The operation of the TEU has already highlighted unresolved problems of financing the second and third pillar actions.

The third issue is the question of a hierarchy of Community norms or acts. The Commission raised this issue during the 1990 IGC and made substantive proposals involving an amendment of Article 189 which set out a number of different instruments of EC law. Although these proposals made no progress, a declaration annexed to the TEU called on the 1996 IGC: to examine to what extent it might be possible to review the classification of Community acts with a view to establishing an appropriate hierarchy between the different categories of act' (Declaration 16 TEU).

The main argument in favour of a hierarchy of norms is that at present all legislation is of the same order. The system requiring a Commission proposal and one or two readings by the Council and EP is used for such highly technical issues as the maximum level of noise for lawnmowers or the addition of a permitted food additive to the existing list. At national level these issues would fall within the realm of secondary or delegated legislation. A hierarchy of acts would distinguish between constitutional acts, legislative acts and implementing acts. Constitutional acts (treaties) would require unanimity by the Council and ratification by national parliaments; legislative acts would be adopted on the basis of a Commission proposal by the EP and Council in a co-decision procedure; implementing acts would be the responsibility of the Commission. Arguments in favour of a hierarchy of Community acts suggest that it would render the business of the Community more accessible and transparent by clearly identifying 'who does what in the system. In addition, it would add to the effectiveness of EU decision-making by tackling the existing medley of decision rules.

Discussion of a hierarchy of Community Acts spills over in the issue of comitology, the existing mechanism for overseeing the Commission' s implementing powers. Some states favour abolishing the existing cumbersome comitology procedures whereas others want to preserve the Council's control over the Commission. Those opposing change in this area are concerned that the introduction of a hierarchy of acts will enhance the state-like character of the Union by establishing a clear separation of powers and by making the Council more like a States' chamber (Reflection Group 1995).

THE EUROPEAN COUNCIL AND THE COUNCIL OF MINISTERS

The Council system which represents the arena where state interests are moulded into collective decision-making is at the heart of the Union system of governance. Debate on the working of the European Council and the Council of Ministers is focused on the role of the European Council as the political motor of integration; the issue of the rotating Presidency; and QMV.

The political importance of the European Council was formally acknowledged in the SEA and strengthened in the TEU which specified that it was responsible for 'general political guidelines' and the 'necessary impetus' for the development of the Union (Article D, TEU). The evolution of the European Council as a 'multi -headed executive' is likely to be strengthened by further reference to its political role.

The future role of the Presidency raises the issue of relations between the large and small states because the formal equality and rotation of the Presidency has been maintained so far. Enlargement would mean that if the present system con- tinues, each member state would have a considerably wider period before it held the Presidency again. More importantly, the expansion of the Union's remit and the demands for international representation have qualitatively altered the chal- lenges confronting each Presidency. There are growing doubts that small and par- ticularly micro states can effectively carry out the obligations of future Presidencies across the range of Union activity. There are proposals for year-long Presidencies of the larger states interspersed with joint Presidencies of regional sub-groups of small states. The election of a President of the Union for external policy has also been mooted. The Ludlow and Ersboll paper on the 1996 IGC suggested 'Team Presidencies' which would allow a Presidency to draw on the resources of more than one member state (Ludlow and Ersboll 1994: 42).

The third and perhaps more intractable issue in relation to the Council of Ministers is the issue of unanimity and qualified majority. The areas requiring the unanimous consent of all member states are likely to be reduced in the light of enlargement. Unanimity could have the perverse effect that a state representing 1 per cent or less of the Union population could veto agreement among the other partners. The debate on QMV revolves around its extension to most areas of law, the voting power of individual states and a dilution of the unanimity requirement in the second pillar. Both the SEA and the TEU expanded the range of issues that could be decided on the basis of QMV but did not lay down the principle that only major constitutional issues should be reserved for unanimity to avoid paral- ysis of the Council system. A majority of states are willing to give QMV a blanket endorsement except for constitutional issues whereas others want to apply a case by case approach to its extension.

Far more problematic is the operation of the QMV system itself. The negotia- tions during the final stages of the EFTA accession talks highlighted just how dif- ficult this issue is. It had been agreed that the EFTA enlargement would involve a mechanical adjustment to the QMV with a blocking minority rising to 27 votes out of a total of 90 (i.e., including Norway). This implied that it would require two large and two small states or two large and a medium-sized state to form a blocking minority. The UK and Spain opposed this adjustment and sought the retention of a blocking minority at 23 votes. The core of the UK argument was the need to protect the position of large states in the Union. The conflict was provisionally resolved in March 1994 under the Greek Presidency with a final solution postponed to the IGC. Under the Ioannina Agreement, the threshold for a blocking minority was raised to 26 but a delaying process was introduced for votes that fell between 23 and 26 votes, whereby the: 'Council would do all in its power to reach, within a reasonable time and without prejudicing obligatory time limits laid down by the Treaties and by secondary law ... a satisfactory solution that could be adopted by at least 68 votes' (*Europe Documents* 1994).

Germany, France, Italy and the UK have a combined vote of 40 which reduced the relative weight of their votes from 57 per cent in the Union of twelve to 46 per cent in the Union of fifteen. The large states can justifiably argue that this amounts to a serious under-representation of their 252 million citizens in contrast to the 115 million in the other eleven. This problem will be exacerbated with an eastwards enlargement because of the preponderance of small states. A report prepared by the Council Secretariat in 1994 concluded that: the relative weight of different states has not changed since the outset apart from Luxembourg after the 1973 enlargement when it got an additional vote; the per percentage necessary for a qualified majority remained stable around 70 percent; a blocking minority represented between 12 and 13 per cent of the population (Charlemangne Document 1994: 64).

However, the high threshold for a qualified majority combined with the membership of many more small states meant that the proportion of the Union's population that could find itself in a minority rose from 30 to 40 per cent. An extrapolation of the existing system to a Union of 28 states would mean that a qualified majority could be attained by a minority of the population of a 28-state Union (47 per cent) and that the newly acceding states of Central and Eastern Europe could form a blocking minority on their own. The large states argue that this undermines the efficiency and democracy of Council decisions. The large states want a reweighting of voting power in the Council so that a large number of countries representing a minority of the Union population could not outvote a small number of countries representing a majority of the population. Karl Lamers, Foreign Affairs spokesman for the CDU and the French UDF MEP, Jean Louis Bourlanges, have proposed the principle of a double majority, a majority of votes and of population. The small states, on the other hand, cling to the principle of sovereign equality to justify the existing allocation of votes (Reflection Group 1995).

THE COMMISSION

The authority of the Commission was weakened during the TEU ratification crisis when it emerged as a primary scapegoat for anti-TEU sentiment. A major goal of President Santer has been to protect the existing role of the Commission, especially its right of initiative (see Chapter 10). There are proposals to change the nature of the Commission as an organization by splitting it into a series of functional agencies. Vibert, for example, has suggested that the functions of the Commission should be 'unbundled' into three main areas: the single market, a treasury board and an external trade commission (Vibert 1994: 26). This would radically alter the nature of the Commission and would emphasize the technocratic element of its vocation. Such a move would downgrade the political role of the Commission and its responsibility for the general European interest.

Three issues dominate discussions on the Commission, namely its size, method of appointment and implementing powers. All three are perennial agenda issues and the subject of considerable contention. To take the issues of size and appointment, it is clear that of the present Commission of twenty members, some Commissioners lack a substantial portfolio. Proposals concerning size range from a reduction from two to one Commissioner for each state, a possible distinction between senior and junior Commissioners, and breaking the link between member state representation and the Commission. In the last case, small states might form a pool to propose a Commissioner. The maintenance of one Commissioner per member state is supported by the argument that without representation, confidence in the Commission could decline in small states. Temple Lang's assertion that: 'small states need an independent Commission most, if they are not to feel coerced by qualified majority voting: the larger states can take care of themselves' should be noted (Temple Lang and Gallagher 1995). One Commissioner per member state could result in a dilution of the independence of the Commission as it might come to resemble the Council. Suggestions that the Commission President would have an enhanced role in the choice of his team might provide a useful corrective to this. So, too, might the changed role of the EP. The TEU altered the appointment process of the Commission by giving the EP a consultative role, which it exercised in January 1995. The EP may well try to enhance that role further in relation to the Commission's appointment.

THE EUROPEAN PARLIAMENT

Since 1987 the EP has assumed a more central role in the Union' s institutional balance. The SEA' s cooperation and assent procedures and the TEU's co-decision procedure fundamentally altered the relationship between the Commission, the Council and the EP. The legislative process is now triangular rather than the traditional Commission–Council dialogue. The enhancement of the role of the EP was not accompanied by a streamlining of decision-making procedures as the new procedures were simply grafted onto the system with the result that there is a plethora of procedures affecting different aspects of cooperation. Article 189b of the TEU specifies that the scope of co-decision may be widened on the basis of a report to be submitted to the Council by the Commission. The declared goal of the EP is to enhance the use of the co-decision procedure which gives it the strongest say and to simplify its operation. It would also like to reduce the number of procedures by abolishing the cooperation procedure and maintaining assent for decisions that require unanimity in the Council and national ratification. The consultation procedure would then be limited to matters of common foreign and security policy.

Enlargement raises the question of the ultimate size of the EP. The EFTA enlargement brought its membership to 626. This is already a very large assembly. If the existing basis for the allocation of seats was to be maintained, it could lead to a Parliament of over 1000 MEPs. The effectiveness of a Parliament of this size must be questioned. Furthermore, as the powers of the EP grow, increasing attention will be paid to the relationship between seats and the size of the national electorates. A capping of the present size of the EP implies an adjustment of representation in the Parliament. The De Gucht Report examined this problem and sought to reconcile the principles of 'one man one vote' with the need to protect small state representation. It proposed the following principles:

- up to 1 million inhabitants: each member state should have a minimum of six seats;
- countries between 1 and 25 million: one seat per 500,000 inhabitants;
- between 26 and 60 million: one seat per 1 million inhabitants;
- over 60 million: one seat per 2 million inhabitants. (De Gucht 1992)

The Parliament itself did not endorse the De Gucht proposals in their entirety but some system will have to be found to allocate seats in a Parliament of 700 which is the number suggested for an enlarged Union by the Reflection Group (Reflection Group 1995). As the Union enlarges, a rebalancing of representation in the EP is desirable to ensure that small state populations are over-represented but that a more equitable relationship is maintained between seats and population.

THE EUROPEAN COURT OF JUSTICE

Given the weakness of many of the traditional sources of public power (budgets, personnel, administrative and coercive capacity) in the Union, law is essential to European integration. The creation of a separate legal order and the transformation of the Treaties into quasi-constitutional documents is one of the great achievements of the Union. The Court of Justice is the central pillar of this legal edifice. There are some signs that the member states are beginning to react to the activism of the Court. The remit of the Court was limited in the TEU when it was given no role in the second and third pillars of the Treaty. Radical proposals such as those prepared by the London European Policy Forum that want to remove the supremacy of Community law over national law are likely to fail (London Policy Forum 1994).

REPRESENTATION OF OTHER INTERESTS

The creation of the Committee of the Regions in the TEU reflected the growing mobilization of regions in the Union and the power of the German *Länder*, the Belgian Regions and the Spanish Autonomous Communities in their respective states. Although its role is simply consultative, the Committee and its strong members want to enhance its role in the Union. This would be resisted by the EP because of fears of a dilution of its representative role.

The politicization of the European question alerted national parliaments to the transformation of European governance since the mid-1980s. Integration has generally tended to privilege executive power over parliamentary power in the member states. National parliaments have woken up to this fact and many of them are now actively monitoring the preparations for constitutional change in the Union. National parliaments want greater access to the European policy process although they disagree on how this might be achieved. The French National Assembly has become one of the most active national parliaments on the issue. As part of the TEU ratification bargain in 1992, the French government inserted a new article (88.4) in the French Constitution which gave the National Assembly and the Senate the right to pass resolutions on European matters. A proposal for a 'third chamber' alongside the Council and the EP have been advocated by the French Parliament but has found no support from other national parliaments or member state governments. That said, formulae that would enhance the association of national parliaments with EU institutions and that would enhance their control over national governments in Union affairs are being explored. One such proposal is to establish a High Consultative Council on subsidiarity composed of delegations of national parliaments.

CONCLUSIONS

The Union has developed a unique institutional system based on an intermeshing of executive and legislative functions at the EU level and an intermeshing of different arenas of governance, European, national and regional. The system has considerable strength, notably its legal base and its capacity to generate collective action among a large number of diverse states. The advantages of membership have led numerable states to opt for a pooling or sharing of their sovereignty in a system of regional governance. Some member states are clearly more comfortable with this than others and for some states there is a relatively easy fit between European and national governance structures. The member states have all accepted, albeit some with reluctance, that they can no longer govern on their own. Member states have increasingly internalized the 'European' dimension in their national systems of public policy-making. However, the lure of autonomous action jostles continuously with pressures for collective action.

The creation of a set of EU institutions that structure interstate and transnational cooperation beyond the domestic level is central to the process of collective action. Since the mid-1980s EU institutions have had to bear the burden of increasingly ambitious collective goals and growing demands from the wider world. All EU institutions have had to adjust their operating procedures and their relations with each other in a rapidly changing institutional landscape. The EU system, lacking as it does many of the traditional attributes of public power, is increasingly overloaded. Yet the efficiency and effectiveness of the system is critical if member states are to be persuaded to invest further in collective institutions.

The quest for effectiveness looms large because of the challenge of incorporating many more states into the system of regional governance. The member states, particularly the smaller ones, are faced with difficult dilemmas about representation, on the one hand, and the functioning of the collective system, on the other. All member states are faced with difficult judgements about how to structure their collective endeavour in a system of governance that is always evolving.

REFERENCES AND BIBLIOGRAPHY

CDU–CSU Fraktion des Deutschen Bundestages (1994) *Ueberlegungen zur europaeischen Politik*. Bonn, September.

Charlemagne (1994) *L' Equilibre Entre Les Etats Membres*. Brussels.

Council of the European Union (June 1993) *Conclusion European Council*, Copenhagen.

— (1993) *Treaty on European Union*.

— (1994) *Conclusions European Council*, Essen.

— (April 1995) *Council Report to the Reflection Group*, Brussels.

d'Estaing (1990) *Report on Subsidarity*. European Parliament, April 1990, no. 83354

European Commission, (May 1995) *Commission Report to the Reflection Group*, Brussels.

de Gucht (1992) Proposals contained in *Enlarged Community Institutional Adapatations*, Brussels, TEPSA.

Hooghe, L. (1996) 'Introduction' in Hooghe, L. (ed.) *The Challenge of Cohesion*. Oxford, Oxford University Press.

Ludlow, P and Ersboll, N. (1994) *The Agenda of the Intergovernmental Conference*. Brussels, CEPS, working paper.

Major, John (1994) 'A Future that works'. Speech at Leiden University, 7 September.

March, J.G. and Olsen, J.P. (1989) *Rediscovering Institutions*, New York, Free Press.

Metcalfe, L (1993) *Trends in European Public Administration*. Swedish white book on the adaptation of the Swedish administration to the EC.

Miller, G. (1995) *Post-Maastricht Legislative Procedures: Is the Council 'Institutionally Challenged'?*, paper delivered to the 4th Biennial International Conference of ECSA, Charleston, South Carolina, May.

Monnet, J. (1976) *Memoires*. London, Collins.

Olsen, J.P. (1995) *Europeanization and Nation-State Dynamics*. Oslo, ARENA, working paper no. 9.

Reflection Group (24 August 1995), progress report on the 1996 Intergovernmental Conference.

Ross, G. (1994) *The Delors Commission*. Oxford, Polity Press.

Temple Lang, J. and Gallagher, E. (1995) *The Role of the Commission and Qualified Majority Voting*. Dublin, IEA, occasional paper no 7.

Vibert, F. (1994) *The Future Role of the European Commission*. London, EPF discussion paper.

Weale, A. (1994) *The Single Market, European Integration and Political Legitimacy*. Paper delivered to ESRC Single Market Conference, University of Exeter, September.

Weidenfeld, W. (ed.) (1994) *Europa '96: Reform Program für die Europäische Union*. Gütersloh, Verlag Bertelsmann Stiftung.

15

THE EU AND WEU:
FROM COOPERATION TO COMMON DEFENCE?

PETER VAN HAM

INTRODUCTION

Article J 4.2 of the Maastricht Treaty on European Union (TEU) stipulates that: 'The Union requests the Western European Union (WEU), which is an integral part of the development of the Union, to elaborate and implement decisions and actions which have defence implications.' The Maastricht Treaty therefore, for the first time, established a formal linkage between the European Union (EU) and the Western European Union (WEU). Article J 4.1 of the Treaty specifies that the Union's Common Foreign and Security Policy (CFSP) 'shall include all questions related to the security of the Union, including the eventual framing of a common defence policy, which might in time lead to a common defence'. By placing Europe's Common Defence Policy (CDP) and Common Defence (CD) within the CFSP, the Treaty has made it clear that the Union's economic–commercial and politico-diplomatic dimension should be complemented by a defence dimension, and, in due course, by commensurate defence instruments.

Although the EU and WEU since 1991 have established a closer working relationship, many questions remain as to how Europe should manage its own security and defence and what role the EU and WEU (as well as NATO) should play. This paper examines the relations between the EU and WEU, especially focusing on the conceptual, institutional and practical aspects of the linkages between the Union's CFSP and a future CDP–CD. It considers the nature and prospects of the development of further European cooperation in the security and defence area, and brings together the main ideas and proposals on these issues and appraises their merits in the light of the EU's Intergovernmental Conference (IGC) of 1996.

THE EUROPEAN UNION AFTER MAASTRICHT

Although the Maastricht Treaty stated boldly that the Union had now established a common foreign and security policy, the CFSP still remains an ambiguous concept and is at times even difficult to distinguish from its predecessor, European Political Cooperation (EPC).

The CFSP: a modest compromise

The Maastricht Treaty was the outcome of fierce debates and battles within and among the member states. The section dealing with the CFSP is riddled with ambiguous language and concepts, reflecting this lack of consensus on Europe's future role. One of the controversies was, and remains, the question how Europe's enhanced responsibility in the field of security should be institutionalized. In the end, the CFSP was given its own 'pillar' within the Union, meaning that decisions are now made by the Council of the Union as well as by the European Council (comprised of heads of state and government), both on an intergovernmental basis.

The CFSP calls for systematic cooperation among the member states on all aspects of security policy, and the gradual implementation of so-called 'joint actions' in areas in which member states have important common interests (J.1.3). Article J.3 stipulates the procedures for adopting such joint actions, making a significant innovation on EPC by introducing the possibility of decision-making through (qualified) majority voting (QMV). However, on the whole, decisions on foreign and security policy continue to be taken on the basis of consensus, although Declaration no. 27 (annexed to the Maastricht Treaty) states that the parties have agreed to 'avoid preventing a unanimous decision where a qualified majority exists in favour of that decision'. Although, in principle, member states are therefore committed to comply with joint actions, an escape clause has been added for those states that have 'difficulties in implementing' certain joint actions (J.3.7).

The Commission is 'fully associated' with the CFSP, participates in discussions and plays a valuable role in ensuring the coherence of the Union's external relations (i.e., among the three pillars). The Commission also has the right to make policy proposals on CFSP matters and a separate directorate-general (DG 1A) has been established to strengthen the Commission's expertise on these issues. It does not, however, have the sole right of initiative (as it does in the Union's other policy areas), neither is it responsible for implementing policy and representing the Union on CFSP issues; this is done by the Presidency (assisted by the other members of the troika – the immediately past and the immediately succeeding Presidencies). The European Parliament (EP) has a rather limited role in the field of foreign and security policy. It has been granted the right to be informed and consulted (it can 'ask questions', make 'recommendations' and hold an 'annual debate' on CFSP matters), but is not directly involved in the decision-making process. However, since all major agreements of the Union with budgetary and legal implications also need the Parliament's assent, the EP does have a say over such important issues such as trade agreements, association and cooperation agreements and the accession of new member states.

Annexed to the Maastricht Treaty are two declarations on WEU, which are not legally binding but do express the political will of governments. The first declaration specifies that WEU is the defence component of the Union which should have a more operational role; it also calls for closer working relations with the EU (as well as with NATO). The second declaration suggests that WEU should strengthen its ties with EU (but non-WEU) member states and European NATO countries. Although WEU remains an autonomous organization (based on the Modified Brussels Treaty of 1954), the Maastricht Treaty has for the first time provided an overall framework for a more coherent West European policy covering economic, political and security as well as defence aspects through creating organic links between the Union's pillars and WEU. It reflects the idea that the EU should play a politico-military role equivalent to Europe's economic weight, and that it is difficult to foresee an effective CFSP which is capable of projecting peace and stability across Europe and beyond, without the option of using military force as a last resort.

The operational capacities of the Union to formulate and implement a CFSP have not developed very quickly. A number of working groups have been formed which deal, among other things, with the formulation of the CFSP and the management of the EU's first joint action: the European Stability Pact. The European Council and the EU Ad-hoc Working Group on Security have produced a number of reports providing a conceptual outline of the CFSP. The scope of these reports has remained modest, stressing the economic, political and social aspects of security in which the EC–EU has traditionally developed expertise and policy. The reports of the Working Group on Security envisaged future EU joint actions on such matters as non-proliferation and the economic aspects of security (i.e., the transfer of conventional weapons).

The 'joint actions' under the CFSP have not been very effective either. A report of a high-level group of experts on the CFSP stated (in December 1994) 'with the possible exception of the Stability Pact these [joint actions] have quickly turned out to be poorly planned, hard to implement and disappointing both in scope and in terms of their meagre results, (High Level Group of Experts 1994: 3). In the Commission's report on the functioning of the Maastricht Treaty (which served as a first contribution to the IGC), it admits that 'the experience of the CFSP has been disappointing so far' (European Commission 1995). Indeed, apart from the joint action on the European Stability Pact, which brought together the nine Central European countries around so-called 'Regional Tables' to discuss minority and border questions, and a joint action concerning the EU's support for the indefinite extension of the Nuclear Non-proliferation Treaty in 1995, the Union has not adopted other major initiatives under the CFSP. The European Commission has prepared several detailed proposals for joint actions (on, for example, an EU policy towards Ukraine), but they have either not been brought to the Council, or the Council decided not to adopt them – at least, not as joint actions.

The CFSP: still at the bottom of a learning curve

It is clear that the Twelve and now the Fifteen have not taken a significant qualitative step towards a common, integrated European policy on foreign and security matters. The CFSP mainly formulates intentions to consult, coordinate and cooperate, without providing a decision-making framework in which member states are obliged to decide on and implement policies on all the security challenges facing the Union. It should be noted that member states have never intended to delegate foreign and security policy to the EU, and that a *Common* Foreign and Security Policy therefore has quite dissimilar aspirations than, for example, the Union's *Common* Agricultural Policy.

Where the CFSP has made an important positive contribution has been in the commitment that the Fifteen will continue to work together in a tighter and more coordinated framework than existed before 1992. This gives European governments the opportunity to harmonize their foreign policy priorities and work out effective decision-making procedures. This, inevitably, is a learning process. For the moment, there are few reasons to assume that the EU member states will follow a steep learning curve; the weak and incoherent response to the Yugoslav crisis is the most obvious case in point. This is probably why European Commissioner Hans van den Broek has called the Union's CFSP a 'misnomer', since the 'CFSP is less a policy in the sense of a specific course of action, than a process' (*Europe* 22 October 1994). Van den Broek has also clearly acknowledged that the Union is faced with:

> the problem [of] how to go beyond joint declarations and really act together to tackle specific international problems ... it is partly a question of political will but partly also because our sense of joint European interests is still insufficiently developed and because we have not yet learned how to take decisions together quickly and how to carry them out. (ibid.)

This highlights the difficulties in overcoming the reluctance of all member states to transfer parts of their sovereignty to Brussels; a reluctance which is especially deep-rooted in the security and defence areas. It has become clear that the differing national interests and foreign policy objectives of major West European states makes it questionable whether Brussels will develop into a unitary actor capable of responding quickly and effectively to impending international crises, even when they occur on the Union's doorstep.

THE WESTERN EUROPEAN UNION AFTER PETERSBERG

WEU's origins go back to the immediate aftermath of the Second World War. Then the fear of a resurgent Germany led France, the UK and the Benelux countries to conclude the so-called Brussels Treaty of March 1948, in which they established a defensive alliance with the general aim to coordinate the policies of the member states in defence matters (and, initially, in economic, social, cultural matters as well). The Brussels Treaty was 'modified' in October 1954, which enabled the Federal Republic of Germany and Italy to join. Assuring the smooth integration of Germany in the defence of Europe and the Atlantic Alliance has been considered one of WEU's most important earlier contributions to European security.

Prior to the accession of the UK to the EC (in 1973), WEU also played a useful role in consultations between the EC founding member states and London. But by and large, WEU was largely a dormant organization during the Cold War.

With the Maastricht Treaty, WEU has been designated as the EU's organization of choice to formulate and implement defence and military aspects of policy. It is clear that for the CFSP to be effective, close cooperation between the EU and WEU is indispensable. WEU and the EU have agreed on arrangements to facilitate coordination of work and policies. The document on EU–WEU relations annexed to the Maastricht Treaty envisages only 'mutual information' and 'cross-participation' of representatives from the two secretariats at CFSP and WEU meetings. For reasons of logistics and symbolism, WEU decided to move its Secretariat-General from London to Brussels (in January 1993). WEU has also reduced the term of office of the WEU Presidency from one year to six months (from 1 July 1994), with the intention also to synchronize the Presidencies of the EU and WEU. Working relations between the EU and WEU have now been established and some synchronization has taken place of Council, the Committee of Permanent Representatives (COREPER) and working group meetings. Of course, both organizations already had links prior to 1992, and the WEU Presidency was regularly informed by representatives of the country holding the EC Presidency. In October 1994, it was agreed that the EC may obtain information from WEU and participate in WEU meetings as part of the delegation of the country holding the EU Presidency in as far as the Commission's competencies under the Union Treaty warrants its presence (WEU C(94)141, 1994).

However, a number of practical steps still have to be taken to improve EU–WEU relations. Most sub-bodies of the CFSP and WEU work without consulting each other, the main exception being the WEU's Special Working Group and the EU's Working Group on Security, which at least encourages a parallel approach between both organizations on the conceptual work for Europe's security policy. But some member states still find it inconceivable that the EC – by many considered the symbol of European integration – can be fully involved in discussions on defence matters and are reluctant to give the Commission full access to all WEU meetings and documents. The division of labour and competencies between both organizations is at times also not clear, especially since foreign and security policy almost inevitably touches upon matters of defence, and vice versa. WEU–NATO working relations, based on the dual principles of 'transparency and complementarity', have been established relatively quickly and satisfactorily (for example, between both secretariats, joint Council meetings, and even a joint WEU–NATO command for 'Operation Sharp Guard' in the Adriatic – see below).

Strengthening WEU's operational capabilities

Only six months after the Maastricht Treaty had been signed, WEU member states adopted the Petersberg Declaration, which can be considered a first attempt to rethink and reformulate WEU's new role as the defence counterpart of the EU.

In order to make WEU an effective instrument to cope with the new post-Cold War security challenges, the Petersberg Declaration stated that apart from its traditional collective defence role (laid down in Article V of the Modified Brussels Treaty), 'military units of WEU member states, acting under the authority of WEU, could be employed for: humanitarian and rescue tasks; peacekeeping tasks; and tasks of combat forces in crisis management, including peacemaking.

These non-Article V tasks of WEU – also known as the 'Petersberg tasks' – clarify WEU's possible military missions which could complement the Union's CFSP (WEU Council of Ministers 1992).

Although the Petersberg Declaration clearly outlined WEU's role in the new Europe, it was also acknowledged that WEU would remain a 'paper tiger' if its operational capabilities would not be enhanced significantly. Since Petersberg, WEU has taken a number of steps towards that end. For example, a 'planning cell' has been established at WEU's Headquarters in Brussels with around 40 military officers. One of the principal tasks of the planning cell (which is under the direct authority of the WEU Council), is to prepare contingency plans for the employment of forces under WEU auspices; prepare recommendations for the necessary command, control and communication arrangements; as well as keeping an updated record of the forces which might be allocated to WEU for specific operations (so-called 'Forces answerable to WEU' (FAWEU), which are frequently those forces which member states have already designated for NATO missions). The planning cell has links with the Chiefs of Defence Staff through the military delegates to WEU. Although the planning cell has improved the military capabilities of WEU, it is still far too small and has only been given a limited mandate to develop an effective and close relationship with its counterparts in NATO.

Another aspect of WEU's operational capabilities is the WEU Satellite Centre, which was opened in Torrejón, Spain (in April 1993). The Satellite Centre has still only a limited operational capacity, but is in a stage of training staff to interpret satellite images. Europe has not yet developed its own satellites, but France and Italy are pressing hard for WEU to officially endorse the Helios-1 military observation satellite (which was launched in July 1995). France has now also started the pre-development phase of the Helios-2 system and anticipates the launch of this satellite around the year 2000. Germany had initially expressed an interest in joining the Helios-2 project but is now reluctant to commit itself due to the high costs (an estimated FF 11.5 billion) and disagreement on the *juste retour* for its defence industry since most high-value contracts have already gone to French companies (*Jane's Defence Weekly* 29 April 1995; *Liberation* 27 March 1995).

In general, given the fact that most Western European governments are cutting their defence budgets, it is not likely that WEU will decide to develop an independent European satellite system in the coming years, despite the fact that more defence cooperation will be essential to develop a viable defence-industrial base on which a European CFSP and CDP–CD can be based (Hodgkinson 1995; van Ham 1995). In this context, WEU is engaged in preparing the development of a European armaments agency (which is mentioned in the Maastricht Treaty), and the Independent European Programme Group (IEPG) – which has dealt with

West European armaments cooperation in the past – has now been incorporated in WEU and continues to function as the Western European Armaments Group (WEAG).

It is clear that the missions identified for WEU in the Petersberg Declaration are very comprehensive. Although WEU has relatively quickly transformed itself into the nucleus of West European cooperation on defence matters, few concrete actions have been taken until now. WEU was involved in monitoring the compliance of shipping (including search actions) with United Nations Security Council (UNSC) sanctions against Serbia and Montenegro in the Adriatic (jointly with NATO in the 'Operation Sharp Guard'). A WEU police and customs operation to support the implementation of UN sanctions has been conducted jointly with Romania, Bulgaria and Hungary. On the basis of a formal request of the EU, WEU has also sent a group of police experts to Mostar (Bosnia–Herzegovina) in support of an EU-led operation to restore public order and security in this city. The operation in Mostar was the first example of how Article J.4 of the Maastricht Treaty could be used, but WEU's problems in providing 180 police experts for the Unified Police Force of Mostar (UPFM) indicate that member states remain hesitant about becoming actively involved in crisis situations.

WEU was conspicuously absent in coordinating West Europe's military and humanitarian and rescue missions in former Yugoslavia and Rwanda. In the latter case, France proposed (on 16 June 1994) to send an interim intervention force for Rwanda, and raised the issue in subsequent meetings of WEU's Permanent Council. Although several WEU member states indicated their readiness to offer practical support for the French operation (of a logistical/technical and humanitarian nature), WEU did not decide to take action itself and only agreed that it would support member states' efforts in crisis management; the planning cell was tasked to serve as a coordination and contact point. But it was France which coordinated the humanitarian mission in Rwanda ('Opération Turquoise'), and not WEU, which again showed the reluctance of nation-states to use WEU's intergovernmental structure. The low profile of WEU in this crisis was partly due to the absence of a common foreign policy towards crisis areas such as in Central Africa, and partly due to the lack of relevant military capabilities to set up complex military operations: WEU has no standing command structure comparable to NATO, and other military assets essential to operate effectively in these crisis areas are either lacking altogether, or are only insufficiently available (such as strategic air and sea-lift capacities and real-time satellite intelligence). In order to resolve some of these deficiencies, WEU intends to set up a Humanitarian Task Force and decided to develop its role in evacuation operations. WEU's Permanent Council is now also elaborating the possibilities of setting up a WEU operational budget which would make swift WEU operations possible without being bogged down in difficult and time-consuming discussions over financing.

WEU's relations with other european countries

WEU has taken several other steps to implement the decisions made in

Maastricht. Article XI of the Modified Brussels Treaty stipulates that 'the High Contracting Parties may, by agreement, invite any other State to accede to the present Treaty on conditions to be agreed between them and the State so invited'. Although entry into the EU does therefore not automatically open the doors to full membership of the WEU, (new) EU member states will be invited to also join WEU. This led to the accession of Greece to WEU in March 1995. Longstanding EU members such as Denmark and Ireland have never applied for WEU membership; Austria, Finland and Sweden are equally unlikely to apply to join WEU in the near future, and in January 1995 acquired observer status. As observers, the five countries may, among others, attend the meetings of the WEU Council and the WEU working groups. Norway, Iceland and Turkey (as European NATO members) became WEU associate members in June 1992. They have the same rights as the observer states, but, as NATO members, are also allowed to be associated to the WEU Planning Cell through a permanent liaison arrangement and they will take part on the same basis as full members in WEU military operations to which they commit forces. Associate members are also connected to WEU's telecommunications system (WEUCOM).

In May 1994, at the WEU meeting in Kirchberg (Luxembourg), the Council decided to offer the status of associate partnership to the Central European (i.e. Bulgaria, the Czech Republic, Hungary, Poland, Romania and the Slovak Republic) and Baltic countries (i.e. Estonia, Latvia and Lithuania). This permits these nine countries, who have all signed so-called Europe Agreements with the EU, to participate regularly in WEU's Permanent Council (on the level of Ambassadors) and working group meetings, and to be present at all WEU Ministerial Councils. These countries also receive regular information about WEU activities, have a liaison arrangement with the WEU Planning Cell, and may associate themselves with decisions by WEU member states on the 'Petersberg tasks', and join ('when it is agreed') WEU operations by committing forces.

The different extent and levels of participation of European countries in the WEU Council and its subsidiary organs, have made WEU an example of 'variable geometry' in European security. WEU can (depending on the topics under discussion) now meet with ten (full members only), thirteen (in the case of WEAG), eighteen (full members, associate members and observers) or twenty-seven states (the full WEU 'family'). It is clear that only the full member states are covered by the security guarantee of Article V of the Modified Brussels Treaty, which stipulates that:

> If any of the High Contracting Parties should be the object of an armed attack in Europe, the other High Contracting Parties will, in accordance with the provisions of Article 51 of the Charter of the United Nations, afford the Party so attacked all the military and other aid and assistance in their power.

However, the scope of Article V has been somewhat weakened with the entry of Greece. Due to the longstanding dispute between Greece and Turkey, WEU was obliged to include in the Petersberg Declaration that the founding treaties of WEU and NATO 'will not be invoked ... in disputes between member States of either of the two organizations'.

WEU now embraces all EU member states, all European countries of NATO, as well as the Central European countries (including the Baltic states), who may join the EU in the decade ahead. This certainly gives added credibility to WEU as the European pillar of the Atlantic Alliance and makes it easier for WEU to interface with the EU. By having all these countries regularly around the table in Brussels, WEU also contributes to the development of a European security and defence identity, not only within the EU and WEU, but also as a more coherent European component within NATO.

FROM COOPERATION TO COMMON DEFENCE?

As the 'European pillar' within the Atlantic Alliance and the defence counterpart of the EU, conceptual thinking on the development of a CDP has inevitably been strongly influenced by the developments in NATO and the prospect of the 1996 IGC. At the Brussels Summit of January 1994, NATO for the first time clearly endorsed the development of a European Security and Defence Identity (ESDI), and welcomed the enhanced role of WEU. At the same time, WEU has also been closely and directly involved in the debate on institutional reform during the run-up to 1996 IGC. The declaration on WEU annexed to the Maastricht Treaty stipulated that 'WEU will re-examine the present provisions in 1996. This re-examination will take account of the progress and experience acquired and will extend to relations between WEU and the Atlantic Alliance'.

WEU's role in a revitalized Atlantic Alliance

At the NATO Rome Summit of November 1991, the importance of an ESDI compatible with NATO was recognized and acknowledged, and the green light was given for West European plans to develop new security and defence arrangements within the EU and WEU. But the historical turning point came at the NATO Summit of January 1994, which set a step towards reducing some of the complexity in Europe's security institutions. For the first time NATO gave its full support for the development of an ESDI, with the EU and WEU as the main tools. NATO proclaimed that the transatlantic link would be reinforced by the strengthening of the European pillar of the Alliance, and that it would enable the European allies to take more responsibility for managing their security and defence. President Clinton gave clear notification that although Europe remains the core of America's security concerns, the 'new security must be found in Europe's integration' (USIS-Defense Special File 13 January 1994), with an important role for both the EU and WEU.

This change in the American attitude towards WEU reflects the greater understanding of the Clinton administration of the relevance of European integration, as well as the fact that the USA is trying to bring its external commitments more into line with its limited domestic potential. Washington now seems to realize that a better organized Western Europe working within effective organizations, will contribute to peace and stability on the continent and beyond, and will hence reduce the need, and limit the costs, of US global commitments.

At the January 1994 Summit, NATO further endorsed the concept of Combined Joint Task Forces (CJTFs) which would be multi-national ('combined') and multi-service ('joint'), capable of being deployed out-of-area for peace operations. The Summit Declaration of 11 January stated that NATO was now ready to make collective assets of the Alliance available (on the basis of consultations in the North Atlantic Council (NAC)) for WEU operations in the context of the Union's CFSP. It was decided that the CJTFs (and their future headquarters) would be adaptable for operations which could be led by WEU. A Politico-Military Working Group has been established to prepare WEU's approach to the practical details of the CJTF concept and at a joint NATO–WEU Council meeting on 29 June 1994 WEU presented a paper on 'Criteria and Modalities for Effective Use by the WEU of CJTFs'. NATO tasked the Provisional Policy Coordinating Group (PPCG), which had been charged with the development of the CJTF concept, to conduct an assessment of this WEU paper. Since the summer of 1994, little practical progress was made, and in the autumn of 1995 both organizations still had to agree on the practical modalities for these new military arrangements. A particular problem was how WEU and NATO might use the existing assets without clarification of the role of Supreme Allied Commander Europe (SACEUR) and NATO's existing command structure in general.

But despite these remaining problems concerning the CJTFs, the January 1994 Summit substantially reduced a source of friction between the USA and Western Europe, meanwhile also facilitating cooperation among the Atlanticist and European oriented member states of the EU–WEU on the development of Europe's CDP. Although there is therefore little disagreement on the overall positive outcome of the January Summit, different interpretations exist of Washington's ultimate strategic aims: does this indicate that the USA is now preparing its withdrawal from Europe? Or is the CJTF concept, on the other hand, part of an American strategy to promote the ESDI while simultaneously retaining a *droit de regard* on Western Europe's security policy by embedding WEU within NATO's structures? Clearly France has felt that Western Europe was not fully independent from the USA as long as it needed the approval of the NAC to make use of NATO assets, and as long as there was an American SACEUR. Paris has also not toned down its insistence on developing independent West European military capabilities alongside NATO. As Jean-Marie Guéhenno, then French Permanent Representative to WEU, stated in October 1994:

> The more the Europeans decide to depend on the Alliance's assets, the more they need to have assets of their own for certain key functions, so that recourse to NATO's collective assets does not lead to WEU and the European Union playing a purely superficial role. (Guéhenno 1994: 12; and see also Guéhenno 1995)

European defence cooperation: practical developments

Within Europe several *ad hoc* multinational formations have already been formed, including the UK/Netherlands Amphibious Force, the Multinational Division-Central (which includes British, Dutch, Belgian and German forces), and the Eurocorps (with forces from Belgium, France, Germany, Luxembourg and Spain). Shrinking defence budgets have encouraged many West European governments to develop functional military partnerships, which range from the joint development of weapons and military equipment, to practical arrangements on the (joint) use of fighter aircraft (e.g. between Belgium and the Netherlands) (*De Standaard* 18 August 1994). The Franco-British European Air Group, which was set up during a UK–French summit in November 1994 in Chartres, was yet another addition to the many bi- and multilateral agreements among West European countries on defence and security matters (*Financial Times* 19–20 November 1994; *Le Figaro* 19 November 1994).

Among these military arrangements, the Eurocorps has attracted most attention. The Eurocorps will eventually consist of 50,000 troops (its aim is to be fully operational as of October 1995), and has its headquarters in Strasbourg. Its missions include collective defence of the allies within the framework of WEU/NATO, maintaining and restoring peace, as well as humanitarian missions. Speaking at the Eurocorps inauguration ceremony (early-November 1993), German Defence Minister Volker Rühe argued that the 'Eurocorps is the central building stone for a European defence. We are creating an instrument for a joint foreign and security policy of the Europeans. At the end of the road Europe's unification will be waiting'(*International Herald Tribune* 6–7 November 1994). General Helmut Willmann, commander of the Eurocorps, was equally clear when he stated:

> for joint political action, one needs common military structures ... In the future, when the Eurocorps is operational, our HQ will be in a position to assume the command and control of European units on behalf of the WEU, if the Europeans have the political will to implement a common security policy. (Willmann 1995: 24).

Initially, a number of West European governments were sceptical about the benefits of the Eurocorps, which could be seen as an unproductive duplication of military cooperation which was already taking place within NATO. However, much of the doubt was removed by the so-called SACEUR Agreement of January 1993, which stipulated that the Eurocorps would be deployed within NATO in case of war in Europe and that it could also be used by NATO for peacekeeping and humanitarian operations (Willmann 1994). In practice this implies that the French troops of the Eurocorps will be subordinated to SACEUR when a crisis demands it. Politically, this was a significant change in French policy towards NATO and has contributed to the dampening of the traditional Franco-American rivalry. Some French observers nevertheless continue to consider the Eurocorps as 'the embryo of a European army' (Baumel 1994), which will provide experience for West Europeans to establish European military cooperation and integration outside the NATO structure. Most other West European countries disagree, and there clearly is no West European intention to set up a distinctive military organization alongside NATO.

For the moment, the Eurocorps is not a unit of significant military importance. Although the Eurocorps can use the air transport capacity of Germany and France – the Transalls (C-160s) and the Hercules (C-130s) of Belgium and Spain – the strategic air transport capacity is very limited. This could change if European countries choose to develop the Future Large Aircraft (FLA); but this is still not decided (Promé 1993). Another problem – which is not specific to the Eurocorps, but is a European one – is the lack of reconnaissance capacity which hampers the autonomous operation of the Eurocorps. General Willmann's comment that 'from October 1995, the WEU will possess a joint HQ that will be capable of commanding air or ground operations on behalf of the WEU or of the countries involved' (Willmann 1995), therefore needs to be qualified.

For the foreseeable future, the Eurocorps primarily has a political role to play, perhaps becoming a model for closer military cooperation between WEU member states. A Mediterranean counterpart to the Eurocorps was announced by France, Italy, Spain and Portugal in May 1995. This new European rapid reaction force called 'Eurofor' will consist of between 10,000 to 15,000 troops that will be 'double-hatted' (i.e., they will be at the disposal either of WEU or NATO, but will remain stationed in their home countries). The four Mediterranean countries plan to contribute infantry and light artillery units and have also agreed to establish a joint naval force ('Euromarfor') (*Le Soir* 16 May 1995). These new initiatives were announced at the WEU Council of Ministers of May 1995 in Lisbon, and were widely seen as a contribution to the development of WEU's operational capabilities.

WEU and the 1996 IGC

The Maastricht Treaty's call for a review in 1996 included the difficult decision concerning the future course of European cooperation in the fields of security and defence. Among the crucial elements in the debate are the relationship between the EU and WEU, and the steps to be taken towards creating a credible and effective CDP and CD.

What the relationship will be between the EU and WEU after 1996, one could conceive three scenarios: (i) the dissolution of WEU and the incorporation of (elements of) the Modified Brussels Treaty in the EU's *acquis*; (ii) gradually strengthening EU–WEU ties with the express aim of promoting, in the long term, the convergence between the two organizations; and (iii) maintaining the WEU as an independent organization outside the EU framework.

The option of merging the EU and WEU would imply that the European Council can no longer only request WEU to take action, but that the EU would acquire independent military capabilities. This option has its most ardent supporters in Bonn, and German Foreign Minister Klaus Kinkel has argued that an eventual merger between the EU and WEU would be a further step towards European integration (*Die Zeit* 10 March 1995).[1] The Dutch government has also indicated its preference for a (gradual) merger of both organizations (Dutch Ministry of Foreign Affairs 1995). A report by the High Level Group of Experts on the CFSP (which was drawn up at the request of European Commissioner Hans van den Broek) also advocated the creation of a sizeable European intervention force, with the necessary command, intelligence and logistical components. This would mean that the forces and military resources now 'answerable to WEU', would be placed at the disposal of the EU to support the CFSP. The report also called for a:

> timetable and a set of minimum requirements for participation, in terms of allocation of forces, integration of command structures and effective support for the concomitant technological and logistical programmes – in other words, additional contactual obligations. (High Level Group of Experts 1994.)

In this option attention is drawn to the fact that in 1998 (50 years after the Brussels Treaty came into force), individual WEU member states have the right, under Article XII of the Modified Brussels Treaty, to cease to be a party to the Treaty (having given one year's notice of denunciation), which might be a suitable occasion to integrate WEU in the European Union.

Giving the CFSP a clear defence component would indeed be a major step towards developing a European 'superpower', and would follow institutional logic and contribute to institutional tidiness. But such a 'great leap forwards' would not only be unacceptable for Europe's main military powers – the UK and France – but would also encounter a large number of practical problems which would seriously hamper such an EU–WEU merger. Most European governments would not be prepared to delegate decisions on defence issues to a supranational body (with a generalized use of QMV or even a restricted system as in the CFSP). Furthermore, one could argue that WEU's 'variable geometry' is essential to accommodate the different interests of the European countries in the field of defence. Squeezing all these interests in one EU straightjacket would be forcing some member states to take a huge leap towards a common approach and common policies, which is hasty and potentially counterproductive.

The second scenario foresees the strengthening of EU–WEU ties, aiming at a final merger of both organizations. In this option it would be necessary to improve the procedures for the decisions made in the CFSP framework to be implemented by WEU. The EU–WEU link should be made more effective and operational, as well as the closest possible harmonization and coordination between all EU and WEU bodies.

In this context the possibility of constructing a defence ('fourth') pillar inside the EU, was informally suggested by the UK in 1994 (though subsequently rejected by London in early 1995). By introducing such a 'defence pillar' inside the Union's structure, which would follow strict intergovernmental rules, the EU would be granted a military dimension without, however, involving the European

Commission and the EP. The model has also been very close to French thinking on future EU–WEU relations since Paris is, like the UK, ardently opposed to introducing supranational elements in the defence field. Both the first scenario (full EU–WEU integration) and the 'fourth pillar' model, give rise to the question whether (and if so, how?) WEU's security guarantee (Article V) can be extended to those EU member states who are not also members of NATO. Would it be possible for a EU/WEU member not to join NATO if WEU could use the collective assets of the Alliance through the CJTFs? Is a security guarantee solely based on the Modified Brussels Treaty credible as long as the operational military capabilities of WEU are limited and remain closely linked to NATO, and as long as there is no 'European' nuclear deterrence?

Another question which arises has been formulated by the Dutch Minister of Foreign Affairs Hans van Mierlo: 'Should there be a WEU-type security guarantee in the revised Maastricht Treaty?' (van Mierlo 1995: 10). There have been some suggestions, by, for example, the Liberal Group in the EP, to insert in the revised Maastricht Treaty a mutual assistance commitment which would bind all EU member states (*Europe* 6 April 1995); this would come close to the option of merging WEU and the EU. Given the reluctance of several European states to add a defence dimension to the EU and especially of merging both organizations, it is unlikely that the Union will have its own 'Article V'. This has been the official reason given by the UK government for rejecting the 'fourth pillar' model. In a memorandum on WEU (made public in March 1995), London also 'rejected the option of simply folding the WEU into the European Union as an intergovernmental pillar', arguing that 'future European defence arrangements should be based on the WEU, acting in a reinforced partnership with the European Union' (UK government, 1 March 1995).

What is more, a number of EU member states do not consider joining NATO and WEU as contributing to their overall security. Some in Finland, for example, would regard joining a Western collective defence alliance a provocation of Russia which would only harm their security and Nordic stability; as the Finnish Prime Minister, Paava Lipponen, put it: 'as far as NATO membership is concerned, it is not on the agenda for Finland ... We have no security deficit' (*International Herald Tribune* 20–21 May 1995). A core element of the traditional Austrian policy of neutrality is the non-participation in military alliances and the refusal to station foreign troops in Austrian territory. Austria's former Minister of Foreign Affairs Alois Mock, has argued that EU membership would suffice to guarantee the country's security: 'The Union's cohesion and solidarity derives from the interdependence and partial fusion of the economies of member states and thus offers to each partner a security guarantee *which might well be more reliable than formal treaty commitments*' (Mock 1995: 17; emphasis added). Although this point is not often raised, its validity is undisputable: it is inconceivable that an EU member state which participates fully in the three pillars of the Union would, in the case of external military aggression, even in the absence of official security guarantees, not be assisted by its European partners. Formal treaty obligations may be worth little in the post-Cold War era if they are not underpinned by strong economic

319

and political ties. The proposals to broaden the scope of US–European relations by adding social and economic aspects to NATO's defence agenda reflects this change in thinking about the nature of security (Bertram 1994). The question nevertheless arises whether this will not result in different zones of security in the EU between member states with a security guarantee (Article V of NATO and WEU), and those which go without such assured military support.[2]

The lack of congruence between the membership of the EU and WEU also affects the debate concerning the Union's institutional reform. At the 1996 IGC, the five EU member states who are not full members of WEU (Denmark, Ireland and the three new members), participate on an equal footing in the debate on EU–WEU relations and the further development of a CDP/CD. In an enlarged EU (with perhaps as many as 25 members), this problem of lacking congruence is unlikely to become less acute. A solution could be found in institutionalizing the concept of 'opting out'. There are several possibilities to apply this concept: whenever there is agreement among the WEU member states within the EU's Council of Ministers to request WEU to act, such a decision could not be blocked by non-WEU EU members. In such a 'coalition of the willing' there would still be a requirement for unanimity, but it would solve the problem that non-WEU EU member states have the power of veto on the EU's decision to make use of WEU's defence capabilities.[3]

A EUROPEAN COMMON DEFENCE POLICY AND COMMON DEFENCE

In May 1994, the WEU Permanent Council was tasked to begin work on the formulation of a common European defence policy, of which the preliminary conclusions were presented at the Council of Ministers in November 1994 in Noordwijk. A WEU special document on European security has been prepared which was approved at the WEU Council of Ministers in Lisbon in May 1995. Both documents have set modest, but nevertheless important steps towards the formulation of a CDP and the development of a common European identity in the fields of security and defence.

Looking for common ground on defence

At the WEU Council of Ministers (November 1994) in Noordwijk, the 'Preliminary Conclusions on the Formulation of a Common European Defence Policy' were accepted. The document was, indeed, 'preliminary', since it tried to answer a number of basic questions concerning the definitions and scope of a CDP, the subsequent role of WEU and its ties with the EU, NATO and the OSCE, as well as the more concrete details of WEU's operational role, the planning requirements and operational capabilities, the decision-making, command, control and burden-sharing arrangements, and the prospects for cooperation in the fields of armaments.

The Noordwijk declaration gave the following definition: 'A common European defence policy will need to incorporate elements on the necessary structures, mechanisms and capabilities, as well as on the definition of principles for the use of the armed forces and armaments of WEU States.' It further, correctly, emphasized that the development of a CDP: 'will require a common assessment and definition of the requirements and substance of a European defence which would first require a clear definition of the security challenges facing the European Union and a determination of appropriate responses'. This, the documents argued, 'will in turn depend upon a judgement of the role the European wishes to play in the world and the contribution it wishes to make to security in its immediate neighbourhood and in the wider world'. Perhaps not very surprisingly, the document was short on explaining how European countries might arrive at such a common assessment of a European defence and a shared definition of the main challenges facing European security. Given the different priorities and foreign policy agendas of the main European countries, reaching a common threat assessment and a common European response is clearly difficult.

The Noordwijk declaration further stressed the need for flexibility in Europe's participation in conflict prevention and crisis management on the continent and elsewhere. It argued that the 'level of involvement of different states can vary according to the circumstances. Decision-making should be sufficiently flexible in order not to frustrate joint activities by WEU states who have expressed the will to undertake such activities'. It also made clear that 'WEU's operational role should be developed in a flexible way, ensuring the capacity to, on the one hand, operate autonomously (where appropriate in close consultation with NATO) and, on the other hand, to operate together with non-WEU countries'.

Although it is clear that a European CDP will remain based on the sovereign decision of each member state whether to participate on a specific operation, an effective CDP presupposes that there is sufficient European solidarity and readiness among the participating states to share responsibilities in the actual execution of the operation tasks. The principles of 'European burden sharing' mentioned in the Noordwijk declaration were: the rotation of forces; the pooling of capabilities and resources; establishing an operational budget to ensure the adequate and timely resourcing and financing of the preparation and implementation of operations; and task specialization. Agreement on such principles is all the more necessary since, as one senior UK official commented 'the "coalitions of the willing" approach is all very well but there is an urgent need to ease the burden of the few States who seem to be willing most of the time' (Bailes 1995: 16).

There is little conceptual clarity as to how a European common defence *policy* would differ from a European common defence. The language of the Maastricht Treaty seems to suggest that a CDP will precede a CD, thereby assuming that the former would be a less advanced form of integration in the defence area. The European Strategy Group in 1995 suggested the following definitions: a CDP could be a 'Common policy with respect to the use of the armed forces of the member states of the European Union', and a CD could be defined as either 'the organisation of the armed forces of the member states in common' (the stronger version), or as 'the organisation of *the activities* of the armed forces of the member states in common' (the weaker version) (Roper 1995). If one accepts these working definitions, it becomes clear that the development of a CD will not be contingent upon the completion of a CDP; elements of both a CDP and a CD can develop simultaneously. One could even argue that it could be more arduous and politically sensitive to agree upon a common policy on *what to do* with Europe's military might, than to arrive at practical cooperative arrangements among the military forces in Europe. To a certain extent, the UK/Netherlands Amphibious Force, the Multinational Division-Central and the Eurocorps, are already examples (on a smaller scale) of common defence arrangements. Deciding on how and when to use these military forces is a political question belonging to the CDP sphere which might be considerably more difficult.

The Noordwijk document did not touch upon more politically sensitive long-term issues related to a CDP/CD, such as the question of a permanent command and control structure of WEU; the costs of the development of a CDP/CD; the nuclear issue;[4] and the joint (development and) procurement of WEU's own military equipment such as strategic transport aircraft; and the nuclear issue. The document did, however, correctly state that the development of a CDP should be based on the joint analysis of Europe's environment and Europe's appropriate policies to address risks and challenges. WEU's Special Working Group was tasked to prepare such a WEU 'White Book'.

Common reflections on European security

At the WEU Council of Ministers in Lisbon in June 1995, a general document presenting 'Common Reflections on the New European Security Conditions' was approved. It provides a comprehensive overview of the common European security interests and its security environment. The document outlined the security challenges for Europe, ranging from instability in Russia, the CIS region and the southern Mediterranean basin, to the risks of non-proliferation of weapons of mass destruction, international terrorism and uncontrolled migration. The general nature of the paper showed clearly that it was a consensus document and it failed to set priorities among Europe's security interests and challenges. WEU countries have attempted to complement the document by seeking to formulate common policy responses to these security challenges in a European 'White Paper' on security and defence.

Probably more important than the specific content of the Lisbon document has been the fact that these issues were discussed among representatives from a very wide range of European countries. The document was prepared over a period of almost six months by delegates of all countries of the 'WEU family', i.e. not only WEU member states, but also associate members, observers, and associate partners. Bringing these 27 countries together to discuss and formulate the premises and problems of European security and Europe's security policy, was a useful exercise in forging a shared assessment of the interests and difficulties that bind Europe. One should keep in mind that the development of a truly European security and defence identity does not only require an institutional framework with clear, efficient and effective rules of decision-making and similar norms for burden-sharing, but also a feeling of common roots as well as a common destiny. Just as the construction of an economic and monetary union in the EU needs the cement of complex interdependence combined with a necessary minimum of solidarity, a European foreign and security policy must have a foundation of common interests and values, a shared assessment of the principal risks, challenges and threats to the security of Europe, as well as the priority with which they should be addressed. Without this groundwork it is difficult to foresee how a truly European identity on security and defence can be formed.

CONCLUDING REMARKS

The 1996 IGC was heralded by some as a 'moment of truth' where crucial decisions would be made concerning Europe's future architecture. Given the reluctance of several key member states to go far beyond the rearrangement of the Union's furniture, expectations should perhaps have remained modest. One can hardly expect that the existing hybrid Gaudian European architecture can be changed overnight into a model of '*Neue Sachlichkeit*'. Experience after the end of the Cold War has shown that international organizations remain impotent as long as member states cannot muster the political will to use the instruments available to them. Especially in the sphere of security and defence a powerful and mature Europe will only emerge when both the institutional and operational infrastructure is in place, as well as the political will of member states to act on a European, rather than on a national level.

This paper has outlined the nature and prospects of European security and defence cooperation in the context of the IGC. It has emphasized developments within the EU's second pillar and WEU. Three points need to be emphasized. First, the dynamic of European integration can only be properly understood in the context of Europe's overall economic, political and security environment. One should remain aware that the development of the CFSP and the CDP/CD is not *sui generis*. On the contrary, it is clearly understood that the future enlargement of the EU towards Central Europe makes institutional reform essential and requires a broader agreement on the future security structure of Europe, including the EU's relationship with Russia. What is more, the conflict in the former Yugoslavia stands as a reminder to European policy-makers that the EU and WEU must become more effective in crisis prevention and management as well as for humanitarian and rescue missions. The uncertain role of the USA in Europe should also concentrate European minds on how to reshape the Atlantic Alliance into a more balanced two-pillar structure.

Second, developments in the EU's second pillar should not be seen in isolation to the other pillars. Disagreements within the Reflection Group suggested that the focus was less on grand designs than on the fine-tuning of the Maastricht three-pillar system. Yet, it is difficult to imagine a Europe with one currency and one monetary policy without an equivalent level of integration in the political and security sphere. Especially Germany and France have been keen on a synchronous progress in these areas. Wolfgang Schäuble of Germany's CDU–CSU formulated this problem succinctly when he argued: 'how can I explain to people that they should give up the D-mark when we cannot stop disputes in Europe' (*Financial Times* 21 March 1995).

That leads to the third and final point: if the experience of the ratification of the Maastricht Treaty has taught us one thing, it is that European integration in whatever sphere should be considered as legitimate by the majority of European citizens. This is only likely when European institutions act effectively and decision-making is transparent. Much remains to be done to achieve these two goals and to make the CFSP and CDP/CP ventures that will receive wide support throughout Europe. Most member states are reluctant to see their national veto diluted in the interest of streamlined decision-making out of concern that this might alienate their citizens. It is characteristic that Britain's former Foreign Secretary Douglas Hurd still argues that security goes 'to the heart of the functions of the nation state', and that 'public opinion' would not understand or accept it 'if these responsibilities appeared to have been surrendered to a supranational body, however worthy' (*Independent* 4 October 1994). This applies equally to France under its Gaullist President Jacques Chirac. What Europe needs most of all today is statesmen who have both the vision and diplomatic skills to construct a powerful and mature Europe capable of managing its own security; without doubt most Europeans will want to ascribe to such a goal.

NOTES

1. Kinkel argued: 'Ein nächster Schritt könnte die Verschmeltzung von Westeuropäischer Union und Europäischer Union sein.'
2. The German Defence Minister Volker Rühe has argued that: 'We cannot allow a situation to evolve where all benefit from the blessings of the Single Market, but only a few shoulder the burdens of common security – organized in a circle by the name of WEU.' Presentation at the 'Security Policy in 1995' seminar of the Federal Academy of Security in Bonn, 20 April 1995
3. This has been suggested by Stefano Silvestri, Nicole Gnesotto and Alvaro Vasconcelos, 'Decision-making and institutions', in Martin, Laurence and Roper, John (eds) *Towards a Common Defence Policy*. Paris, The European Strategy Group and the WEU Institute for Security Studies, 1995, pp. 63–5. Silvestri, Gnesotto and Vasconcelos consider this an aspect of what they call 'variable unity' (a term which describes in a 'positive way' the concept of variable geometry).
4. France, especially has seemed keen to include it in the debate about a European CDP/CP, the French Prime Minister, Alain Juppé, arguing in February 1995, for example: 'Pour le long terme, il est indispensable de réfléchir aux étapes du développement de l'Europe de la défense, y compris la mission – sujet sensible – des forces nucléaires nationales' (Juppé 1995: 6).

REFERENCES AND BIBLIOGRAPHY

Bailes, Alyson (1995) 'Britain's security-policy agenda: an official's view', *RUSI Journal*, February.

Baumel, Jacques (1994) 'Le Corps européen: un premier pas vers une défense de l'Europe', *Défense*, no. 65, September.

Bertram, Christoph (1994) at the 40th General Assembly of the Atlantic Treaty Association in The Hague, on 26 October 1994.

Dutch Ministry of Foreign Affairs (1995) 'Het gemeenschappelijk Europees buitenlands, veiligheids – en defensiebeleid: naar een krachtiger extern optreden van de Europese Unie' 30 March 1995.

European Commission (1995) *Preparing Europe for the twenty-first century*, IP/95/465 Brussels 10 May.

High Level Group of Experts on the CFSP. (1994) *European security policy towards 2000; ways and means to establish genuine credibility*, report at the request of European Commissioner, Hans van den Broek. Brussels 19 December.

Guéhenno, Jean-Marie (1994) 'France and the WEU', *NATO Review*, October.

—— (1995) 'Sécurité européenne: l'impossible statu quo', *Politique Etrangère*, vol. 60, no. 1, Spring.

Hodgkinson, Keith (1995) 'Defence industries: the urge to merge', *International Defence Review*, vol. 28, no. 4, April.

Juppé, Alain (1995) 'La France et la sécurité européenne', *Defense Nationale*, vol. 51, no. 4, April.

Mock, Alois (1995) 'Austria's role in the new Europe', *NATO Review*, vol. 43, no. 2, March.

Promé, Jean-Louis (1993) 'Europe's FLA: dream or necessity?' *Military Technology*, December.

Reflection Group (24 August 1995), progress report on the 1996 Intergovernmental Conference.

Roper, John (1995) 'Defining a common defence policy and common defence', in Martin, Laurence and Roper, John (eds) *Towards a Common Defence Policy*. Paris, The European Strategy Group and the WEU Institute for Security Studies.

Rühe, Volker (1995) Presentation at the 'Security Policy in 1995' seminar of the Federal Academy of Security in Bonn, 20 April.

Silvestri, Stefano, Gnesotto, Nicole and Vasconcelos, Alvaro (1995) 'Decision-making and institutions', in Martin, Laurence and Roper, John (eds) *Towards a Common Defence Policy*. Paris, The European Strategy Group and the WEU Institute for Security Studies.

van Ham, Peter (1995) 'The development of a European security and defence identity', *European Security*, vol. 4, no. 4, Winter.

van Mierlo, Hans (1995) 'The WEU and NATO: prospects for a more balanced relationship,' *NATO Review*, vol. 43, No. 2, March 1995.

WEU Council of Ministers (1992) *Petersberg Declaration*. Bonn, 19 June.

WEU Document (unclassified), C (94) 141 revised, 3 October 1994 'Relations with the European Union, modalities for information and consultation between the European Commission and WEU'.

Willmann, Lt. Gen. Helmut (1994) 'The European corps – political dimension and military aims', *RUSI Journal*, August.

—— (1995) 'Eurocorps: "condemned to success"', *International Defence Review*, no. 2.

UK government (1995) 'Memorandum of the United Kingdom Government's approach to the treatment of European defence issues at the 1996 Inter-Governmental Conference', made public 1 March.

16
EUROPEAN UNION – JUSTICE AND HOME AFFAIRS: A BALANCE SHEET AND AN AGENDA FOR REFORM

JÖRG MONAR

JUSTICE AND HOME AFFAIRS IN THE INTEGRATION PROCESS

Justice and home affairs are relatively new areas of European policy-making, which attracted comparatively little attention in the run-up to the 1996 Intergovernmental Conference (IGC). Yet a prominent voice has already identified them as a possibly decisive battlefield in the struggle between the predominance of the nation-state and supranational integration in Europe. In his memoirs, the former British Home Secretary, Kenneth Baker, writes that a collision with the European Community (EC) over the central justice and home affairs issue of maintaining of national frontier controls 'will be the ultimate test of "who governs?", the national or the supranational state' (Baker 1993: 442-3). Such a test is certainly the last thing the often tense relationship between London and Brussels needs. Yet Baker's phrase points to a fundamental problem of justice and home affairs as areas of Union policy-making: more or less all aspects falling within these areas concern the internal security of member states, and traditionally the enormous concentration of political, administrative and financial power of the modern state has found one of its main reasons of legitimacy in the guarantee of the internal security of its citizens. As a result, justice and home affairs are intimately linked to the traditional concept of national sovereignty: even the slightest renunciation of national control over state instruments in this area seems to question the nation-state in one of its most essential functions.

It is hardly surprising therefore that progress in the area of justice and home affairs has proved to be even more difficult to achieve than progress in the foreign and security policy area. Whereas certain aspects of external security had already been brought within the ambit of the Treaties by the Single European Act (SEA) of 1986, justice and home affairs have been formally introduced into the integration process only with the entry into force of the Union Treaty in November 1993. And even this late step was taken rather cautiously. In spite of some member governments who favoured a more ambitious step forward, justice and home affairs were introduced not as areas of a 'common policy' according to the EC model but only as 'areas of common interest'. They were thus outside the integrated political and legal system of the EC and within the framework of intergovernmental cooperation now commonly referred to as the 'third pillar'.

A question of forbearance?

Given the fairly recent introduction of Title VI of the Union one may be tempted to look at the functioning of the third pillar with some forbearance. Practitioners participating in the process have stressed the fact that ministers and officials concerned have been working in the new framework for a very short time compared with their colleagues involved in the first or even second pillar and that therefore some expectations have been unrealistic and probably even unfair (Fortescue 1995: 25). Yet for at least two reasons such forbearance at the performance of cooperation in the fields of justice and home affairs can hardly be justified.

First, the entry into force of the Union Treaty in November 1993 was actually not the 'zero hour' of intergovernmental cooperation on justice and home affairs. In the area of the fight against terrorism the member states had already begun to cooperate in the mid-1970s in the European Political Cooperation (EPC) substructure which had become known as 'TREVI'. In the second half of the 1980s, the single market programme and the gradual abolition of internal borders led to the setting up of a whole range of new cooperation mechanisms and bodies which at the beginning of the 1990s covered nearly all the areas presently listed in Article K.1 of the Union Treaty. All these structures, having been set up on the basis of *ad hoc* decisions rather than as the result of a comprehensive strategy, suffered from a lack of coordination and transparency. Responding to the obvious weaknesses of this proliferation of cooperation structures already in place, the third pillar was much more a codification and partial reform of existing cooperation on justice and home affairs than a 'first step'. The member states, in other words, have already had quite some time to gain experience with intergovernmental cooperation, not just since November 1993 but in most areas for five or ten years, or even longer.

The second – and more important – reason why a forbearing view of the third pillar does not seem justified is that in all 'areas of common interest' listed in Article K.1 of the Union Treaty, the member states individually and as a group face ever-increasing challenges. Already many of these areas are among the central problem areas of national politics. To give only a few examples: immigration and asylum policy as well as questions of internal security were among the key issues of the French presidential and parliamentary elections of 1995. In the UK, new restrictive measures introduced by the government in 1996 to curb the number of asylum seekers led to a broad public debate and defeats for the government both before the Court of Appeal and in the House of Lords. In Germany and Austria, the new forms of organized crime in Eastern Europe and the CIS (especially as regards the smuggling of drugs, nuclear materials and stolen cars) have led to a new security threat perception and asylum and immigration issues figure high on the national and regional political agenda there as well. Due to the

327

intensity of national debates on these issues, it often appears as if these are still mainly national problems. Yet whether it is migration pressure, the abuse of the asylum system, international drug trafficking, money laundering or the growth of international organized crime, in all these areas the member states face challenges which are of an essentially trans-boundary nature and therefore require common responses. Clearly none of the member states are any longer in a position to tackle any of these growing challenges effectively on their own. For all these reasons the Union can simply not afford to grant any sort of 'period of forbearance, to the third pillar.

With the publication of the EU institutions' reports on the functioning of the Union Treaty, if not earlier, it became obvious that so far the third pillar has not been able to meet these challenges. Even the report submitted by the EU Council, normally a defender of intergovernmental mechanisms, admitted that there were serious problems with the functioning of cooperation under Title VI (Council of the EU 1995: points 74–83). The need to reform the third pillar was also clearly emphasized in the report of the Reflection Group of December 1995. Yet the report did not provide any deeper analysis of existing weaknesses and remained rather general and in part inconclusive as regards concrete proposals for reform. In order to clarify the actual need for reform it seems useful to proceed to a brief critical analysis of the performance of the third pillar so far, both in respect to the decision-making system and its instruments and to results achieved in the various policy areas.

THE DECISION-MAKING SYSTEM AND THE INSTRUMENTS OF JHA

As regards the decision-making system of cooperation in the fields of justice and home affairs it is important not to underestimate the progress made with the introduction of Title VI. The rather loose and fragmented set of existing working groups was streamlined and divided up in three clearly defined sectors (asylum and immigration, police and customs, judicial cooperation). The activities of the working groups in all three sectors are coordinated by specific 'Steering Groups' composed of senior officials. The so-called 'K.4 Committee' acts as the supreme coordinating body of the third pillar and also prepares the decisions of the Justice and Home Affairs Council (JHA), although it remains formally subordinated to the Committee of Permenant Representatives (COREPER) with its overall responsibility for preparing the Council's work (under Article 151 of the EC Treaty). In order to provide administrative support to the whole cooperation framework a new directorate general ('H') was set up in the Secretariat General of the Council, and in the Commission, too, the responsible unit in the Secretariat General was upgraded to a special 'Task Force'. All this has led to a more uniform and systematic structure of bodies and procedures and has greatly eased continuous cooperation and information exchange between the national ministries.

Nevertheless there have also been problems with the new decision-making system. One is that, with its five levels of decision-making (working groups, steering groups, K.4 Committee, COREPER, Council), the new structure is even more heavy than the one in the EC framework, which, in most policy areas, has only three levels. Another problem is the relationship between the K.4 Committee and COREPER which has not been sufficiently clarified in the Treaty and which has led on a number of occasions to frictions between both bodies over competences and procedures. Both problems tend to slow down the decision-making process and to increase the workload of coordination inside the Council machinery and at the national level.

As usual in the intergovernmental sphere decision-making procedures under Title VI are dominated by the unanimity rule. It is true that the Treaty gives member states the possibility of deciding by qualified majority on measures implementing a 'joint action'(Article K.3(2)b), but this provision has not so far been used. Some member states – in particular the UK – have well-known objections to the principle of using majority voting in the intergovernmental sphere. As all the 'matters' listed in Article K.1 touch upon core areas of national sovereignty, the maintenance of the unanimity requirement seems understandable. Yet one also has to see that this is clearly one of the major weaknesses of the whole third pillar structure. Here, as well as in other policy areas of the Union, the unanimity requirement regularly leads to agreements at the level of the lowest common denominator. This means that in most cases the process of negotiating a text looses a large part of its substance[1] and/or that important issues are addressed in the form of legally-non-binding texts such as 'resolutions' and 'conclusions' (see p.330). In cases of persistent differences, agreement on a text of major importance may even be endlessly delayed. The conclusion and entry into force of a whole range of important conventions (among these the EUROPOL Convention), for example, has been delayed because of the objections of the British government to the jurisdiction of the European Court of Justice (ECJ) in the framework of these agreements.

The non-exclusive right of initiative of the Commission is also of importance for decision-making in the third pillar. Although the Commission – unlike in the EC framework – has to share this right with the member states, it nevertheless increases its potential role in decision-making which can also contribute to the consistency of third pillar measures and EC policies. Yet the Commission's right does not extend to three important areas of the third pillar: judicial cooperation in criminal matters, customs cooperation and police cooperation (Article K.3(2) TEU). In practice, this, as well as the non-exclusive nature of the right of initiative and the unanimity requirement, effectively limit the Commission's weight in decision-making. Its actual influence depends heavily on its tactical ability and on any specific expertise it may be able to bring into the process. Probably with the aim of avoiding counter-productive polarization and conflicts among the member states, the Commission has so far made only rather carefully drafted proposals such as the ones on the new Draft External Frontiers Convention of December 1993 (COM(93) 684 final) and the Drug Action Plan of 1994 (COM(94) 234 final). In effect, the Commission has been limiting itself largely to facilitating the intergovernmental decision-making process through additional expertise and mediation among member states' positions (Myers 1995). This means that, at least so far, in the third pillar the Commission is far from playing the role of a 'motor' of the integration process, which has been one of its traditional functions in the EC framework. It also means that – as a result – the possible driving force in the further development of the third pillar is largely absent. The role of initiator is left mainly to the Presidency but its possibilities are limited, as well, because of the half-yearly rotation and the often actual or suspected link of any initiative with specific national interests.

Hardly less important than the decision-making system are the instruments it can use, and here, again, the third pillar has brought certain innovations. Besides the classic and already frequently used instrument of 'conventions' under public international law, the Union Treaty also provides for 'joint positions' and 'joint actions' (Article K.3). The creation of specific instruments marks an important step forward in principle. Yet the terminology used in the Treaty and the question of legal binding force have proved to be problematic. Both the joint positions and the joint actions have obviously been taken over from the terminology of the Common Foreign and Security Policy (CFSP). But in the CFSP, the two means of pursuing foreign policy postures make sense (even if in practice, the distinctions have been rather blurred). Justice and home affairs, however, covers areas which are by nature fields of legislative action rather than external posture so that here the meaning of 'positions' and 'actions' is much less clear. It is hardly surprising that the meaning of joint positions has given rise to rather different interpretations, and this is one of the reasons why this instrument has been used only once so far (on a harmonized application of the concept of 'refugee' (*OJ L* 63, 13 March 1996)). Joint actions have also been used only rarely (as in the case of the extension of the mandate of the Europol Drugs Unit (*OJ L* 62, 20 March 1995)), although there is no question about their legal binding force. In general, the member states have so far preferred to use classic non-binding texts of intergovernmental cooperation such as 'resolutions', 'statements' and 'conclusions' rather than the new legal instruments created by the Union Treaty. As a result the legal *acquis* of the third pillar has remained extremely limited.

Article K.1 of the Union Treaty does not create a Union competence for the individual policy fields listed therein which would, in any way, be similar to the supranational competences of the EC but it creates an intergovernmental framework for action in these fields. Here, as well, problems have emerged. Some of the areas of Article K.1 clearly overlap with Community competences. This is particularly true in respect to the rules governing the crossing of external borders where there is an overlap with Community competence for visa policy and a uniform format for visas (Article K.1(2) Treaty on European Union (TEU) and Article 100c EC Treaty), the fight against drug addiction, where the Community can take action as well under its public health policy (Article K.1(4) TEU and Article 129 EC Treaty), and the fight against fraud on an international scale, an area in which the Community can take action as well in order to protect its financial interests (Article K.1(5) TEU and Article 209a EC Treaty). This overlap has not only led to uncertainties as regards the division of competences, but they also mean that certain closely interrelated issues such as the rules governing the crossing of external borders and visa policy have to be dealt with on different legal basis and under different procedures. This, too, can cause frictions and slow down the decision-making process.

Article K.9 of the Union Treaty gives the Council the possibility to transfer a number of the areas listed in Article K.1 partially or totally into Community competence. In order to do so it has to decide unanimously to apply Article 100c of the EC Treaty to action in one of the first six areas listed in Article K.1.[2] The European Parliament (EP) has repeatedly urged the Commission to use its right of initiative under this provision to pursue a further communitarization of the third pillar. In a first reaction, the Commission declared in November 1993 that it considered it not appropriate to use Article K.9 before some further experience had been gained with the application of Title VI, a position which was, not surprisingly, fully endorsed by the Council (SEC(93) 1687). Under pressure from the EP, the Commission in November 1995 submitted a second report on the question. In this the Commission advocated a communitarization of all areas of the third pillar with the exception of police and judicial cooperation in criminal matters but took the view that this objective would have better prospects of being achieved in the framework of the 1996 IGC. It declared the K.9 procedure would be too cumbersome, that it could overlap with the IGC and that it could create the impression that a reform of the third pillar would also be possible without a major revision of the Treaty provisions (COM(95) 566 final). Another reason may have been that, for tactical reasons, the Commission wanted to avoid a polarization of member states on the question of communitarization at least before the start of the IGC. Nevertheless one might regret that the opportunity to use this rather unique instrument for a revision of the division of competences without a Treaty revision has been missed. The particularly ponderous process of an IGC with its exposure to all sorts of political package dealing is not necessarily the best way to arrive at a more efficient division of competences on justice and home affairs.

THE RESULTS IN THE DIFFERENT POLICY AREAS

Whatever may be the deficiencies of the political decision-making system, the ultimate performance test is a look at the results it has achieved. The balance sheet of the third pillar since the entry into force of the Union Treaty can be summarized as follows.

Asylum policy

Some basic results were achieved in this area such as the Council Resolution of June 1995 on minimum guarantees for asylum procedures and the Resolution of March 1995 on the harmonized application of the definition of 'refugee' for the purposes of Article 1A of the Geneva Convention. Some progress was also made as regards the formalities of asylum procedures such as the agreements reached on a common form for the determination of the state responsible for examining an asylum application under the Dublin Convention and the use of evidence in asylum procedures. Yet the Dublin Convention itself, which is of central importance for the further development of EU asylum policy, has still not been ratified by all the member states. Negotiations on a comprehensive common definition of the term 'refugee', common conditions for admission of asylum seekers, on a common system for the exchange of fingerprints of asylum seekers and on burden-sharing among the member states have also not yet led to decisive results. In addition, representatives of the UN High Commissioner for Refugees and of the European Council of Refugees have severely criticized the EU for using so far a rather limited concept of refugee.

Rules governing the crossing of external borders

A major step forward on rules governing the crossing of external borders was achieved not in the third pillar framework but in the Community context. This was the agreement in 1995 on a uniform format for visas and on a list of the third countries whose nations must be in possession of a visa when crossing the external frontiers of the member states. Yet due to the controversy between Spain and the UK over the status of Gibraltar and a couple of other unresolved questions, the Draft External Frontiers Convention proposed by the Commission in December 1993 – the centrepiece of EU policy in this area – still remains under negotiation.

Immigration policy

The member states were able to agree on certain restrictions on the entry of third country nationals seeking employment in the Union, on conditions of entry for students and self-employed persons, on travel facilities for school pupils from third countries resident in a member state and on a common model for readmission agreements to be concluded with third countries. In view of the enormous challenges of global migration these few elements of progress make a particularly poor record. In its 1994 Communication to the Council and the EP on Immigration and Asylum Policies, the Commission had favoured a comprehensive approach to the challenges of immigration. According to the Commission, the Union should aim at attacking the root causes of emigration in third countries using, *inter alia*, instruments of development and commercial policy and should, in addition, combine instruments of immigration control with a more active policy of integration (COM(94) 23 final). Between 1993 and 1996, unfortunately, the Union has made hardly any progress towards such a comprehensive policy.

The fight against drugs

The new Europol Drugs Unit was able to start its work in 1994 and the Madrid European Council of December 1995 agreed on the principles of a comprehen-

sive five-year action plan. Yet the Europol Drugs Unit is so far limited to the collection and exchange of data on drug trafficking and the implementation of the
action plan has not yet fully started. A positive element, however, is the extension
of EU action to cooperation with third countries (especially with the USA and
Canada in the Caribbean and Latin America) which was reaffirmed by the
Florence European Council of June 1996 (*Europe* No. 6755, 23 June 1996).

Judicial cooperation

Here the picture is a rather mixed one. On the one hand, some progress has
clearly been achieved with the signing of the Conventions on a simplified extradition procedure between the member states (March 1995) and on the protection
of the financial interests of the EC (July 1995). On the other hand, however, the
member states have not yet been able to agree on a more comprehensive convention on extradition (mainly because of the problems with political infractions
as justification for refusing extradition and with the extradition of nationals), to
apply the Convention on the protection of the financial interests of the
Community (because of the controversy over the role of the Court of Justice under
this Convention) and to make any decisive progress in such areas such as the
meaning and notification of judiciary documents and the fight against corruption.

Customs cooperation

A central topic in the area of customs cooperation has been the use of information technology for customs purposes. Yet the agreement reached in July 1995 on
the Customs Information System (CIS) is still not yet fully operational because
here, as well, the controversy over the role of the Court of Justice has still to be
sorted out. On 19 March 1996 the Council was able to agree on a new customs
strategy at external borders providing for the organization of joint control operations but this strategy covers so far mainly air and maritime traffic and not yet
road and postal traffic.

Police cooperation

Police cooperation has been developed not only through the signing – after very
difficult negotiations – of the EUROPOL Convention (July 1995) but also by a
number of recommendations and declarations of intent (mainly in the form of
'Resolutions' and 'Conclusions') on the fight against money laundering, on trade
in human beings and various aspects of international organized crime. Yet so far
police cooperation is mainly limited to information exchange. No operational
powers have been granted to EUROPOL. The problem of the role of the Court
of Justice which has delayed the entry into force of the EUROPOL Convention
was only resolved by a hardly satisfying compromise (see p.334–5). Further
deficits are a lack of coordination and interaction between the areas of police and
judicial cooperation and a still rather low level of cooperation with third countries

where most of the member states still prefer to go their own ways.

The balance sheet makes it apparent how fragmented and limited in substance the results achieved by the third pillar still are. More comprehensive policies or strategies – which the size of the challenges require – are either totally absent or take the form of vague declarations of intent. Most of the progress achieved has taken place only in the areas harmonization of procedures and increased exchange of information. Too little progress has been made in respect to an increased operational capacity of the third pillar and the harmonization of fundamental national legislation.

TWO CONSTITUTIONAL PROBLEMS: DEMOCRATIC AND JUDICIAL CONTROL

Any assessment of the third pillar would be incomplete without mentioning two problems of constitutional nature: the democracy deficit of cooperation under Title VI and the lack of judicial control.

Pursuant to Article K.6 of the Union Treaty the EP has to be informed of discussions in the areas of Title VI and to be consulted on the 'principal aspects of activities' in these areas. It is hardly surprising that the Council and the member states have interpreted these provisions in a rather restrictive sense. In most cases, information and consultation of the EP comes late or covers only part of the relevant activities. Attempts by Parliament to improve the possibilities of its control by way of an inter-institutional agreement have foundered in the Council. The obvious lack of effective democracy at the EU level is not compensated by the national parliaments because many of these also receive rather limited information and are often enough faced with accomplished facts (Monar 1995). The Union's democracy deficit is a well-known feature of the first and second pillars as well. Yet in the third pillar it can be regarded as particularly serious because almost all areas of Article K.1 have a much more direct impact on the individual citizen than most other EU policy areas and also because the complexity and the many facets of justice and home affairs make it anyway more difficult for parliaments to effectively scrutinize decision-making and measures taken.

Hardly less serious is the question of judicial control. Although the areas covered by the third pillar bear a considerable potential for violations of the rights of the individual (to protection of data of individuals in the framework of police cooperation is only one example among many), there is no judicial control at the EU level because under Article L of the Union Treaty the third pillar has been excluded from the jurisdiction of the Court of Justice. This creates dangers not only for the protection of individuals but also for a uniform legal interpretation of measures adopted under Title VI (Neuwahl 1995). The existing possibility (not obligation) of giving jurisdiction to the Court within certain conventions (Article K.3(c)) is clearly insufficient. It should be mentioned also that in the case of the EUROPOL Convention this provision has led to the unfortunate precedent of an à la carte jurisdiction. According to the compromise reached at the Florence

European Council of June 1996, each of the member states is free to state in a protocol whether it accepts the authority of the Court for issuing preliminary rulings on the interpretation of the Convention (*Europe* No. 6755, 23 June 1996).

THE MAIN AREAS OF POTENTIAL REFORM IN THE FRAMEWORK OF THE 1996 IGC

Any policy finds its final legitimation in the results it achieves. Today this must be particularly true for the EU which since the crisis of ratification of the Union Treaty is clearly under pressure to justify its policies before its citizens more than ever through concrete results. So far the third pillar has certainly not passed this test of legitimacy. Its performance has been as poor as it has been fragmented and far from meeting the challenges the Union has to face in these areas. Simplistic patterns of explanation, such as all its deficits can be traced back to the unanimity requirement of intergovernmental cooperation have to be avoided. The negative factors surrounding the development of justice and home affairs cooperation are manifold. The different legal systems and political traditions of the member states in the policy areas of Article K.1, their national sovereignty implications and their prominent place in domestic politics make it more difficult for the member states to agree on substantial measures here than in many other EU policy areas. One also has to see that the Schengen process, often described as a 'laboratory' for the EU, has not necessarily helped the development of cooperation under Title VI. It offers the members of the Schengen group the possibility of arriving at their common aims by 'eluding' the third pillar rather than by insisting on a solution within it. These and other basic factors affecting the development of EU justice and home affairs cannot simply be 'reformed away', let alone by an IGC which is burdened by so many other difficult tasks.

Yet our assessment of the third pillar has shown that cooperation in the fields of justice and home affairs is also affected by a number of clearly identifiable deficits resulting from the present treaty provisions. It is here that the IGC as a 'treaty revision conference' can find its proper domain to act. If one assumes the persistence of Title VI as a pillar of the Union distinct from the EC framework – something which has not been put into doubt by the Reflection Group Report – the following areas of potential (and desirable) reform can be identified:

First, so far there is clearly a lack of clearly defined aims for the further development of EU justice and home affairs. While the Union Treaty is certainly not the appropriate place to define the substantive elements of policies there can be no doubt that the definition of a number of general objectives (such as the gradual formulation and implementation of a common asylum and immigration policy) would be of considerable help in the setting of priorities and strategies. The fixing of a catalogue of aims (one may think in this respect of provisions similar to Articles 2 and 3 EC Treaty) whose completion could be linked with a timetable would mark a major step forward but is still rather controversial among the member states.

Second, some progress should be made as regards the transfer of parts of the third pillar into the EC framework. Political arguments on this issue are, unfortunately, often dominated by the ideological connotations of any communitarization. Yet what really counts here are not doctrines but the criterion of efficiency. In all areas of the third pillar where there is already some (overlapping) Community competence, communitarization makes sense because it will increase the efficiency of measures and the coherence of action taken by the Union. This is certainly true, for instance, for the rules governing the crossing of external borders (Article K.1(2) TEU) which are closely linked to the abolition of internal borders in the internal market and to EC competences in the area of visa policy. There are also areas where the link to existing EC competences is less prominent and where for other reasons as well a communitarization appears to be more problematic. A majority of the members of the Reflection Group declared itself to be in favour of a communitarization of asylum and immigration policy (Reflection Group Report 1995: para. 49), and the Italian Presidency, in its Progress report on the IGC of 17 June 1996, also mentioned asylum and immigration as the most suitable areas for incorporation into the Community sphere (Council Document CONF 3860/1/96, 17 June 1996). Yet national legislation and political traditions in the member states are still very different in these areas and many of the key issues are highly controversial in domestic politics, certainly more so than most of the present EC policies. One may therefore raise the question whether the Community system would not – at least in the next few years – be overcharged by a full communitarization of these areas and may then only end up, once more, as a scapegoat for unresolved conflicts and problems at the national level. From this point of view a gradual communitarization according to a set timetable appears much more sensible.

Third, the structure of the decision-making system should be simplified. Here a major step forward would be the reduction of the number of decision-making levels. Even the British government in its White Paper on the IGC of March 1996 has declared itself in favour of such a reform (HMSO 1996: para. 53). Possible solutions might include a strengthening of the position of the K.4 Committee as the central preparatory body below the JHA or a removal of the Steering Groups. In the first months of the IGC even a removal of the K.4 Committee itself was discussed as an option, yet having regard to the heavy agenda of COREPER in the EC framework and the specific expertise of the K.4 Committee this seems to be a less obvious solution.

Fourth, the possibilities for taking decisions by majority should be increased. Some member states (not only the UK) have considerable difficulties with any progress on this issue, and it would certainly be unrealistic to aim at generalized majority voting all over the third pillar. Prospects for some sort of an intermediate solution may be better, and even such a more moderate progress could still make a qualitative difference in decision-making under Title VI. Such an intermediate solution would be, for instance, to make qualified majority decisions obligatory on all measures implementing joint actions and to introduce a timetable for making majority voting obligatory on other decisions as well in some or eventually all areas of Article K.1. This could be combined with an extension of the Commission's right of initiative to all areas of the third pillar as this has already been proposed by the Commission in its opinion on the IGC of February 1996 (COM(96) 90: para. 17).

Fifth, the instruments of the third pillar, partially taken over from the CFSP, should be adapted to its real needs. In most cases the member states will continue to take decisions which need to be implemented by national legislation. This decisions should wherever possible take a legally binding form. Therefore it would be sensible to introduce the EC instrument of the directive into the third pillar where it could be placed alongside the existing joint positions and actions or (better) replace them. In the first months of the IGC the idea of introducing a new legal instrument called a 'common measure', which in its effects would be rather similar to an EC directive was generally welcomed (CONF 3860/1/96, 17 June 1996). A sensible reform would also be the introduction into the Treaty of specific procedures and instruments for the cooperation with third countries and international organizations since international cooperation has become a key element of effective policies in nearly all of the third pillar areas.

Sixth, the role of the EP should be strengthened. Here, a minimum reform would be to introduce a mandatory consultation of the Parliament on all legally binding acts and action programmes coming up for decision in the Council. In cases where legally binding texts will not have to be submitted to the national parliaments (as is the case with joint measures, for instance) the Parliament should be granted a right of co-decision or, at least, assent. Yet in the first months of the IGC only some member states have advocated a strengthening of the Parliament's role and these have been in favour of mandatory consultation only. More backing was given to various proposals for strengthening the participation of national parliaments in the third pillar process (ibid.: 17).

Seventh, the jurisdiction of the Court of Justice should be extended to all legally bindings texts adopted within the framework of the third pillar and as well to the interpretation of all provisions of Title VI. This not only for reasons of judicial protection and of the unity of the EU legal system but also in order to prevent the endless series of controversies which have emerged during the negotiation of third pillar conventions until now. However, because of the stiff opposition of the British government against any extension of the role of the Court this is certainly one of the most difficult points on the IGC's third pillar agenda.

Eighth, the Schengen system as a whole or in essential parts should be transferred into the third pillar in order to avoid the risk of a further growth of this 'parallel system' and in order to bring the progressive elements of Schengen into the Union framework. It seems that in the first phase of the IGC such a major reform has at least been taken into consideration (ibid.: 19).

OUTLOOK

The first months of the IGC have shown that the negotiating parties accept the need for a reform of the third pillar and this has already been the object of serious discussions. Yet differences between the member states on the elements and on the extent of the reform have proven to be as great as ever. So far there is little evidence which suggests that the IGC will fundamentally change the intergovernmental basis of the third pillar. Nevertheless some progress as regards the decision-making system and some of the policy areas listed in Article K.1 seems possible.

Progress in the areas of justice and home affairs is needed. Not only because the external and internal challenges which have been mentioned are becoming more and more important. The political relevance of the third pillar extends beyond the achievement of greater efficiency. One of the few points on which there was a clear consensus within the Reflection Group was that a key element for the success of the IGC would be 'to place the citizen at the centre of the European venture by endeavouring to meet his expectations and concerns, that is to say, to make Europe the affair of the citizen' (Reflection Group 1995: para 29). The policy areas covered by the third pillar are clearly of direct relevance to some of the major concerns of the citizens of the EU. There can be little doubt that issues like internal security, the combat against drug addiction and organized crime and the problems of immigration are much closer to immediate interests of the citizens than, for example, the question of a common currency or of a more efficient common foreign and security policy. Consequently these are areas in which the Union has a chance to prove that it takes citizens' concerns seriously and that it can produce effective policies in response to major new challenges. What is at stake in the reform of the third pillar is therefore not the efficiency of institutions and procedures but also the political credibility of the Union in the eyes of its citizens.

NOTES

1. The Convention on simplified extradition procedure between the member states of the EU of 10 March 1995 (*OJ C* 78, 30 March 1995) is a good example in this respect: originally it should have been a text covering most aspects of extradition between the member states but in the process the text was watered down to rather limited aspects of procedures.
2. These areas are: asylum policy, the rules governing the crossing of external borders, immigration policy, the combat against drug addiction, the combat against fraud on an international scale and judicial cooperation in civil matters.

REFERENCES AND BIBLIOGRAPHY

Baker, Kenneth (1993) *The Turbulent Years*. London, Faber and Faber.

Cullen, David, Monar, Jörg and Myers, Phil (1996) *Cooperation in Justice and Home Affairs: An Evaluation of the Third Pillar in Practice*. Brussels, European Interuniversity Press.

Fortescue, Adrian (1995) 'First experiences with the implementation of the third pillar provisions', in Bieber, R. and Monar, J. (eds) *Justice and Home Affairs in the European Union*. Brussels, European Interuniversity Press.

HMSO (1996) 'White Paper on the 1996 IGC.'

Myers, Phil (1995) 'The Commission's approach to the third pillar: political organisational elements', in Bieber, R. and Monar, J. (eds) *Justice and Home Affairs in the European Union*. Brussels, European Interuniversity Press.

Monar, Jörg (1995) 'Democratic control of justice and home affairs', in Bieber, R. and Monar, J. (eds) *Justice and Home Affairs in the European Union*. Brussels, European Interuniversity Press.

Neuwahl, Nanette (1995) 'Judicial control in matters of justice and home affairs', in Bieber R. and Monar, J. (eds) *Justice and Home Affairs in the European Union*. Brussels, European Interuniversity Press.

17
EPILOGUE

ALFRED PIJPERS AND GEOFFREY EDWARDS

The preceding chapters have sought to place the 1996 Intergovernmental Conference (IGC) in the longer-term perspective of European integration. It is clear that Maastricht challenged a number of ideas about that process and that the 1996 IGC was, initially at least, looked on as an opportunity to put right what had gone wrong or had been overlooked, and to renew and strengthen the commitment of the member states to the process in the face of further enlargement eastwards and southwards. Whatever the actual agenda of the Conference, the profoundly difficult issue of enlargement is only one of a number of interrelated and equally challenging issues that include the legitimacy of the contemporary nation-state as well as of the European Union (EU), large-scale unemployment, over-burdened social welfare systems, racial tension, and a wide range of foreign policy and security problems very close to Europe's borders.

This problematic, bewildering European reality has here been organized around the theme of the 1996 IGC. We divided it into three parts, the setting, the players, and the agenda, with chapters by nineteen authors, from eight countries in Europe and from the US. The authors are from different academic backgrounds, though the majority fall within the disciplines of international relations and political science. All the authors show, within the common framework of the project, the usual individual, sometimes idiosyncratic characteristics of academics, and the editors have certainly not attempted to smooth these out in order to create a harmonized perspective even if they could agree between themselves on how to do so.

Yet despite this variety of styles and approaches, one may nevertheless discern some common features in the description of Europe's fate over the past few years. Apart from the many shared viewpoints on the necessity of treaty reform, the required institutional adaptations, etc. (they speak for themselves) one may group these common European features under two broad headings that relate, first, to governments, people and the legitimacy of the European integration process and, second, to the nature of this process, particularly the issue of differentiated integration.

Governments, people and the question of legitimacy

In many of the chapters of this volume there are references to the increased tension or gap between government and the people. On the one hand, governments, central banks, and the leadership of political parties have (on the whole) been pressing for further integration. On the other hand, ever larger segments (so it seems) of the public in the member states seem resistant to this process. In one sense, the gap is not a new phenomenon in the history of European integration. As Weiler recalls in his chapter, the European Coal and Steel Community (ECSC) treaty was conceived almost entirely without any public debate, and the subsequent evolution of the EC, too, is generally considered to have been largely an élite affair. In the 1960s and 1970s, the larger part of the population in most member states appeared to accept EC policies (with one or two well-known exceptions, though even in, say, the UK, hostility to the EC/EU among the public can easily be exaggerated), forming a silent or 'permissive majority'. Even as governments were launching new, potentially profound intitatives, that broad popular consensus in favour of further integration seemed to crumble. As Laursen has pointed out, there has been a steady decline in voting turn-out in the elections for the European Parliament (EP) as well as the critical reception of Maastricht by large groups of citizens in France, Denmark, and even Germany. There is also the growing number of sceptical voices heard – among élites as well as the broader public – in member states with an unspoken federal vocation in the past; Germany and The Netherlands are cases in point.

What has compounded the problem is the somewhat paradoxical phenomenon first suggested by Stanley Hoffmann some 30 years ago (Hoffmann 1966), that the process of European integration, while creating a number of supranational features, has in some respects strengthened the very institution it was supposed to undo: the nation-state. The very need to be in continuous negotiation over an ever-widening range of issues has placed a premium on the ability of national ministries to coordinate policy stances. Given the nature of policy-making in the EU, of compromise and package deals that sometimes stretch beyond particular sectors, the need (not always met) for administrations to be tightly coordinated within and in close touch with organized outside interests without, has become all the greater. At the same time, however, this widening of the numbers of the national policy-making élites has created counter-pressures. As more are involved so there have been increasing incentives – encouraged by the Community's central institutions – to link up with functional counter-parts within the other member states. There is therefore considerable tension, at the national level, in these rival pressures for centralization and fragmentation. In neither case, though, has it meant any greater transparency in decision-making or the involvement of general publics.

This growing divergence between government and governed on European issues can perhaps be seen as an element of a much wider, more basic gap between rulers and ruled that is a common (natural?) part of political life, national or international. A similar 'gap' in the EU, therefore, is in itself not a reason for deep concern. But the gap within many member states seems to be widening. The relative wealth, prosperity and security achieved by so many in the advanced industrialized states of Western Europe may have been challenged in the 1970s, but by the 1980s and 1990s there were few complacent about the prospects of overcoming widespread unemployment and of maintaining the full panoply of the welfare state. Establishing and developing that state may have been a vital factor in the creation of the Communities (Haas 1958), but trying to maintain or ease the consequences of having to slim down and dismantle key parts of it has not created the same sort of agreement among Western European governments. Some governments, including the British governments under Thatcher and Major, have positively welcomed the opportunity to 'roll back the state'; others have found stimulus only in the need to meet the criteria laid out in the Maastricht Treaty for participation in the single currency under EMU. In both instances, the EU has inevitably, become a factor in domestic electoral calculations. A similar process seems to be at work when, as Szukala and Wessels have pointed out, the identification of the EC/EU with modernization brings the EU within the purview of domestic politics, creating another complex interaction that needs to be taken into account.

In such circumstances of change and uncertainty, the EU's role has clearly become an ambiguous one – the harbinger of new opportunities or the constraint on traditional policy solutions. Without being too cynical, it is clear that the latter view has often been particularly useful to governments facing adverse conditions, difficult decisions or electoral problems. The EC/EU as scapegoat is hardly a new concept; the problem lies in the fact that the EU has moved into an ever-wider range of policy areas, including, with Maastricht, areas previously very closely identified with the prerogative of the nation-state. As the involvement of the EU and its institutions has expanded, but without any complementary shift in the sense of involvement and identification of the electorate so the opportunities for being critical of the EU increase and questions are raised about its very legitimacy.

That has problematic consequences for governments as they negotiate in the IGC. As others have pointed out, the problems of ratifying Maastricht came as an unwelcome surprise to many. Some governments have responded by seeking to establish a public debate – or at least disseminate more information more widely – even in the preparatory stages of the 1996 IGC. Most seem also to be taking very much greater notice of public opinion during the negotiations. There is in a very real sense a two-level negotiation taking place, among governments on reviewing and reforming Maastricht, and among governments and their electorates – or at least key groups within them – on what is desirable and acceptable.

Differentiated integration

Another significant aspect of the 'reality' of the integration process, which springs from nearly every page in this volume, is the highly differentiated nature of the process. Differentiated integration in all its institutional forms of 'multi-speed' Europe, *géométrie variable, formation à la carte*, core groups, or flying geese (Wallace and Wallace 1995), has accompanied, or rather shaped European integration ever since the Second World War. The smaller groups of the Benelux may have led the way in certain sectors but there have also been the inner Six and outer

Seven (of the EC and European Free Trade Association (EFTA)), the wider concentric circles of the Council of Europe and the CSCE (now OSCE (Organization of Security and Cooperation in Europe)), or the many more specialized intergovernmental European organizations like the European Space Agency or the Independent European Programme Group (IEPG) now the Western European Armaments Group (WEAG), a part of another European organization, the Western European Union (WEU). With their great variety of councils, committees and assemblies, all have contributed to the management of the European system in a vital way. They have also been supplemented and complemented by bodies such as the North Atlantic Treaty Organization (NATO) or the Organization for Economic Cooperation and Development (OECD) with its broader membership. The dialectics of history and space in Jonathan Story's felicitous formulation is indeed very much part and parcel of Europe's way of life.

The present dialectics differ, however, from the earlier post-war experiences. During the first decades after the war, the various integration or cooperation schemes not only diverged in terms of speed or the level of integration, but they were also conducted in separate international organizations. The organizations of Western and Eastern Europe were even part of completely different market and security systems, effectively separated from each other by the Iron Curtain and huge trade barriers. The current patterns of, and proposals for, differentiated integration take place increasingly within the single context of an expanding EU as part of an open pan-European system.

Within this single integration framework, there are, however, continuities as well as profound differences. The Franco-German tandem, analysed by Szukala and Wessels, is an example of a core function still considered – by the governments themselves as well as by others – as a vital mechanism in a much enlarged Union. But the Benelux, too, have regained some importance in this respect, though now in a rather more subordinate than pioneering role (see Pijpers and Vanhoonacker). Likewise, the position of the UK *vis-à-vis* the core of Europe has remained, as George points out, sometimes alarmingly consistent over the years; a central player in the various security arrangements (including bilateral ones with, for instance, France), but adopting an attitude of aloofness towards the European Monetary System (EMS) (with only a brief and unhappy interlude within it) and Economic and Monetary Union (EMU). The Southern pattern allows for more variation as the years have gone by, but here as well cooperation patterns based on certain joint Mediterranean interests follow a similar course as in the past, as Tsakaloyannis shows. Only in the case of Italy can one see an example of a founding member of the EC which has gradually manoeuvred itself partly outside the inner circle, at least for the time being.

What has also remained largely the same in terms of differentiation, are the disjointed circuits of sector integration. While there was some differentiation within the EC framework, especially in monetary integration, there was from 1972 until Maastricht unanimous agreement on the ultimate, albeit somewhat vaguely defined, goals of EMU. That differentiation was, however, complemented by the almost completely different integration speeds between that first pillar, the

EC and the second and now the third pillar. Economic integration and security cooperation have always been a couple dancing apart from each other on the same dance floor. Despite the recurrent crises and setbacks, the process of economic integration has tended to follow the neo-functionalist logic of the expansiveness of sectoral integration. It may not have been a linear development, but the establishment of the customs union was followed by the development of common trade and agricultural policies (among others), the establishment of the exchange rate mechanism, the further removal of internal trade barriers, cohesion and social policies, etc. All these policies were accompanied by, sometimes led by, institutional development.

European security cooperation has always lagged behind in this respect, both in substance and procedures. Having been established in such intergovernmental bodies as the WEU – itself a fairly moribund subordinate partner to NATO – cooperation remained largely absent from the EC as such, until the mid-1980s. While the Single European Act (SEA) brought a breakthrough in the decision-making rules of the internal market, European Political Cooperation (EPC) (minus defence – movement in that direction had failed with the Genscher–Colombo initiative) was only codified on an intergovernmental basis. While WEU may have been revitalized in 1984 (Tsakaloyannis 1985) it was largely still without substance and so was not a part of the *relance européenne* later that decade. Maastricht only confirmed this mixed record, of substantial integration in the first pillar, combined with only restricted progress in the second, though the introduction of a prospective common defence was in itself a novel feature in the history of the Community treaties.

Again, during the run-up to the 1996 IGC there were few signs that any further treaty revision would have a very different result. The proposals tabled by the various member states showed conflicting positions on, for instance, the links between the EU and the WEU, or on a 'Monsieur PESC', but a true European security and defence identity has a long way to go, despite, as van Ham has pointed out, the progress made on a European pillar within the NATO framework. This is partly because of the conflicting security interests among member states, and their consequent reluctance to concede sovereignty in this area, but it is also because, unlike all the protestations to the contrary in past years, the role of the USA in the post-Cold War period has turned out to be less restrictive than many had predicted (or feared). This may change, of course, depending on the nature of future crises, but the limited evolution of European thinking on security and defence that van Ham describes is perhaps surprising.

The long-standing discrepancy between policy-making in the first and second pillars has found its equivalent in the gulf separating the Community method from decision-making in the field of justice and home affairs. The picture showing most member states preparing to enter an advanced stage of economic (and monetary) integration remains the same; it contrasts particularly with cooperation in adjacent fields that remain limited if not stagnant. This, in the case of the third pillar, is surprising in so far as the areas of the internal market and of the free movement of people are functionally closely related to each other. However, as

Monar has shown, the problems of the third pillar are to a large extent due to the fact that cooperation in matters of crime prevention, asylum, and justice touch upon the core functions of national states, where governments, in this case particularly the British, remain reluctant to concede ground.

The process of contemporary European integration, thus, partly follows a familiar course, laid down by the Paris and Rome Treaties, but has also developed several new dimensions even closer to the traditional prerogatives of the European nation-state. We have pointed above to the fact that many of these new areas of European activity created not simply increased public awareness but also a growing concern – whether over the deepening of integration to include such issues as a single currency, or the increasing saliency of the EU's foreign and security policy with its larger impact on both the performance and legitimacy of the EU, or greater cooperation on crime prevention and police cooperation. However intergovernmental the decision-making process may be, it is perhaps clear that the framework of cooperation has significantly altered. Within the new system, and partly in response to it, there has been a decline in the support for a federal vocation, at least as an ideology, and an open resumption of much more nationalistic aspirations, at least in terms of the language being employed. At the same time, the existing structures and balance of costs and benefits are challenged by the prospect of further enlargement with, in its wake, an ever stronger call for drastic institutional revisions and for variable forms of integration.

A note on theory

Academics are frequently brought up with the assumption that such issues can or should be explained or understood with the help of theory. Integration theory is not the subject of this book, and yet we cannot leave it completely untouched given the EU's complexity and the confusion of theoretical explanations for it.

We did not ask the contributors to build their reflections on the IGC and the EU's future agenda around a particular theoretical approach. It would have been difficult to do so for there is no single theoretical approach to integration, at least not in the sense of a readily available set of hypotheses, concepts, etc., on which there is a consensus among the academic community. This state of affairs may be normal in the social sciences, but it is not particularly helpful for our understanding of European integration. Some 40 years ago, for example, Haas defined political integration as 'the process whereby political actors in several distinct national settings are persuaded to shift their loyalties, expectations and political activities toward a new centre, whose institutions possess or demand jurisdiction over the pre-existing national states' (Haas 1958: 16). So how should we define (and explain) a process whereby many political actors in the member states have shifted much of their political activity to Brussels, negotiating on a whole raft of issues on a semi-permanent basis within common institutions, yet appear reluctant to declare, at least publicly, any shift in loyalties and remain ambivalent about expectations? Since Haas, the theoretical discussion has sometimes revolved around the question of supranationalism *versus* intergovernmentalism, with, inevitably, much depending on the questions being asked. Natural prejudice, sometimes ennobled by an -ology of some sort or another, has determined a great deal, not least in terms of outcomes and the assessement of the predictive qualities of theory. In other cases, a synthesis of different perspectives has been sought on the basis that no single approach or theory can fully explain the process of integration (see, for example, Cameron 1992). In yet other cases, theorizing as such has been eschewed in the interests of description, the deliberate parsimony of so many theories being considered unhelpful. In other words there has been a proliferation of theorizing, model-building, metaphor-making, etc.

Precisely because the EU itself has entered the more sensitive fields of national political and economic life, theoretical reflections, too, have spilled well beyond the borders of the international relations discipline, where the primary concern has been to explain why states might integrate, into comparative politics in order to focus more closely on decision-making within the EC/EU. The assumption is made that, even if not a discrete and identifiable political system in which there is an authoritative allocation of values, the EC/EU frequently acts as if it is one, which makes insights and concepts derived from comparative politics relevant and valuable (Hix 1994). Theories of democracy, legitimacy, citizenship, electoral behaviour, lobbying, nationalism, or culture all claim their share in the quest for knowledge on the EU, as the contributions of Weiler, Mazey and Richardson, Story, and others in this volume testify.

Given the richness of approaches in this volume, we cannot argue in this epilogue that any one approach provides more insights than any other. Nor do we propose to rehearse the variety of theories currently on offer. In choosing to focus on an intergovernmental conference and in suggesting that the treaty-revision process seems to be approaching a permanent feature of European politics – at least since the 1980s – almost a fourth intergovernmental 'pillar', it is perhaps inevitable that the emphasis has been on states and governments. The thrust of the book might therefore seem to give support to those who have sought to explain the EU and the integration process in terms of a series of inter-governmental bargains – not least, of course, Moravcsik (1993). And yet, from a reading of the chapters presented here, it is clear that, however sophisticated the liberal intergovernmentalist position may be, questions remain. In the area of *political cooperation*, for example, Moravcsik suggests that his model is more difficult to apply, since the 'costs and benefits created by political cooperation for private groups are diffuse and uncertain' (ibid.: 494). And he speaks of a 'troubling neofunctionalist anomaly, namely the manifest importance of ideologically motivated heads of state ('dramatic-political' actors) in matters of foreign policy and institutional reform' (ibid.). The European scene is, of course, riddled with 'ideologically motivated heads of state' setting goals and targets within the framework of the European Council for the IGC as well as foreign policy. On institutional reform, too, Moravcsik sees 'only a loose public or élite opinion constraint' (ibid.: 495). Given the difficulties of ratifying Maastricht, that looseness has taken on a far greater significance; the legitimacy of the bargaining process becomes a vital factor.

Because of our choice of subjects within the broad framework of the 1996 Conference, we are, perhaps, open to the charge that we would in any case question some of the conclusions of liberal intergovernmentalism. After all, we considered it important to cover the European Commission and the Parliament as indicative of the role of the EU's central institutions. Both contributed to and participated in the discussions leading up to and during the IGC. They also appear, of course, as items on the Conference's agenda. But it is simply not enough to suggest that the EC institutions come into play where they 'increase the efficiency of interstate bargaining' by reducing the so-called transaction costs of governments (ibid.: 508). We also thought it important to examine the role of interest groups: after all, whereas there might be disagreement on their role in the negotiation of the SEA (Green Cowles 1995; Sandholtz and Zysman 1989; Moravcsik 1991), there is a general consensus that their role was limited in the move to Maastricht. Given their importance in the ordinary decision-making processes of the EU – even if that importance varies among the three pillars – it is particularly necessary to try to assess their role in the 1996 IGC.

What emerges particularly clearly in many of the chapters is the importance of domestic politics in the post-Maastricht integration process. This is also, of course, highlighted by Moravcsik. His bargaining model has essentially two stages or dimensions: (a) governments first define a set of interests, the process of national preference formation, whereby the 'foreign policy goals of national governments are viewed as varying in response to shifting pressure from domestic groups' (Moravcsik 1993: 481), and whereby the 'costs and benefits of economic interdependence are the primary determinants of national preferences'; (b) the process of 'interstate negotiation', whereby governments try to realize their 'goals that are defined domestically' (ibid.). The process is essentially sequential, unlike that suggested by Putnam in his approach to two-level games (Putnam 1988). Maastricht showed only too clearly the danger of governments being out of touch. One of the lessons of Maastricht has been, i.e., that instead of a sequential process, governments had to be looking continuously over their shoulders to their domestic audience, not just in national parliaments but in the country as a whole. As Weiler points out, the role of the German Constitutional Court proved of no little significance during the Maastricht ratification process.

Moreover, it might also be argued that the logic of interdependence reduces the ability of governments to define national preferences so straighforwardly as might be suggested. Changes in global investment patterns are very largely out of the hands of governments however much some may try to influence outcomes. Similarly, the revolution in communications has had profound implications for the role of government as gate-keeper in maintaining at least a degree of control over information flows. Language barriers may still be a major obstacle within Europe but there are now a multitude of alternative sources of information to those simply supplied by government briefings, not least those provided by transnational interest groups. Finally, the pressures from domestic groups may no longer be so simply determined primarily by the costs and benefits of economic interdependence. That is not to suggest that they do not remain of critical importance, but that in so far as Maastricht extended the EU's remit to cover security and potentially defence, citizenship issues, police and questions of immigration, other factors may enter the equation.

These examples are not given to reject out of hand some important ideas from mainstream integration theory. On the contrary, both the older and more recent concepts of, for instance, neo-functionalism (Tranholm-Mikkelsen 1991), 'dialectical functionalism' (Corbey 1993), or even realism (usually in the case of the second and third pillars, though see Grieco (1995) for an application of neo-realism to Maastricht and EMU), remain in many respects useful for the understanding of certain elements in the European integration process. A satisfying single model of European reform cycles, however, will probably become more elusive as – or when – integration proceeds. The constant interaction of volatile domestic settings within the EU with its sometimes crisis-ridden external environment, makes for an unsteady journey. It is not just the Community treaties which need repeated repair, so, too, do the academic assumptions of the integration process, itself.

REFERENCES AND BIBLIOGRAPHY

Cameron, David (1992) 'The 1992 Initiative: causes and consequences', in Sbragia, Alberta (ed.) *Euro-politics*. Washington, DC, The Brookings Institution.

Corbey, Dorette (1995) 'Dialectical functionalism: stagnation as a booster of European integration', *International Organization*, vol. 49 (Spring), pp. 253–84.

Green Cowles, Maria (1995) 'Setting the agenda for a new Europe: the ERT and EC 1992', *Journal of Common Market Studies*, vol. 33 (December), pp. 501–26.

Grieco, Joseph (1995) 'The Maastricht Treaty, Economic and Monetary Union and the neo-realist research programme', *Review of International Studies*, vol. 21 (January) pp. 21–40.

Haas, Ernst (1958) *The Uniting of Europe*. London, Stevens and Sons.

Hix, Simon (1994) 'The study of the European Community: the challenge to comparative politics', *West European Politics*, vol. 17 (January), pp. 1–30.

Hoffmann, Stanley (1966) 'Obstinate or obsolete: the fate of the nation state and the case of Western Europe', *Daedelus*, vol. 95 (summer), pp. 862–915.

Moravcsik, Andrew (1991) 'Negotiating the Single European Act' in Hoffman, Stanley and Keohane, Robert (eds) *The New European Community*. Boulder Colorado, Westview.

Putnam, Robert (1988) 'Diplomacy and domestic politics: the logic of two-level games', *International Organization*, vol. 42 (summer) 1988.

Sandholtz, Wayne and Zysman, John (1989) '1992: recasting the European bargain', *World Politics*, vol. 41, pp. 95–128

Tranholm-Mikkelsen, Jeppe (1991) 'Neo-functionalism: obstinate or obsolete?', *Millenium*, vol. 20 (spring), pp. 1–22.

Tsakaloyannis, Panos (ed.) 1985 *The Reactivation of the Western European Union: the effects on the EC and its institutions*. Maastricht, European Institute of Public Administration.

Wallace, H. and Wallace W. (1995) *Flying Together in a larger and more diverse European Union*. The Hague, Netherlands Scientific Council for Government Policy Working Documents W87.

INDEX

349